MEN AND EVENTS

OF

MY TIME IN INDIA

MEN AND EVENTS

OF

MY TIME IN INDIA.

SIR RICHARD TEMPLE, BART.

GYAN

Published by

Gyan Publishing House
5, Ansari Road
Daryaganj, New Delhi-110002
Phone: 011-47034999, 9811692060
E-mail: books@gyanbooks.com

Distribution Network
gyanbooks.com
India, USA, Canada, UK, Australia, France

ISBN : 978-81-212-9496-6 (PB)
First Published, 1882

2nd Impression 2023

Printed at: Gyan Press, Delhi.

MEN AND EVENTS
Author: SIR RICHARD TEMPLE

MEN AND EVENTS

OF

MY TIME IN INDIA.

By SIR RICHARD TEMPLE, Bart.,
G.C.S.I., C.I.E., D.C.L.

LATE FINANCE MINISTER OF INDIA; LIEUTENANT-GOVERNOR OF BENGAL, AND GOVERNOR OF BOMBAY; AUTHOR OF 'INDIA IN 1880.'

SECOND THOUSAND.

1882.

BY THE SAME AUTHOR.

INDIA IN 1880. *Second Edition.* With Maps. 8vo. 16*s*.

TO

HER MOST GRACIOUS MAJESTY

THE QUEEN,

EMPRESS OF INDIA,

THIS IMPERFECT NARRATIVE,

RELATING TO SOME AMONG THE MOST ILLUSTRIOUS OF HER MAJESTY'S SERVANTS AND SUBJECTS

IN THE EAST,

AND TO MANY OF THE GREAT RESULTS ACHIEVED, DURING HER MAJESTY'S AUSPICIOUS REIGN,

IN THE INDIAN EMPIRE,

IS WITH HER MAJESTY'S PERMISSION

HUMBLY DEDICATED

BY

THE AUTHOR.

PREFACE.

This work presents to the world a picture of the men and events that have passed before me during the thirty years of my life in India. The objects and limits of the undertaking are set forth in the beginning of the introductory chapter, and therefore the preface may be brief. My last book, 'India in 1880,' related to external things, to measures of national improvement, to results produced by diverse trains of causes, to the character and disposition of the Natives in masses. But it rarely or never comprised any delineation of individual character. This book, on the contrary, is mainly devoted to the description of particular men in their public capacities, or to summaries of their official conduct, and of their idiosyncrasies as displayed in the manner whereby they served the country. More or less of space is allotted according to the importance of the parts they played, or the magnitude of the sphere in which their powers found employment. The account given of them is derived from personal knowledge, and not from annals or records. It therefore is not absolutely complete as a chronicle either of them or of the circumstances in which they moved. For I cannot pretend to know everything about the many persons who are noticed in this work, or to have been acquainted with all the men and affairs of a whole generation, in so wide an empire as India. Consequently some well-known events, or some affectionately remembered episodes may be found to have been omitted from the narrative, and may therefore be missed by those who are familiar with the time to which it refers. But unless I have actual cognizance of these cases, I do not trouble the reader with any history of them, however interesting they may be.

Still, having been thrown into many arenas of labour, and been brought into contact with many men who have since become famous, I am necessarily conversant with much that may well be stated for the general good. At a time like the present, when the British people take a conscientious interest in the Eastern empire, it behoves every Englishman who possesses knowledge to communicate it to his countrymen in as popular and readable a form as possible. Though I trust that the story, so far as it extends, will be found correct by critics already acquainted with India, yet it is absolutely free from technicalities or from any local expressions which might not be intelligible to the public in England. Though the composition will, I think, stand the tests which Indian readers may apply, yet it has been studiously designed to suit the English reader.

While I hope that my work contains much that will be pleasing to those concerned, I am confident that there is nothing to cause pain to any one. Those have been chosen for mention who from greatness in deed or in station, from nobility of disposition, from proved service, or from excellence of conduct, deserve to be remembered. As I am writing from recollection —verified wherever necessary by reference to records—it is to such characters that my memory clings, and it is the career of such persons that can be most readily recalled. On the other hand, men of types different from the above doubtless have at various times passed along the stage. But I cannot undertake to describe them, or to recollect the faults into which they may have fallen, and the errors which they may have committed. Certainly some national mistakes or shortcomings have to be acknowledged upon a comprehensive retrospect of affairs. In such instances I have endeavoured to explain how these deviations happened, in order that the explanation may help in establishing sign-posts for the future.

The most salient feature of the book perhaps is the description of several among the greatest Governors-General that have ever held supreme command in India. Chapters VI., VIII., XIV., and XVI. afford a succinct, though I trust a tolerably full, analysis of the administration and the official character of four

Governors-General, namely the Marquis of Dalhousie, Earl Canning, Sir John Lawrence, and the Earl of Mayo.

My intimate connection officially with John Lawrence, first as his Secretary in the Panjab, next as the Foreign Secretary to his Government of India, and then as his Financial Councillor, may perhaps impart the character of a monograph to my account of him; and this account comprehends not only chapter XIV. mentioned above, but also chapters IV. and V. Further, in chapter IV. there is included a portrait of his celebrated brother Henry.

Some portions of the administration of three Governors-General, namely Viscount Hardinge, the Earl of Northbrook and Earl Lytton, are set forth in chapters II., XVII. and XX.

The careers of two provincial Governors, namely James Thomason and Sir Bartle Frere, are mentioned with some fulness in chapters III., and XII., and considerable reference is made to that of a third, namely Sir George Campbell, in chapter XVIII.

In chapters IX. and X. the financial policy is explained of two Finance Ministers who, after having acquired a reputation in England, were appointed to direct the finances of India, namely James Wilson and Samuel Laing, under both of whom I had the advantage of serving in a confidential capacity. My official intimacy with Wilson during his, too brief, service in India, has enabled me to pourtray accurately the closing passages of his most useful life.

Allusion, in some detail, is made to other men of distinction, namely Sir Robert Montgomery in chapters IV., V. and VII., Sir Arthur Phayre in chapter X., Sir Philip Wodehouse in chapter XX., Sir Henry Durand in chapter XVI., Sir John Strachey in chapters XV. and XVI., Bishop Cotton in chapters XI. and XIV., and Sir Seymour Fitzgerald in chapter XX. Throughout the book there are many scattered notices of those whose names will hereafter be inscribed in the roll of Anglo-Indian worthies.

Some tribute is paid, in chapters XIV. and XVI., to the services rendered to India by two English jurists, Sir Henry Sumner Maine and Sir James Fitzjames Stephen.

Several of the missionaries whose talents were equal to their zeal and piety, namely Alexander Duff, William Smith, Stephen Hislop, John Wilson, and Bishop Sargent, are duly mentioned in chapters II., III., XI., XII. and XIX. Emphatic testimony is borne to the efficacy and success of the Christian missions in India.

Further, in the belief that my countrymen desire to know something in regard to the character of those Native princes, who have proved themselves the loyal feudatories of the empire, I have given a sketch of the Maharaja of Pattiâla, the Maharaja of Jhînd, the Nizam of the Deccan, and the Maharaja of Jyepur—all deceased—in chapters VII. and XIII. Some portraiture also is included, in the same chapters, of eminent Native statesmen, namely Sir Salar Jang, Sir Dinkar Rao, Sir Madhava Rao, and Jang Behadur. Interspersed throughout the book, are notices of Native worthies who are well known to the European community in India, namely the Rev. Krishna Mohan Banerji, the Rev. Lal Behari Dey, Keshab Chunder Sen, Karsundas Mulji of Bombay, Kristo Das Pal of Calcutta and many others. Thoughtful Englishmen will readily perceive that in a vast and progressive community like that of India, there must be numerous individuals among the Natives, who, though unknown to fame in England, are exercising a potent influence among their countrymen and upon the society in which they move.

For all names and topics, whether European or Native, an index has been prepared which will, it is hoped, be found sufficiently copious to help the reader in referring to particular points without looking through any chapter entirely.

The chapters depicting the life, which is really lived in the interior of India, are VII. on the war of the Mutinies, XI. on the Central Provinces, XIII. on the Indian Foreign Secretaryship, and XVIII. on the administration of Bengal. Chapter XIII. also pourtrays the court and camp in a Native State of the first rank.

Although the book is not written at all for the purpose of describing the beauties of nature or of art, which have been already described in 'India in 1880,' still there are some delineations of the scenery in the vale of Cashmir, the eastern

Himalayas, the river kingdom of Bengal and the Western Ghât mountains.

Lastly, although the work is meant to comprise narrative rather than disquisition, yet there is in the introductory chapter a summary of the progressive results achieved during the last generation, and of the evils which still remain to be remedied; while the concluding chapter XXI. contains a specific discussion of the questions, social and political, which most nearly concern the welfare of the Natives and the position of the British Government.

R. T.

THE NASH, KEMPSEY *near* WORCESTER,
January 27th, 1882.

CONTENTS.

CHAPTER I.

INTRODUCTION.—CONTRAST BETWEEN THE CIRCUMSTANCES OF INDIA IN THE YEARS 1847 AND 1881.

CHAPTER II.

(1847.)

CLOSE OF LORD HARDINGE'S ADMINISTRATION.

CHAPTER III.

(1848–1853.)

THOMASON'S GOVERNMENT IN THE NORTH-WESTERN PROVINCES.

CHAPTER IV.

(1849–1853.)

DUUMVIRATE IN THE PANJAB OF THE LAWRENCE BROTHERS.

CHAPTER V.

(1854–1856.)

JOHN LAWRENCE ADMINISTRATOR-IN-CHIEF OF THE PANJAB.

CHAPTER VI.

(1848–1856.)

DALHOUSIE THE GREAT PROCONSUL.

CHAPTER VII.

(1857–1859.)

THE WAR OF THE MUTINIES.

CHAPTER XI.

(1862–1866.)

THE CENTRAL PROVINCES.

CHAPTER XII.

(1862–1866.)

SIR BARTLE FRERE AND WESTERN INDIA.

CHAPTER XIII.

(1867–1868.)

THE INDIAN FOREIGN SECRETARYSHIP.

CHAPTER XIV.

(1864–1868.)

JOHN LAWRENCE AS VICEROY.

MEN AND EVENTS OF MY TIME IN INDIA.

CHAPTER I.

INTRODUCTION.—CONTRAST BETWEEN THE CIRCUMSTANCES OF INDIA IN THE YEARS 1847 AND 1881.

Aspect of affairs in 1847—Respecting public establishments—Internal administration—Condition of the Natives—Improved aspect of affairs in 1881—Administrative changes—Foreign trade—Advancement of the Natives—Development of resources—National progress generally—But many evils still existing—Encouragement for the future.

In this work some account will be given of the statesmen I have met or known, and of the events with which I have been acquainted, during my time in India from 1847 to 1880. Without attempting any autobiography, I shall have occasionally to mention my own proceedings in order to explain my knowledge of the affairs described. The narrative will be confined to what I have seen and heard, or what was gathered at the place and the time of the occurrences. I do not, therefore, undertake a contemporary history which would be prepared after reference to records and annals; although I hope to contribute towards such history some testimony of use and interest. My contribution will, indeed, relate to many of the most important men and affairs during the time under consideration. Still, if this story shall be found to omit the notice of some men and events, or to mention others but imperfectly, my explanation must be that I was not so fortunate as to meet those men at the time, or did not happen to witness those events. In brief, I shall state only what I can attest personally, and not what might have been ascertained from study or investigation. Even with this limitation, however, the subjects which present themselves in relation to a chequered and eventful period are numerous and diversified.

The time under review comprises one whole generation of men, perhaps the most important that has ever passed over India. In it are compressed more striking changes than in all the preceding times of British rule, or in any of the recent ages before British rule. Other generations had seen wars, conquests, and revolutions, the annihilation of ancient institutions, and the substitution of new systems. This generation also beheld events of a like nature, though perhaps on a greater scale; for it witnessed the collection of the largest British force ever assembled on a single battle-field in India, and the fall of several kingdoms of the first rank among Native States. More than all this, however, it felt the shock of a mutiny and rebellion which convulsed half the Indian empire and shook the British power to the very foundations. It saw, too, the abolition of the East India Company, the grandest private corporation that ever existed, and the assumption of direct administrative functions by the Queen of England as Empress of India. Further, it has known changes, moral and material, of which previous times afford no example. The magnitude and rapidity of these changes can be appreciated only by contrasting the circumstances of India in 1847 and 1881.

In 1847 the time-honoured East India Company had consolidated what was then in effect, and has since been formally styled an empire under the Crown of England. The Company had completed the pacification of these widely extended territories after a protracted anarchy, so that order had everywhere replaced disorder, and the "pax Romana" was reigning throughout the country. The European soldiers were comparatively few in number, and bore a much smaller proportion to the total armed force of the country than they now bear. They were lodged in barracks which would nowadays be condemned.

Though in bravery and endurance they attained a standard which will scarcely be surpassed, their habits were often intemperate, and some of their surroundings were objectionable. While the greater part of these troops belonged to the Royal army, the remainder were raised separately in England for the service of the East India Company. On the other hand, the Native army was maintained in imposing strength, vastly outnumbering the European troops, and confidence was generally placed in its fidelity.

While the religion, the customs, and even the prejudices of the Natives were scrupulously respected for the most part, still some social reforms had been introduced, some semi-barbarous rites and usages suppressed, and some extraordinary crimes extirpated. A series of laws termed Regulations had been elaborately framed by non-professional hands; it was only in the department of criminal law that the basis of legislation was scientifically laid. At the Presidency towns there sat Crown tribunals, styled Supreme Courts, separate from the courts established by the Company. The supremacy of the civil law had been established, and a judicial system after a fashion was set up. All that proved good in the Native management of the land revenue had been studiously preserved, and many evil practices eliminated. Large proprietors of land, after the model of English landlords, had been long previously created in Bengal proper, and some adjacent provinces. Peasant proprietors had recently by a formal settlement been recognized in the North-western Provinces. The principle of fixing the revenue demand for long periods was declared, so that the landowners might enjoy the fruits of their improvements; and similar settlements for western and southern India were being prepared. Tenant-right, though much discussed, yet remained in a doubtful and precarious condition. A multitude of transit-duties and other imposts which fettered trade had been removed, but a long inland customs line for salt and sugar was organized in the heart of the country. The three Presidency seaports of Calcutta, Madras, and Bombay had been developed; the foreign trade was growing to dimensions which were then esteemed to be large, but would now be thought small. The overland route by Egypt had been established for passengers, letters and valuables; but the bulk of the merchandise was still carried by sailing ships round the Cape of Good Hope. Measures were adopted for the introduction of the tea-plant, but tea-planting was not really established, and coffee-planting had hardly begun. The exportation of jute-fibre was unknown; and the manufacture of cotton piece-goods after the European model by machinery was not contemplated. Coal was believed to exist, but no mines or seams were worked to any appreciable extent.

The rules framed for enabling the European officers of the Government, both civil and military, to restore their health after sickness, were liberal indeed, but antiquated in principle, and unsuited to the circumstances of the time. A sick officer might repair to Australia, South Africa, or the Mauritius, but not to Europe or to his native land. Members of the Covenanted Civil Service were still nominated under the patronage of the Directors of the East India Company.

The antiquities of the country had been explored by researches which will ever remain famous, and which, if they be equalled in the future, will hardly be surpassed. The study of Oriental languages was promoted, and superior education introduced among the upper and middle classes on European principles, the palpable errors of the Asiatic system having been abandoned. But primary education for the masses had hardly been attempted, and a department of public instruction was not as yet set up in each province. Though one important sect of Hindu religious reformers had arisen, still the vast majority of educated Hindus continued to profess the Brahminical religion; and the Hindu faith had not thus far been shaken at the principal centres of civilization. Female education had scarcely begun among the middle and lower classes; while among the upper classes the apartments of the ladies were closed against educational enlightenment. Christian missions had been established by missionaries whose labours adorned the annals of the Protestant church. But the mission-stations were few and far between, the Native converts were in scattered congregations mustering a few hundreds in this province or in that, and numbering perhaps some tens of thousands in the whole country. Postal lines had ramified throughout the land, but the increase of correspondence was impeded by a costly postage varying according to distance. The speed of communication was very poor; a letter required a week to arrive at a destination which is now reached in a day. The police had been established on the old Native modes, and was not only corrupt, but destitute of such organization as might be expected to produce efficiency. The prisons were conscientiously managed according to the light of those days, but their construction was faulty, their management unscientific, and their supervision incomplete in reference to the notions of the present time. Medical instruction was afforded to Native students in limited numbers, also a body of Native surgeons and physicians had been organized as subsidiary to the corps of European medical officers. Dispensaries had been opened at many places, and vaccination was introduced. But sanitation, as now understood, had not yet been contemplated. The emoluments of native *employés* were indeed higher than they had ever been under Native rule, but yet insufficient to secure integrity. From this cause, in conjunction with other causes, corruption was the rule and honesty the exception; even the Native judges were for the most part distrusted. Native officials were not advanced to any appointments of authority or importance in the service of Government, nor admitted to the ranks of the Covenanted Civil Service. Private and independent Native gentlemen were seldom entrusted with honorary functions for the public good.

Attention had been given to material improvement so far as was possible with the limited means at the disposal of the Government. The principle of borrowing capital for reproductive public works had not been entertained. The old works of irrigation originally constructed by the Native rulers had been maintained for the most part, and, in some cases, improved. One new canal, that of the Ganges, was in progress; but the great system of irrigation, which is now so famous, was then in its infancy. Road-making in a professional style had been undertaken; macadamized roadways to a limited extent existed in some provinces; but of the trunk lines, which are nowadays the veins and arteries of the country, few had advanced beyond the initiatory stage. Steamers were plying on the rivers of Bengal, and rendered to the community much service, which is now better performed by the railroads. But coasting steamers for the extensive and populous coasts were unknown, and the only convenient communication for travellers between Calcutta, Madras and Bombay was by the fortnightly steamships of the Peninsular and Oriental Company. Much of the postal mail-line between Bombay and Calcutta ran through forests sparsely inhabited, abounding in malaria, and infested by wild beasts. The introduction of railways was being discussed in general terms only, but no definite arrangement had been formed. Under all these circumstances the difficulties of communication and travelling at that time between the widely distant parts of those vast territories were such as would hardly be conceived. In an empire containing a million and a half of square miles—where, owing to unavoidably frequent changes, the necessity for locomotion was constant—journeys several hundred miles long were of common occurrence. Such journeys used to be performed during the night-time, at the rate of forty miles in each twenty-four hours, the traveller resting during the day-time, and halting at intervals. The passage from Calcutta to Delhi, which now takes forty-eight hours by rail, then took from three to four weeks. The ordinary means of conveyance was a palanquin, holding one person, and borne by eight men, relieved by relays of bearers at stages of ten miles. In the North-western Provinces only was there seen the transit in vans drawn by ponies.

For the conservancy of forests a beginning had been made; but generally the trees, both for timber and fuel, were wastefully felled, without due thought for reproduction, and no department of forestry was established.

Municipal life had not yet sprung into existence; in the interior of the country municipalities were almost unknown; even in Calcutta and Bombay the municipal organization was quite imperfect, and those great cities were ill-drained and dimly lighted.

With some bright exceptions, the Native States, comprising more than one-fourth of the empire, were not managed at all after the example of the British system, and were indifferently governed even according to the Oriental standard. In some of them misrule more or less prevailed, while in several the troubles and evils were such as would be deemed intolerable at the present time.

Lastly, respecting the finances of British India, no budget was annually produced, nor was any explanation of the public accounts given periodically to the public in India.

In 1881 either a marked change or a decided improvement is found to have occurred in every one of the national particulars above mentioned.

The East India Company has passed away, leaving a memory which, though disparaged by some opponents, is beloved by the great majority of those who are best informed, and respected by the Natives. Its conduct and policy will probably receive a favourable judgment from the historian. Under the direct administration by the Crown, public reverence for British rule has increased and personal loyalty among the Native princes has been quickened. Much progress also has been effected, socially and politically. But in fact the foundations for improvement were laid by the great Company; and there would have been a quick rate of advance, whether under the Crown direct or under the Company subject to the control and guidance of the Crown.

The Native army is now to the European forces in the proportion of two to one, instead of being in that of six to one. The Company's local European force has ceased to exist; and the European troops now belong entirely to the Royal army. The improvement in the barracks, sanitary surroundings and general condition of the European soldier is a source of satisfaction and thankfulness. Though confidence is still reposed in the Native army, the British power is understood to be really based on the strength of European troops.

Legislative Councils have been established, consisting in part of European members, holding their sessions in public, instead of legislative proceedings in the cabinet. The laws are systematized, developed, or codified in a scientific and professional manner. The old Supreme Courts of the Crown have been amalgamated with the High Courts which control all Indian courts whatsoever.

The Native portion of the judicial establishment has been improved in a mode which augurs well for the moral and mental progress of the Indians. The Native judges are now generally well-educated, upright and honest, instead of being too often the reverse.

The principle of recognizing and confirming the status of peasant proprietors, and of fixing for long terms of years the land revenue payable by them, has been largely extended. Tenant-right, though not universally recognized, has been to a considerable extent established.

The inland customs line for levying the salt-duties has been at length swept away. Care, too, has been taken lest, under the guise of octroi levied for municipal purposes in towns, some of the evils of the obsolete transit-duties should revive. The three Presidency seaports already great, have risen and prospered, till the population of Calcutta has grown to half a million and Bombay has become in respect of population the second city in the British empire. The foreign trade of India has increased by more than 400 per cent. in this one generation, a ratio hardly surpassed in the annals of any nation. An important part of the merchandise is now carried by the Suez Canal route which competes largely with that of the Cape. Tea-planting and the cultivation of coffee have become great industries. The jute-fibre is both exported abroad and manufactured at home. The manufacture of cotton goods by machinery is so successful as to excite the apprehensions of manufacturers in England. Extensive coal-mines are now worked in several provinces.

The Covenanted Civil Servants are appointed under the system of open competition; the men thus appointed form the great majority of the service; a minority only consists of those who were nominated by the Directors of the East India Company. Sick officers, both civil and military, instead of being virtually compelled to seek health in Australia or South Africa, and prevented from resorting to Europe, may now, without any difficulty, return to their native land.

Primary education for the masses has been established throughout the empire, however much the system may need development. A department of public instruction is established in every province. Three Universities have been incorporated by law, and an extensive class of highly educated Natives has arisen. The high or superior education is found to produce happy results in respect of trustworthiness of disposition and moral integrity. The sect of Hindu religious reformers has increased many-fold, and been powerfully stimulated by the progress of education. Many educated Hindus no longer believe in or even profess the Brahminical religion. The Hindu faith has been shaken at the centres of Indian civilization; but retains its hold over the masses of the people, and the system of caste has not suffered any serious inroad. The education of women, though not far advanced as yet, has taken root among the middle and humble classes, and among the upper classes the female apartments are often entered by European ladies who therein diffuse the light of knowledge.

The Protestant missions now count their native Christians by hundreds of thousands; their colleges supply candidates for the University examinations, and an important system of Christian vernacular education has been set on foot.

A cheap and uniform postage has been established, the number of post-offices nearly trebled and the speed on the principal lines increased six-fold, while the covers delivered amount to 135 millions annually.

The police instead of being roughly formed, as before, after the Native fashion, are regularly organized, and constituted upon the English model.

The prisons have been for the most part rebuilt; many of the new structures are planned and arranged in the approved English style, with the necessary adaptations for the eastern climate. Humane and enlightened principles are to some extent adopted in respect of the moral as well as the physical discipline of the prisoners.

While medical instruction is much developed, the principle of sanitation, for all the towns and for some of the larger villages, has been introduced. A sanitary department is established as an integral part of the administration in every province.

The emoluments of Native *employés* have been augmented by at least 30 per cent., and in some instances by 50 per cent.; generally with a marked result in respect of integrity and efficiency.

Natives are now advanced to positions of consequence in the service of Government. They have been appointed to be district judges and even to sit on the bench of the High Court; they are also chosen as members of the several Legislative Councils. Their admission to the ranks of the Covenanted Civil Service partly by competition and partly by nomination is secured, though that great Service is still, for the most part, manned by Europeans. Independent non-official Native gentlemen exercise many unpaid functions for the public good, serving as honorary magistrates, judges of conciliation courts, jurors, members of road-fund committees, municipal commissioners, governors of educational institutions.

Those who survey comprehensively and accurately the character of the Native officials, judicial and executive, as it was in 1847, and as it is in 1881, must feel thankful in the contemplation of a moral improvement, greater than perhaps was ordinarily expected.

The prices of food and other necessary articles have increased by 50 per cent., and even more in many cases. Though the wages of labour are still lamentably low in many localities, still there is a corresponding increase in the remuneration of many among the labouring classes.

It is in material improvement and works of public utility that 1881 offers the most palpable contrast to former times.

The system of irrigation, though still insufficient for so great a country, is nevertheless one of the wonders of the land. Not only have European works been engrafted, as it were, upon all the old native works of irrigation, but new canals have been undertaken of great capacity, breadth and length, probably the grandest, certainly the most scientifically constructed, in the world. Nine thousand miles of railway are open for traffic, connecting together the principal places in the country. All the main lines of road are now macadamized; in many places where men cannot travel by rail, they use conveyances drawn by horses or ponies; and the much-enduring race of palanquin-bearers has taken to other pursuits, like the old coach-drivers and post-boys in England. Efficient lines of steamers ply right round the coast, stopping at the numerous sea-ports. A net-work of electric telegraph lines has been spread over the whole country. Telegraphic communication with Europe is now secured by two lines, one running across Asia the other by the Red Sea, and has been opened with China, Australia, and South Africa by means of submarine cables.

The conservancy of forests has been undertaken tardily indeed, and not always effectually; still scientific forestry, mainly on the French and German models, is introduced on a large scale. The total area of the forests thus preserved is perhaps the largest to be found under any government in the world, but is yet not considerable relatively to the vastness of the country.

The municipal principle has spread itself among the towns and cities throughout the empire, the rural municipalities have specially attended to the water-supply as the first desideratum, and scarcely a town is destitute of waterworks professionally constructed. The municipalities of Calcutta and Bombay are powerful corporations, whose revenues are extensive and whose debentures command a good price in the money market. These two great cities are lighted with gas; their drainage has been nearly completed according to the principles of sanitary engineering, and their waterworks may well be compared with those of the largest cities of Europe.

The Native States are for the most part fairly well governed, instances of misrule being comparatively rare. Many of them conduct their administration after the British model, and in some the improvement has been marked.

Lastly, respecting the finances of British India, either a normal budget is introduced into the legislative council, or a financial statement equivalent to a budget is published for public information.

The general statistics of the empire afford the best proofs of its growth within this generation. In 1847 the population for the whole country, including both the British territories and the Native States, was estimated at 190 millions; in 1881 it is known by census to amount to 252 millions. In 1847 the British territories had an area of 800,000 square miles, and their population was reckoned at 100 millions; in 1881 this area has been augmented to one million of square miles, and the population to 200 millions. Four kingdoms, namely, those of Sattara, the Panjab, Nagpur and Oudh, besides the Burmese province of Pegu, have been incorporated in the British dominions. In 1847 the annual revenue of British India stood at 37 millions sterling; in 1881 the budget shews the total receipts as 65 millions. In 1847 the value of the foreign trade of the Indian empire amounted to 26 millions sterling; in 1881 it stood at 120 millions, or had nearly quintupled. It now stands at 140 millions. In 1847 the capital laid out by the Government on the permanent improvement of the country by reproductive public works, consisted of a few sums doled out sparingly year after year from the current revenues. By 1881, the Government had invested not less than 150 millions sterling in railways and canals for irrigation.

On the other hand, many evils exist to humble our national pride and keep alive an anxious foreboding.

Uncertainty of season prevails, ofttimes affecting large and populous areas. Its results may be mitigated by irrigation and communication, but cannot be wholly prevented. Desolating famine occurs periodically, and the gigantic efforts put forth by the Government to meet it are attended sometimes with success but often with failure. Reflection upon the millions sterling spent to avert famine, and yet the millions of lives lost from hunger,—fills the minds of administrators with despondency. Notwithstanding the happy issue of relief operations in some instances, it remains to be seen whether the Government will prove itself able to prevent starvation occurring on a large scale in one province or another from time to time. In many districts the population already too dense is becoming denser, and although there is much cultivable waste within the empire, the people are slow to migrate. The agriculture of the couhtry is so backward that the land produces less than two-thirds of what it is capable of producing. While most classes are growing in wealth and strength some large sections of the population still are, as they ever have been, insufficiently nourished. The wages of some at least among the labouring poor are deplorably inadequate. The rate of mortality is high, the epidemics are destructive, and the deaths from preventible causes demonstrate the want of sanitary measures. Yet there is no hope of a sufficiently far-reaching sanitation being adopted for a long time to come. Notwithstanding the system of public instruction, female education is in its infancy, the mass of the people are still unlettered, and the land-owning peasantry care not to learn. Despite the improved standard of rectitude among educated Natives, the reform of public departments and the prevention of violent offences, there is much of petty corruption and oppression exercised not only by private persons but also by the Native officials upon their helpless fellow-countrymen. Great as the works of material improvement may be, the country is still in manifest need of many additional works for which capital can hardly be found. Therefore the unimproved condition of the empire in several respects must remain an abiding source of regret. Generally the country is not rich enough to meet the administrative demands of a progressive age. The silver standard, also, places the Government at a disadvantage which has caused and at any moment may again cause financial trouble. Though peace reigns throughout the land in an unexampled degree, yet now and again internal disturbances occur which, however isolated, serve to warn us that our hold on the country is far from being perfectly strong. Treasonous conspiracies are not unfrequently formed close to the very centres of authority, illustrating the eastern proverb that the darkest spot lies immediately beneath the candle. Fanaticism and bigoted hate still exist and are apparently irreconcileable by any policy which the Government could adopt. Though the Native press is with outspoken candour loyal in the main, yet some of its utterances have been gravely disloyal, proving that the fruits of education are not always sweet, but may sometimes even be bitter. The settlement of the land with all its social benefits, essential justice and economic soundness, has yet left discontent rankling in the minds of several classes holding a territorial position. In some provinces many thousands of tenants are still without the rightful protection accorded to their more fortunate brethren elsewhere. The peasantry in several districts have by indebtedness placed themselves at the mercy of money-lenders and thus become the slaves of a legal tyranny more galling perhaps than forcible oppression. Many opposing elements exist of which the activity may remain dormant or be quickened according to circumstances, and would spring into life if any crisis were to arise. But it is doubtful whether the influences arrayed on our side are at the best more than passive. Even the mass of peasant proprietors for whom our rule has done more than for any other class will—as an eminent authority once said—continue cultivating stolidly without thinking of politics till the crack of doom. The ease whereby political falsehoods are circulated and the credulous spirit in which mischievous rumours are received, indicate that the public mind is seldom in a condition of satisfactory stability, and has been by long tradition familiarized with the thought of revolutionary change. Some of the very blessings which the Government is conscientiously affording to the people may sow the seed of ultimate trouble. Highly educated men often fail to obtain employment worthy of their talents and acquirements. The old-established professions become overstocked, yet new spheres connected with scientific and practical pursuits are developed but slowly. The Western teaching with all its enlightenment and elevating power, may induce some classes to indulge aspirations which cannot be satisfied in the immediate future. The realization of such hopes, if it ever be possible, is so remote as to be outside the range of practical politics. For these classes much is being and yet will be done; their accession to high offices in the State is already permitted, and still further concessions may eventually be made. Their entrance into public life, with its functions and responsibilities, will be facilitated, and they will be allowed a larger share than heretofore in the administration of the country. With respect to local and municipal affairs the upper and middle classes may be invited to exercise that elective franchise which has been tried with a fair measure of success in the capital cities. Many however will seek for something more than all these things, and failing to find it, will be dissatisfied. Such discontent the Government must with calmness and self-possession be prepared to face.

Thus, notwithstanding the progress and grandeur of India, there are skeletons in the imperial chamber and spectres haunting the visions of statesmen. When all that may be favourable or unfavourable has been summed up we fail to reach beyond the familiar conclusion that the country is like other dominions, a strange mixture of good and evil.

The contrast, then, between 1847 and 1881 is not drawn in a boastful or vain-glorious spirit. Those who are the best able to remember accurately the onward movements which have been made within this generation will be the most conscious of the backwardness which continues to retard the national progress, and of the darkness in which so many classes of the people are steeped. Indeed when India, as she exists, is compared in imagination with India as she ought to be, a feeling of despair supervenes. But courage revives when a retrospect is taken of the latest and most progressive generation which has yet been seen. If the ratio of progress in the generation between 1847 and 1881 shall, under Providence, be maintained during the coming and again in the succeeding generation, then an illimitable vista will open itself before the mind. The various questions as to the directions in which improvement is likely to move, may excite much interesting speculation. This chapter however is confined to a *résumé* of facts as introductory to the narrative of deeds performed by many illustrious men.

The great results already seen are not indeed wholly attributable to individuals, and are in several respects beyond human control. Nevertheless a series of statesmen in succession, and parties of administrators acting in combination, have helped to bring about the progress and prosperity which are witnessed to-day. I shall essay to chronicle such of their deeds and proceedings as have fallen within my cognizance or observation. Most of the larger actions have been noble in intention and successful in result; therefore the narrative will pourtray these in the colours which are appropriate. Some cardinal errors also must be acknowledged, but endeavour will be made to explain how these arose. Again, disputed proceedings will occasionally have to be recounted in which the conduct of statesmen is alleged by some to be wrong, and by others vindicated as being right; in such cases the conflicting views will be summarized so that justice may be done to the disputants on both sides. But after abatement has been fully made on account of everything that can be deemed unfavourable, there will remain a favourable balance on a truly grand scale. The retrospect must convince every impartial observer that despite mistakes, failures, shortcomings, omissions, there has been much of wisdom, courage, justice and nobleness in the management of affairs; and that although there have been instances of feebleness, apathy, remissness or incapacity, still those on whom the control of the helm devolved have, for the most part, proved to be men of benevolent aspirations, potent energy and patriotic virtue. Among them are many who have been fortunate in the opportunity of doing work, or privileged to render service, which may entitle them to the regard of their countrymen in England, and to gratitude from the people of India. Some are still surviving in health and strength, with high capacity for national service; and when reference is made to the living some reserve is unavoidable. Others have passed away regarding whom praise may be declared without stint or reservation,—

> "Can honour's voice provoke the silent dust
> Or flattery soothe the dull cold ear of death?"

For them it may be truly said—

> "Manibus date lilia plenis
> Purpureos spargam flores."

But I hope that it may not be necessary to add—

> "Et fungar *inani*
> Munere."

For, to commemorate their examples, is to light beacons for the guidance of ourselves and of those who come after us.

CHAPTER II.

(1847.)

CLOSE OF LORD HARDINGE'S ADMINISTRATION.

East India Company's College at Haileybury in Hertfordshire—Overland voyage to India—Calcutta in 1847—Daniel Wilson, Bishop of Calcutta—Alexander Duff and Scottish Free Church Mission — Marshman and Baptist Mission at Serampur—Remembrance of Lord Ellenborough—Lord Hardinge Governor-General—His campaign in the Satlej—His general administration—Public sentiment regarding him—My journey in the Gangetic valley.

WHEN a young man had received from one of the Directors of the Honourable East India Company a "writership" or nomination to the Covenanted Civil Service, it used to be necessary that he should obtain a certificate of moral character from the head of one of the schools in England. This certificate was given me by Archibald Campbell Tait, the successor of Arnold as head-master of Rugby, and now the Archbishop of Canterbury. The persons thus nominated to the Civil Service had to spend two years in the Company's College at Haileybury in Hertfordshire, and to pass many examinations in both European and Oriental knowledge before proceeding to India. In 1847 the College was in its prime. The Principal was Henry Melvill, afterwards Canon of St. Paul's, a preacher famed for impressive eloquence. James Amiraux Jeremie, the Dean and Professor of Classics, had a refined and delicate mind which imparted an air of æsthetic culture to all his teachings; he subsequently became Regius Professor of Divinity in the University of Cambridge and Dean of Lincoln. Richard Jones, the Professor of History and Political Economy, was the author of a book on Rent, a work which at that time had much repute. William Empson, the Professor of Law, was also the editor of the

Edinburgh Review. The Examiner in Sanskrit was Horace Hayman Wilson, one of the men who by learned and renowned labours had thrown resplendent light on the antiquities of the Hindu race. Monier Williams, who was then our Professor of Sanskrit, is now Regius Professor of that language in the University of Oxford. Major J. W. J. Ouseley, the Professor of Persian and Arabic, belonged to a family distinguished in Asiatic affairs. Edward Eastwick, the Professor of Hindustani, afterwards published a work on Persia, the outcome of his diplomatic experience in that country, and represented Falmouth in Parliament. According to the light of those days the curriculum of the College was extensive, and in many respects suitable for its purposes. The variety of subjects, however, relating to the West and the East, had a somewhat distracting effect upon those who studied hard, and, as Jeremie once said to me, was "enough to tear a student's brain to pieces." All things considered, a man, who at the age of twenty or twenty-one years passed through the College successfully, in order to join the Company's service, had enjoyed the benefit of a comprehensive education. On one of the half-yearly visitations of the Court of Directors, the Chairman, Sir James Hogg (then a member of parliament), told us students that the Company had striven to collect at the College a body of professors hardly to be surpassed in any similar institution in Europe. The friendships and associations formed at College constituted one of the several bonds of comradeship among all the Civil Servants during their administrative careers, and helped to maintain an elevated standard of thought and feeling in the Service as a *corps d'élite*. Every Civil Servant on first landing in India imagined himself to be a member of the most highly organized body of functionaries that the world had ever seen. Before sailing from England I, with some of my comrades, went to the East India Office at Leadenhall Street, in the City of London, to formally take our leave, and the sitting Director, Colonel William Henry Sykes, then distinguished by his statistical researches, entreated us with much earnestness to think kindly, even fraternally, regarding the Natives of India, adding an assurance that, if inferior to us in moral robustness.

of character, they would prove to be intellectually our equals. On the whole, many circumstances conduced to send us forth from our homes, on a strange and distant service, in that frame of mind which England should desire for those who are to represent her before the nations of the East.

We felt youthful wonder at the normal incidents of the overland journey, as it used to be made in those days—the equinoctial gale in the Bay of Biscay, the distant summit of Atlas forming a background to the view of Gibraltar, the peaks of the Spanish Sierra Nevada looming dimly over the Mediterranean horizon, the city and villas of Algiers gleaming under the glare of African sunlight, the gloomy magnificence of the Church of the Knights of St. John at Malta, the matchless prospect of the Nile delta from the citadel of Cairo, the gallop on Arab horses to the Pyramids, the long jolting of the vans across the Egyptian desert, the frowning volcanic rocks of Aden, the surf dashing right up to the cocoa-nut groves of Ceylon. Fortunately among our fellow-passengers were Bartle Frere and William Muir, then regarded as rising men in the East India Company's service. Frere would recount experience among the Mahrattas in the Deccan, and Muir would tell of the language, history, and tenures of north-western India. Their conversation confirmed my ideas respecting the quality of the Civil Service I was about to join, and helped me to form a mental standard towards which I should strive to raise my future work in India.

As our vessel entered the mouth of the Hughli the first place at which she stopped was Kedgeri, and there the captain received news that his wife had died from cholera at Calcutta after an illness of a few hours. We were told that this was the point where sad messages had often been delivered to passengers on their first touching the shore of Bengal.

On arrival at Calcutta my first care was to engage a Hindu as valet, and a Muhammadan as butler. Both these men remained in my service for a quarter of a century; the Hindu died the other day in the receipt of a small pension from me; for the Muhammadan a place was obtained in the Minister's household at the Nizam's capital in the Deccan. In those days it was common for an European officer to retain some of his Native servants for life, their younger relatives afterwards serving his son in similar capacities. Good Native servants in India still remain with their European masters for terms of which the length recalls the traditions of olden times in other lands.

The city and environs of Calcutta did not then seem to me so beautiful as they certainly are now. The noble river crowded with ocean-going vessels, and thick with a forest of masts both Indian and foreign—the suburbs, richly wooded with the casuarina, the bamboo and the plantain—the "maidan" or green grassy plain called "the lungs of the place"—the strings of carriages passing up and down the mall on the river-bank in the cool of the evening—were all there indeed. But the palaces of which we had read so much appeared scarcely palatial, though as dwelling-places they were built in an architectural style admirably suited to the climate. The drainage was execrable, causing among other evils a constant plague of mosquitos. The jackals would wake the nocturnal echoes by howling in chorus. The imperfect lighting served only to render darkness visible. There were but few public vehicles, and palanquins with their sets of bearers, hardy fellows, not from Bengal, but from Orissa, were in readiness at their stations in the streets, as cabs have their stands in European cities. It will be shewn in a future chapter how these things have been altered for the better.

The Governor-General, Sir Henry (afterwards Lord) Hardinge, was far away, near the banks of the Satlej, completing the arrangements consequent on the first Panjab war which had been recently concluded. The senior member of his Council was at Calcutta, conducting the government of the surrounding provinces of Bengal, Behar, and Orissa, the separate government for those provinces not having as yet been constructed. As newly arrived Civil Servants we were for a time attached to the College at Fort William, an institution which, at the beginning of the nineteenth century, had been designed by the great Lord Wellesley to raise on the banks of the Hughli some imitation of the classic models on the Cam and the Isis, but which was then lapsing into the state that preceded its final abolition.

I made the valued acquaintance of Sir Lawrence Peel, a relative of the Prime Minister (Sir Robert Peel). He was Chief Justice of the Supreme Court, a tribunal set up by the English Crown, separately from the East India Company's courts, but now merged in the High Court. He had long been one of the legal luminaries who vindicated the character of English law, despite the disadvantages which beset its administration in the east. His social virtues, charitable munificence, and scholarlike attainments, were worthy of the illustrious name he bore.

Daniel Wilson was then Bishop of the Calcutta diocese, and Metropolitan over the other Bishops in British India, a blunt, plain-spoken and earnest man, of the evangelical type in the best and largest sense of the term. He used to warn us, with impressive solemnity of manner, to be spiritually on our guard, as we had come to a land of sickness and death. Without any pretension to graceful gifts or accomplishments, he was a working prelate and a powerful minister of religion. He had induced the Government to found and endow a cathedral at Calcutta, without however any establishment of dean and chapter. I was one of the congregation on the day that he consecrated this new cathedral. The structure is not imposing architecturally, but it contains, among many relics and memorials now becoming historic, his own remains, underneath a tablet with the inscription (in the Greek) "God be merciful to me a sinner." He was often saying that a warmer zeal must be kindled in his clergy—the chaplains who ministered among the English community—and that the number of clergymen maintained by the state being inadequate, ought to be augmented by private effort. To this end he procured the formation of the Additional Clergy Society, which is still, though with some difficulty, kept up, and supplies pastors for the little English flocks scattered among the remote parts of India. He also was striving to infuse vitality into Bishop's College, founded by his predecessor, Bishop Middleton, for training Native clergymen. This institution had been established in the preceding generation, with far-sighted care, to meet a want which in the present and coming generations will be widely felt, namely, that of men qualified for the ministry among the fast growing congregations of Native Christians. It was then, however, languishing, with a tendency towards the decadence which has since ensued; and the want it was designed to meet is being supplied by many missionary institutions.

At Calcutta I made the acquaintance of Alexander Duff, then in the zenith of his usefulness as a missionary of the newly formed Free Church of Scotland. While zealously interesting himself in missionary work among the population of the interior, he was Principal of the Scottish school and college at Calcutta for the education of Native youths in the vernacular and in English. Of the scholars some were converts, and many were still heathen while receiving Christian as well as secular instruction. Those who saw him in his latest years labouring as Convener of the Foreign Missions at Edinburgh, and heard the voice of the old man eloquent, can imagine the vivacity with which, during his prime, he lighted up the severest discussions on eastern philosophy, on Native superstitions, on Oriental ideas. Having just completed his book upon Indian Missions, he was fond of explaining orally to us his listeners, what he had so well set forth in that work, namely, the effect which the vastness of the landscape in India, the grandeur of the scenery, the magnificence of the atmospheric phenomena, had wrought through many generations upon the Hindu mind. He thought that thereby the fancy had been over-stimulated, and the imagination, as it were, inflated, that some faculties had run riot in excessive luxuriance, while other and more important powers had become stunted or shrunken. He thence inferred that sound and precise knowledge would pave the way for the reception of religious and moral truth. Thus he relied much on the bracing efficacy and the sobering influence of high education. It was mainly to such instruction that he applied himself with signal ability and with a success which at that time was pre-eminent. Other missionaries in the several Protestant demoninations may have surpassed him in Oriental acquirements, or in evangelistic labours among masses of Natives, but in the work of superior education, with the view of leading youths towards higher and holier truths, he has hardly been equalled by any missionary in this generation. His influence was not confined to the Natives; he was in himself, for many years, a power among the European community of Calcutta; if any movement for good was to be impelled forward his eloquent advocacy was invoked. In after years, when the University of Calcutta was constituted, he became one of the most influential members of the senate, and assisted effectually in determining the standard or the curriculum for the higher walks of education. The last time I heard him speak in public was on the occasion of a severe famine in some districts of northern India, and rarely has the cause of suffering humanity been pleaded with more pathetic earnestness.

Near Calcutta was Serampore, the old mission station of the Baptist community, redolent with the fragrance of memories left by the elder Marshman and by Carey. At that time the younger Marshman, afterwards known as a popular historian of India, and as the biographer of Havelock the hero, was conducting the *Friend of India* newspaper, and was acknowledged to be at the head of Anglo-Indian journalism. Many of those who witnessed the sudden decline of this journal subsequently, will have hardly realized the influence it once possessed, from the soundness of its information, and the literary merit of its articles in the time of Marshman and his successors Meredith Townsend and George Smith.

Our life at Calcutta, though not favourable for acquiring knowledge of the Indian people, except secondhand from the educated Natives at the capital, did yet enable us to gather the best thoughts of the English community, official and non-official, regarding the state of the Government and the course of events.

The late Governor-General Lord Ellenborough was remembered with warmth of admiration by some, but in a cold and critical spirit by others. He was understood to have evinced an unaccountable dislike to the Covenanted Civil Service. In proof of such dislike the case of the Nerbudda territories was cited, where he had dismissed the Civil Servants in a body, sending them back to the older provinces, and replacing them with officers selected from the army. The Civil Servants, it was argued, were personally able and efficient officers; if he found them erring or mistaken in their management, he could have set them right by revised instructions, but to change the entire *personnel* in that way was to make a child's play of government. Whether a feeling adverse to Civil Servants had really been entertained by him or not, the belief in its existence naturally caused him to be jealously criticized by the leading members of the Civil Service, who possessed influence in many quarters. These critics would call his proclamations bombastic, his movements meteoric, his opinions enigmatical, and his conduct theatrical. By them even his share in the successful termination of the first Afghan war was disputed. The Generals, especially Sir William Nott of Candahar, were said to have restored the dignity of British arms and policy, despite the discouraging tenour of their instructions from the Governor-General. This passing criticism, as expressed at the time, has since been, and may yet further be, tested by historical investigation. There was one man, Major (afterwards Sir Henry) Durand, who, having as Private Secretary fully enjoyed the Governor-General's confidence, could, beyond all others, have done justice to Lord Ellenborough's views, intentions and policy in India. But his untimely death extinguished any hope there might have been that this task would one day be performed by him. Still the best-informed persons of the time would say that in several respects Ellenborough possessed real genius, that many of his ideas were statesmanlike, and that he ofttimes shewed solid judgment. The rhetoric of his polished oratory commanded the admiration of both friends and opponents. By the officers of the army he was beloved, being regarded as the special protector of their interests. The non-official community deeming him to be "dignus imperii," felt regard for his conspicuous and popular qualities. The indignity he unavoidably suffered, when recalled from his post by the Court of Directors, caused public sympathy to be drawn towards him. And the valedictory entertainments, given to him on his departure from

Calcutta, expressed the general regret that the bright promise of his career in the East had been prematurely destroyed.

Sir Henry Hardinge, succeeding Lord Ellenborough, was a man of quite a different mould. He was lacking in the brilliancy of his predecessor, and was quiet, unassuming and soldierlike. He had not a definite ambition politically nor a preconceived policy in civil affairs; his desire was to discharge to the utmost those arduous duties which the current of events in the East might cast upon him from day to day. He may perhaps have heard of his predecessor being unpopular with the Civil Servants, inasmuch as he apparently tried to reassure them by judiciously considerate language. He was quite free from any angularities which might provoke friction with any class of the community. His military knowledge was soon called into play by the political conjunctures which ended in the first Panjab war. When the hostilities began he had, in addition to all his ordinary cares of state, to take an active part in the organization of transport for the army advancing across the weary plains between Delhi and the Satlej. In that affair he largely availed himself of the services of John Lawrence, then Magistrate of Delhi. After reaching the banks of the Satlej, he actually worked in a military capacity in the field, assuming the functions of second in command to the Commander-in-Chief, Sir Hugh Gough. In taking this extraordinary step, he was justified in public estimation by the successful result; nevertheless, that step was unprecedented, and not consistent with the ordinary relations between the Governor-General and the Commander-in-Chief. It was manifest that both these high functionaries must have displayed wonderful tact, temper and forbearance. But irrespective of the question as to how Sir Henry Hardinge, as head of the Government, came to be in the field of battle, actually leading a wing of the army in action, the praise of his conduct when there was on the lips of all men. On the night after the battle of Ferozshah he was wakeful all through the nocturnal hours, moving about among the troops who lay bivouacking on the ground. With quiet and cheerful demeanour he was telling the private soldiers that they must rise at the dawn and finish beating the already half-beaten enemy, but warning those in his confidence that if the attack should not succeed in the morning there was nothing left for them but to die honourably on the field. The anecdote that he had on this night taken the decorations from off his breast so that they might not be among the trophies of the enemy, was hardly credited; but it was known that he had ordered his papers to be destroyed in the event of defeat. It was believed that the 21st December, 1846, the date of Ferozshah, was the most perilous day that had passed over India since the beginning of the century. Never before had such stout and valorous resistance been offered by Indian troops to the British army. The enemy possessed what might have proved victorious advantages of which he forbore to make use—a forbearance which was attributed to treachery among his leaders. If the force under Hardinge and Gough at Ferozshah had been overwhelmed by superior numbers, there was nothing to stop the Sikh army from overrunning the North-western Provinces down to Allahabad, and hardly any intermediate strongholds which could have been successfully held against them. Their further advance towards Calcutta must have depended on the Gurkhas of Nepal, who would probably have descended from the Himalayas to ravage Behar and northern Bengal, and thus the English might have been driven back to their base on the sea-coast. Such in the, perhaps exaggerated, apprehension of that day was the peril from the very jaws of which the British had been saved by the narrow chances of war. Disasters in Afghanistan and elsewhere were, indeed, borne in mind, still immediately after them none doubted that the British power remained erect. But most people thought that if any disaster had occurred at Ferozshah, this power would have been shaken seriously.

There were some brilliant passages in the campaign on which all men dwelt with pride and hope; some of the foot regiments had in the assaults evinced all the traditional qualities of British infantry; the exploits of the cavalry regiments, the 3rd Dragoons and the 9th Lancers, resounded in public commendation, and people recalled the famous memories of Assaye and

Laswari, when great military results were won by a few hundred English sabres.

Fierce invectives had been hurled from some quarters against Sir Henry Hardinge for his alleged want of preparation before the Sikh army crossed the Satlej and burst like a swollen torrent upon upper India. Well-reasoned rejoinders were made by his friends to such animadversion; but most prudent men suspended their judgment. The truth was that he did his best with the means at his disposal; it was vain to blame a statesman for not being perfectly prepared when he had not the resources for adequate preparation. In that as in so many other conjunctures the Government had not enough of English troops in the country; but this error, instead of being punished by defeat, was luckily followed by glorious victory; so the policy of keeping the European armament at too low a scale was maintained.

The treaty made with the Panjab State after this campaign on the Satlej was generally approved; and Hardinge, by establishing a regency under British supervision and annexing an important part of the Panjab to the British dominions, was thought to have made a good bargain for his Government, inasmuch as he was obliged to conclude peace speedily. For his force, though flushed with victory, was scanty in numbers, the fortresses of the Panjab were still untaken, and the hot weather was fast becoming too inclement for operations.

One part of his arrangements was however bitterly criticized, namely, the gift of Cashmir to Golab Sing. The allegation that this beautiful territory was sold to Golab Sing for a paltry sum of money was absurd; the real argument was that the grant of territory had been considered desirable in order to establish the new regime in the Panjab and its dependencies. This reason was seldom admitted by the public at the time, and is still much disputed. Such a discussion is however to be deprecated as being likely to raise doubts regarding the faithfulness of British intentions. Manifestly a gift, once made, cannot be recalled because it is regretted.

Sir Henry Hardinge was anxious to be relieved of his high

office when much of the ordinary time of incumbency remained unexpired. Thus he did not allow to himself full space for running a political and administrative career. Despite the shortness of time, however, he attended to several of the important matters which came into prominence under his successor. He visited the Ganges Canal in order to satisfy himself before sanctioning any outlay for the works. He advocated the plan of entrusting to a company in England the construction of the first railway to be undertaken in India. He recommended a reform of the Post-office with a view to the equalization of postal charges. He supported Thomason, who was striving for manifold improvements in the North-western Provinces. He first brought to the front three men who rapidly rose to eminence, namely, Henry Lawrence, John Lawrence, and Henry M. Elliot. He was often mentioned by the Bishop as having set a Christian example before the world. He was deemed to be a discreet, practical and conscientious ruler. When he was elevated to the peerage, as Viscount Hardinge, and eulogized in Parliament by the Prime Minister (Sir Robert Peel), his countrymen in the East raised a responsive applause. The public gratitude was attested by the statue which was then entrusted to the sculptor Foley for execution, and which is now admired as among the most artistic ornaments of Calcutta. Among the men whom he had befriended and trusted was Henry Lawrence, by whom the best-informed record of his career was subsequently written.

Having spent at Calcutta several months in the study of Oriental languages, and thus acquired by quiet study some knowledge which could hardly be gathered amidst the stir and bustle of the life which was so soon to follow, I proceeded on my way to upper India. The journey now takes two days by railway; it then took two or three weeks for the traveller borne in a palanquin—aptly described as "a box carried on men's shoulders"—by relays of eight Native bearers at each stage of ten miles. Midway in this journey, as we approached the place where the railway station of Rajmehâl now stands, the swamps were still spongy after autumnal rains. My much-enduring palanquin-bearers struggled in the mud all through that moonlit night. Next day an European medical officer warned me that "jungle" fever might be the consequence of the exposure to such a malarious atmosphere during the nocturnal hours. He described the symptoms which would herald the approach of the dreaded malady, such as a creeping sensation in the spine and a seemingly iron band around the forehead. As the scenery was interesting and the weather lovely, I began to take what might prove to be my last look at the beauties of nature; but fever did not come, and the apprehension passed away. The chief local authority conducted me to the tomb of Cleveland, in whose memory the Government had set up an epitaph declaring that he had established British dominion in the hearts and minds of the neighbouring hill tribes. Shortly afterwards I stood before the stately monument over the grave of the Marquis Cornwallis, the Governor-General who died at his post, after having introduced the Permanent Settlement at the end of the last century, a measure which was expected to naturalize the landed institutions of England among the Natives of Bengal, but which has certainly failed in some of its main objects, and is regarded by many authorities with mixed feelings. At length the pinnacles, cupolas and minarets of Benares came into view, and then I had entered the limits of the North-western Provinces.

CHAPTER III.

(1848–1853.)

THOMASON'S GOVERNMENT IN THE NORTH-WESTERN PROVINCES.

City of Benares—Church of England missions there—First impressions regarding the Natives and the country—Life in camp—Scenes at Agra and Allahabad—Second Panjab War—Popular estimate of Lord Gough—Thomason Lieutenant-Governor—His personal characteristics—His method of governing—Objects of his policy—Land settlement—Village communities—Primary education—The Ganges Canal—Training of Natives as civil engineers—Thomason's death—Affectionate respect for his memory.

STAYING at Benares some little time, I observed the working of the Mission belonging to the Church (of England) Missionary Society, and conducted by the Reverend Missionaries William Smith and Charles Benjamin Leupolt. The conversation of these self-denying and experienced men was most instructive to a young officer. They impressed me with their charitable considerateness towards the faults of the Native character, and their appreciative discernment of its virtues. They shewed me what were the ways of native thought, and how those ways could best be approached by moral and religious influences. They explained the characteristics of Hindu priests, and the results of a caste-system which dominated the popular superstitions. Their mission was a very important one, as it related to the most sacred seat of the Hindu religion and the greatest abode of Brahminical learning. The sight of their work taught me, at the outset of my career, the salutary lesson that something more was to be expected from British rule than military success, political management, material prosperity and intellectual education. Then the reflection was brought home to me that when England sent forth men to the East, some to lead her armies, others to collect her revenues or construct her public works, and again others to manage her trade or industrial enterprises,—she could also provide many for higher and more blessed purposes than these.

William Smith had a command of colloquial Hindi and Hindustani which had seldom or never been surpassed by an Englishman in northern India. His preaching among the heathen was most interesting and suggestive to Europeans as well as to Natives. Early in the morning he would drive me in a gig from the Mission station to the city of Benares; then he would conduct me for a walk in the crowded streets, stopping at points where the Natives most did congregate, to preach for a while; then arriving at the bank of the river Ganges, he would shew me the dying carried down to the water's edge to breathe their last near the holy stream, and the corpses reverently laid on the flaming pyres. Sometimes, too, he would take me on board a boat soon after sunrise, so that we might drop gently down the sluggish current, and thus leisurely admire the unrivalled spectacle which the city displays at that hour of the day, when the slanting rays of the sun light up cone-shaped temples, glittering finials, stone carvings, grotesque frescoes, lattice windows, palaces and housetops rising one above the other, and successive flights of steps. The gayest part even of this bright scene, however, was the crowd thronging the river-bank, clad in white diversified with all sorts of colours from red to blue. Countless bathers, too, were disporting themselves in the water, swimming, plunging, diving, floating.

Sometimes, again, we visited quieter scenes; the thatched cottages of the Native Christian village, amidst bamboos and creepers; the boys in the school-house; the girls knitting or sewing and singing hymns; the little church, with its spire bearing witness to God in a strange land; the divine service in the vernacular; the altar, with the Native communicants. Or again, we entered the class-rooms of a mission school, where scholars were being examined in Bible history, or studying the map of the world, or reading English poetry, or acquiring the rudiments of science, or learning the classical language of their own country.

Little was then being done by the State for primary education among the Natives, and the efforts of Government were confined to the higher branches of instruction. There was at Benares a college mainly for instructing Native youths in Sanscrit; of this Ballantyne was the principal, and his Oriental acquirements greatly conciliated the regards of the learned classes among the Hindus of the city.

Journeying onwards from Benares I met, at Cawnpore, John, the elder brother of William Muir, who has been already mentioned. Though much occupied with his judicial duties, he was prosecuting his researches into Hindu antiquities, and acquiring fast that Sanscrit learning for which he has since become famous.

At that time all well-informed persons whom I met, concurred in advising me to seek employment, in a district where the principal officer was a man possessing marked ability himself, and also disposed to educe and cultivate whatever capabilities might be inherent in his subordinates. With this view I obtained an appointment in the district of Mathra (near Agra) under Edward Thornton, the Magistrate and Collector, who was a man of high repute. The Magistrates and Collectors are well known as forming the most important class in the Civil Service, and being the representatives of British rule before the people in every-day life. Of this class Edward Thornton was a worthy example; he was a capital rider, a good judge of agricultural products; a prompt, careful and accurate man of business; versed in the tenures, customs, traditions of the land-holding classes and possessing a sound knowledge of the Natives generally; an adept in unravelling the skeins of a complicated dispute, which so often occurs between one village and another, and in gathering up the threads so as to arrive at a conclusion; patient in listening to grievances, and imbued with a never-failing sense of essential justice, so far as it could be meted out amidst the conflicting considerations which spring up in Native society. He was full of zeal, not only for doing well himself, but also for making others do the like; and he heartily attended to the task of instructing me and his other assistants. He taught us what to observe, and how to note it exactly; he enjoined us to search for our facts, to remember them precisely, and to rely on ourselves rather than lean on our Native subordinates, reminding us that such self-trust would be useful only when we were well grounded in our knowledge. He strove to make us care personally for the Natives, guard their interests, and enter into their troubles and anxieties. Through the vista of years I look back with gratitude to the official tuition then received from him.

Thornton soon despatched me into the interior of the district to supervise a registration of landed tenures which was being made, and live in tents among the villages. Then I saw for the first time that camp life which every one must wish to live who would understand India aright and feel the exhilarating effect of contact with rural affairs. My tent would be pitched in one of those umbrageous groves of the mango which are amongst the chief ornaments of the country, or on the ridge of a steep bank overhanging a river, anon under the spreadin branches of a banyan tree, amidst—

> "the ample shade
> Cloistered with columned dropping stems and roofed
> With vaults of glistening green."

The district was classic ground to Hindus, as there the scene was laid of some among the events in their sacred mythology. Picturesque rocks crowned with temples here or there cropped up in the midst of the cultivated plain; and among these were embosomed sacred tanks. The margin of such a tank would be crowded with pilgrims and visitors on festival days or other gala occasions. Sometimes there were illuminations at nightfall, causing the outline of rock and building to be reflected in the water.

While the Muhammadan mosques had imposing dimensions, the Hindu temples seemed small and overlaid with ornamentation. Grateful was my surprise when near Mathra I found a half-ruined fane built in a grand style which almost called to mind the nave and transepts of a church, but having a material of purple stone which could hardly be matched in Europe.

Adjoining the district of Mathra was that of Agra, whither I now and then made short excursions to see the famed marble tomb of the Mogul empress in its pure glory; to spell out the epitaph on the tomb of Akber the Great; to wander among the desolate quadrangles, pillared halls and sculptured recesses; to scan the towers which kings ascended for viewing the royal battues; to stand beneath the lofty domes, mount the minarets, and pace the long stretching arcades of the deserted mosques. There, too, I visited the Christian villages, inhabited by those who had been left orphans during the last famine, and rescued by the missionaries.

The city of Agra, built on the bank of the Jamna, used then to be approached by a bridge of boats thrown across the stream when the water was low. But the river is now spanned by a railway viaduct, from which there is a fine view, comprising the city, the great mosque, Akber's fort, and the Tâj mausoleum in the distance. As we wandered about the fort, admiring its architecture and beautiful material of red sandstone, or stood on the balcony of its palace, we little thought that within a few years this place would be the refuge of our countrymen during the crisis of the mutinies and an abode of grief to many English families.

Sometimes I was able to visit the neighbouring Raja of Bhartpur surrounded by his half-barbaric pomp, watch his gaudy cavalcades, witness the combats in the arena between elephants and other animals, enjoy the beauties of his pleasure-gardens irrigated by artificial watercourses, and his summer-houses with their graceful architecture of richly carved stone.

The manner in which a Native prince received his European guests or visitors excited my curiosity. The Natives seemed to be masters of scenic effect, with the diffusion of chastened light over masses of rich ornamentation, colours gorgeous yet possessing what artists term quality, and the perspective of columns and arches. Then the prince and his suite out of deference to us would seat themselves awkwardly on European chairs, instead of sitting comfortably cross-legged on the carpet. But all the same the carpet was there and had its uses, for upon it would be laid trays of sweetmeats, tinsel ornaments and indigenous fabrics,—the trays being scrupulously arranged in sets for presentation to the visitors, each set being graduated in its size and contents according to the official rank of every visitor.

I was surprised to find the country literally strewn with relics, ruins and remains, indicating the existence of dynasties and of social systems, regarding which no other record was discoverable. It seemed that—

> "Where'er we tread 'tis haunted holy ground,
> No earth of thine is lost in vulgar mould,
> But one vast realm of wonders spreads around."

Then, looking at these sights, one felt tempted to exclaim—

> "Chaos of ruins! who shall trace the void,
> And say, here was, or is, where all is doubly night."

Thus the ways of the Natives, both high and humble; the toils and anxieties, the simple-minded happiness of the peasantry; the course of the seasons; the seed-time and harvest; the colts, fillies, steers, heifers, kids and lambs; the strings of carts laden with merchandise, dragged by bullocks along the deep ruts of the dusty roads—became familiar to me. In the day-time there was a sense of glare and aridity; in the afternoon my tent used to be crowded to suffocation with men wrangling about their boundary-marks, their quotas of revenue, their ancestral shares. But in that winter season nothing could exceed the cheering glow of the unclouded sunrise, morning after morning, or the serene loveliness of those moonlight nights. To my English notions, November evenings were shrouded in damp mist; but here I found the November moon to be the most auspicious in the year, when the rains were over, the autumn crops garnered, and the husbandman gladdened by the sight of the young wheat rising to form his future spring harvest.

Though for many days consecutively I never heard the English language spoken, yet occasionally I was fortunate in the companionship of a brother officer. Among my companions at that time was Ensign Brownlow, who was afterwards distinguished both on the north-west and north-east frontier of the empire, and is now General Sir Charles Brownlow, one of the Secretaries at the Horse Guards in London.

The daily converse of the Natives was, however, full of interest and novelty; if a man in authority talks with them much, they are skilful in enlisting his sympathy in their concerns, and they have an inexhaustible fund of amusing personalities. So I felt regret when, compelled by the heat to return to the head-quarters and to the house, there to sit in darkened rooms, behind grass mats which were kept constantly wet, so that the burning wind as it played upon them might be made to cool the inner air.

While at the head-quarters of the district, and occupied all day long in hearing disputes, I saw and heard of the dark part of the Native character almost to the exclusion of the bright one. Forgery, tampering with documents, swearing and counter-swearing, perjury on one side or the other, perhaps on both sides, the striking of the balance for truth between conflicting statements, the bewildering search for some clue to fact amidst mazes of falsehood—these were the staple themes for my consideration during the greater part of the day. When out of court or office, I had executive duties to perform which led me into confidential conversation with many Natives. Their besetting fault seemed to be a capacity for hating one another; no doubt every man had his friends, and felt kindly towards his fellow-countrymen in general, but still appeared to entertain a mortal spite against individuals. It was painful to note this irresistible tendency, not so much to open slander, but rather towards secret backbiting. There were many shocking features in the crimes which came before the magistracy; on the other hand, there was no wife-beating, nor any of the brutal circumstances which in other countries attend intemperance. The men seemed very jealous and sensitive regarding the honour of their women. Nevertheless, partly from the out-of-doors life which the women of humbler classes lead (in contradistinction to the women of the upper classes), conjugal infidelity was not uncommon, and usually caused sanguinary or deadly feuds. It was astonishing to see the readiness with which men took up iron-headed staves for the bloody arbitrament of agrarian disputes, indicating that the fervid and violent temper produced by war or revolution, and transmitted through many generations, had not yet subsided. The thing which weighed oppressively upon the mind of a young officer was the consideration that very few Native officials could be trusted, and that a pleasant address and an impressive manner were but too often the cloaks of deceit or corruption. We were warned of this by all experienced persons, and palpable facts frequently forced it upon our unwilling conviction.

But if reluctantly receiving unfavourable impressions while at the head-quarters, I rapidly gathered favourable notions when encamped among the villages. It soon became apparent that there were countless good people who would mind their own business in their humble homes, and seldom enter a public office, or see the face of authority. The rural folk evinced much of domestic virtue, fraternal fidelity, social cheerfulness, charity towards the needy. If questioned regarding a disputed point, while near home, and in the presence of their neighbours, they would speak the truth. Among the Native officials, too, men were found who formed bright exceptions to the prevailing corruption, and whom, after the lapse of years, I still remember as honourable men and pleasant companions.

It is indeed important that junior civil officers should be employed under canvas in the interior of the country, so that their minds may not become prejudiced, nor their sympathies alienated by the scenes of a police office or a magistrate's court, and that they may learn from observation of the villagers at home that there are many elements of good in the Native character. Thus will be acquired that sympathizing faculty, without which they cannot become successful rulers over masses of Natives.

From Mathra I proceeded to Allahabad, which, situated on a tongue of fertile land near the confluence of the Ganges and Jamna, was then thought one of the prettiest stations in the country The historic fortress dominating the point of confluence, the sacred bathing-places frequented on festival days by myriads of Hindus, the united floods of the two rivers in the rainy season, the long lanes shaded by mango groves—confirmed the pleasurable impression already made upon my mind by Indian scenes. But the quiet graceful place as it then was, is hardly to be recognized in the Allahabad of to-day. Its commanding situation geographically and politically has caused it to become a large military cantonment, a central railway station, and a seat of civil government. The river is crossed by a grand latticed bridge, the fields, lanes and groves have been taken up for rows of barracks, public departments and palatial structures.

While our thoughts were thus devoted to the labours of peace, news came of renewed trouble in the Panjab. At Multan, with the connivance of the Sikh governor Mulraj, the political officers Agnew and Anderson had been treacherously murdered while predicting with their last breath that the deed would be soon avenged by a British army. A besieging force despatched against Multan was obliged to suspend the siege and await reinforcements. Several Sikh chieftains, taking courage at this, raised an army in revolt against the British control, as set up by Lord Hardinge. The new Governor-General, Lord Dalhousie, hastened from Calcutta towards the then British frontier on the Satlej; and on his way held a large levée at Agra. He looked fresh and youthful for his great office, but vigilant and self-sustained. We wished him god-speed on his grave enterprise, for all knew that a struggle was impending, on the issue of which the tranquillity, indeed the safety, of the British territories in northern India must depend. The martial classes of the Sikh nation, and the greater part of their feudal aristocracy, had risen with a resolve to shake off, if possible, that yoke which the British Government was equally determined to maintain. The warlike reputation of the Sikhs, always high, had been raised by their conduct in the first Panjab war. They declared bitterly that they would have beaten and pursued right through upper India the Native troops of the British Government, had it not been for the prowess of the European soldiery. They were feared by the Native population of the British territories; and feverish speculation was arising in the Native mind regarding the outcome of the second war, of which the opening events had been unfavourable. Still the public mind was reassured by the sight of many thousand troops hurrying past, some to re-inforce the besiegers of Multan, others to form an army under Lord Gough for operations beyond Lahore. The eyes of all were turned chiefly towards Gough's forces opposed to the Sikh leaders and all their chivalry on the bank of the Chenab. After some actions, partially successful on the British side, the Sikhs retired towards the river Jhelum, close to the classic spot where Alexander the Great attacked Porus. Soon it was proclaimed that in this position at Chilianwala, Gough had attacked the Sikhs victoriously and captured some of their guns. The rejoicing was, however, speedily dimmed by the information which arrived in painful detail. The victory proved to be of a Pyrrhic character. The enemy had been assailed while posted in a jungle, offering every disadvantage to the assailants. The British right wing suffered defeat, while the centre and the left wing were successful. The 24th Regiment, reckoned to be the flower of the force, had been half destroyed; out of its twenty-five officers who went into action at noon, thirteen were laid out dead in one tent by the evening. The 14th Light Dragoons, a regiment of historic fame, fell into confusion amidst the jungle, and was carried back in a stampede upon our own artillery. The enemy had closely pursued our cavalry, and riding about amongst our artillery had sabred the gunners at their guns. The British centre and left had indeed victoriously seized a large part of the enemy's position, capturing many guns, but were unable, by reason of the supervening darkness, to make good their advantage. Shortly afterwards the enemy retook most of their guns, leaving a few only in our hands. The night, after the battle, was spent by the British army in distress and confusion. Next morning the enemy retired, the British not renewing the attack, nor making any pursuit. It further appeared that the British army had come up within sight of the enemy during the forenoon, and Lord Gough was believed to have formed a judicious plan for giving battle on the next morning. Some movements on the part of the enemy induced him to alter his plans and deliver the attack at once, before the intervening ground could be properly reconnoitred. Once again, it was said, the old mistake had been committed of beginning the action too late in the day. To this mistake were attributed the unfruitful result of that victory—which, despite partial failure, had at one moment been really achieved—the impossibility of securing all the captured guns, and the nocturnal confusion which jeopardized the safety of the whole force.

It is difficult to pourtray the grief and astonishment which these tidings excited in the public mind. Indignation ran high against Lord Gough, who was believed to have allowed his hot blood and natural impetuosity to overcome the dictates of his professional judgment. His so-called "Tipperary tactics," in precipitating the battle, were freely denounced. It was expected that the war would drag its tedious length along, and that he would be superseded by orders from England. The newspaper press teemed with lampoons and satires upon the conduct of the campaign; and when the British despatches describing the battle appeared in the Gazette, counter-despatches were satirically framed and published, as if coming from the Sikh commanders, and relating in humorous terms the partial discomfiture of the British.

The winter season, favourable for operations in the field, was advancing towards its end, while Multan was still untaken, and the main Sikh army was unbroken. But there soon came the welcome tidings that Multan had fallen, and the rebel Mulraj had surrendered himself after the British sappers had approached the very gateway of his fortress, and when the storming party was about to advance for the final assault. Then were announced, first the crowning victory won by Gough at Gujerat after an action deliberately fought, next the brilliant pursuit of the flying enemy by Sir Walter Gilbert, and finally the utter collapse of the Sikh insurrection. There was general rejoicing because Gough had been so fortunate as to put the finishing stroke to the war before any successor to his command could arrive from England. For Gough, despite transient dissatisfaction at his hotheadedness (real or supposed), was beloved by the whole community, whether civil or military, both by those who were and those who were not acquainted with him personally. He was known to be quite aflame with martial ardour, and to be as generous and self-devoting as he was resolute and enduring. When his blood was cool, he was declared by all competent observers to be an able strategist and tactician. His energetic forwardness in action despite increasing years, the dignity of his character and the nobility of his career endeared him to his countrymen in the East. His promotion in the peerage as Viscount Gough set the seal of royal approval to the popular esteem.

Meanwhile it became known that Sir Charles Napier had been appointed Commander-in-Chief. The public judgment in northern India had never been pronounced regarding his political conduct in Sind; but whatever were the merits or demerits of his proceedings there, he was believed to be the hero of several hard-fought battles, and considered one of the best soldiers living; so his arrival was hailed with a hearty welcome.

The war being over, there ensued a brief suspense respecting the disposal of the Panjab, now finally subdued. The obstacles to annexation were thought in diplomatic circles to be considerable; and it was expected that Henry Lawrence (the Resident at Lahore) would do his best to save the Sikh dynasty. Still the prevailing opinion was that Lord Dalhousie would, indeed must, procure sanction from England to annex the whole Panjab. Thus when he declared the province to be annexed he seemed to be announcing that which was a foregone conclusion in the public mind.

The annexation having been proclaimed, British officers were immediately nominated for the administration of the new territory. The principal among these officers were taken from the North-western Provinces, because the Panjab was contiguous to those Provinces, having a partial (though not entire) affinity with them in respect of race and language. Further, John Lawrence, upon whose recommendation the selection of civil officers for the annexed country was made by the Government, thoroughly believed in the superior advantages of the North-western Provinces, as a school for administration, over any other part of India. Knowing well the qualities of the men in the ranks whence he himself had been drawn, he sent for the best among his old comrades to man what were at that moment regarded as the posts of civil honour. Consequently several of the foremost officers in the North-western Provinces, Edward Thornton (already mentioned), Robert Montgomery and Donald Macleod, regarding both of whom more will be written hereafter, and others, were summoned to the Panjab. These events raised the spirits and enlarged the ambition of the public service in the North-western Provinces, of which Mr. Thomason was then the Lieutenant-Governor, and made us all think that there was no chief like him, and that to be counted among his men was a passport to future distinction.

James Thomason had been Foreign Secretary to the Government of India, when he was chosen by Lord Ellenborough to be Lieutenant-Governor. When Ellenborough's judgment in state affairs was sometimes called in question it would be urged in reply that at least he shewed discernment and sagacity in appointing Thomason to the highest post then in the gift of the Governor-General. Thomason towered, metaphorically and actually, a head and shoulders above his fellows; his figure was tall and spare, his brow massive, his countenance thoughtful, his utterance gentle. Though permanently lamed by an accident, he preserved his bodily as well as mental energy. Being the son of a well-known missionary, he had, as might be expected, a devout and reverent bearing in all matters relating to religion. His religious sentiments, though never manifested in any obtrusive way, permeated his whole existence. His Christian example, adorning a high official station, and forming an attribute of one so renowned for successful achievements, had an influence which was not the less potent from being indirect.

Underneath a mild and somewhat reserved manner he maintained an intensity of will, and a tenacity of purpose. He took a pleasure in exercising his faculty of patient and continuous thought; and having thus formed his resolves, he adhered to them with unyielding perseverance. Having set before himself certain objects of policy, he prosecuted them unfalteringly, despite delay and disappointment, to their beneficent end. He was slow and cautious in giving his confidence, but it was unreserved when once given, and those who enjoyed it knew that they could depend upon him absolutely. Though simple in his tastes and habits, he was generously hospitable; and in respect to all works of charity, of benevolence, of moral and religious improvement, he was unostentatiously and judiciously munificent. His habitual composure and unbending demeanour in public prevented him from becoming popular with his own countrymen. While he lacked some of the external qualities which are usually associated with leadership, being generally possessed by the *ἀναξ ἀνδρων*, and though he failed to arouse enthusiasm on his side, he was in effect a leader of men.

His acquirements in several branches of Oriental learning were considerable, and but for his devotion to state affairs, he would have become a great scholar. His loving pursuit of antiquarian research was interrupted by his distracting avocations. Though excelled by some in knowledge of India as a whole, he has never been surpassed by any Englishman in acquaintance with the Natives of northern India, both agricultural and commercial. He felt a charitable considerateness for the failings and faults of the Natives, a sympathetic appreciation of their merits and virtues, and benevolent aspirations for their moral advancement. He burned with a desire to elevate the masses of the population by improving their material condition and by educating the younger generation. He breathed into those who came in contact with him something of his own passion for the national weal and of his own faith in the future of the people. While uniformly gracious towards the poor and the weak, he showed towards the Native aristocracy a stiffness of manner and a reserve which might sometimes have been mistaken by them for indifference or unkindness, though he never intended to be otherwise than kind and sympathetic. While his name was pleasantly familiar to the millions who lived under his government, he hardly attracted the personal regard of the upper classes.

It is therefore doubtful whether he would have been successful if thrown into the thick of political combinations and diplomatic discussions in which persuasive address and unfailing adroitness were needed. Perhaps his mind was not disposed to turn towards those affairs which inevitably require the cold eye and the iron hand. Though duly solicitous regarding the management of the police and the repression of crime, he scarcely evinced as much talent and aptitude for these as for other branches of the administration.

He was actively assiduous in making tours and marching from village to village and town to town throughout the whole country, till at length there was hardly a place or a road in an area of 70,000 square miles, scarcely a clan or tribe in a population of 30 millions, with which he was not acquainted.

The practical quality in which he was quite unrivalled may be summed up as the faculty of systematizing. He set himself laboriously to learn how each kind of complex business should be performed from beginning to end, from the lowest to the highest step; having done that, he would reduce all his knowledge to lucid statement, so that what had perhaps been hard to him might be made easy to others. When he had thus instructed his officers of all degrees, he was extraordinarily patient and watchful in seeing that they acted up to his instructions. His manuals for the guidance of settlement officers and revenue officers, though partially superseded by the march of events, are still monuments of sound erudition, and should be read by all who would understand aright the peasantry and yeomanry of northern India. He had caused to be prepared under his own eye the draft of a Revenue Code which comprised all the rules relating to the land revenue, and which would, if passed into law, have given stability to the landed institutions of the country. Many of the matters embraced therein have subsequently been taken up by the Legislature.

He did not indeed originate the celebrated settlement of the North-western Provinces, whereby the land revenue was fixed on a scientific basis, and the rights and interests in land were secured. The credit of that truly belongs to Holt Mackenzie and Robert Mertins Bird. But he took up this great work, carried its intentions into full effect, and rendered all its benefits available for the good of the people. Upon it, too, he founded a complete yearly registration of tenures, village by village, for the whole country. In his belief, the constitution of the village communities in northern India possessed peculiar advantages, derived power from its connexion with the historic past, was suited to the clannish disposition of the most industrious castes among the Hindus, maintained a spirit of self-help, a fraternal sentiment and a bond of peace among the members of widely extended families. He thought that in it there lay the germs of self-government, the village being the social unit. He was persuaded that its organization with the elders and hereditary office-bearers might become the means of effecting local or municipal improvements, and of performing a mass of work which, though demanded for the progress of the country, could not be done by any other agency. Some of his best minutes were written in vindication of the village system when it was attacked as involving the principle of joint responsibility, whereby the brotherhood or community became responsible for the fiscal obligations of the thriftless or insolvent members.

He was strict in defining the powers and duties of landlords, the relations between superior and inferior proprietors, the rights of occupancy cultivators, the position of tenants at will. Being, on the whole, a decided advocate of tenant-right wherever existing by local usage, he was anxious that this right should involve fixity of tenure with a fair rent, and was vigilant to curb the tyrannical by protecting the weak. Apprehending that in the then state of rural society there would be danger of extortion or oppression being occasionally practised by landlords, he acted essentially as the poor man's friend. His policy was, after enquiry, to determine and define what the superior might demand from the inferior, so that the former might know the limit of exaction and the latter might be secure against any transgression of that limit. He regarded indefiniteness of demand as one of the banes of the past and as the fruitful parent of tyranny. He deemed it his mission to see that certainty was substituted for uncertainty in this respect, a measure which would prove the palladium of the feeble against the strong. Such ideas were approved by the majority of the best men of his day; but soon after his death opinion veered round towards the view that this policy had gone too far in a direction adverse to the upper classes, was calculated to provoke some reasonable discontent, and might even be fraught with political risk. Thus distrust began to be expressed by some regarding what was called "the Thomasonian school" of administrators. Had Thomason lived, he would have employed all his consummate knowledge and argumentative power to prove that his enquiries had been fairly conducted respecting matters into which the Government was equitably bound to enquire, and that while vindicating the status of the inferior he had shewn due consideration to the superior. Having established the equity of his case, he would have told his assailants to be just and fear not.

All authorities aver that the agricultural classes gladly acquiesce in British rule, and, as was afterwards proved by many instances during the disturbances of 1857, entertain a friendly feeling towards the English officers who have been employed among them. But none believe fully that even by the most thoughtful and benevolent management can those classes be induced to render an actively patriotic support to any foreign Government. Thomason however was nearer to this belief than any statesman I ever met. His ambition was to attach the masses heartily to our rule as one for which it was worth their while to fight if required; and had such a result been attainable by any English ruler in India, he would have attained it.

An ably written article on the purposes, progress, completion and results of the settlement was written in the *Calcutta Review* by the trusted and valued Secretary to his Government, John Thornton. This treatise should be consulted by all who are interested in the social and economic affairs of northern India.

Thomason was the father of primary education by the State in northern India; no matter lay nearer to his heart than this. In those days there were no departments of public instruction nor any educational funds, but by earnest importunity he obtained a permanent grant from the treasury for education, and caused a moderate rate to be imposed on the land for the support of village schools. He held that men would never be fit for the position of peasant proprietors which had been assured to them by the recent settlement, until they acquired the rudiments of knowledge.

He took to heart the lessons of the famine of 1837, having witnessed the consequences of that visitation, and did his utmost to promote the artificial irrigation of thirsty soils by excavating wells and damming up streams so as to form reservoirs or lakes. He was the influential and persistent advocate of the large system of irrigation represented by the Ganges Canal. Although the honour of originating the project of that great canal belongs mainly to those who designed the works, yet the engineers would have been the first to acknowledge their obligations to him on whose co-operation the fulfilment of the design so much depended. It was chiefly through his advocacy that the Government of India, then under Lord Ellenborough, and afterwards under Lord Hardinge, was induced to sanction the preliminary outlay necessary for this undertaking. He met with a more ready and sympathetic response from the next Governor-General, Lord Dalhousie, and then the affairs of the canal advanced with the full tide of fortune. He founded a college of civil engineering at Rurki near the head works of the Ganges Canal, an institution which bears his name. Its main purpose was to train the Natives for taking part in the material improvement of their country, and for doing useful work as engineers and surveyors on canals and roads. He paid so much attention to the bridging and macadamizing of the roads, that in his jurisdiction the communications were the best of their day in all India, greatly facilitating the through traffic with Calcutta, until in their turn they were superseded by the railway.

He can hardly be said to have formed the great school of administrators in the North-western Provinces, which was virtually established by some of those who preceded him, especially by Mertins Bird. But he developed and confirmed it, identifying himself with its ideas, and securing for it that fame and consideration which are among the passports to public success. He had just been appointed Governor of Madras by the Court of Directors, and a new æra of administrative vigour was anticipated for southern India, when he died after a few days' illness in the midst of the provinces he had loved so well. The Governor-General, Lord Dalhousie, commemorated the event in a "Gazette extraordinary" with words of nervous yet graceful eloquence. The crash of events consequent on the war of the mutinies, and the changes which thereupon swept over the land, probably prevented a full history of his masterly administration being prepared at the time. A brief but very interesting memoir of him appeared in the *Calcutta Review* from the pen of William Muir, who was Secretary to his Government at the time of his death, and copious selections from his public despatches were published. He perhaps became regarded as one belonging to a bygone æra, though truly his example is one which ought to be kept before the eyes of coming generations of public officers. But even the best memoir would fail to express adequately the affectionate respect for him which survives in the recollection of those who saw him doing his daily work. In their memories his conversation, whether fired with zeal for the common welfare, or gently beaming with charity and benevolence, forms a sunny spot on which perpetual light seems to rest. John Lawrence in the days of his greatness would often declare that as a civil administrator he drooped his flag to Thomason. When receiving decorations in after years, Montgomery said that he felt almost unworthy, because Thomason had died undecorated. In considering Thomason's place among the British worthies of India, we must remember that he was essentially an administrator in time of peace, that he was not tried in those grave emergencies and political crises wherein eminent Civil Servants in India have often been engaged, that he had not to coerce martial tribes, nor to pacify turbulent territories. He will therefore be placed in a rank different from that of such Anglo-Indian statesmen as Warren Hastings, Charles (Lord) Metcalfe, Mountstuart Elphinstone, and John (Lord) Lawrence, who have shone under difficulties other than those of quiet times. His proceedings in many controverted matters relating to landed tenures have been assailed, and his authority in some questions has been disputed, but his policy stands the test of time in the judgment of the best informed. He set before himself certain objects—the completion of the land settlement, the registration of tenures, the beginning of primary education, the extension of irrigation, the improvement of roads and communications, the instruction of the Natives in civil engineering—and he accomplished them. These things he intended to do, and he did them all before he died, though his death was sudden and premature. Thus in discharging the strictly professional duties of the Civil Service in the widest field, in managing extensive provinces, in promoting the cause of progress and enlightenment among the Natives, he was one of the strongest men that ever served the British Government in the East.

CHAPTER IV.

(1849–1853.)

DUUMVIRATE IN THE PANJAB OF THE LAWRENCE BROTHERS.

Journey to the Panjab—First visit to Simla—Settlement work—Impressions regarding Lahore—Board of Administration for the Panjab—Henry and John Lawrence, contrast between the two—Transition from Native to British rule—Trans-Indus border and Panjab frontier force—Protected Native States—Native aristocracy under the British system—Internal administration—Development of material resources—Provincial finance—Popularity of system pursued by the Board—Its characteristics and results.

I TARRIED for three years in the North-western Provinces, in order to complete my official education under Thomason; and then joined, in 1851, John Lawrence's party in the Panjab as one of the settlement officers for the newly annexed country. There was a twofold attraction impelling young Civil Servants towards this change of masters. To us the Panjab loomed grandly as the land of promise; it afforded scope for displaying individuality, and perhaps for carving out the path of a considerable career. The very atmosphere of the country nourished a spirit of adventure; the people were known to have in their character the hard grit and high stomach which demand the governing faculty that Englishmen instinctively love to exercise. Then the "settlement" was esteemed as the "blue ribbon" of civil employment. To be chosen for it by John Lawrence was an honour which made the pulse beat high. The land revenue was to be assessed for a term of thirty years, and the landed tenures were to be determined after the model of the North-western Provinces. These various operations were comprehended under the term "settlement." Thus the importance of the work entrusted to a settlement officer was manifest in a country where the agricultural interest overshadowed all other interests.

Having received a farewell letter from Thomason, which still shines like the evening star in my recollection, I started for the Jalander district, lying between the rivers Satlej and Beas. On my way I saw the Ganges Canal, that wonderful channel which attests the engineering genius of Sir Proby Cautley. The canal leads the river gently from its bed near the sacred Hardwar—next carries it by tunnels through opposing spurs of hills, then underneath one stream, again by an aqueduct over another, and so through deep cuttings in undulating ground to the open country at last. Within the plains I admired its breadth of 200 feet, its belts of umbrageous trees on either bank, and the zone of verdure which marked its beneficent course through thirsty tracts. Travelling on, I passed the Satlej without difficulty; its bed was some miles in breadth, and intersected by several parallel streams which were crossed by boat bridges. It is now spanned by a long railway viaduct, the erection of which has cost infinite trouble by reason of the destructive floods. The journey being made in the lovely weather of an Indian winter, I caught my first view of the Himalayas just after a fall of snow had whitened the hillsides. Like many other travellers I instinctively raised my hat to salute the peerless mountains.

Arrived at Jalander I received charge of the settlement from Hercules Scott, who was about to return to England by reason of ill-health. He was a man much esteemed by John Lawrence and very popular with the Natives, quite one of the Panjab school of administrators which was then being formed. Having after several busy and laborious months brought my work to a forward stage, I repaired to Simla to make the personal acquaintance of John Lawrence, and to be presented to Lord Dalhousie. At this time I also met Sir Charles Napier, who having arrived in India as Commander-in-Chief was busily inspecting the troops and their stations, and zealously supervising all matters relating to the welfare and discipline of the army.

At Simla the season had passed when the mountain-side is reddened with the flower of the rhododendron; but the woods, consisting of cedar, pine and oak, struck my sight so long accustomed to scantily wooded plains, and the forest-clad summits made me realize the beauty of the Homeric epithet "εἰνοσίφυλλος." At some hours the horizon displayed itself in a long line of snowy peaks glistening from afar in the sunlight. Then the rainy season was ushered in by thunder-claps reverberating through the mountains, while clouds gathered in stately masses. I felt bewildered by the mighty scale of the scenery and the magnificence of the atmospheric phenomena. Thus I descended to the familiar plains once more with my memory full of the grandest images and my nerves braced for resuming work.

Returning to my station at Jalander, I proceeded with the work of the settlement, visiting the villages and becoming acquainted with the rural chiefs, the village communities, the peasant proprietors and the cultivators. The district had now been for several years under British rule. The people seemed to me to be more manly and straightforward than those whom I had left behind me in the North-western Provinces. Their idiosyncrasies were strongly marked; their physique was large and powerful. In many villages the men were tall enough to furnish recruits for grenadier regiments. As the territory lay near the junction of two rivers (the Satlej and the Beas), the land was fertile, the cultivation and the crops were good, and the homesteads were thriving. I shortly afterwards went to see my superior officer Donald Macleod, the Commissioner, who was at Dharmsâla in the neighbouring Himalayas. Dharmsâla is at the head of a lovely valley, which has quite a network of watercourses for the irrigation of the rice-fields. Around it are the forest-clad sides and spurs of precipitous mountains, above which in open weather there shine the everlasting snows. It is now memorable as the place whither Lord Elgin, stricken by sudden illness, was carried to die. On the way the hill fortress of Kangra was seen rising up, a mass frowning in the midst of a gorge and overhanging a hill torrent. While I was at Dharmsâla, Macleod earnestly impressed on me the importance of assessing the land revenue in a moderate manner, and of consulting the opinions of the best-informed native agriculturists after making my own calculations.

In the Jalander district the magistrate was Lieutenant (afterwards Sir Herbert) Edwardes. He had been in diplomatic employment on the Trans-Indus frontier, when there occurred at Multan that outbreak which led to the second Panjab war. He subsequently published a graphic narrative of his experience at that critical time. A disciple of Henry Lawrence, though much attached to John Lawrence also, he was a typical man of the then rising Panjab school. His companionship was diverting and enlivening; his racy and humorous conversation lent a peculiar charm to his society. Though still young in years he was a soldier of proved courage and capacity, and a diplomatist of much experience among turbulent native tribes. He was a bright-gleaming man, with a rich imagination, a poetic temperament, and a rare talent for English composition with choice language and lucid array of facts. Yet he was a steady counsellor in grave conjunctures, and full of fire in the presence of danger. Afterwards, as Commissioner of Peshawar, he proved a tower of strength to the state during the crisis of 1857. He was esteemed by John Lawrence to be a man equal to very high offices, and worthy of the Lieutenant-Governorship of the Panjab in due course if opportunity should offer. Later he began to write a life of Henry Lawrence—to him a labour of love—with complete knowledge of his most interesting subject, and with much historic skill. But untimely death snatched him away while he was in England, during the flower of his age, cutting short his literary work and the promise of his political career.

The settlement being nearly completed at Jalander, I proceeded, in the beginning of 1862, to Lahore, the capital of the Panjab, in order to conduct similar operations in the adjacent districts. On the way the sacred tank of Amritsur was visited, where men are baptized into the Sikh faith, and in the midst of which there stands the gilded temple dazzling the sight in the noonday glare, and venerated by the Sikhs as the holiest of holies. Approaching Lahore I saw the elaborate but somewhat gaudy tomb of Ranjit Sing, the Lion King, as it nestled quietly in the shadow of a towering fortress. Near at hand stood the mosque erected by a Mogul emperor in a sombre and massive style; it then was, as it had long been, used for a military magazine, but has since been restored to the priests for worship. Then crossing the river I visited the mausoleum of which the minarets form landmarks for many miles round, and which was erected by the Mogul empress (one of the heroines in Moore's *Lalla Rookh*) in memory of her imperial husband, after he died on his way down from Cashmir. The river Ravi close by was then crossed by a bridge of boats; it is now spanned by a railway viaduct. The contemplation of interesting objects like these imbues a young officer with affection for the province to which he is about to devote his energies.

At Lahore I reported myself to the Board of Administration, to whom the management of the Panjab had been entrusted by Lord Dalhousie. The President of the Board was Sir Henry Lawrence, the senior member was John Lawrence; the junior member was Robert Montgomery, who had recently succeeded C. G. Mansel in that capacity. The Board had then been at the head of the province for two years and a half, and the time had come for them to render an account of their stewardship by causing a general report to be prepared. I was employed under their immediate direction in preparing the document which became afterwards known as "the first Panjab Report." Thus I was brought into confidential communication with Henry Lawrence, and had close relations with John Lawrence and Montgomery.

Taken all in all, Henry Lawrence was one of the most gifted men whom this generation has beheld in India. His appearance betokened an impulsive disposition and a restless energy. His manner though sometimes shadowed by melancholy, was often brightened with Hibernian vivacity. His active and somewhat attenuated frame seemed a prison-house which had been gradually worn away by the fluttering of the eager soul within. Though far from precise in trivial matters, he had a natural dignity of mien. In the field or on horseback he was indefatigable, evincing much endurance in all vicissitudes of weather. In the cabinet he would despatch affairs by spasmodic exertion, rather than by system or method. He was ambitious in the pure and lofty sense of the term; for he wished to earn praise by deserving gratitude. Though generously hospitable, and anxious to maintain the state suitable to his position, he was simple in his tastes and almost Spartan in his habits. He had an imaginative temperament, something of poetic inspiration, and an aptitude for literary culture. His arguments, whether oral or written, were incisive, his language always racy, and his phrases sometimes sarcastic. He knew mankind individually and collectively, both English and Indian. He could analyze the elements of Native thought and sentiment, and his discernment of the temper of Native chiefs and courts was unfailing. His letters and despatches regarding the disposition and tendencies of Native States were striking and instructive. His ear was sensitive to the voice of distress when he moved among the humbler classes of the Natives. His compassionate benevolence extended to all whose circumstances were fraught with difficulties and temptations. He took a deep interest in the welfare of the European troops in India, and devoted much of his hard-earned means to institutions for the benefit of soldiers' orphans. With him sentiment was allowed quite as much play as reason, the two holding, as it were, equal sway—a "divisum imperium." It would be but feeble praise to say that he confronted danger with moral courage, for he was inflamed with ardour to encounter grave emergencies, though he calmed down to sober judgment when actually face to face with them. Having much military knowledge, some diplomatic and political experience of the best sort, a general acquaintance with civil affairs, and a far-reaching ken of most public questions,—he thoroughly understood the elements of danger or security, strength or weakness, which pervade our Eastern empire. His prime faculties were an insight into the characters of men, and a power of endearing himself to all whom he had chosen as coadjutors. No Anglo-Indian statesman within living memory has had so distinguished a clientèle as he; a truly noble company, consisting of officers whom he had selected for their qualities of head and heart, to render service in arduous fields of duty or in enterprises of moment. With them the ordinary motives of subordination were merged in the feeling of affection for him. In fine, throughout his nature there burned the unquenchable flame of genius.

In his estimation of administrators he naturally leaned towards those who, like himself, had been drawn from the army; such men as Herbert Edwardes, James Abbott, Edward Lake, John Nicholson, Reynell Taylor, John Becher, Hugh James, Frederick Mackeson, George Macgregor, who were worthy of the confidence placed in them, who were typical men of the "soldier-civilian" class– to borrow Sir Charles Napier's expression—and of whom some are remembered by history. There were also Covenanted Civil Servants who won his regard by reason of their popularity with the Natives; such men were George Barnes, Arthur Cocks, George Christian, and, at a somewhat later date, Charles Raikes.

John Lawrence, though possessing some qualities in common with his brother—zeal, energy, resolution "rebus in arduis"—was yet a man of a different type. His career appealed in a lesser degree to the popular imagination. His genius did not manifest itself quite so quickly. The fire within him did not kindle so readily, and, when excited, burnt slower. He had not the same glow of sentiment and aptitude for literary expression. But he was a bold and vigorous writer, as Lord Dalhousie, an excellent judge on such a point, used to declare. He was, in his inner mind, much impressed by the solemn truths of religion, and year by year his thoughts seemed to assume more and more of a religious cast. Those who saw him only during the latter part of his life may have found his physical form somewhat shrunken. But in those days he had a broad, stout and powerful build. His face, already furrowed by the lines which mental and moral effort often imprint on the features, was frank and open. His manner and conversation, though somewhat stern when he was actually at work, were cheerful, almost jovial, when he was at leisure. In civil affairs he was imbued with all the knowledge characteristic of Thomason's school in the North-western Provinces already described. During recent years he had acquired political and diplomatic experience under circumstances of severe trial. He had been brought much in contact with soldiers, and would bestow all the time and attention he possibly could upon military affairs. While he preached the doctrine that civil employment is a profession demanding lifelong devotion, and thoroughly practised his preaching, yet at times he seemed almost to have mistaken his profession, so much aptitude and fondness did he display for the art of war.

The prevailing sentiment in his public life was a love for duty. Though his temper was strong, and on occasion warm, yet in his nature judgment and reason reigned supreme. As a subsidiary element, caution was present with him in the highest degree, and there never was in India a more cautious statesman than he. It being an object of the first importance with him to foresee the course of all affairs, he remembered that prescience could be acquired only by careful reflection. He was never tired of affirming that forethought was among the primary duties of public servants, and that the man who was endowed largely with the power of exercising such forethought, possessed one of the essential requisites for success. To weigh both sides of every question evenly and strike the balance, to eliminate passion favour prejudice or misleading sentiment, and fix the gaze on exact justice alone, were maxims uppermost in his mind. He acted according to this principle in judging of the conduct and character of officers whose fate he held in the hollow of his hand. Individuals may be sometimes condemned and set aside altogether on account of some salient faults, notwithstanding their deserts in many respects; but he would say, such and such an one, though having this or that imperfection no doubt, had real merit in other ways, and therefore must not be excluded. Again, men may be, on account of some conspicuous qualities, placed in positions where success is marred by some failings which ought not to have been overlooked; but he, while recognizing the high qualification, would duly note the counter-balancing defect. But to those who, notwithstanding their gifts and accomplishments, lacked the fundamental condition of zeal for public duty, he would shew no consideration. In equitable discrimination of the diverse moral and intellectual qualities of the numerous subordinates under his command he has not been surpassed by any man of his generation in India. He did not at that time arouse so much enthusiasm as his brother among large numbers of men, nor win so extensive a popularity. But he was respected by all, admired by most, and beloved by many.

While the third member of the Board was pushing on the wheels of administration, there was in many respects a duumvirate of the Lawrence brothers in the Panjab. Nevertheless the "par nobile fratrum" did not look at all public affairs from the same standpoint. Henry was proud of his position as President, and anxious to keep it. If only he could have his way in some matters deemed by him to be paramount, or in respect of certain interests which he felt bound to guard, he was willing to lean on the support of his brother in civil affairs. But John was not quite satisfied with his position as senior member of the Board. While admiring his brother's policy in many respects, he thought it to be fraught with some tendencies likely to embarrass the administration. While fully holding his own in civil affairs, he could seldom brook interposition on the part of the President. Sometimes when he had been stationary at Lahore working up some difficult question, his brother, who had perhaps been making tours beyond the Indus or on the Cashmir frontier, would arrive at headquarters and raise his voice in the matter. Thus John began to entertain the desire of exchanging his post for one of lesser status, where he could exercise a limited but comparatively absolute sway. At one time it was believed that both brothers had intimated to Lord Dalhousie their willingness that one of them should quit the Panjab, leaving the field clear for the other. But the Governor-General apparently thought that the presence of each was needed for the general good of the province, and that the time had not yet come for parting them. Although the friction never caused any estrangement, still both brothers grieved at it, and strove to prevent its appearance before the world. Henry respected John's opinion, and was anxious, if possible, to have it arrayed on his own side. John admired Henry's genius, and was glad, whenever he conscientiously could, to bring his solid aid to its support. They believed themselves, when united, to be more than a match for all comers. For instance, Sir Charles Napier having formerly vanquished many opponents with his speech and pen, as well as with his sword, ran a tilt of words against the Panjab Board. Then, indeed, the Lawrence brothers rose together for their common defence, and repelled the doughty old warrior with masterly and conclusive minutes.

It is well to summarize here the points whereon Henry and John Lawrence were agreed and those on which they differed.

They were in the main of one mind, then, as to the necessity of holding the new British border trans-Indus in fully armed strength, conciliating those tribes which were tameable, and punishing those untameable tribes which gave us unjustifiable offence, the principle being:—

"Parcere subjectis et debellare superbos."

There was entire accord between them respecting the military defence and occupation of the province, and regarding the measures necessary for the speedy establishment of order amongst a sturdy population in some degree barbarized by wars or disturbances. There was a tolerable, though not perfect, agreement betwixt them regarding the political relations with the larger Native States comprised within the Panjab and its dependencies, the preliminary steps for the settling of the land revenue, and the initiation of public works for material improvement. They were both anxious that the administration should be rendered popular with the Natives. Henry preferred the patriarchal style, whereby the European officer sitting in the shade of a banyan tree might dispense justice while in familiar converse with the rustic throng around him. John, as might be expected, knew that besides riding about the country an officer must be for hours at his desk poring over returns, and patiently sit on the bench hearing Natives argue about the meaning of a regulation. Still they both agreed that contact with the people out of doors, and also assiduous attention to business indoors, were necessary to make an administrator efficient. They were entirely united in their hopeful desire that "forwards" should be the motto of the Panjab administration, and that their province, profiting by all the valuable experience of the past, yet avoiding the mistakes which, despite good intentions, had been made elsewhere, should move in the very van of all the provinces in India.

But they differed primarily in respect to the treatment of the Native aristocracy on the introduction of British rule. The question as to how much should be conceded by the State to these important classes, and how much withheld from them, has ever been, perhaps still is, the crux of the British Government in India. Such conflicting principles form a sort of dilemma from which there is no complete escape. Some compromise between these principles has been attained during recent years, chiefly through the operation of time. But in those days the difference was sharply defined, and Henry took up one of the opposing principles while John held to the other. The root of the matter, around which so much controversy raged, may be stated in this wise. Under Native rule the land revenue belonged to, and was the mainstay of, the State. The ruler or sovereign would assign temporarily to his chieftains the land revenue of certain villages, or whole tracts of territory, on the condition of feudal service, chiefly military, being rendered. This service is not wanted under British rule, and cannot be maintained; then the question arises whether the assignment of the land revenue is to be continued. Similarly, allowances in cash from the State treasury are made to local chiefs in consideration of duty nominal or real being performed. This duty cannot be accepted under British rule, and a discussion springs up regarding the extent to which the allowances are to be upheld. When these cases exist on a large scale, involving extensive interests, it will be seen at a glance that there is much room for divergence of opinion between statesmen equally able humane and conscientious. Henry thought that liberal concessions ought to be made to these feudal classes, for the sake of the moral effect to be produced on the people by the example of considerateness on the part of the conquerors, and for reasons of policy in allaying discontent among influential sections of the community. The greater part of the former grants ought to be continued, although the obligation of service might be remitted. This must be effected, despite the financial cost which such arrangements might involve. John would rejoin that these grants must at once be curtailed, and provision should be made for their cessation on the demise of present incumbents. The Government could not bear the double expense of continuing grants for the old service just dispensed with, and of defraying the charges of the new service then to be introduced. Justice to the people at large required an economical management of the finances, without special regard to any particular class.

Regarding these affairs the opinions of John, rather than of Henry, found favour with Lord Dalhousie, and in the end prevailed. Henry, however, displayed to the Chiefs all the compassion of a friend who had known them in better days. When the concessions claimed for them had been in part refused, he would still beg something more for every one of them, and would contest for them their losing cause. It was said of him that he looked as if he bore the scars from the countless wounds of disappointment suffered on behalf of his Native friends.

Next there was some difference of opinion between Henry and John, respecting the land revenue, the largest of all internal matters in the province. Under Native rule, this revenue had been collected sometimes in cash and sometimes in kind. After the annexation, the British Government proclaimed that it should be levied always in cash; and, inasmuch as the collection in kind was notoriously liable to oppressive abuses, this proclamation was in the first instance well received by the people. But two years later, the showers, usual in winter, were extraordinarily abundant and propitious; consequently the yield on poorly cultivated lands was luxuriant, equalling that of fields on which agricultural capital had been expended. There was an unprecedented glut of grain in the market; prices were unremunerative to the producers who had temporary difficulty in realizing cash wherewith to pay the revenue. The tax-payers then having more grain on their hands than they could conveniently dispose of, desired to pay their fiscal dues in that commodity, and began in many places to agitate for a return to the old system of payment in kind. Henry having heard much of this agitation during his tours, was inclined to yield to it, in some districts at least, in order to satisfy the people. John set his face against any inroad being attempted upon a fundamental part of the British system, affirming that payment in cash was based on the results of universal experience in India, and that the policy of the Government would be stultified if it were partially abandoned on the first shock of difficulties which, with patience, could be overcome.

The third point of divergence related to financial management. Henry ardently aspired to initiate and push forward all improvements conducive to progress and civilization. He knew indeed that these would be expensive, but he anticipated that difficulties on the score of expense would sooner or later right themselves, and that the State would ultimately recoup itself for its outlay by the benefits which must follow. John equally desired the improvements, but he held that the prosecution of all such projects must be regulated by the financial means available in the country. He was convinced that the province ought to be made to defray from its revenues the cost of the civil and political administration, and also contribute something towards the charges for its military defence. He feared that his brother's policy, if unchecked, would interfere with the consummation of this result.

Notwithstanding all these circumstances, I found no difficulty during 1852 in drafting a general report on the Board's administration in which its three members concurred, and of which they themselves wrote some portions. Nothing could be more cordial and laudatory than Lord Dalhousie's reply acknowledging the vast work which the Board had accomplished in a short time. The narrative of facts, when published shortly afterwards, was regarded by the public as redounding to the honour of the Board and of its many subordinates. It was believed, however, in other parts of the empire that the Panjab officers entertained, though they did not express, a faith in the superiority of their province over its neighbours. This caused inter-provincial emulation which was healthy, also some jealousy which led to detraction of the Panjab. Nevertheless the land of the Lawrences was known by all men to be the most advancing province of India at that time.

Early in the following year, the news came like a thunderbolt to the effect that Henry would be translated to a great political and diplomatic post (in the States of Rajputâna), that the Board was to be abolished, and in its place a new administration set up with John as the sole chief. Though the secret had been well kept, Lord Dalhousie must for some time have been maturing this intention. In most of the discussions between Henry and John, the Governor-General had probably agreed in the main with John's views. He deemed that the conditions which demanded Henry's special experience and ability were passing away, and that the development of the province would require the trained aptitude for civil affairs which John pre-eminently possessed.

The divergence between the brothers respecting some official matters in nowise affected their fraternal regard. The points whereon they differed were not nearly equal to those whereon they were in accord. Two men of powerful and independent minds cannot always agree in affairs involving diverse principles. Their discussions served to bring out into strong relief the noble qualities belonging to each of them. There never was a brighter example of mutual love and admiration between brothers than that afforded by Henry and John Lawrence.

The third member of the Board was C. G. Mansel, whom I never met; he was succeeded by Mr. (now Sir Robert) Montgomery, with whom I was so fortunate as to become intimately acquainted.

Montgomery was also an officer of the Thomason school, and had a thoroughly practical acquaintance with every part of his profession. Benevolence and good-humour beamed in his countenance; while cheerfulness brightened all his ways. He was an excellent man of business, ever ready and dexterous, without disturbing himself or others. This unhesitating promptitude gave him a remarkable power for despatching affairs in the mass. His moral courage was soon evinced on many occasions of anxiety. Experience afterwards shewed, in May 1857, that he would rise to the level of emergencies with alacrity, yet with calmness, and confront the most critical danger with a smiling face. In respect to religion he was unostentatiously devout, setting a good example to the community. He enjoyed a wide popularity among all classes; and by those who had close relations with him he was beloved. During his boyhood he had been brought up at the same school with Henry and John Lawrence. It was a strange chance that brought him now in contact with them during these important stages in their careers; and he was peculiarly suited to mediate in questions between them. John Lawrence always spoke of him as his brother in old association and comrade in administration.

Such was the character of the men who were at the head of the administration in the Panjab during several years after the annexation. That administration had great credit on the spot and much fame throughout India; it received warm commendations from the Governor-General and the authorities in England; also it is regarded, on an historical retrospect, as a brilliant episode in British Indian annals. The particulars of it, however, become gradually lost to memory from lapse of time; and enquirers may now ask what where the causes which led to its celebrity.

The primary cause was the rapidity and facility with which British rule was established in a province which had made by far the most formidable resistance ever offered to our arms in India. Thus a territory which had been expected to be a scene of chronic trouble and revolt was converted into an abode of prosperity and a source of strength. The next cause was the reforming spirit displayed from the very outset. It was supposed that the progress of civilization would be slow and precarious among people of a rude and rugged nature, and that the improvements established in the older provinces after repeated trials and failures could be but gradually introduced into this new province. But actually the best form of administration, according to the known models of that time, was seen to have been set up *per saltum*, as it were. The third cause was the comparative cheapness with which successful results were attained. There had been fear lest the addition of a territory fraught with difficulties should prove financially burdensome to the empire. The province, however, was found to be paying its way and contributing a share towards the imperial defences. The fourth cause was the enthusiastic pride which officers of the Panjab school felt in their work. This attracted to their province the critical notice and the jealous though still admiring regard of the public. It may be well to explain briefly the operation of these several causes.

The principal secretary then with the Governor-General (Lord Dalhousie) was Sir Henry Elliot, one of the most learned and accomplished men in the Civil Service. Under Dalhousie's directions Elliot prepared a letter of general instructions to the Board regarding the policy to be pursued by them. It is a letter redounding to Dalhousie's honour as a historic document, its perusal is still instructive, and being addressed to persons of the mettle above described it must have produced an electrical effect. Thus the Board started with a charter enjoining them to accomplish great things.

The annexation was proclaimed in March of 1849, just as the spring harvest was ripening. It was important to arrange the time, so that the land revenue for the year, which largely depends on these crops, might be duly collected. The hot season was then advancing apace, and European officers were hastily collected to conduct the administration in the interior of the province. On reaching their districts they had the utmost difficulty in sheltering themselves from the burning heat, there being no houses suitable for European habitation. In the unavoidable hurry of the occasion, they had not time even to bring tents with them. Thus severe privations had to be endured by Englishmen during their first summer in the Panjab, though their minds were diverted by the exciting novelty of their duties. Their hardships were cheerfully shared by the faithful Native servants whom they had brought with them from the North-western Provinces, and to whom the Sikh people were almost as strange as to their masters.

The principal officers were chosen judiciously from among the best and ablest men of the older provinces, as the members of the Board had much knowledge of the *personnel* of the public service. Lord Dalhousie was naturally anxious that persons should be selected who would, humanly speaking, ensure the success of an annexation for which he had to bear a grave responsibility. Most of the selections answered fully the expectations which had been formed of them. But, among many men, some failed; and wherever an individual shewed signs of inefficiency the Board were instant in procuring his removal.

The first step to be taken was the disbandment of all that remained of the late Sikh army, and of all the quasi-military retainers of the Native Government. These large bodies of men submitted to disintegration with a resigned composure which under other circumstances would not have been evinced. It happened then, however, as has so often proved the case in India, that the minds of men were overawed and their spirit stupefied by the sense of recent defeat and disaster. Thus the soldiery, once so turbulent as to be uncontrollable by their own chiefs, bowed submissively to what they regarded as their fate. Next, the people at large, by a disarming proclamation, were required to give up their arms; this they did without hesitation or murmur, and without fail. For although they might, while surrendering some weapons, have secreted others, experience proved that they must have produced all or nearly all. Upon these sturdy and courageous people the British victories seemed to have acted like a spell.

It was immediately necessary to provide for the external

defence of the province, and for the preservation of internal order. Of the European troops which had been engaged in the recent campaigns, a considerable portion was retained within the province, and stationed near the most important towns. The distribution of these troops caused some discussions between the Board and Sir Charles Napier, then Commander-in-Chief. Napier was disposed to declare or to imply that if a stronger police were organized, and the local administration were altogether rendered more efficient, a smaller force than that which was then cantoned within the Panjab would suffice. He was generally believed to be influenced by jealousy of the Lawrence administration, and to have aspired to be Governor of the Panjab after its annexation, as he had been Governor of Sind after its conquest; there is, however, great risk of error whenever any attempt is made to analyze motives of this nature. But whether this belief were correct or not, there was beyond doubt a disposition on his part to visit everything Indian with an unsparing criticism, from which he by no means exempted the Panjab. In the discussions which thus arose there was included the allotment of European troops to this province in relation to neighbouring provinces. In the end it was decided to retain in the Panjab a large portion of the whole European force at the disposal of the Government, even at the risk of comparatively denuding the old provinces. In principle the whole empire was being guarded by the protection of the north-west frontier, and the maintenance of absolute order in the territories between the Satlej and the Indus was one of the most potent means of assuring peace and security to India at large.

Then a separate force was organized for guarding the border, namely the territories intervening between the river Indus and the mountains which surround the Peshawar Valley and separate Afghanistan from India. These special troops constituted the Panjab frontier Force, and were organized, both horse and foot, in the same manner as the irregular troops of India. They were however placed, not under the Commander-in-Chief of the army, but under the Board of Administration. The frontier was inhabited by wild races, and was subject to frequent incursions from still fiercer tribes dwelling in the adjacent hills. The repression of marauding and plundering was the first duty of the frontier administration, but could not be executed without the aid of troops. Such troops must be at the call of the civil officers on the instant, without any of the delay which might be occasioned by a reference to the ordinary military authorities. Substantially these were the reasons why the Panjab frontier Force was placed under the civil administration which was thus *pro tanto* vested with a military capacity. Accordingly a military department was included in the secretariat of the Board. The frontier service became popular with the officers of the army, as affording a school for soldiers, and opening a field for distinction. Thus the Board were able to select many of the most promising young officers of the day for regimental duty in the Force, and to procure the appointment of some of the ablest commanders in the country for supervising it in quarters or leading it into action. The Native soldiers were recruited from among the most martial tribes in the Panjab itself, and especially in the border mountains. The Native officers were chosen for personal merit and social status, there being fortunately no scope in a newly raised force for promotion by seniority alone. Thus with its commanders, its European officers, its Native officers, and its soldiers, the Panjab frontier Force soon became perhaps the finest body of Native troops ever arrayed under British banners in India, being equally excellent in its cavalry and in its infantry. Its mettle and prowess were frequently tried in expeditions against the fierce and warlike offenders on the border; its endurance was constantly tested by the watch and ward in scattered outposts at the foot of the hills. It held the whole border, five hundred miles in length, from Hazara in the Himalayas near the upper Indus, down to Sind in the south. Its annals were adorned by such names as Neville Chamberlain, Harry Lumsden, John Coke, Henry Daly, Charles Brownlow and others.

Within the Panjab some military police was organized by

the Board, consisting partly of foot, but chiefly of horsemen organized to some extent in a military fashion and fairly well mounted. The rest of the police, that is, the main body, had a purely civil organization in the then Indian fashion, which was only a development, with some slight improvement, of the old Native police. The idea of reforming the Indian police in the style of the English constabulary did not then exist in the minds of Indian statesmen. Thus regarding its police arrangements the Board were not so far in advance of their time as they proved to be in many other respects. They were, however, very successful in constituting their magistracy. Active and energetic men, European officers, were stationed in the right places, a high standard of discipline and order was upheld, a wise severity in heinous cases such as gang-robbery was meted out, and sentences of a deterrent character were passed. Violent crime was rife in a province always containing turbulent elements, and recently disturbed by war and revolution, but the magisterial vigour of the Board, and its results in the suppression of crime, were subjects of common remark and congratulation at the time.

Despite its preoccupation with the general defence of the province, the Board was obliged to give instant attention to its political duties. The Maharaja Golab Sing had been confirmed as ruler of the Jammu territories, that is, the sub-Himalayan dominions of his territory, and to this kingdom had been added the fair domain of Cashmir. Having long been one of the first among the Panjab chiefs, he still possessed much influence with the political parties in the province, and represented the Rajpût element, which was in some degree a counterfoil to the Sikhs and Muhammadans. The proximity of his dominions to the northern part of the Indus frontier gave him additional consequence. It was important at the outset to place the relations of the British Government with him upon a satisfactory footing. At this time he was engaged in internal strife with a powerful member of his own family who seemed likely to dispute the succession to the throne. To the south, near Multan, there was a rebellion in the State of Bahawalpur, and the rebels were appealing to the British Government. In the Cis-Satlej States lying between Delhi and the Satlej the minutiæ and intricacies of feudal tenures were causing complications which, if not unravelled and settled, would lead to internal disturbance. The Himalayan regions overhanging the Panjab were held by hill chiefs governing their own territories, but living under the shield of the British Government and having close relations with its representatives. With the intractable tribes, which formed an independent cordon between the long trans-Indus border and Afghanistan, the Board and its officers had almost daily transactions, which were usually of a troubled character. Several military expeditions had to be despatched against the tribes near the Khyber Pass. But with Afghanistan no communications had as yet been opened; that country having been left to itself since the conclusion of the first Afghan war.

The next object aimed at by the Board and its officers was the safe and judicious transition from Native to British rule throughout the interior of the Panjab. The Native system existing there had been founded roughly indeed, but firmly, by Ranjit Sing. He was the very embodiment of that practical sagacity which achieves great things despite the disadvantages of unlettered ignorance. That system helped those who could help themselves, but provided scantily for the feeble and friendless. It afforded strong meat for the sturdy, but as for the poor it sent them empty away. It was liked by the overbearing and the masterful; but even on the hardy it imposed a burden quite as heavy as they could bear; still its yoke, though onerous, was not galling, It took little account of the weak, and for them it virtually gave effect to the doctrine of the survival of the fittest. Its justice was rude, its injustice was tempered by the power and resolution of the people to resist such oppression as transgressed endurable limits. It left an aristocracy accustomed to arbitrary absolutism on occasions, but prone to have its own way for the most part; a yeomanry prepared to sacrifice much to tyranny, but jealous of its essential rights; and a peasantry inured to hardship, but clinging tenaciously to the ancestral fields and homesteads. Under it the property in land survived despite all changes and revolutions, and the village communities preserved their constitution intact.

From the outset it was necessary to guard against the occurrence of fanatical outbreaks. For the Sikh faith, though it had ceased to be triumphant, was still militant, being supported by many bands of armed monks, while the Muhammadan community was numerous and self-asserting. There was a specially irritating cause likely to provoke collision, as for instance the Muhammadans were eaters of beef while the Sikhs carried to an extreme the prejudice against the killing of cows. Therefore the authorities had to arrange that the slaughtering of kine should be so conducted as to avoid unnecessary offence.

The treatment of the Native aristocracy has been already mentioned in the statement of the views held by Henry and John Lawrence respectively. In no part of India had this aristocracy held a more important position territorially than in the Panjab. The Sikh system had been in a large measure feudal; the greater part of the country was no doubt under the direct management of the central government at Lahore; but a considerable part was under local chiefs of various degrees. Many of these chiefs were petty, others influential, while some were actually powerful; and their estates were held under every sort of feudal tenure. Of these tenures some were hereditary; but many were temporary, granted for special objects which might or might not last, and were therefore resumable at will by the ruler of the day. The holders were ordinarily entitled to collect as their income the land revenue which was due from the lands, and which would otherwise be collected by the State. Notable among the nobility were the members of the late council of regency which governed the country for Dhulîp Sing, the infant prince, under the advice of the British Resident, up to the time when war and rebellion caused the annexation of the province. Some of them had joined the enemy, but many remained loyal, and now had the highest claim to consideration. A careful enquiry was instituted into all these tenures, from the largest to the smallest. Those which had any real character of perpetuity or permanency were respected accordingly; though naturally there was often much discussion as to what constituted this permanency. Those which had only a temporary character were continued in part or in whole for the lives of the incumbents, and sometimes for one generation afterwards. Those which were wholly dependent on temporary service, now to be dispensed with, were still continued in part, though subjected to curtailment. In some cases it was thought desirable to commute a limited tenure of land, to a cash allowance from the treasury. Again many were in receipt of pensions or other allowances in cash from the treasury; the pensions were generally continued by the British Government; but the continuance of other cash allowances depended on the surrounding conditions. In these several classes of cases, there was almost boundless scope for difference of opinion as to what under all the circumstances constituted liberality or illiberality, or what was meant by strictness in a judicious or an undue degree. On the whole a moderate measure of liberality was allowed, and certainly there was no error in the direction of over-generosity or extravagance. Thus the interest of the public as opposed to that of individuals or classes was properly guarded. Disappointment was felt by the Natives at the decisions as a whole, and with some even a stronger feeling prevailed. A government which is conscious of having conceded as much as was consistent with the public weal must be prepared to face such objections. This, too, was the feeling of the Board, but the President, Henry Lawrence, shared in some degree the sentiments of regret and dissatisfaction which were feelingly, even touchingly, expressed by the Natives in private interviews, though seldom declared openly. These important measures, matured after deliberations lasting over many months and extending to many thousands of cases, passed off quietly, and the decisions were accepted with overt loyalty, notwithstanding inward murmurs. Subsequent experience has abundantly proved the result to be good.

The religious endowments—Hindu, Sikh, Muhammadan, tens of thousands in number, some extensive and many minute, to be found in every village—were treated in the same considerate and conscientious spirit. The expense incurred in this investigation if computed must be found very considerable, but the care and labour devoted to the task would baffle description. It were vain to hope that the decisions gave satisfaction, for in these affairs concessions beget hopes which can never be satisfied. Still the decisions of the Government were accepted by those concerned with at least apparent acquiescence. Here, again, experience has ratified the justice and expediency of the principles then observed.

The Hindu priesthood was generally mild and inoffensive, but the Muhammadans were numerous and often disposed to be fanatical, and there was danger of quarrels arising between them and the Sikhs. The priesthood of the Sikh sect was militant and dominant before the introduction of British rule. Having been elated by the political ascendency which had accrued to its faith, it was proportionably depressed by the recent military defeats, the ruin of the indigenous dynasty, and the substitution of foreign rulers. To the Sikhs the word "Khalsa" meant church and state; their state indeed had fallen, but their church still stood, though with glory dimmed and influence lowered. While the Sikh faith was professed by the Government of the day the sacred precincts were thronged with candidates for baptism according to Sikh rites. Men were Hindus by birth, but became Sikhs afterwards by being baptized. Therefore Hindu soldiers on being enlisted to serve the "Khalsa," and commanders on receiving their appointments, were frequently admitted into the dominant sect. Now, however, the number of baptisms declined utterly, and only those applied for admission whose fathers or ancestors had been Sikhs. The priests, still, had a high stomach and a haughty look while their subordinates assumed a sour and aggressive demeanour.

The judicial system was framed on the principle which has subsequently been termed patriarchal. It was said that in the older provinces the laws (technically styled "regulations") were unsuited for the dispensing of substantial justice, the rules of procedure prolix or expensive, and the courts unpopular. The institution of a separate body of judicial officers caused the dispensation of justice to be out of harmony with the rest of the administration, and prevented the judges from having full sympathy with the practical needs of the people. Undue scope or encouragement was afforded to Native practitioners who fostered litigation and instructed the suitors in chicanery. It was therefore decided to place the executive and the judicial administration in the hands of the same officers; to have a short, simple and inexpensive procedure; to follow the "regulations" in their spirit only, without adherence to their letter; to discourage Native practitioners; to aim at dispensing substantial justice and rendering the courts popular; and to induce the litigants to settle disputes out of court or to refer their causes to arbitration. This was known as the "non-regulation" system for which the Panjab soon became famous. Whether it proceeded from a correct idea, or whether it would suit a more advanced stage of even Indian civilization, may be questioned. But beyond doubt it suited the then existing state of the Panjab, and rendered the courts of justice comparatively popular. The number of cases settled out of court by arbitration or otherwise was remarkably large at first, though it decreased as years went on. The Board maintained a strict supervision over the courts, both those which exercised original jurisdiction and those which had appellate powers. Moreover, circular instructions were issued for the guidance of the courts in all classes of cases wherein the regulations were not exactly to be followed.

The prisons being at first little more than temporary makeshifts, were soon filled with criminals under the vigorous magistracy which had been established. The Board exerted itself strenuously to effect improvement, and Henry Lawrence especially took a humane interest in the proceedings. Dr. Charles Hathaway was the officer chiefly employed in this work, to which he devoted professional science as well as zeal. Attention had recently been paid to prison reform in the neighbouring North-western Provinces, and the experience gained there was used for regulating the Panjab prisons from the outset in the most enlightened manner then known. The substitution of indoor for outdoor labour, the good-behaviour system, the classification of prisoners, the construction of central jails for the worst offenders, the introduction of elementary education, were from the beginning carried into effect throughout the Panjab with greater efficiency than in many of the older provinces.

Some foundation was laid for general sanitation in the towns and cities. Municipalities were aroused to the need of drainage and conservancy, dispensaries were opened, and medical instruction was afforded to a few educated youths.

The country being somewhat destitute of vegetation, much care was bestowed upon arboriculture, and trees were planted in great numbers, on the road-sides, near wells, around towns and stations, and on other suitable sites. An impetus was given to these proceedings by the publication of a minute on this subject from the pen of Lord Dalhousie. A beginning was made with forest conservancy, in order to secure the timber supplies drawn from the Himalayan regions to the north of the province.

The fundamental measure, on which the Board laid the utmost stress, was the settlement of the land revenue. For the first year or so, the land revenue was summarily assessed upon such data as were available. In other words, the amount levied by the Native Government was generally demanded by the British, but with some abatement. The operations for the settlement were immediately set on foot, whereby the revenue was to be settled for long terms of twenty to thirty years, and the rights, tenures and interests in the land determined. To this end a professional survey of every village or parish was undertaken, shewing all the details of the ground, cultivation, habitation, roadways, waste, jungle, watercourses; and serving all topographical purposes, besides being the basis of the settlement. This was followed by an unprofessional field survey, like the cadastral survey of estates in Europe, exhibiting every field; and as these maps received much rectification from the professional survey, they were fairly correct. Thus, for every village or parish, the area was ascertained with all its details, so much cultivated, so much cultivable, so much rich or poor soil, so much under each kind of crop, and so on. Then the land revenue was scientifically assessed on absolute data, and with due consideration of all surrounding circumstances. Its amount was considerably less than that which has been collected by the Native Government. But its main advantage consisted in the equitable distribution, whereby each parish had to pay what was right in reference to that which its neighbours were paying. Whereas the main disadvantage of the Native assessment had been this, that in the absence of any knowledge of area, one parish would pay more, another less, than it ought, according to error, accident, fear or favour.

Then the "record of rights" was undertaken, whereby the property of the people in the land was formally recognized, and the rights or interests of every man, superior or inferior, direct or collateral, were determined. The prevailing tenure was the one which is well known in northern India as that of the village community. These wonderful communities, which have been noticed by the greatest writers on the growth and formation of human society, displayed their largest and yet their minutest development in the Panjab. Although in their main constitution there was a generic resemblance between them all, yet specific varieties existed in almost every one. The record of all these for each member of the brotherhood, and for the whole community in every parish, was undertaken, shewing what every individual had to pay, and the exact amount of his share or holding. Next the unwritten rules and customs, which from time immemorial had governed the affairs of the fraternity were reduced to writing. The revenue was assessed by the settlement officer on the whole village or parish, and the village community then distributed the burden among themselves. This distribution being sanctioned by the settlement officer was duly recorded. Many disputes, questions and local complications arose, all which were authoritatively decided. Such a registration was necessarily complex and elaborate; the people were often careless and inaccurate in affording information; consequently after the record for whole parishes had been drawn up, errors or discrepancies in detail would be discovered which vitiated the whole. Thus patience had to be exercised in rectifying, recasting or re-writing, with much cost and trouble, the papers which had been drawn up. At length, after much revision and modification, a full and correct record was accomplished.

At the same time tenant-right received a due share of consideration. Some cultivators admitted themselves to be tenants at will; but others claimed that their holdings should constitute tenancies, that they were not liable to eviction while they paid their rent, and that if an enhancement of rent were demanded it must be judicially fixed. As some principle was needed whereby these claims might be settled with uniformity, it was held, after reference to local customs, that the status thus claimed should, as a rule, be allowed to those who had been for twelve years in uninterrupted possession.

Next after the land revenue settlement the matter to which the Board attached the greatest importance was material improvement. They were fortunate in obtaining for the direction of the public works the services of Robert Napier (now Lord Napier of Magdala), an officer of the corps of Bengal Engineers.

The first project was to open a main line of trunk road from Delhi to Peshawar. The viaducts over the Five Rivers were to be postponed, but the bridging of all lesser streams in the champaign country was to be undertaken, and especially a good passage made through the rugged region between the Jhelum and the Indus. The road-makers, under Lieutenant (now Sir Alexander) Taylor, of the corps of Engineers, immediately grappled with all the engineering difficulties over the whole length of this extensive line, connecting most of the important stations of the Province with each other and with the older provinces of India. From this trunk line there radiated branch lines in every direction. Among these the most noteworthy was the road from Lahore the capital, leading southwards to Multan, and ultimately connecting the Panjab with Sind.

In the land of the Five Rivers it was natural that artificial irrigation should occupy a prominent place. This subject had been brought to the notice of Government by Baird Smith, of the corps of Engineers, a talented and accomplished officer, whose elaborate report proved very suggestive. A new canal was now undertaken, to be drawn from the river Ravi, near the foot of the Himalayas, and to water the territory near Amritsar and Lahore. This territory was the home of the Sikh nation, and called by them the Manjha; it was esteemed to be the most important part of the whole province. These canal-works, under Lieutenant Dyas, of the corps of Engineers, were designed in the best manner known to engineering science, and executed in the finest style. Simultaneously the numerous Native canals, chiefly styled inundation canals, were in many parts of the province repaired improved or enlarged.

The Sikh Government had levied numerous taxes on trades, manufactures, professions, and especially upon articles in transit. Most of these imposts were remitted, and commerce was set free by the abolition of the transit-duties. The old salt-tax, levied on the salts excavated from the mines between the Indus and the Jhelum, was brought under a reformed management.

Education is one of the few subjects to which, according to the principles of the present day, it might be thought that the Board should have given earlier attention. Schools were indeed established at some large places; but as regards elementary instruction the proceedings did not go beyond the stage of enquiry. Primary education had at that time hardly been introduced into India; though some strenuous efforts on its behalf were being made by Thomason in the North-western Provinces. But even there an experiment on a limited scale only had been tried, and its result was being awaited by the Panjab authorities before making an attempt in the same direction. This circumstance may serve as a landmark to indicate how fast the ideas of men have subsequently advanced in respect to the education of the people.

Side by side and *pari passu* with all these measures, whether of a military, political or civil character, was the management of the provincial finances, on which the Board bestowed continuous attention. It might have been feared that, amidst all the schemes for improving a new country to which much public interest was attached, the administrators would be apt to overlook considerations of cost. The Board, however, resisted that tendency, and strove to manage the territory not only well but economically, even cheaply, to make it pay its own expenses and yield an annual sum towards the general defence of the empire. The cost of the regular army stationed within the province was not reckoned among the provincial charges, as that army defended not only the country beyond the Satlej, but all India which lay behind. It was acknowledged, however, that the revenues of the province, after defraying all administrative charges, must contribute a due share towards the cost of the army. Accordingly the Board frequently occupied itself in balancing the accounts of its incomings and outgoings, and forecasting the financial results of their measures. The income was found to amount to 1½ million sterling annually, therefore their policy was to keep the provincial expenditure down to 1 million if possible, or at all events to 1¼ million, so that the contribution towards the imperial expenses of the army might be in a favourable year half a million, or at the least a quarter of a million in an unfavourable year; and this result was, with vigilant supervision, attained.

The Board were anxious that the administration in all its branches should be popular with the Natives. Some unpopularity with certain of the political classes must inevitably be incurred, though even that was to be mitigated as far as possible. But to the millions who toiled with their brains and hands British rule was to be rendered suitable and acceptable. This principle is, indeed, the pole-star of British officers in all provinces, old or new; but it was inculcated in the Panjab with an efficacy which I have never seen equalled anywhere in India. The officers were instructed not only to receive representations, but also to listen to the people and engage in familiar conversation with them. The European official, who could induce the country folk to open their hearts to him, acquired thereby a reputation for ability. Certainly the Panjabis were not slow in responding to this considerateness. The Natives of India are everywhere adepts in the art of importunity; the unsuccessful petitioner sitting persistently at the gate of authority is an ordinary spectacle. But in the Panjab the vociferous, though good-humoured vehemence with which the people would press their wishes, and the persistency with which, after receiving an unfavourable reply, they plagued the authorities until something satisfactory was extracted, quite baffle description. Some compromise would ultimately be attained between them and the authorities, the latter conceding all that was properly permissible, and often something more. Thus a mutual understanding sprang up between the officers and the people; and these good relations, which exist more or less in all provinces of India, were throughout the Panjab sustained in a happy degree.

Such, in brief, are the chief matters to which the Board set their minds and hands; but in commemorating their conduct it would not be just to separate them from their superior, Lord Dalhousie, or from their subordinate officers. The various parts of this human machine worked harmoniously, each in its due place. The Board insisted upon every man being kept up to at least their minimum standard. Many rose to a degree higher than that standard, but some few fell below. With the latter no compromise was possible, and they were released from service in the province with as much consideration as the circumstances allowed. It was this absolute intolerance of feebleness half-heartedness or inefficiency, that perfected the style of the public service throughout the territory.

The work must be regarded as a whole, in order that its effect may be appreciated. Many a thing, taken singly, which the Board did in the Panjab, had been done elsewhere before. Many measures, which its members adopted well, have since been effected in other places better still, and will hereafter be managed with increasing excellence as the age improves. But the cardinal merit lay in this, that the Board did all those things simultaneously in what was then regarded as an incredibly short space of time. Again, the work must be viewed in the light of those days, not in that of the present and more enlightened day. Many points towards which the Board struggled laboriously were then obscure, uncertain or disputed, though now perhaps clear, certain and indisputable. In two respects great advantages were enjoyed; first, the experience of all the older provinces was available; secondly, there was a *tabula rasa* on which to operate. Many an ambitious man has sighed heretofore, and will sigh in the future, for such chances as then fell into the very lap of the Panjab. Thus the Board owed something to its star and its fortune, though it derived still more from its own courage and constancy. Then identifying itself with all the best contemporary ideas, it succeeded in effecting a progress which proved to be in advance of the furthest limits reached up to that time.

CHAPTER V.

(1854–1856.)

JOHN LAWRENCE ADMINISTRATOR-IN-CHIEF OF THE PANJAB.

John Lawrence appointed Chief Commissioner—Montgomery, Edmonstone and Macleod his coadjutors—The Panjab Civil Code—Completion of the land revenue settlement—Progress of material improvement—Military expeditions on the Trans-Indus frontier—Afghanistan and Central Asia—Summary of John Lawrence's policy and conduct in the Panjab—Advance of the province morally and materially.

In 1854 I was in charge of the Gujerat district, where, as already mentioned, Gough won his crowning victory over the Sikhs. The summer rains of that year had begun to fall when I received a missive from John Lawrence, the Chief Commissioner, ordering me to join him immediately as his Secretary at Lahore, a vacancy having suddenly occurred by death of the incumbent. I had just returned from an inspection of the battle-field where the action of Chilianwala, mentioned in the previous chapter II., had been fought. The scene of the battle was marked by a monumental obelisk, bearing an inscription, believed to have been penned by Sir Charles Napier, and recounting in vigorous, though somewhat high-flown, language the deeds which were done that day. On visiting the jungles where the Sikhs were posted, and wherein some of the British troops became entangled, the spectator is enabled to realize the events as they occurred. The place, also, is fraught with classical associations, being probably close to the point where Alexander the Great crossed the Jhelum to attack Porus, the Indian king.

It was necessary with all speed to obey the Chief Commissioner's mandate, and to cross the river Chenab, then swollen by the rains and the melted snows of the Himalayas to a width of nearly five miles. The boat-bridge having been removed when the flood season set in, crossing over in boats occupied all the hours between morning and evening. This mighty river is now being spanned by a great railway viaduct. Shortly after my arrival at Lahore, John Lawrence was attacked by a violent pain in the head, whereby his general health and strength were much reduced. There had been premonitory threatenings at times during several previous years; but after this attack he did not fully recover, and thenceforward his arduous labours had to be conducted under the disadvantages of occasional distress and depression.

He was now, as Chief Commissioner, exercising the sole administrative command in the Panjab and its dependencies. The government of the province still pertained to the Governor-General in Council, who then was Lord Dalhousie. But the Chief Commissioner performed on his own authority the greater part of the work of governing, and regarding the remainder he submitted recommendations for Lord Dalhousie's sanction. The judicial business of the province was supervised by a Judicial Commissioner, then Robert Montgomery, already mentioned, who had the functions of a high court of judicature. The fiscal and financial affairs were managed by a Financial Commissioner, who was first George Edmonstone, and afterwards Donald Macleod. When Lord Dalhousie selected Edmonstone to be Foreign Secretary to the Government of India, Macleod succeeded to the Financial Commissionership of the Panjab. In general terms, the Chief Commissioner represented the Government, retaining in his own hands the control of the political service, of the public works and of some other departments, but having in the Judicial and Financial Commissioners two departmental heads over the main branches of the civil administration. In all other respects the administrative machinery of the country remained the same as that described in the last preceding chapter.

Besides the leading men just mentioned there were others whose names became familiar to the people. In the first place Edward Thornton, already mentioned in chapter III., had cast in his lot with this province. Charles Raikes was summoned from the North-western Provinces; there he had endeared himself to the Natives by his sympathetic acquaintance with their habits and traditions; he had also illustrated their tenures and agricultural customs by his graphic and picturesque writings. Robert Cust was one of the earliest *élèves* of the Panjab school; he loved his work and his profession with that ardour which men ordinarily shew in regard to art, sport or other favourite pursuits; and he surpassed his contemporaries in official proficiency and literary aptitude. Indeed he possessed that talent for methodizing and systematizing which, as shewn in chapter III., was conspicuous in Thomason. Arthur Roberts was essentially a popular man, of high courage yet steady judgment, most useful in troublous times. Philip Sandys Melvill was esteemed to be an excellent officer in all respects; he afterwards became Governor-General's Agent at Baroda. Henry Davies was already marked out for distinction in the future; he became Secretary to Government and ultimately Lieutenant-Governor of the Panjab. These were all members of the Civil Service, but several eminent officers had been drawn from the army for civil employ, besides those already mentioned in chapter IV. as members of Henry Lawrence's school. Such officers were George Hamilton, Philip Goldney, John Clarke, and others.

John Lawrence's management of the Panjab is held to be among the brightest parts of his now historic career, and constitutes one of his titles to posthumous fame. As a witness, I shall here offer some account of what he did and what he was as a ruler.

His policy when he became Chief Commissioner was to develop the management and system which had been established by the late Board of Administration, as described in the preceding chapter, and in which he had taken so large a part. He made progressive movements in every direction, but no organic change anywhere. There were no oscillations of policy, and the march of affairs went onwards at a steady pace.

The first important measure completed under him was the

preparation of the Panjab Civil Code. The summary system of civil justice established by the late Board of Administration has been already mentioned. For the then existing stage of society something like equity was secured in a rough and ready though substantial manner. The prolix procedure of the Regulations was abandoned, and some brief rules were substituted. The Board and its officers soon began to improve and amplify these rules of procedure mainly with the object of confronting personally the litigant parties and their respective sets of witnesses before the judge, who would thus gather the truth that is sure to come out in verbal discussion when question and answer, rejoinder and repartee, are fired off, as it were, shot for shot, before either side have time to concoct allegations. At that time, too, the Legislative Council in Calcutta, at the instance of Mr. (afterwards Sir Henry) Harington, were considering a draft Act for the same purpose. The Board at Lahore, however, began to take action, and first George Barnes, an officer of John Lawrence's own school and entirely after his liking, drafted some rules of procedure. It was then determined that a procedure should be framed to which was to be added a code of such substantive law as might suffice for the courts of justice in the Panjab; and the preparation of this short code of law and procedure was entrusted to me. Shortly before this the Board had been abolished, and I was ordered to undertake the codification under the immediate direction of Montgomery, the Judicial Commissioner. The procedure was so framed as to be simple, and full effect was given to it by the courts. Its operation proved successful for several years, until it was superseded by the procedure prescribed by the legislature for all British India; and in that legislation its best principles are embodied, though clothed in a more scientific form. The substantive law comprised mainly such extracts from the Hindu and Muhammadan laws as might be needed for the determination of questions relating to the social usages of the Natives, together with some plain directions taken from the English law of contracts, and various rules which experience in the province had already shewn to be necessary. This substantive law, so far as it went, was followed by the courts for many years, until the legislature passed an enactment specifying the laws to be regarded as having force within the Panjab. Though several digests and analyses of Hindu and Muhammadan law had been in former days prepared in English by William Jones, Colebrooke, Macnaghten, Strange and other eminent men, the British Regulations directed the courts to refer to the Native law officers all disputed questions of Native law. This Panjab Code was the first attempt to prescribe authoritatively the principal maxims comprised in the Hindu and Muhammadan laws. Its effect was to render the English officers better acquainted than they otherwise would have been with matters pertaining to the very heart and structure of Native society. Montgomery afforded constant supervision to my work in preparing the Code, and John Lawrence gave cordial encouragement. The promulgation of the Code required the sanction of the Government of India, which was received in due course. To the according of that sanction there probably would have been obstacles had not Lord Dalhousie interposed to smooth the way for a measure which had his full approval.

Another primary object of John Lawrence's policy was the development of the land revenue settlement which was then in progress. The principles on which this great operation proceeded have been already sketched in the previous chapter IV. The work, at once comprehensive and minute, was spread over the whole province within a space of four years commencing from the year after the annexation. Thus the people began immediately to feel the benefit of the new assessment whereby the land revenue was fixed at a lower amount than before on the area already cultivated. The sum total however did not fall so far short of the former standard as might have been anticipated, after a diminution in the general rate of assessment. For the spread of irrigation brought into existence many superior products which were specially chargeable with a higher rate of revenue and new lands were brought under cultivation. The large number of yeomen and peasants who, on leaving their employment in the court and camp under Sikh rule, betook themselves to the fields and crops, gave a wonderful stimulus to agriculture, and strengthened the village communities with fresh vigour. Wells were excavated by hundreds; miles and miles of watercourses were conducted from the nearest canals; ploughs increased by thousands, and cattle by tens of thousands. A cycle of bounteous seasons, with copious rains in summer, and timely showers in winter—the like of which had not been known for many years, and has not been seen since—imparted fertility even to sandy soils. The grain markets became glutted, and as the facilities for exportation were but slight then as compared with the present time, there was embarrassment from a plethora of stores. Thus prices fell to rates which, however beneficial to the non-agricultural class, reduced greatly all agricultural profits. Thus the cash assessments under the new settlement were not favoured with so auspicious a beginning as might have been expected in a time of plenty, for the peasantry had difficulty in selling their stocks of grain. Assets in kind they had in quantities, but they found it hard to obtain money. The rates of assessment were, however, repeatedly reviewed, and not unfrequently lowered in reference to the diminution of profits from the fall in prices. In the end the assessment fixed mainly on the recognized varieties of land—one rate for the black loamy soil, another on the red soil, another on the sandy soil, and so on—was found to operate equitably, as the relative productiveness of these various soils was well known to the people. In India the peasantry are no more satisfied with a new assessment than are the farmers with the weather in other countries; but on the whole this assessment gave quite as much satisfaction as could reasonably have been expected.

Apart from the fiscal operation of the settlement, it has been already stated in chapter IV. that there was the Record of Rights, or registration and determination of landed tenures. This most important work involved infinite trouble, the result of which was at first far from satisfactory. The difficulty of obtaining accurate information from a people unused to such enquiries caused errors to creep into the elaborate registers of complex tenures and extensive village communities. Thus (as explained in chapter IV.) much work done once with great labour and expense had to be re-done. Indeed, to effect a complete registration in the then state of the people seemed an almost hopeless task. Little daunted however, the officers proceeded with the rectification until at length a veritable Domesday book of the Panjab was prepared. The peasant proprietors seemed to fully appreciate the ownership of their lands, now recognized as vested in them; in their modes of culture they evinced an improving spirit, and in their village system shewed aptitude for self-government. Sums began to be advanced to them by the money-lending classes on the new security afforded by the property in land; but the privilege was not abused, nor did any extensive indebtedness set in.

John Lawrence hoped by this settlement to elevate the character and status of the peasant proprietors, whom he regarded as the mainstay of the country; and in this respect he was entirely successful.

A similar settlement was made in the numerous estates wherein Native chiefs were authorized to collect the land revenue which would otherwise have been due to the Government. These estates were generally called "alienated" by Europeans, because the Government had alienated the land revenue in favour of the chiefs; and were termed "Jagirs" by the Natives. But under the chiefs the peasant proprietors were justly entitled to have an equitable assessment made of the revenue payable by them, and to see their proprietary title secured. That was now done for these estates in the same way as in the rest of the province: the measure was not popular with the chiefs, but its justice was indisputable.

Under the proprietors there were tenants to be found almost everywhere; of these tenants many possessed rights which had yet survived, though often trodden down and trampled upon, and of which the marks, though frequently obscured, were still traceable. For this mass of tenant-right a record was made and included in the settlement. As mentioned in chapter IV., it had been decided by the Board that, in the absence of special cause to the contrary, those tenants who had held possession for twelve years should be treated as tenants having occupancy rights. An occupancy tenant was not liable to an enhancement of the rent recorded for him at the settlement, without his consent, and in the event of his disputing such enhancement it could not be imposed without a decree from a court of justice. But he had not the right of selling his tenancy without the consent of the landlord. John Lawrence took much interest in the matter of tenant-right, which he regarded as subsidiary to the determination of property in the land. The treatment of this important subject, as then ordered, held good for many years until it became disputed. It was in or about 1867 that a reaction in some parts of India seemed to set in against tenant-right. Thereupon a law was introduced into the Legislature to place upon a legal basis the tenant-right in the Panjab as fixed at the settlement.

John Lawrence then took up with his wonted vigour the work of education, one of the very few departments, perhaps the only department, in which delay, as explained in chapter IV., was suffered to occur. Authority had been received in the Panjab, in common with all other provinces in India, to set on foot a department of Public Instruction. Besides the establishment of superior and normal schools for training Panjab schoolmasters, due attention was, as will be readily imagined, given to primary education, and village schools were thoroughly organized. The first Director of this department in the Panjab was William Arnold, a son of the great Dr. Arnold of Rugby, and known as an author; he was a man of thoughtfulness and originality, specially qualified for his new duties. Had he lived he would have left the impress of his mind upon the rising generation of the Panjab; but the promise of his career was cut short by untimely death.

A complete census of the population was taken; the inhabitants of the province were all counted in a single night, tribe by tribe, caste by caste, profession by profession.

The prosecution of the public works relating to material improvement generally, and especially to canals and roads, next demanded John Lawrence's attention. Some sketch of these works has been already given, according to the scale on which they were initiated under the late Board. A further expansion of the public works department took place when Lord Dalhousie finally entrusted to the several provincial Governments the management of these useful works in every province. Robert Napier, already mentioned as Civil Engineer for the Panjab, became under the new arrangement Chief Engineer, and made, with the strong support of John Lawrence, strenuous efforts to complete the works, especially the grand trunk road from Delhi to Peshawar and the canal from the Ravi to beyond Lahore, called the Bari Doab Canal. Accordingly such progress was made in a short time as redounded to the honour of the Engineer officers, to the good of the country and to the fame of the administration. But these operations proved very expensive, especially in the basin of the Satlej, the upper valley of the Ravi, and the rugged tracts between the Jhelam and the Indus. For some time the Government of India supplied funds without stint; but the general treasury began to suffer depletion, and it became necessary to raise a loan for the public works which were being prosecuted in many provinces besides the Panjab. Consequently restrictions were imposed on the Panjab expenditure; thus John Lawrence and Robert Napier were to their extreme regret forced to check the rapidity of their operations. Much progress, however, continued to be made not only for the principal works of communication and irrigation, but also for lesser works and public buildings, court-houses, prisons, public offices, schools, dispensaries, staging stations, resting places for travellers, and the like. At length in every corner of the country there were traces visible of the improving hand of the British Government. The crops and the land revenue were secured from vicissitudes of the seasons, commerce, both local and provincial, was stimulated, the public accommodated, and a spirit of improvement diffused among the people.

At this time John Lawrence paid much attention to projects for navigating the Five Rivers of the Panjab with powerful steamers of small draught, and for constructing a railway from Lahore to Multan; which projects represented, as he would say, the crying wants of the province. Already he rejoiced that the scheme was afloat for carrying the railway from Calcutta to Delhi onwards to Lahore and so connecting the Panjab with the older provinces. But he seemed to lay still greater stress on connecting his province by steam communication with Sind and the mouth of the Indus. His eyes were gladdened before he quitted the Panjab by the sight of the first sod being turned on the railway to Multan; but the navigation of the Indus and its affluents never attained much development. In this instance the river cannot compete with the rail.

The affairs on the Trans-Indus frontier continued to demand armed interposition from time to time. Complaints reached Lord Dalhousie to the effect that the tribes had been treated with unnecessary severity. He did not credit these complaints, but directed that I should, as Secretary to John Lawrence, prepare a history of these transactions, which was accordingly done. During the six years which had passed since annexation, there had been fifteen of these expeditions. In every case it was shown that the offences were such as could not be passed over, that every reasonable alternative had been tried in vain before resort was had to arms, that those who suffered from the hostilities were really guilty, that the chastisement always caused cessation of the offences, and that peace had ensued in all those quarters where a salutary example was made of offenders. It was proved that the British Government had behaved towards these tribes in a neighbourly manner, recognizing their independence, throwing open its markets to their traders, allowing their people to settle on its land, and taking many of their members into its service. Notwithstanding these occasional disturbances, the general pacification of the long line of frontier, the mitigation of the violent aggressiveness among most of the tribes, the growth of local trade, the encroachment of cultivation upon the rugged wastes, were patent to all observers.

At that time General (afterwards Sir Neville) Chamberlain commanded the Panjab frontier Force, which was engaged in these expeditions. He was a soldier of great merit, having much experience of border warfare, and considerable knowledge of this frontier, possessing the confidence both of his superiors and of the troops he led in action.

About this time the invasion of the Crimea by the allied armaments of England and France startled the minds of Englishmen in the Panjab, even of those who were most absorbed in the works of peace. The Panjab people received the news with an interest less keen than might have been expected. The fall of Sebastopol, however, which Lord Dalhousie took care to proclaim in striking terms, produced a considerable effect on their minds. The city of Lahore was illuminated in honour of the victory; and when the Native spectators assembled in vast crowds, John Lawrence, after scanning their faces, remarked to me that they seemed to be really glad that Russia had for once been well beaten. Even at that time the idea of Russia making a diversion towards Central Asia, in order to counteract any measures which England might adopt towards Turkey, was much discussed. John Lawrence was earnestly opposed to any retaliatory movement being made from the British side through Afghanistan towards Central Asia, and was most unwilling to meet Russia in any such manner. It may have thence been inferred by some that therefore he was prepared to tolerate Russian proceedings in Central Asia which might be manifestly hostile or menacing to England; such however was not the case. He thought that there were certain points beyond which indirectly hostile proceedings on the part of Russia should not be endured by England, and that if Russia then persevered she should be threatened, not in Asia, but in Europe. He thought that Russia could be so menaced in the Baltic and the Black Sea that she must needs desist from any attempt to harass India from the quarter of Central Asia.

In these days, the Khan of Kokand perceiving the steady advance of the Russians from Siberia towards his territories, and foreseeing the future absorption of his little kingdom in the empire of the Czar, sent a deputation to the Panjab to ask for assistance by arms and money being given to him, and more especially by British officers being deputed to drill his troops. John Lawrence submitted these proposals to Lord Dalhousie, but gave a very adverse opinion respecting them; he thought that if any Englishmen were so venturesome as to enter the Khan's service, nothing but misery and disappointment would be their lot, ending perhaps in a wretched death. The deputation was kindly entertained for some time at Peshawar, and then carried back to their master the negative reply of the British Government. The Khan's anticipations of his absorption into the Russian empire were realized soon afterwards.

Then the Amir of Caubul, Dost Muhammad, intimated a desire to renew with the British Government the relations which had for nearly fifteen years been suspended. He sent Gholam Hyder, his favourite son and heir-apparent, to Peshawar, whither John Lawrence repaired with the necessary instructions from Lord Dalhousie. The Amir, through his representative, professed much fear of Persia being backed by Russia. The reasons for this fear turned out afterwards to be more valid than was then supposed by the British authorities. His immediate object was to obtain the moral support of the English alliance before making his meditated annexation of Candahar. He ultimately agreed to a treaty binding himself to be the friend of our friends and the enemy of our enemies, but imposing no corresponding obligation on the British Government. Two years later, John Lawrence again proceeded to Peshawar to render the relations with the Amir closer, in consequence of the war which England was about to undertake against Persia by reason of Persian aggression upon Herat.

The character of John Lawrence, in contrast to that of his brother Henry, has been sketched in the preceding chapter; it now only remains to complete the summary of his management and policy in the Panjab while he conducted the administration there alone.

He deemed himself happy and fortunate in his two colleagues, Robert Montgomery and Donald Macleod. Being fond of interpolating Hindustani words into his familiar speech, he spoke of them as his "bhais," or brethren; and this feeling was reciprocated by them. They not only concurred in his policy, but had the highest esteem for his prescience and resolution, also the kindest affection towards him personally. They saw how anxious he was that the work of the province should be well done, according to the highest standard that could reasonably be displayed, and were prepared to support him heartily. Montgomery, he thought, combined all the qualities of mind, temper and disposition necessary for the administration, and also an extraordinary promptitude in the despatch of affairs. Macleod was, he considered, admirable as an officer, accomplished in all knowledge pertaining to the civil profession, and intellectually one of the most gifted men that ever crossed the Satlej; he grieved, however, over the delays which Macleod occasionally allowed to occur in the disposal of complicated affairs. He believed that both his colleagues possessed much popularity with the Natives, and he had the fullest reliance on their knowledge and experience.

John Lawrence's official life was a continuous protest against the maxim "ce n'est que le premier pas qui coûte." He was all for making a beginning in every affair, and, in that sense, duly valued the importance of the first step, but he appreciated that step in reference to the second, third and other steps which were to follow. He was instant in business, abhorring dilatoriness, and declaring that procrastination was the thief of efficiency as well as of time. He was not in the least satisfied with a good beginning, and became immediately intent on following it up. It is a maxim in war that when a breach is to be stormed the first line of stormers must be immediately followed by another, and again by another, just as wave succeeds wave; and this was exactly his principle in prosecuting civil measures to a successful issue. He would give orders on a particular subject knowing that the execution of them must take weeks or months of watchful labour on the part of those concerned. He would after a short interval enquire whether progress was being made, and after another interval repeat that enquiry, especially noting whether unforeseen obstacles were presenting themselves, or any defects in the operations were perceptible, and so on to the end. It is well to prepare sound instructions, he would say, but better still to see that they are actually carried into effect. It was to his unswerving persistency in this respect that he owed much of his success as an administrator. This principle of his may at first sight seem trite, but it ceases to be commonplace when it has to be applied with sleepless attention to affairs many in number, varied in character, complex in detail, large in scale.

Consequently in the despatch of public business he was wonderfully efficient. The late Board, of which he was a prominent member, had set on foot all manner of useful measures, and had floated almost every good scheme that could be thought of according to the knowledge existing in those days, and he had now singly to carry them all to their legitimate conclusion. The difficulty consisted not only in there being so many things to be done, but also in there being little time for him wherein to do them. He must needs insist on having for his province whatever the older provinces had. But then the administrators in those provinces had inherited the results achieved during many previous years, and had entered into the labours of their predecessors, whereas he found nothing ready made to his hand, being obliged to make everything *de novo*, and inheriting little save the consequences of Sikh misrule.

While he looked for the quantity of the work, which had often to be done against time, he also regarded its quality with intense eagerness. He had in the highest degree that disposition commonly attributed to the English mechanic, namely, pride in turning out his work in the best possible style. Thus, if an enquiry has to be made it must probe to the bottom; if a statement has to be put forth it must be *teres atque rotundus;* if a fact is even mentioned it must be verified; if a proposal is offered it must be supported by all available data luminously arranged; if a course be taken every obstacle must be provided against. These ordinary precautions he adopted with an extraordinary regularity. The Foreign Secretary of the Government of India (George Edmonstone), who saw the work of all the provincial Governments in the empire, told me that no administrator equalled John Lawrence respecting the manner in which affairs were despatched, or the style in which work was sent forth by the administrative machinery.

John Lawrence felt that success must depend not only on what he did himself, but also on what he could induce others to do, and that an administration is a human machine whereof all the component parts are intelligent beings. His constant thought, then, was to supervise all the workers, and to keep them up to the mark or standard of efficiency, and also to hold them in hand. With this view he closely studied the various tempers and dispositions of the men, spurring the slothful, reining in the impetuous, encouraging the industrious, and applauding the zealous. They all knew that he was a ruler and a guide who would note merit as well as scan shortcomings, and who would sooner or later make his presence felt in every one of the many departments. Herein he followed, indeed, the example of all great administrators; his grand peculiarity, however, consisted in the degree to which he carried this system.

Not content with enforcing rules and principles both in generalities and in particulars, he paid the utmost attention to individual cases. If in any department a failure occurred, or errors were detected, or misconduct on the part of an officer was reported, he would bend his whole mind to the subject. He believed that the tone of the entire administration was affected by the manner in which such cases were treated. If the disposal and decision of them should be regulated with strictness after searching investigation, a sense of duty would pervade the public service. But if the treatment were perfunctory, and if the just opportunity of meting severe measure were passed over, then deterioration would set in.

Though inclined to be what his admirers termed strict, and his detractors called severe, still he unquestionably was, above all things, anxious to hold an even and equitable balance; to avoid going too far in this direction or in that, to go ahead quickly but not too fast, to study details without being over-minute, to pick out every particular and yet never lose sight of the essential substance, to take up every case earnestly and yet not make too much of it; in short, to weigh every matter well. The idea of weighing was always in his mind and frequently on his lips. He thought that the mental faculty of securing equipoise was much appreciated by the Natives when found by them in their English rulers. He once was told by a Native of position that certain officers held the scales exactly, not delighting nor even pleasing any one very much, but, on the other hand, not displeasing nor causing discontent to any one. He considered that this indicated the golden mean, of which the attainment is to be considered fortunate by those who are arbiters between various interests, conflicting, diverging, colliding.

In dealing with the Natives, his abiding thought was to render the majority of them contented; their vernacular for contented is "râzi," and this word came oftener to his lips than any other expression. He would never spare evil-doers, and to the ill-disposed he presented a rigid front. But among the peaceful, quiet and industrious masses he was resolved, if possible to secure contentment; that was one main *raison d'être* for him, and unless this result were obtained he would consider himself to have failed altogether. He would be thankful if, over and above this, he could actually please the well-disposed, but, looking to the uncertainties of human temper, he did not feel sure of winning such favour. Here again his balancing power was called into play; the customs, the manners, even the prejudices of the Natives must be respected, everything good in their ancient institutions must be scrupulously observed; there were many evils in Native society which might for the present be regarded as irremediable, and for which a remedy must not be attempted. On the other hand, British rule was worth nothing unless it constituted a distinct improvement upon Native rule. Many remediable evils existed in Native society, and to these some efficacious remedies must be applied. Wherever a change was for the better, might prove suitable in practice and would meet with a sufficient degree of acceptance—it must be introduced. He was amused with the barbaric pomp and circumstance of Native rule, and took a friendly interest in popular *fêtes*, ceremonies and amenities conducted after the Oriental style. These things he thought were very well in their proper place, but external glitter must not be mistaken for solid merit, and the British Government should turn its face towards the sterner matters of the law. He hardly expected that his officers should aim at a factitious popularity, which if won might not be sustained. But he wished that they should make themselves acquainted with the requirements of the people, by conversing familiarly on every suitable occasion with persons of each class, from the highest to the humblest, not only with the influential and intelligent, but also with the rude and ignorant, who, if they could explain nothing else, could at least tell where the pinch of oppression or of remediable evil was felt. At the same time he held that there were some Natives of loyalty and of judgment who would, if asked, give sound information as to the state of popular feeling and the actual effect of the change from Native to British rule. But discrimination must, he thought, be exercised in choosing such advisers, because the suggestions of specious and misleading confidants form some of the most dangerous among the pitfalls which beset the paths of British administrators. He was fond of listening for a moment to the statements made to him casually on the wayside, and of receiving the numerous petitions which Natives habitually present on all imaginable subjects to those in authority. He well knew the *granum salis* with which all such allegations must be taken; still he wished to weigh them, *quantum valeant*, in order that his information might be abreast of current affairs in the country.

Thus labouring, often despite indifferent health up to the eve of the war of the mutinies, John Lawrence had made the Panjab the most famous province ever known in the annals of British India. Extraneous circumstances beyond his control doubtless contributed to elevate that reputation, which nevertheless rested on a solid basis. This once martial and turbulent province had become peaceful and contented; the staunch soldiery were converted into peasant proprietors; the military leaders who in past times had formed committees (Punchayets) for dictating to their masters, settled down as village elders; here, indeed, if anywhere, the sword was turned into the ploughshare. The prosperity had been unprecedented, and cultivation so increased that clamour arose for enlarged means of exporting surplus produce. The old works of irrigation had been enlarged, and new canals of the most scientific type carried through the very heart of that territory which was the birthplace of the Sikh nation. A sympathetic bearing was enjoined on the European officers in their treatment of matters affecting the prejudices and peculiarities of the people. Trade and industry were fostered by the abolition of transit-duties, also by the opening out of roads. A wild frontier of great length had been reduced to quiet, and brought under some sort of civilization by armed expeditions against the incorrigible, by rigorous measures tempered with mercy towards the wavering, and by a friendly policy towards the comparatively well-disposed. In the interior of the country the violent crimes incidental to a rude state of society were stamped out, the highroads rendered safe from robbers, life and property secured against overt attack. A cheap, simple and speedy system of civil justice had been established. The land revenue, being direct taxation, was kept down by reduction of assessment; but the salt-tax and other indirect taxes had grown and prospered by spontaneous increase. The expectations originally formed regarding the provincial finances were fulfilled; the province had year by year paid its own expenses, and contributed a surplus towards the imperial charges. That surplus would have been much larger but for the beneficent expenditure on material improvement. The people in the mass were contented, and imbued with the utmost respect for British prowess and capacity. The prevalence of these sentiments was soon to be proved by their demeanour during the war of the mutinies. The change from Native to British rule was unavoidably displeasing and disadvantageous to the political classes which largely depended on the Native Government; these classes were, however, dwindling in importance. On the other hand, British rule was eminently suitable to the yeoman, the peasant proprietor, the trader, the artisan and the labourer. A spirit of progress had become the *genius loci* of the province; an elevated tone was preserved throughout the public service, and a school formed of administrators among whom many were destined to serve or rule subsequently in the older provinces, and thus to carry into other spheres, and spread among distant parts of the empire, the principles they had learnt in the Panjab.

The first and the second Panjab Reports were submitted to the discriminating yet sympathizing eye of Lord Dalhousie, the third was laid before Lord Canning. When presenting the last-named document to the new Governor-General, John Lawrence took occasion to do what he could not have so well done before, namely, declare the obligations he owed to the departed Governor-General Lord Dalhousie "for support and guidance which, firm and considerate from the first, were extended to the end, and proved essential to the success of the administration."

CHAPTER VI.

(1848-1856.)

DALHOUSIE THE GREAT PROCONSUL.

Popular estimate in India of Lord Dalhousie—Varying between extremes of favour and disfavour—His published Minutes—His several annexations of Native States—His faith in British rule—His military arrangements—His controversy with Sir Charles Napier—His measures for the pacification of newly annexed Provinces—His policy regarding Public Works—His plans for railways and the Electric Telegraph—His reform of the Indian Post-office—He gives effect to educational scheme of Sir Charles Wood—His policy respecting legislation—His general conduct—His personal capacity.

In the background of the picture presented by the foregoing narrative there has been one imposing figure, namely, that of the Governor-General, the Earl (afterwards Marquis) of Dalhousie. In those days I was too young an officer to see much personally of the head of the Government; but being Secretary to John Lawrence, who was one of Lord Dalhousie's right-hand men, I enjoyed many facilities for understanding the character of the Governor-General. John Lawrence was in constant communication with Lord Dalhousie; and in consequence of this almost daily interchange of thought, the substance of the Governor-General's wishes, the style of his ideas, and the tone of his instructions, became familiar to me as Secretary. Occasionally I had the honour of conversing with the Governor-General himself, and was much impressed with the kind way in which he made me, a young man, feel at ease. He seemed, indeed, to be particularly careful in encouraging even very subordinate officers from whom hard work was to be demanded. In some respects he may have been reserved; but in regard to public policy and duty he was entirely frank. Conscious of a great mission to be fulfilled, he intended so far to be thoroughly known and understood, and he wished that all men concerned should keep their eyes fixed on his guiding hand. I shall ever value a farewell letter received from him shortly before his departure; nor is it possible to forget my grateful surprise at his having found time to write to me, when he must doubtless have been writing to many others, at such a busy season.

Dalhousie sailed from Calcutta on his return to England in March 1856, amidst the blaze of popularity and thunders of applause. If there was disapproval in the Native States, or among some of the Native aristocracy, it was hardly perceived at the capital cities and central stations of British India. If here and there an Anglo-Indian politician intimated doubt regarding some of the measures of annexation which had been taken, most men regarded them as imperial deeds of a beneficent character. The public sympathy was intensified by the knowledge that the departing Governor-General was suffering from an incurable and most painful malady, against which he had long sustained himself, amidst all his burdensome cares, with courageous constancy, and would consequently be precluded from taking any part in valedictory ceremonies. But eulogistic addresses, of extraordinary variety, poured in from every influential quarter, and from all sorts of communities. The title of "Great Proconsul" was set forth in the public press, and circulated in the mouths of men. With the exception of the Marquis Wellesley, there never had been a Governor-General so widely eulogized on his departure; even Wellesley had perhaps not been greeted with such manifold approbation. Nor was this a sudden outburst of public feeling; for the sentiment had been growing and gaining strength during several years. Dalhousie had fully appreciated the moral effect of public approval, and had uniformly striven to do well, to make that well-doing patent to his fellow-men, and to justify his ways before the world. Partly from natural aptitude, and partly from his education at Harrow and Oxford, he possessed a marvellous facility for recording in lucid array the facts and arguments relating to his proceedings in large and complex affairs.

These records were comprised in Minutes which he frequently allowed to see the light. First appeared his Minute regarding the annexation of the Panjab. Then the controversy which had been forced upon him by Sir Charles Napier (the Commander-in-Chief) was published. Afterwards, from time to time his writings upon the many administrative questions, then agitating the country, were given to the public, by whom they were read with avidity. Indeed for several years the appearance of a Minute from his pen used to be anticipated with interest and pleasure as one of the events of the day. The "trace of the Roman hand" was a phrase frequently applied to him and his proceedings. When his incumbency was drawing near its close he began to compose a very elaborate Minute which summarized his whole administration from beginning to end. No document more comprehensive than this has ever been penned regarding Indian affairs. Thus he had courted "the fierce light which beat" upon himself, and to the close of a long career his conduct had well stood that test.

But in less than two years after his departure India was convulsed by mutiny and rebellion. Then the estimate of him passed rapidly from the height of favour to the depth of disfavour. The multitude desired to pull down their idol from its pedestal, and declared the former hero of success to be in truth the author of misfortune. This transition shewed that no trust can be placed in the "arbitrium popularis auræ"; and the pendulum, after that violent oscillation, has not even yet swung back. Nevertheless public opinion in the British empire is generally just in the end, and respecting Dalhousie's memory all reasonable allowances will be made for the difficulties presented by the conjunctures of his time, while the grand features of his administration will assume their permanent place in history.

Dalhousie seemed to feel himself wronged by this temporary reversal of public opinion, and to expect a continuance of reprobation from the contemporary generation, when he forbade by his last will that his papers should be opened until fifty years after his death, which occurred in 1860. Many documents, therefore, which may serve to vindicate his proceedings and policy will not be publicly known before the year 1910. Meanwhile, some passages in his career offer salient points for discussion, irrespective of whatever information may hereafter be gathered, while others may be commemorated whenever the information regarding them shall be complete.

The allegations respecting Dalhousie in his governing capacity were, first, that by annexing several Native States he disturbed the minds of the Native Princes and the upper classes in the British territories; secondly, that during his time there had been in the Native army of Bengal some mutinous manifestations which ought to have put him on his guard, but to which sufficient heed was not paid when the proportion between the European and Native forces was adjusted; thirdly, that, having enlarged the British dominions by conquests in war, also by annexation of Native States, he omitted to secure the presence of an adequate European force, and, owing to that omission, rendered it possible for the sepoys to revolt successfully in 1857.

There was also another allegation to the effect that he permitted certain laws and projects of laws to be brought forward which, however well meant, threatened some of the religious or social usages of the Natives. This was adduced after the outbreak of the mutinies, as a subsidiary reason to account for events which seemed almost unaccountably strange. It never had any real foundation, and, after the lapse of time, is hardly worth discussing.

Referring to the first allegation, namely, the annexation of Native States, I was not present at any of the discussions which led to these measures. But it so happened that in after years I had to govern or administer several of the States thus brought under British management, namely, Nagpur, Berar, Sattara, Sambalpur, to assist in the executive government of the Panjab, and to be for a time officially connected with British Burma. Thus I necessarily became conversant with the views of those who were on the spot and had been intimately concerned in these affairs, both European and Native. I also heard the particulars in favour of, or in opposition to, the proceedings discussed by those who had the means for closest observation.

When the annexations were under consideration, some grave remonstrances were made by men of weight and authority, notably Sir George Clerk, Governor of Bombay, in the case of Sattara, and Sir John Low, member of Council, in that of Nagpur. These were calmly weighed by the public at the time as the opposing arguments which must always arise in great causes. Soon, however, objections of quite a different class began to be urged in less measured terms. The families of the late rulers in the annexed States remained on the spot to plead in persuasive language their alleged wrongs and sufferings in the ears of European gentlemen, who were from disposition likely to sympathize with these representations, and also able by voice or by pen to publish their opinions. There was necessarily much in these circumstances to move compassion and to arouse an imaginative sympathy. Thus the murmurs, which were audible even while Dalhousie was present, swelled into a chorus after his departure, and gained intensity when the occurrence of the mutinies gave them at least a plausible appearance of truth. Then opprobrium was commonly and violently cast upon the name of Dalhousie, so much as to temporarily obscure the memory of his other great deeds. Although the resounding noise of disapprobation grew fainter as years rolled on, still the prevailing opinion seems to regard Dalhousie as having erred in these matters. Such phrases as "the evil days of annexation have passed for ever," or "the spectre of annexation has been laid," the "terrors of the right of lapse" are seen in publications of recent date. On the other hand, closely reasoned vindications of Dalhousie's conduct have appeared. Nevertheless the times have been, perhaps still are, unfavourable for dispassionate consideration.

The debateable point respecting these annexations was the question whether an adoption made by the Prince of a dependent Native State, who had no heirs of his body, should be recognized by the British Government respecting the succession to the kingship and the devolution of governing power.

It has been earnestly argued that there was cruelty in withholding the recognition of an adoption which was binding by Hindu law and possessed religious efficacy. This point has sometimes been debated with an almost moving eloquence and surrounded with a sorrowful interest. As regards sacred rites and private property, however, the adoption was undisputed, and needed no British recognition. Thus the religious and social points in the argument are at once met conclusively.

This, then, was apart from the one question before Dalhousie, namely, whether the adoption should receive British recognition for succession to the power of the State. That question related only to dependent Native States, which had been created by, or were by clear agreements subordinate to, the British Government. It did not concern the Native States in the first rank of importance which have been recognized as allies of the Government, or are in a certain sense independent, though under general control politically. Some of these States are believed to have made enquiries at the time on this point, and to have received satisfactory assurances.

Now, with the dependent Native States, as above defined, Dalhousie was technically within his right in proposing to withhold recognition. None disputed that the recognition of the British Government, as paramount power, was necessary, according to well-established Indian usage. But some urged that the recognition was formal only, and must be conceded; Dalhousie denied this, adducing precedents under British rule to the contrary. The precedents, however, though quite relevant, were not important cases; and the real controversy had never been brought to a decisive issue, until the previously pending question of conceding or refusing recognition of the Sattara adoption came to be decided shortly after the arrival of Dalhousie in India. As is well known, he recommended refusal, and that recommendation was accepted by the East India Company and the Queen's Government on their responsibility. The matter of right was clear; the questions of wisdom and policy were open to a debate, on both sides of which there was much to be said, and wherein agreement or absolute certainty was unattainable.

The decision of the Sattara case governed that of Jhansi and of other lesser cases where the Government refused to recognize the adoptions which had been made by the ruling chiefs.

These cases occurred, as will be recollected, before the war of the mutinies. Some years subsequently, and after that war, the right of adoption was in general terms recognized by Her Majesty's Government in favour of the chiefs and princes who were governing their own territories. The then Governor-General, Lord Canning, gave a "sanad" or patent to every chief to whom this right was to pertain, so that there might be no doubt as to who should, or should not, possess it. The right was expressly limited to the cases where the adoption had been made by the chiefs or princes themselves.

In favour of this change in policy there were then, in 1859, several reasons which hardly existed in the beginning of Dalhousie's time, say in 1848. During the convulsion which ensued on the mutinies of 1857, the authorities rejoiced to find that the Native States constituted a conservative element in the country and a bulwark of the British Government, whereas formerly the reverse might, perhaps, have been anticipated. To this consideration was superadded the desire to reward a most important class, which had (with some exceptions) behaved loyally during a time of national danger despite many temptations to disloyalty. It was found also that Native States could be administered properly, and would fall more and more under European influence in this respect; whereas formerly misgovernment was the rule rather than the exception in these States.

In the case of Nagpur the Raja died without making any adoption, having, for reasons never exactly known, refrained from taking that step; so in his case the right of adopting never was brought to the test. The only question was whether his widow should be permitted to adopt an heir to the throne; and Dalhousie recommended that this should not be allowed. Now, the right to make such an adoption has not to this day been conceded to the widow when the prince had in his lifetime failed to adopt. By the terms of the patents granted later, in Lord Canning's time, the Nagpur State would be regarded as having lapsed, and as being liable to annexation. As a matter of grace or of policy it may be that the Government would forego insisting upon annexation if a similar case were to recur; but the precise position of the existing rule ought to be remembered, when Dalhousie's conduct, at that time, comes now to be judged.

Although, *coram publico,* Dalhousie has borne almost exclusively the odium attending these annexations, it is to be remembered that he had not to decide, but only to recommend; the decision lay with the Court of Directors, subject to the control of Her Majesty's Government. When the Court of Directors had, in the execution of their duty, to perform unpopular acts, it was but too often the fashion to deride their authority. Therefore the assailants of Dalhousie would probably not have admitted the sanction of the Court as an argument on his behalf. But in these grave matters the successive Presidents of the Board of Control, Lord Broughton, Mr. Herries, and Sir Charles Wood, also the successive Prime Ministers of that time, must have finally approved the decision. Thus they must have been in the wrong equally with Dalhousie if he were really blameworthy. He, indeed, would have loyally claimed a full share in the responsibility, but his opponents hardly perceived, perhaps, that in accusing him of tyranny and injustice they were involving in the accusation several statesmen who were members of English Cabinets.

The annexations of the Panjab and of Pegu in British Burma, as the results of war, were never questioned. For the annexation of Oudh Dalhousie was never charged with the sole responsibility even by his opponents, as it was known that there misgovernment had reached an intolerable climax, and that he had recommended a somewhat milder measure regarding the Native ruler than that which had actually been adopted by the Government in England.

Berar, though not annexed, was brought permanently under British administration by a treaty with the Nizam. This measure was necessary in order to defray the charges of the Hyderabad Contingent, a body of troops absolutely needed for preserving order within the Nizam's dominions, and for curbing the unruly bands of foreign mercenaries which had during the course of many years been collected by His Highness' authority. The British Government had from time to time advanced large sums for the pay of the Contingent, until the debt reached a stage when a settlement for the past and a material security for the future became indispensable. The Nizam then signed the treaty whereby he made over the administration of Berar to the British Government, retaining his titular sovereignty, and being entitled to receive the surplus which might remain financially, after the expenses of governing the province and of maintaining the Contingent had been defrayed; the said expenses, however, being entirely at the discretion of the British Government. There was no alternative left except that of taking over territory; the troubles in the Nizam's government having gathered and thickened during many years, at length reached a stage when his relations with the British Government were compromised and the safety of his State imperilled. But since the completion of the arrangement by Dalhousie regarding Berar, these difficulties have entirely ceased, and in no part of the empire has a change for the better been more apparent than in His Highness' dominions.

In regard to the policy of bringing under British administration those Native States which might be fairly regarded as having, by failure of heirs, lapsed to the British Government, or which had become disposable on the termination of war, the conclusion of treaties and the like, Dalhousie believed in his conscience that the transfer of a people from Native to British rule was productive of blessings moral and material. He was much impressed by the reports received of Native misrule. The administration of Native States has so much improved since his day, that the argument as it struck him will hardly be appreciated now in its full force. But after full allowance has been made for possible amelioration of Native rule on the one hand, and for practical defects still remaining in British rule on the other hand,—no well-informed person can doubt that in securing British administration for the Panjab, Pegu, Sattara, Jhansi, Nagpur, Berar, Oudh, and several lesser States, Dalhousie was instrumental in conferring countless benefits upon a population comprising many tribes and races. The total population of all these States amounts to more than forty millions of souls, of whom a section only, numerically small though politically influential, is discontented with the change, while the great mass is happier, healthier and altogether better than before. Although a great good was thus attainable and has been actually attained, that would be no justification for evil, if indeed any wrong were proved to have been committed in the acquisition of these territories. But this good may be adduced when the acquisition, being within the limits of strict right, was questionable only on grounds of policy regarding which different opinions were held, and may still be entertained, by conscientious men. It is true that subsequently there has been a change of public opinion respecting the policy; but this change was consequent on extraordinary events which happened after Dalhousie's time. In order to form a proper judgment on his conduct it is necessary to review the circumstances as they appeared in the light of those days in which he lived.

The annexations in Dalhousie's time were considered by some to have helped to bring on the crisis which supervened upon the outbreak of the mutinies in 1857. It must be admitted that the absorption of so many Native States did agitate the minds of some classes of the population, both under Native and British rule. The sympathy felt by the subjects of the British Crown in India for the Native States, for the Native rulers, courts and camps, is more clearly perceived nowadays than in Dalhousie's time. The faith of the Native princes was sorely tried by sinister representations from many quarters to the effect that the British Government aimed at the direct administration of all India; and the phrase regarding "the red line" on the political map became familiar to them. Notwithstanding this, the question remains as to whether the loyal confidence of the principal Native States was shaken or seriously impaired by Dalhousie's policy and conduct. No candid critic can say that it was thus shaken or impaired in the face of the events which followed the mutinies of 1857, less than two years after his departure. During that crisis the great Native rulers, the Nizam, Sindhia, Holkar, the Gaekwar of Baroda, the Maharaja of Jammu and Cashmir, the Begam of Bhopal, the Rajput princes, the Protected Sikh chiefs, and many others of similar rank, remained faithful to the British cause. Their fidelity was indeed so valuable that some observers feared lest without it the British Government could not weather the storm. Whether the fact possessed this high degree of importance or not, it proves at all events that the confidence of the Native princes as a body had not at all been alienated from the British Government by the policy of Dalhousie.

These acquisitions of territory were not supposed to have caused the sepoy revolt, which was seen to have arisen from independent causes, but they were alleged to have aggravated that crisis. The direct charge of so many additional provinces, containing in all nearly 200,000 square miles and 45 millions of inhabitants, did certainly augment the difficulties of the British Government on that most grave occasion, without always affording, in proportion, fresh strength for encountering them. An addition of 4½ millions sterling annually had, however, been made to the revenues of British India by the annexations. One of the new provinces, indeed, the Panjab, furnished martial resources, and proved a tower of strength to the Government. If it had not been annexed and had remained under Sikh rule, the British cause during the war of the mutinies would have been in a much worse position than it actually was; and Dalhousie is entitled to his share of national gratitude on this account. Pegu and Berar remained quiet, throughout the period of disturbance; and mischief was avoided in Nagpur and Sattara. At Nagpur, however, a Muhammadan conspiracy formed with Mahratta collusion, was frustrated by a timely discovery; this danger might possibly not have arisen had the Mahratta rule been still existing there. At Sattara a mutiny was prevented, owing to the memorable march of seventy miles in a single night by a squadron of British cavalry despatched under the orders of Lord Elphinstone, then Governor of Bombay: this danger might have arisen whether Sattara had been annexed or not. At Jhansi the ex-Rani headed an outbreak which had a very evil effect in that part of the country; this event would probably have been averted if the State had not been annexed.

The effect of the annexation of Oudh upon the course of the Sepoy revolt remains to be considered. This important annexation did not indeed contribute to bring about the mutinies, but did aggravate the effect of the mutinies after they had broken out. The insurrection began with the high-caste Hindu sepoys, but advantage was taken of it by the Muhammadans both inside and outside the army for organizing a conspiracy against the British Government. Thus the rising flames of Hindu discontent were fanned into a blaze; and when the outbreak became general the province of Oudh placed itself in the very van of rebellion. Some of the prime movers in the Muhammadan conspiracy were men connected with the late Native court and camp in Oudh. Had that province not been annexed, the Muhammadan king, himself effete and helpless, must have clung to the skirts of the British Government, also the leading chiefs in the province would have stood by him for the sake of his dynasty. Thus Oudh, instead of being one of the worst quarters of danger, might have remained comparatively quiescent, like the other principal Native States. The retrospect need not cause, however, any regret for the annexation, which measure the British Government was morally obliged to undertake with all the attendant risks.

The second allegation, respecting the insufficient heed paid to the mutinous symptoms in the Bengal army before the general outbreak in 1857, arose from the circumstances discussed in the once celebrated controversy between Dalhousie and Sir Charles Napier, then Commander-in-Chief. Certain orders had been given by Napier, respecting the pay of the sepoys in the Panjab, in excess of his proper authority, and to these orders Dalhousie objected. Thereupon Napier took offence and resigned his command, justifying his conduct on the ground that there had been danger of mutiny. A controversy followed, during which Napier averred that 40,000 men had been in a mutinous state; Dalhousie characterized this as gross exaggeration, uttered in the heat of argument. Still there had been decided symptoms of mutiny in several regiments, and one whole regiment (the 66th Native Infantry) mutinied, mainly because the Government, having granted extra allowances for foreign service during the campaigns in the Panjab, withheld those allowances when that province had become British territory. The difficulty soon disappeared however, and the 66th Regiment was disbanded. A belief prevailed at the time that the regiment had endeavoured to seize the fort of Govindgarh near Amritsar, and Napier shared that belief. Further enquiry, however, showed that this case had been somewhat overstated, and Henry Lawrence, who was on the spot almost immediately afterwards, deemed that the affair, though bad enough, wore a less serious complexion than was at first supposed. These events occurred at the end of 1849 and the beginning of 1850; and there was no further trouble with the sepoys in that quarter till 1857. The only other occurrence of this nature was in 1852, when one sepoy regiment being ordered to sail for Burma, objected to do so, on the ground that by their terms of service they were not bound to go to sea, which was technically true. The Government did not insist on their sailing, and made them march by land to their destination; but the symptom was unsatisfactory. All the other sepoy regiments on that occasion proceeded to sea without demur. Napier's successor, Sir William Gomm, served for five years in Dalhousie's time, and was generally satisfied with the conduct of the Native army.

The third allegation, to the effect that Dalhousie failed to secure the presence of an adequate strength of European troops in dominions which had been enlarged by warlike conquests and peaceful annexations, cannot be definitely discussed at the present time. Many expect that this is one of the points on which light will be thrown by the papers, which, as already seen, cannot be published for many years to come. The insufficiency of European troops in India was frequently observed by Dalhousie at different times during his incumbency. Towards the close he recommended some augmentation of the European forces, simultaneously with a diminution of the Native troops. If he could have had his own way unfettered, he would have left the country safer from a military point of view than it actually was. But nothing that he could have proposed with the slightest chance of success, in the then state of opinion, would have averted the general mutiny which soon ensued. The event shewed that a great error on the part of the British Government had existed for many years; in that error Dalhousie participated together with the rest of his countrymen.

The short and plain truth is that the great mutiny of 1857 arose because the British Government in India had for a long time maintained a Native army much too large, and an European force much too small. The Government thus unwittingly placed itself in the power of the sepoys. This, and this alone, was the main cause of that tremendous event; other secondary and subsidiary causes there were, and these will be mentioned in a future chapter; but to dwell on them at this present is apt to obscure the main, indeed the all-important, cause. The sepoys may have had grievances, or been moved by some particular alarm; but they would never have revolted unless they felt themselves able to do so with some chance of success. The disproportion between the European and Native forces was an error for which the British Indian Government was near paying with its very life, and for which the country suffered a dire penalty. To trace the origin of this national fault would require an historical review extending over a century; and the responsibility pertained to all the statesmen and commanders who had been connected with or served in India from the beginning. The responsibility is, indeed, so wide-spread that the British nation at large is involved in it. The insufficiency of European troops is of old standing and has produced peril in many other quarters besides India, and at many other epochs besides 1857. It was not reasonable to single out Dalhousie as the one man who should have foreseen and provided against the sepoy revolt. Doubtless as the last of the Governors-General before the outbreak, and as possessing the best means of judging and foreseeing, he had as large a share in the responsibility as any one, and would assuredly have been ready to acknowledge his full portion.

Whatever judgment may be formed respecting the disputed points in Dalhousie's career, there was very much in his military and civil administration which must be regarded with national gratitude and admiration, beyond the reach of controversy. His management of affairs relating to war commanded the confidence of men in India, who had been long habituated to the spectacle of campaigns conducted with that vigour which arises when the commanders in the field are supported with all the resources of the general government. He gave the brightest promise of vigour and efficiency very shortly after his arrival in India, by the arrangements he made for despatching forces to the Panjab and providing transport. The distances were in those days tediously long, and their length can hardly be realized now by those who are accustomed to railways and do not possess actual experience of what India was before the introduction of communication by rail. Subsequently, having supervised personally the transport by sea of the force to Burma, he despatched that expedition with unsurpassed promptitude and efficiency. It used to be said at the time, with much truth, that he was his own minister for war. Ability and energy of this nature are common, though in various degrees, to all Governors-General. India, too, is a land fertile in military administrators; and in no country is the art of making war-like preparations more studied and understood. Even there Dalhousie is remembered as one of the greatest men that ever directed affairs of war or organized military resources in the Eastern empire. There also patriotic and enthusiastic Englishmen pray that whenever the national safety shall be menaced by formidable danger, a spirit like his may be present with the counsels of the Government.

His measures for the pacification and settlement of provinces newly added to the British dominions are to be ranked amongst his greatest achievements. Other Governors-General had successfully introduced British rule into newly acquired provinces, but none of them had equalled him in this respect. The system which he caused to be adopted in the conquered or annexed districts became at once equal to the best that had ever been seen in British India. It formed a fresh starting point in Indian administration, and imparted an impulse even to the management of the older provinces. Having chosen leading men for this work, he gave them clear outlines of the policy to be pursued; made them feel that the results of progress were expected; taught them to look to him for guidance, strive for his approval and dread his displeasure; supported them in their efforts for improvement, and left them to select the subordinate officers as their instruments.

In the distribution of troops which followed upon the acquisition of fresh territories, he desired to see spacious and airy barracks erected for the European soldiers in the best permanent style by the earliest possible date. No spur or stimulus was needed by him in this respect; had any such been needed it would have been supplied by the caustic and incisive language with which Sir Charles Napier used to condemn most of the then existing barracks. Due credit must be assigned on this account to Sir Charles Napier, who was one of the first, if not the very first, to cause an enlarged style to be adopted for the barracks in supercession of the former structures. These old buildings, although good and sufficient at the time when they were erected, had ceased to fulfil the requirements of a progressive age. Then Dalhousie took up the work with a vigour and originality all his own. He desired that no nation should be able to shew better quarters for its troops than those which the Government provided for its European soldiers in the East. Having worked upon this principle in the new territories, he extended it to the older provinces. The work being one of time, was very far from being completed during his incumbency; and the efforts which had subsequently to be made in this direction will be mentioned in a future chapter; but a decisive beginning was made by him. Besides their lodging, all matters concerning the food, the drink, the recreation of the soldiers, the increase of temperance among them, the accommodation for their wives and families, the education of their children, and kindred matters, received his sympathetic care. Much more was effected in these ways during his time, than at any previous period.

Further in respect of military administration he signalized himself by the reconstruction of departments; and was popularly called "the crusher of Boards." Several branches of the public service now administered by separate departments, the public works, the commissariat, the ordnance, the army clothing, were all under one body, namely the Military Board. It is difficult after the lapse of years to recall in expressive terms the notoriety which surrounded this Board in those days. It was truly a monster institution, charged with duties so multifarious as to be beyond its power; it was a typical instance of the defects which are popularly ascribed to Boards, and which such a writer as Charles Dickens would have loved to pourtray. Dalhousie, as might have been expected, procured its abolition, and devised a vastly better control for the several departments which had been under its management.

Among the departments under the Military Board, as has just been seen, was that of the Public Works. The fact may seem strange, but it was a relic of the early days of British rule, when the Government was fighting for existence, and when the only buildings, roads, or other works, for which means could be found, were those relating to the army. There was, indeed, a corps of Engineer officers, of high professional ability; but they were military, though some of them had won, or were fast winning, distinction in constructing works of a purely civil character. On the abolition of the Military Board, Dalhousie constituted formally a Public Works Department for each of the several provincial Governments into which India was divided; and the department had two branches, one civil, the other military. The charge of Public Works was for the first time entrusted to the provincial Governments, subject to the control of the

Government of India. The recognition of the civil element in the public works rendered it necessary to introduce Civil Engineers from England. That was accordingly done, and thus was founded the profession of civil engineering which has since become so conspicuously useful in India.

Dalhousie was not content with constituting a department of Public Works, but resolved that it should be fruitful in results and well supplied with funds. He declared that the revenues of India, while sufficient for all ordinary charges, were necessarily insufficient to meet the capital outlay required for works of improvement. The Government would be essaying an impossible task if it attempted to construct such works out of the current revenue; such a task was not undertaken in any civilized country. Either improvement must be indefinitely retarded, or else an annual deficiency incurred avowedly for that purpose, and such deficiency must be met by loans. In other words the Government should be prepared to borrow the capital for works of material improvement. At that time it required courage and firmness on Dalhousie's part to avow and enforce such a principle as this, which in these days is readily acknowledged. He derived, however, much support from public opinion in India, and more particularly in England. The growth of trade attracted towards public works the attention of merchants and other well-informed persons. They used to transmit their views to statesmen in England who would urge the matter both in Parliament and in the English press. Much reproach was then, with but little of justice or consideration, levelled at the Court of Directors, who, pressed by war and by administrative exigencies, had always done their best with limited means, but had been naturally anxious to keep their finances in order, and had never felt themselves authorized to borrow money for anything save war. They now supported Dalhousie in what was really borrowing for works of improvement; and during the two last years of his incumbency the annual expenditure on this account rose to 2½ millions sterling; an amount which in relation to the then revenues is quite as great proportionably as any outlay which has been allowed subsequently in these progressive times.

He was not in the least indifferent to financial considerations; on the contrary, he adopted the idea of reducing the rate of interest on a part of the public debt from five to four per cent., and thereby obtained a saving of £300,000 annually, setting an example which Indian financiers have subsequently followed. Within two years however he was obliged to raise a "public works loan" at five per cent. interest to meet the outlay on material improvement, and then much dissatisfaction against him arose in financial circles. The holders of the four per cent. stock were chiefly those who holding the old five per cent. stock had accepted instead new stock at the reduced, or four per cent., rate. They found their property somewhat depreciated when soon afterwards the Government brought out a new loan, offering a higher rate of interest.

Among the objects, to which Dalhousie directed the outlay for improvement, was irrigation. Many noble canals in different parts of the country he caused to be begun, such as the Bari Doab canal in the Panjab at the instance of the Lawrence brothers, of Robert Napier and Baird Smith. He also secured the vigorous prosecution of the Ganges canal in the North-western Provinces, at the urgent request of James Thomason and Proby Cautley. The Ganges canal had been commenced in the time of Ellenborough and Hardinge; but it was Dalhousie who really sustained the movers in that splendid enterprise and supplied them with nearly the whole of the financial means.

There were three great improvements made upon the English model, with which the name of Dalhousie is permanently associated, namely, the introduction of railways, the establishment of the electric telegraph and the reform of the post-office. These were measures demanded by the public opinion of that time, and the like of them had been recently accomplished in England. For a certainty, therefore they would have been introduced into India at some time or other, whoever had been Governor-General. Dalhousie may be therefore regarded as fortunate in that the execution of such beneficent schemes fell to his lot. To say that he performed the task with his accustomed vigour and success would be to accord but feeble commendation. He did more than this; for, possessing special experience, he propelled these improvements with personal diligence, at a rate of progress which probably no other man of that age could have attained. Indeed it is possible that, judged by an ordinary standard, he hastened their accomplishment by several years. Among all who are concerned in the railways the electric telegraph and the post-office in India, his memory is cherished with extraordinary respect. I recollect the hearty response which was elicited when years afterwards, in 1860, on the occasion of the railway being opened from Calcutta to the Ganges, Lord Canning with characteristic generosity reminded his audience of the obligation which the nation owed to Dalhousie for the speedy introduction of railways.

Every measure proposed by local authorities for investigating or developing the resources of the country used to receive from Dalhousie an approval more cordial than would ordinarily have been expected in those days. Some of the earliest steps for geological enquiry regarding supplies of Indian coal and iron were taken at his instance. The culture of tea in the Himalayan regions was much promoted by his assistance. He was the first ruler who attended earnestly to the supply of timber and fuel; he also laid the foundation of what has become the department for conservancy of forests.

The establishing of national education and the constituting of a department for public instruction, were measures introduced into India during Dalhousie's incumbency. But the origination of them must in the main be ascribed to Sir Charles Wood, now Lord Halifax, then President of the Board of Control in London. Dalhousie greatly favoured the cause of education; supported in the North-western Provinces the educational policy of James Thomason, whom he justly called the father of primary education; sanctioned Thomason's plans for founding a college for Native civil engineers; maintained at his own expense the school for Native girls at Calcutta on the death of Drinkwater Bethune, its founder; and urged the Court of Directors generally to allow educational expenditure. But he did not venture to hope that so large a scheme would he allowed as that prescribed in Sir

Charles Wood's famous despatch. After receiving this general authority he caused the new department to be organized for every province of the empire within the shortest possible time.

Amidst all his avocations he found time to prosecute measures for social amelioration, such as the prevention of female infanticide among high-caste Hindus and the suppression of the human sacrifices practised by semi-barbarous mountaineers.

A legislative council for India was established during the latter part of his incumbency. He often presided at their deliberations, but seldom took an active part in their proceedings. In legislation he was assisted by several English jurists or lawyers in succession, Hay Cameron, Drinkwater Bethune, Charles Jackson, Barnes Peacock. He prided himself in the thought that his was a busy time in respect to the framing of useful laws, such as those relating to municipal conservancy in town and country, joint-stock companies, courts of small causes, Native emigration, Indian marriages, the protection of Christian converts in the possession of their property; and the laws concerning several of the measures already mentioned, namely, railways, the electric telegraph, the post-office.

Lastly, Dalhousie is to be remembered as having procured the establishment of the Lieutenant-Governorship of Bengal, which is the largest provincial Government in the British Empire, being placed over a population of 65 millions of souls, and collecting a revenue for local and imperial purposes together of nearly 20 millions sterling annually. He found this vast local administration added to the general cares of the Government of India, and receiving consequently a share only of attention from authorities otherwise preoccupied. The affairs of Bengal, which were previously backward, have subsequently made rapid strides onwards.

For a due appreciation of Dalhousie's merit as a man of progress and as a ruler with consummate capacity for despatching affairs, the circumstances of his time must be recalled to the imagination. So fast has the march of affairs since become that many things which are now easily practicable were in his days difficult, and would have been quite unattainable but for the extraordinary zeal and energy which he brought to bear on them. Many truths, which in this time of enlightenment are obvious, were then obscure, and would not have been reached but for his persistent enquiries. Many fair superstructures of improvement upon which India now gazes with admiration were really first founded or devised by him, and would not have been raised so soon but for his enterprising disposition. In short, living at an era when improvement and progress were ushered into Europe with startling rapidity, he was in unison with the advancing tendencies of his day, and for India he was much ahead of the age. Whether in some respects he drove the chariot of Indian Government too fast and too far, will always remain a matter of controversy. But there is no doubt that in many respects he imparted to India a decided impulse and moved the hands on her dial by several degrees forwards.

Some men are found who while severely exacting obedience from their subordinates are unwilling to render it implicitly to their superiors: Dalhousie was not one of these. He was invariably courteous and respectful to the Court of Directors; while he evidently felt grateful for the support so consistently afforded by them. On their part they were equally considerate to him, and approved his proceedings almost without exception; a circumstance the more remarkable because they had sometimes differed with some of the most eminent among their servants, such as the Marquis Wellesley. It is creditable to Dalhousie's tact and discretion that he should, though a very progressive ruler, have retained to the end the confidence of so cautious a body as the Court of Directors.

Again, some men of the greatest resolution and energy are constitutionally indisposed to listen to opposing arguments, and apt to adopt one side of a complex question without adequately considering its other side; Dalhousie was not one of these. He had indeed an aspiring and ambitious disposition, together with a proud and sensitive temper; but he was schooled and disciplined by self-control, and anxious to understand objections. He desired to choose his line with patient care, because he intended to follow it decisively, when once it had been taken. He fulfilled, probably, the ancient idea of a dictator, but his dictatorship would have been guided by judicially reasoned considerations. In cases where he had a right to be masterful, he was prompt to vindicate authority; and whenever he received a provocation justly to be resented, he had quite a special faculty for making his displeasure dreaded. By those who had served him loyally he was regarded as a trustworthy friend, but even they looked up to him with a certain awe. Towards his colleagues and all those in daily official relations with him he was considerate and obliging. Every one who had business with him felt that intercourse to be a pleasure, the harder the affairs the greater the satisfaction, so completely trained was his capacity for administration.

In stature he was somewhat short and slender, but erect; his glance was piercing and his profile aquiline; his voice in public speaking was clear and commanding; his aspect denoted a disciplined temper and a trained habit, with an unbounded reserve of energetic resolution and an unconquerable will. It used to be said of him at the time that, though his height was not imposing, he looked every inch a king.

During the greater part of his intensely busy time he was suffering from a malady lying between the knee and the foot which, despite all preventive or curative measures, grew upon him gradually. It was for this reason that he sometimes went to sea, cruising round Indian shores, or dwelt at Chini in the heart of the Himalayas, or resorted to the Nilgiri hills in southern India. He suppressed as much as possible any manifestation of his distress or suffering; and the public was scarcely aware that his strength and life were gradually but surely ebbing away. His wife, proceeding homewards round the Cape of Good Hope, died on board ship within sight of the English shore from weakness following upon protracted sea-sickness. This most distressful intelligence reached him at Calcutta, and he naturally shut himself up for some time in Government House; it was understood that then his malady grew worse. Towards the close of his time, he found it hard to appear much in public, and sometimes was scarcely able from pain to stand up for replying to valedictory addresses. Though his illness had become well known to all, yet few understood that the hand of death was really on him. Many even anticipated that, as he was then only forty-five years old, and comparatively young for the great part he had played, his Governor-Generalship in India would form only a grand episode in a long career of statesmanship; but, alas! *dis aliter visum.*

It is difficult to pronounce what was the estimate formed by the Natives regarding his character. He certainly never could have acquired the popularity which grew around some Governors-General, such as Lord William Bentinck and Lord Canning. Among certain of the classes connected with the Native States he was unavoidably a subject of dread. By some Natives, again, who objected to much of his policy he was admired for his boldness and patriotism. For instance I recollect hearing a Native gentleman of high ability say of him "well, he was a wonderful Englishman; he did mighty things for his Government." The frequent seclusion enforced upon him by his malady prevented him from moving among the people as much as he would have wished, and thus winning popular regards. But among the educated classes at Calcutta and elsewhere the many bright points of his enlightened policy were fully appreciated. Native addresses of farewell were presented to him, and a vast multitude watched his departure.

The estimate formed of him by his fellow countrymen in the East has been already described; the high tide of favour having fallen to its ebb, is now apparently in its refluence rising towards the flow. Apart from moot points of his policy, respecting which there is much difference of opinion, it will be admitted on all hands that as an imperial administrator he has never been surpassed and seldom equalled by any of the illustrious men whom England has sent forth to govern India.

CHAPTER VII.

(1857-1859.)

THE WAR OF THE MUTINIES.

Spread of mutiny in the Native army wholly unexpected—Colin Campbell (Lord Clyde) encamped at Cawnpore—Delhi after its siege and recapture by the British—Memory of General John Nicholson—General Sir Neville Chamberlain—The Mogul ex-Emperor—The loyal Sikh States—The ruler of Jammu and Cashmir—Able conduct of Sir Robert Montgomery—Sir Bartle Frere in Sind—Effect produced upon the Panjab by the war of the Mutinies—Excitement among the Sikhs—John Lawrence's prudence during this critical time—His views regarding Peshawar—Proclamation of the assumption by the Queen of the Government of India—Mutinous behaviour of some of the East India Company's European troops—Visit to Cashmir.

It must be acknowledged on a retrospect of the grave events of 1857 that the spread of mutiny among the Native army of India was unexpected and unforeseen even by the more experienced members of the Anglo-Indian community. Sudden and temporary outbreaks of a mutinous character, sometimes dangerous in extent, were not, indeed, unknown. The importance of the Native soldiers to the maintenance of British rule was remembered, and perhaps estimated more highly than it is nowadays. The possibility of their rising *en masse* to overturn the Government was recognized, though regarded generally as an abstract idea. Hasty and petulant expressions were casually uttered by individuals to the effect that the sepoys would one day rise to rend their foreign masters and drive the British Government into the sea. But the fear that any one of the three Native armies would ever, as a whole, revolt was not seriously felt by any class among the English in India, or by any of the British authorities. A belief prevailed that whatever the sentiments of the sepoys might be, their interests, means of livelihood and prospects were associated with the British Government by ties which no temptations could dissolve.

I quitted India towards the end of 1856 in a fever-stricken condition, intending to remain in England for a twelvemonth. There was not, at that time, any symptom whatever of internal upheaval in India. In the language of meteorology no approaching "disturbance" in the political atmosphere was predicted, and regarding storm-warnings it might truly be said that there were "none issued." While travelling in Italy during the summer of 1857, I first heard of the thunder of mutiny resounding in a sky which, though not cloudless, had been but little overcast. Returning hastily to London, I learnt that the mutineers had seized Delhi, the old imperial capital, and had set up the titular Great Mogul in room of the English Queen; that nevertheless the Government of India stood firm, and that European troops were converging from several quarters on Delhi to vindicate British authority. There was no electric telegraph between India and England in those days, consequently this intelligence was six weeks old before it reached London. I was considering whether by returning to India immediately I should be able to pass up the country as far as the Panjab, and so rejoin my post on John Lawrence's staff, where great opportunities of service would doubtless present themselves, when I was again affected by fever disabling me as regarded active duty. It turned out, however, that every road to the Panjab was utterly closed.

When returning to Calcutta, towards the end of 1857, I learnt that Delhi had been recaptured, and that thereby the backbone of the rebellion had been broken, though the limbs of the monster still retained a terrible vitality. Travelling rapidly from Calcutta to the North-western Provinces, I passed through the scenes of the rebellion which certain chiefs had raised in Behar from special motives of self-interest. Arriving at Allahabad, I found Lord Canning encamped and unattended by his Council. He was then conducting the local administration of the North-western Provinces, in addition to his imperial duties as Governor-General.

Thence I proceeded to Cawnpore and saw the sights for which that place will ever be remembered with sadness; the barracks riddled with shot where the English held out so long against overwhelming odds; the river-bank whence the mutineers fired on the boats laden with fugitives; the room (now demolished) where our captive countrymen and country-women were massacred with the sword; the well into which their bodies were flung, then freshly filled in with earth, but now surmounted with a noble monument and adorned with a blooming garden. Sir Hugh Wheeler, who ably commanded the brave but hapless garrison, was well known to me in the Panjab as a very smart and active officer devoted to his profession.

At Cawnpore I met the Commander-in-Chief of the army, Sir Colin Campbell (afterwards Lord Clyde), encamped on the left bank of the Ganges. He had recently crossed over the river from Oudh in order to retrieve the partial defeat which had been suffered by General Windham. He was about to recross in order to advance against Lucknow; and he gave me some explanation of his plans, in order that it might be conveyed to John Lawrence. He evidently commanded the confidence of military men generally, and the business of his head-quarters, both in the cabinet and in the field, was known to be admirably conducted by Sir William Mansfield, then Chief of the Staff and afterwards Lord Sandhurst. He was thought to be unsurpassed in the professional knowledge of fighting, and his presence at critical points of action rejoiced both the officers and the men. As a strategist, however, he was at this time unfavourably criticized by the public, who, having been accustomed to the brilliant movements of John Nicholson, Hugh Rose or Robert Napier, were disposed to call him the "cunctator" and to ridicule his Fabian strategy. Ultimately, as his fighting qualities and acquaintance with war were unquestionable, his prudence became duly valued, and the meed of popularity was accorded to him as a sagacious and trustworthy commander.

My desire was to go immediately to Delhi, there to resume work as Secretary to John Lawrence, who was administering the affairs of that city and its adjoining territory, in addition to his duties as Chief Commissioner of the Panjab. The road being closed for traffic, owing to the disturbed state of the country, transport was obtained for me from the Quarter-master-General's department. Thus I drove as fast as postal ponies could canter along the Grand Trunk Road, once thronged with peaceful traffic, but now temporarily deserted. The sound of distant cannon could be caught by the listener, as fighting was in progress all around. The road lay through some of the most richly cultivated parts of the country, and the season was one when the young crops should be rising. It might have been supposed that after the fighting, the marching, the plundering, the harrying, of the last few months, there would be many signs of desolation and much land thrown out of cultivation. But at that moment the cereals or other products were flourishing almost as of yore, and from a cursory inspection the eye could hardly discern any difference in the breadth or area of land under crop.

Arriving at Delhi, I found John Lawrence in camp, close to that Cashmir Gate where the deathless deeds of the storming party had been recently performed, and where the marks of the cannon-shot were still fresh. He seemed none the worse for the trials he had undergone, and was both brighter in spirits and more buoyant in manner than when I had last seen him in 1856 before the mutiny. Having been magistrate of Delhi in his younger days, he rejoiced, after such a political hurricane, in restoring to order a place which was endeared to him by many associations. He regarded the recapture of Delhi as the turning-point in a national crisis. He took the greatest pride in the courage and endurance of our countrymen, who achieved supreme success even despite the depressing consciousness that they were but a handful against overwhelming odds, notwithstanding also the physical prostration from heat, damp and malaria. He was amazed, too, at the errors which the mutineers had committed from their own evil point of view, and the chances which they had thrown away of success in their bad cause. He used to say that having revolted they became demented in their manner of proceeding with the rebellion. It seemed as if some avenging fury was scattering their senses and confounding their devices. Often if they had pursued any other course than that which they did pursue, they must have succeeded in defeating the British forces. He was devoutly thankful to the Almighty Power which, in his belief, had extricated us from difficulties humanly insuperable.

We remained in camp for a fortnight at Delhi, which in that cold season, the winter of 1857–8, presented innumerable objects of historic interest. But we had little leisure to study the remains not of a single city but of several cities, one succeeding the other on nearly the same site, the long rows of stately mausolea, the fallen fortresses, the deserted caravanserais, the canals old and new, and the sublime column of the Kutab Minar. Our thoughts were full of recent memories, as we were studying the rocky ridge which had been the position of the British forces, and moving about the city which had been plundered and for a time deserted, but to which the inhabitants were fast returning. The place though pillaged had not been burnt; the marks of shot were fresh on the walls the gateways and some of the principal buildings, but the private houses were all standing and the streets uninjured. There was something of gloom and desolation in the celebrated street "the Chandni Chouk," which had been in its day the most brilliant thoroughfare in all Asia, the focus of splendour and the centre of all that was gayest during the zenith of the Mogul empire. In the equally famous "Jama Mosque," justly esteemed the finest place of worship ever erected by Muhammadan hands, a battalion of Sikh infantry was quartered. This beautiful building was soon restored to the priests for its proper uses. Public confidence was fast reviving, and day by day the place was quickening with the stir hum and bustle of returning animation. When riding along the ridge whence a prospect was obtained of the recent battle-fields, John Lawrence's thoughts often turned towards those who had fallen during the siege.

"Think," he would exclaim, "of all the genius and bravery buried here."

While John Lawrence was encamped before Delhi, his conversation turned repeatedly on the wonderful circumstances of the siege, and many points were brought into prominence.

He thought that there had been some delay in the advance of the British force for the recapture of Delhi after the outbreak of the mutinies in May. The Commander-in-Chief, General Anson, was personally anxious to move, but had been overruled by the difficulty of procuring carriage for all the articles required by European troops on a march during the hottest weather. Whether the circumstances justified the General in incurring the risk of moving the troops with insufficient baggage at such a season, was a military question which no unprofessional person could determine. John Lawrence, however, thought that in this case speed was so important as to justify any risk which could reasonably be braved. If only the British forces could have at the outset appeared before Delhi, the place would have succumbed and woes unnumbered would have been avoided. He was highly satisfied, however, with the conduct of George Barnes and Douglas Forsyth, the chief civil officers on the line of military communications, in procuring carriage for the troops; and he eulogized the loyalty of the Sikh principalities through which the British army had to pass.

He would say "On these occasions the great thing is to advance, to stand still is fatal; precautionary consideration before moving is no doubt necessary, but that consideration should be quickly taken, and thereupon the decision must be instant. Dangers which might be dissipated by a forward movement, will thicken beyond possibility of retrieval if there be any pause or hesitation." The word "advance" was constantly on his lips as comprising a maxim for the guidance of men suddenly confronted with political danger in India.

He deemed it very unfortunate that so many European troops had been stationed in the Himalayan mountains out of immediate reach when dangers arose in the plains of northern India;

and from this he gathered a warning. Sanitary reasons, indeed, there were of which the importance was not to be overlooked; but in the disposition of troops, military and political considerations should be paramount. When the mutiny broke out in May, there were three European battalions in the hills near Simla; had they been in the plains at that time the rebellion might have been crushed at the outset.

In support of the view that in India difficulties melt away before British power if it moves and presses forwards, he would refer to the battle of Badli Serai, the first action fought by the British troops near Delhi. He believed from his information that had it been possible for the European troops after fighting victoriously during the day to push on to the city that very evening, they would have found the gates open and the defenders frightened into surrender; a result which, if attained, would have been of priceless importance. This, however, was not practicable, as the men, after fighting all day with valour and endurance under a burning sun, were unable from thirst and exhaustion to move further.

He used to make the most honourable mention of Lieutenant (now Sir Alexander) Taylor, of the Engineers, for having set up silently in the dead of night, and in the very teeth of the enemy, the batteries which made the breaches whereby the city was stormed. He declared that Taylor was remarkable for skill and science, and "as brave as a lion." Taylor has been mentioned in a previous chapter as the officer who, in the early days of the Panjab administration, projected and constructed the trunk road from Lahore towards Peshawar.

The very highest opinion used to be expressed by John Lawrence regarding the qualities of John Nicholson, as those of a real hero. In Nicholson were combined ardent courage, lofty aspirations, indomitable will, unswerving perseverance, unfaltering coolness, unflagging zeal, and to these moral qualities was added the advantage of enduring strength. But he had an imperious temper and was hardly tolerant of even reasonable and necessary control. When commanding a moveable column in the Panjab, he had intercepted a large body of mutineers by conveying European soldiers over a considerable distance in a space of time which would have been deemed almost incredible. The city of Amritsar (near Lahore) abounded in little chaises drawn by ponies; the whole place was scoured for the collection of chaises in hundreds, upon which the soldiers were then placed and seated. These vehicles were driven all day under the scorching sun, and soon the mutineers were confronted to their dismay by British infantry supposed to be far away. Few commanders save Nicholson could at that moment have effected such a movement; had it not been effected, the mutineers would have passed on to light a flame in the heart of the Panjab. This exploit gladdened the hearts of many administrators anxiously engaged in preserving the public order. After executing other movements with vigour and success, Nicholson marched with his column to strengthen the British forces on the ridge before Delhi. The British siege train was coming from the Panjab, and the mutineers detached a force to stop it; to Nicholson was confided the task of scattering that force. In order to do this he had to march his troops across a broad swamp, which would have been ordinarily deemed almost impassable. Nevertheless his men waded and struggled to victory through miles of deep mud and water. This achievement brought joy to the hearts of the British troops before Delhi. When the time approached for assaulting the city, Nicholson's counsel was added to that of the enthusiastic men who were in favour of action. Indeed the autumnal season had become so malarious, that unless the assault were delivered without any delay, it could not be managed at all, for the soldiers were falling sick by hundreds daily. At the best, so scanty were the numbers, that after the storming parties had victoriously entered the city there was for nearly a whole day much difficulty in preserving communication with the camp outside. I visited the spot where Nicholson fell shortly after the city gate had been stormed. The street was narrow, with houses on both sides, from which musketry was being poured into the advancing column; he was standing forward to guide his men, and dropped mortally wounded. John Lawrence never ceased lamenting the untimely death of Nicholson, and exclaimed, "The memory of his deeds will never perish so long as British rule endures."

General (now Sir Neville) Chamberlain was at that time in camp with us at Delhi. In early life he had been known as one of the *beaux sabreurs* of the Bengal army. He had subsequently been Commandant of the Panjab Irregular Force already described in chapter IV., had brought that fine body of troops into a condition of disciplined efficiency, and had led it with skill and forethought in several expeditions against offending tribes on the mountainous frontier between the British territories trans-Indus and Afghanistan. He had been appointed to command a moveable column which was formed in the Panjab to prevent the mutinies from spreading to that province. After the force had been formed for the recapture of Delhi from the rebels, he was appointed to act as Adjutant-General of the army, and during the operations of the siege had received a severe wound in the arm, from which he was still suffering. He told us many particulars regarding the British camp during the siege, the night attacks frequently made upon it by the enemy, the incessant strain upon the vigilance of the officers and the patience of the men in the defence of a widely-extended position with insufficient numbers, besides the depression caused by sultry heat and humid ground through many weeks of the rainy season. But although the enemy in front was greatly superior in numbers, and sufficiently enterprising to inflict constant annoyance, while the country on both flanks was more or less in insurrection, still the communications in the rear were kept open, and the supplies of meat, drink and ammunition never failed. The Native troops, chiefly Panjabis and Gurkhas, vied with their European comrades in steadfastness; seldom has the excellence attainable by Indian troops been better illustrated.

The conduct of the British troops, European and Native, inside the city after its recapture was reported on all hands to have been satisfactorily good. There was no plundering, nor any maltreatment of the inhabitants of either sex, and very little drunkenness. Great precautions had been taken by the commanders, with happy success, to prevent any such misbehaviour.

During our stay at Delhi, it became my duty to prepare the evidence for the trial of the ex-king of Delhi, which was then impending. With this view I visited him in his place of confinement, examined his papers and questioned persons who had been his confidants. It was a strange sight to see the aged man seated in a darkened chamber of his palace. The finely chiselled features, arched eyebrow, aquiline profile, sickly pallor of the olive complexion, nervous twitching of the face, delicate fingers counting beads, muttering speech, incoherent language, irritable self-consciousness, demeanour indicating febrile excitability—altogether made up a curious picture, upon which no spectator could look unmoved who was acquainted with Asiatic history. Here sat the last of the Great Moguls, the descendant of emperors two centuries ago ruling the second largest population in the world, who had himself, though a phantom sovereign, been treated with regal honours. He was now about to be tried for his life by judges whose forefathers had sued for favour and protection from his imperial ancestors. I looked at the lattice window where at the dawn of that fatal 11th of May he stood to hear the vows of allegiance from the mutineer troopers as they stood in the dry fosse below; at the cabinet whence he issued edicts as if the Mogul empire had been restored; at the hall of audience where he reproached his new followers for their rudeness in the imperial presence; at the old tree in the palace precincts where the European prisoners were executed with his sanction; at the shrine whither he fled for asylum when he found that the British had stormed the city gates. His own signatures, annotations, and orders after the outbreak shewed him to have possessed more capacity than would have been expected from a man who had been immured all his life as a titular king in his ancestral palace. Though he had not originated any movement, he welcomed the event as offering some chance for his political revival. Though he probably did not desire to shed blood, he had authorized the execution of the British captives; perhaps he thought it impossible to save them from his bloodthirsty adherents. He was found guilty of a capital charge, but the Government wisely spared his life and sent him into captivity beyond the seas.

Among the ex-king's papers which fell into our hands, there were letters and reports from priests or other enthusiastic Muhammadans, describing the results of the great outbreak. These writings were couched in the most vigorous and striking phraseology, and the perusal of them confirmed what I had previously believed, namely this, that fanaticism is a volcanic agency which will probably burst forth in eruptions from time to time. It would be difficult to reproduce the imagery with which the scornful exultation over British discomfiture was expressed. The infidel tyrant had been dethroned in an instant like the twinkling of an eye, the flashing of a scimitar, the striking of a knell. He whose glance had once struck terror into the hearts of a myriad time-servers was cast out with contumely, to die of hunger in the jungle or of thirst in the desert. He whose very shoes the faithful had been long forced to lick, was now himself grovelling in the dust!

Before the mutinies, Delhi with its adjacent territory had formed part of the North-western Provinces; after its recapture it was placed by Lord Canning under John Lawrence, and thus became incorporated in the Panjab jurisdiction. Accordingly John Lawrence was now, in the beginning of 1858, restoring peace and order to the distracted place. His first care was to reintroduce the regular police, the magistracy and the criminal law, whereby all accused persons should be brought to formal trial before being punished. During the terrible times which followed the mutiny, and the confusion which existed after the recapture of the city, the criminal law had been virtually suspended. Many Europeans had been murdered or maltreated after the outbreak; the mob committed countless excesses; hundreds of persons were known to have perpetrated outrages and treasonable acts; the villages of the neighbourhood teemed with predatory or lawless characters, and plunder had been rife. Thus it happened that many persons were seized and punished after a brief enquiry, which, though it satisfied the punishing authority, did not amount to trial; many, again, having been caught red-handed, or *in flagrante delicto*, were punished straightway. Under the emergency and pressure of the time, prisoners were executed in a summary manner which would not have been tolerable under any other circumstances. This rapid process, or rather the absence of procedure, during times when the minds of men are excited by tremendous events, must inevitably be dangerous and cause injustice to be unwittingly done in some cases. The local authorities doubtless acted in good faith, according to their judgment so far as it could be exercised under agitating conditions. But there is always fear lest a summary procedure should be prolonged after the actual necessity has ceased or the emergency passed by. If, however, such a procedure be permissible, while all the bonds of society are unloosed, it ought certainly to cease the moment that law and order can be restored. Now, John Lawrence, deeming that such proceedings were being carried too far, interposed with his usual vigour and firmness to stop them, and substitute the normal procedure of the criminal law. As many prisoners were awaiting trial he appointed special tribunals to dispose of all pending cases, so that the fear of wild retribution might be removed from the Native mind.

The conduct of the Native population, at the outbreak of the mutinies both around Delhi and in other parts of the North-western Provinces, had been unsatisfactory and discouraging to those who hoped that British rule in the course of two or three generations would alter the character and disposition of the masses. Though much of mildness and submissiveness is found in the people as a whole, there are also elements of fierceness and savagery. The mob in Indian cities, and especially in the bazaars which cluster round military cantonments, is vicious and ruthless. Such a rabble broke out in wild excesses at all places where the civil authority had been paralyzed by military disturbance; and the rioters were speedily joined by plundering bands from the interior of the country. Had these bands consisted only of the thieves and robbers who are at all times wandering or lurking about the country, there would have been no reason for surprise. But the gangs in many places, and especially in the districts around Delhi, were in part formed by villagers who owned flocks and herds, or who tilled land as peasant proprietors. Several tribes or castes had acquired predatory habits in former generations when this part of the country was one of the great battle-fields of Asia. The plundering instinct had been transmitted as if by hereditary descent, and, though so long dormant, now burst forth on the relaxation of general order, just as if wars and revolutions had continued unceasingly up to the most recent time, and as if more than two generations had not intervened between the traditions of the past and the conditions of the present. Then with almost electrical swiftness the demon of mischief issued forth. The jails were broken, and a flood of criminals was let loose to swell the tide of disorder. Court-houses and public offices were attacked, public records consigned to the flames, dwellings of the Europeans unroofed dismantled or burnt. The treasuries were not rifled by the ruffians, because the treasure had fallen into the hands of the mutinous soldiery. Among the records destroyed were the elaborate papers comprising the detailed surveys village by village even field by field, containing also the registration of proprietary tenures and tenant-right, in short everything which pertained to the land revenue settlement. This destruction, however, proved to be not so fatal as might have been expected, for in the villages the old institution of Native accountant existed in greater vigour than ever. Every accountant had copies of the settlement papers relating to his village, and these copies he almost invariably preserved with all the secretiveness characteristic of the Natives in times of revolution. Thus after a time the losses caused by the burning of records were for the most part repaired. Certain critics who disliked the policy of the settlement seemed to see in the destruction of these papers some proof of the supposed unpopularity of that great measure. Discontented individuals probably did take the opportunity of wreaking their spite upon the records; but this destruction was, in the main, nothing more than a part of the general and indiscriminate spoliation committed by a raving multitude.

It was my duty, among many other things, to enquire into the truth or error of the shocking stories current regarding the maltreatment and indignities inflicted upon the European victims of the mutineers and the mob; also to award compensation on behalf of Government to those European ladies and gentlemen whose houses and effects had been plundered or destroyed. The cases of outrage were found often to be exaggerated, and sometimes quite baseless; they loomed, indeed, sadly from afar, but on the spot and in contact with positive information they seemed to dwindle away. Murders of European men, women and children, alas, there were; but the murderers generally did their work offhand with horrid eagerness, seldom pausing to add torture or prolong agony. Yet if many of the alleged sufferings proved to be fabulous, the real misery of but too many Europeans of both sexes was not, and never will be, fully known, the undescribed, perhaps indescribable, anguish of anxiety felt by men, not for themselves, but for the helpless ones around them, the terrified imagination of the women, the protracted vigils conjuring up phantoms of horror, the exposure of delicately nurtured people to the blinding blistering sun, their frames fevered by thirst sleeplessness and poverty of sustenance.

In those days we were anxiously awaiting news regarding the final recapture of Lucknow by Sir Colin Campbell. The special correspondent of the London *Times* with the army was William Howard Russell. The Anglo-Indian community were delighted by his power of noting mentally all that passed before him and of depicting it graphically. His word-paintings of the scenes inside Lucknow after the storming hold a high place in the picture-gallery of Indian history.

When John Lawrence moved his camp from Delhi in the spring of 1858 and marched towards Lahore, I accompanied him. Our line of march lay through the territory known as the "Protected Sikh States," which half a century before had been rescued by the British Government from the devouring jaws of Ranjit Sing, then called the "Lion of the Panjab." The Chiefs of these States had been foremost among the loyal during the outbreak and crisis of the mutiny, and formed a political breakwater between the loyal Panjab and the rebellious Hindostan. Between all these good men and John Lawrence there was an interchange of congratulations on the happy issue of events.

First among them, the Chief of Pattiala, had personally done much to sustain the public confidence. His position between the Panjab and Delhi enabled him to shew of what stuff he was made. Thereupon he evinced that steadiness and calmness upon which the English justly pride themselves. He was then a fine-looking man, nearly six feet high, with a commanding presence, and in the prime of life. He said that his house had always been faithful to the paramount power from the day it received its patent of chiefship from the Durrani sovereigns of Afghanistan to the time when it did good service in the wars waged by the British. He was ready either to march to Delhi or to maintain order in the country intervening between that city and the Satlej. It was decided that he should stay at or near his capital and employ his troops in guarding the trunk road leading from the Panjab to Delhi, or escorting the stores and munitions in the rear of the British force besieging that city. Some five thousand troops of his were thus employed for many weeks, thereby enabling the British authorities to send every soldier of their own to the siege. The extreme value of his service will be appreciated when it is remembered that for some time the besiegers held their own with difficulty and were themselves almost besieged. Afterwards when the British fugitives from neighbouring districts passed through his capital, he displayed a cheerful bearing and assured them of his faith that European troops would soon arrive from England to regain all that had been lost. All this time he maintained absolute order in his own territories although they were ofttimes nearly catching fire from the sparks or firebrands falling into them when the contiguous Hindostan was ablaze with rebellion.

Next, the Chief of Jhind was the handsomest Native prince I ever saw. His height was much above six feet, and he had the flowing grey beard which Sikhs regard as the best of manly ornaments. He instantly took up arms against the rebels, declaring that he should fight for the British, under whose shadow he and his had enjoyed security for fifty years; and he was the first man who appeared in the field with an armed force on the British side. In order to take every available man with him into the field, he left his little capital quite defenceless. With his troops he remained under canvas before Delhi throughout the siege, and his men took part in the final assault. Though a thorough Sikh, he possessed many of what would be considered sterling British qualities, frankness, truthfulness, fidelity, resolution.

If hereafter a national crisis shall arise, may there then be Native chiefs possessing such strength of character, and bound to the British Government by such ties of gratitude as the chiefs of Pattiala and Jhind in 1857! They deserved to be, as they actually were, regarded by many Englishmen with fraternal sentiments. It is no mere form of words to say, peace be to their ashes, for indeed their gallant memory will be preserved together with that of the British worthies.

Among the lesser magnates were the descendants of the Kythal chief who bore the title of "Bhai," which indicates priestly rank and corresponds to "Fra" in Roman Catholic countries. At the beginning of the century he attended a meeting of Chiefs who intended to make overtures to the British for protection against Ranjit Sing. According to the Native story he expressed himself in this wise, "Brethren, it is death for us in either event; if we are caught in the grip of Ranjit Sing we shall die with the sharp pangs of Asiatic cholera; if we come under the shadow of the British we shall pine away of slow consumption." Strangely the prophecy was verified in his own case, for his possessions did lapse from failure of heirs; but it was falsified in the cases of those whom he addressed, as their descendants now have a position firmer than ever.

The political officer in charge of these Cis-Satlej chiefs was George Barnes, who has been already mentioned. Of all the officers in the Panjab there was none who commanded the confidence of John Lawrence more than he. His insight into the

Oriental character, his mastery of affairs however difficult, his sagacious judgment in momentous conjunctures, his power of managing Natives of all ranks from the highest to the humblest —gave him great influence both with his civil superiors and with the military authorities. After the recapture of Delhi he received the official thanks of the Commander (Sir Archdale Wilson) for the manner in which the resources of the Cis-Satlej States had been disposed so as best to subserve the plans of the General and to supply the needs of the army. He was next appointed Foreign Secretary by Lord Canning, and had his life been spared would have rapidly risen to the highest posts. I was with him during his fatal illness; and afterwards John Lawrence spoke to me with affectionate solicitude in respect to the closing moments of his old friend, enquired regarding the administration of the last offices of the church, and expressed a fervent hope for his eternal welfare.

After leaving the Cis-Satlej States, John Lawrence paid a visit to Jammu, at the foot of the Himalayas. Here was the capital of Maharaja Golab Sing, the ruler of the Jammû-Cashmir State which had been established by the British Government after the first Panjab war. Golab Sing came forth to meet us with a procession of elephants, crossing the stony bed of the river which flows beneath the forest-clad bluffs. High above us on the crest of the cliffs stood the palaces and temples of Jammu. The historic antecedents and personal celebrity of Golab Sing struck the imagination. His pomp and equipage forming a fit foreground to the sub-Himalayan scenery, the mountain called "the three-peaked goddess," rising up grandly in the background, and the snowy range in the distant horizon, made up an animated scene. This preliminary meeting was a gay prelude to the ceremonies which were to follow and the felicitations which were to be exchanged. For the Jammû troops had marched right through the Panjab, and appeared before Delhi in the very crisis of the siege, under the command of Colonel Richard Lawrence the youngest of the Lawrence brothers. The sight of these troops moving against the mutineers in the darkest hour of British fortunes produced a moral effect on the

Panjab people. Golab Sing had a character containing some good or strong elements but profoundly subtle and hard to fathom. Extraordinary stories were current regarding the intrigues in which he had been engaged and the cruelty he had practised. Doubtless there was exaggeration in these, but he had lived in times when such things were rife, and it is necessary to realize the surroundings and temptations of a man when judging his conduct. Though now stricken in years he was well-preserved; his features were still handsome, and he had all the air of his Rajput lineage. The phrase "mellifluous speech" is quite translateable into Persian, and was applicable to the courtly and euphonious diction which he used whenever occasion might demand it. He retained a grateful recollection of Henry Lawrence, whom he regarded as his political patron, and whose recent death at Lucknow he lamented as a personal loss. On this occasion, alluding to Richard Lawrence, he said, "I see in his face the likeness of Sir Henry, and my heart becomes full."

On our return to Lahore it became necessary to prepare for the Governor-General a report on the events of the mutinies in the Panjab. For this purpose I had many conversations with John Lawrence, and he wrote some important memoranda for incorporation in the report. He pondered over the causes of the great mutiny and rebellion, so that if they should be traceable to national error, a salutary lesson might be learnt for the future.

While ready to vindicate the character of his country and the grand qualities displayed by her sons on the whole in dealing with the mutinies, he was far from thinking that these qualities had been displayed by all his countrymen. On the contrary he knew that a cardinal vice in the then existing system was the placing of incapable officers in high command by reason of seniority. The consequences were signally illustrated by the incompetent proceedings of the authorities during the outbreak at Meerut. Even at Ferozpur on the Satlej, where the local commander was esteemed an able man, much disappointment had been felt at the ineffectual manner in which the mutiny was dealt with, though no absolute failure or actual disaster occurred. Still none of the errors committed by individuals exceeded that chargeable to the Government itself in leaving such a place as Delhi in the custody of a large Native garrison without European troops. Sanitary reasons doubtless induced the authorities to prefer keeping the European troops elsewhere. But in truth, when such considerations were allowed to override the clear dictates of political prudence, then incapacity in statecraft was displayed.

As to the origin of the great mutiny, the sum and substance of John Lawrence's opinion was this, that the sepoys had become too numerous and powerful in proportion to the European army. The State was virtually in their hands, therefore they wished to displace their foreign masters, and set up a national Government of which they would be the controllers. Their numerical preponderance, he thought, was aggravated by the situations in which they had been placed. "Was it to be expected," he would exclaim, "that the Native soldiery, who had charge of our fortresses, arsenals, magazines, and treasuries, without adequate European control, should fail to gather extravagant ideas of their own importance?" Again, he would say, "it was the sense of power that induced them to rebel;" and herein, according to him, lay the warning to the Government for the future. This cardinal and abiding cause having been established, he regarded other causes as secondary and casual. He believed that the sepoys, when they first began to rise, were actually alarmed for their caste and religion, that their apprehension regarding the greased cartridges was not feigned at all, but was quite real, and that had no novel cartridges been issued there would have been then no mutiny. But the question was in his judgment one of time only; some other provocative cause would sooner or later have arisen, for with a sepoy army fancying itself master of the situation, it was hardly possible for an alien Government ultimately to avoid collision. Though positive upon this most material point, he was less confident respecting the collateral questions whether the time for the outbreak was in part determined by the annexations of Native States which had taken place, or by measures legislative and executive which, however right, had been unpopular. Less weight was attributed to these causes by him than by some other authorities. He thought that the Government, while maintaining the utmost caution and considerateness in these matters, must be prepared sometimes to face temporary unpopularity for the sake of permanent good. But he would hardly deny that the annexation of Oudh, happening when it did, must, however just and necessary, have had a disturbing effect.

He admitted that the composition and system of the Bengal Native army had been faulty. When an organized system has existed for many years, there gather round it many influential persons, whose sentiments prejudices and interests compel them to gloss over its defects and repel its critics. Occasionally fault had been unreasonably found with the sepoy army and some conclusive answer would then be given. But even well-founded criticism would have been indignantly spurned by the numerous authorities who were concerned in the maintenance of things as they were. Still, no degree of perfection in these matters could have averted the ultimate catastrophe. For the event depended not so much on the organization of the sepoys, as on the might of their numbers.

The English are subjected to the irremediable disadvantage of being aliens; do what they may, they can hardly make themselves popular, for Natives, though submissive outwardly, are inwardly swayed by national sentiments, and though they may respect and acquiesce in a foreign Government, will hardly love it. John Lawrence did not attribute to the Natives that ingratitude with which they are but too often charged. "Give them much to be grateful for," he would say, "and they will evince gratitude." Still he felt that no tangible benefits which the English could confer would be of avail, if an opportunity were really to occur of driving them into the sea which girdles India; the sepoys may be faithful at least to the British pay, up to a certain point, but this fidelity would be flung away by them if they saw a positively favourable chance of setting up with their bayonets a ruler of their own kith and kin. Therefore, he thought the British must rule to the best of their ability; hoping for the best from moral influence, trusting, however, in the last resort, to physical power. He would refrain from answering categorically the question, why the mutiny had not broken out before 1857, when the main cause, as explained by him, had existed for a long time. If a thing is destined to occur there is an element of chance in the time of occurrence; it is impossible to say when a spark may ignite a combustible body, or when disease may break out after morbid conditions have been established. The practical issue, in his view, was to rectify the old error by lessening the Native forces and increasing the European, in order that the physical, as well as the moral, power of the country should be in British hands.

After due reflection upon the great mutiny of 1857, he declared these opinions in the beginning of 1858, little thinking perhaps that they would receive confirmation before the last-named year was out. For the Government were near committing a similar error in entertaining too many Panjabi troops, and fears in regard to a like consequence began to arise.

In reviewing the events of 1857 in the Panjab, he assigned the utmost credit to Robert Montgomery, General Corbett and Colonel James Duncan Macpherson for the prompt disarming of the sepoys at Lahore; also to Herbert Edwardes and General Sydney Cotton for maintaining order at Peshawar. The disarming of the Sepoys at Lahore on 13th of May, 1857, was one of the most remarkable events in the history of the mutinies. Corbett in the exercise of the soundest judgment assumed a perilous responsibility, and Macpherson played his part excellently well. But the chief credit is due to Robert Montgomery, who rendered a priceless service to his country. Had this measure not been taken with the requisite promptness, the sepoys certainly would have revolted. Whether such a revolt would have succeeded is a question which the boldest might tremble to answer; the chances of its success were considerable. Had it occurred, the course of affairs in the Panjab might have been disastrously altered.

In the general course of affairs John Lawrence considered the support of the Field Force before Delhi to be the turning point of his policy. There was no matter on which he so often dwelt in conversation as this. Though Delhi was outside the Panjab, still he thought that the Panjab must in the end stand or fall according as Delhi should be recaptured or should hold out against us. He felt sure that the Panjabi people would expect soon to hear of Delhi being recaptured, but would not withstand the temptation to revolt if that expectation should not be fulfilled and the rebellious front which had been raised in the imperial city should not be beaten down. Not only might the Panjabi people rise, but the Panjabi troops might swerve from their fidelity; and yet these were the troops upon which the Government depended after losing the Bengal sepoys. Therefore, at all hazards, Delhi must be retaken speedily; and with this view he despatched thither the flower of the Panjab Frontier Force, and raised many Panjabi regiments. His Military Secretary, Colonel Macpherson, already mentioned, did true yeoman's work in the organization and equipment of the new regiments. Then it was found that this would not suffice, and that some European troops must be sent. So John Lawrence despatched Nicholson's column to Delhi, notwithstanding that he thereby lowered the European force in the Panjab to an almost dangerous minimum, as the best part of that force was stationed beyond the Indus. He declared plainly that he was thereby "playing the final card," that he was "gleaning the last man," that he was "draining the cup to the uttermost drop." When told that there was danger for the Panjab in sending the column, he would rejoin that there was still more danger in not sending it. If it were sent, there was some hope of Delhi being recaptured and of the Panjab standing firm, but if it were not sent, then there was no hope of Delhi being recaptured, and the Panjab must fall sooner or later. He was fond of saying that he did not "care to be among the children whom the ogre ate up last." He noted that during the month preceding the recapture of Delhi several untoward symptoms had manifested themselves in the Panjab, and such manifestations would have become more frequent during every month, perhaps every week, that Delhi remained untaken.

He had a most thankful sense of the aid afforded to him throughout that critical time by Bartle Frere, the Commissioner in Sind, and would declare that, had Sind been a part of the Panjab, the co-operation for the public safety between the two provinces could hardly have been more perfect than it was. Indeed Frere, more than once, sent reinforcements, especially European soldiers, to support the Panjab, thereby almost denuding Sind, his own province, of troops, and reducing his available resources to a minimum. Notwithstanding occasional differences of opinion between them concerning the management of the Trans-Indus Frontier or other topics, John Lawrence felt the highest regard and respect for Frere, and deliberately considered him to be one of the most capable rulers that this generation has produced in India.

It was in these days that John Lawrence gave me instructions for drafting the despatch regarding the attitude of the British Government towards Christianity in India. He took the strongest interest in the subject, and conned over and over again every paragraph as it was drafted. The production of the despatch arose from some questions in respect to placing the Bible in the libraries of all Government Schools for the study of those who might wish to read it; and he determined that this step should be taken. Religious feeling had been more and more gaining strength in his mind for many years past, and now formed the main-spring of his whole being. He apprehended that things intended to be Christian were often performed in an un-Christian way, and thus lost the true character of Christianity. He held that Christian things done in a Christian way could never be politically dangerous in India. Any hesitation which might have formerly existed in this respect was swept away by the recent cataclysm, and by the victory which had been mercifully vouchsafed. The Government should be more explicit than heretofore in avowing its Christian character while adhering to the resolution of scrupulously abstaining from interference in the religions of the people. Education and private effort might produce their legitimate fruit, and yet the motives of the Government would be appreciated.

In the spring of 1858 the political sky in the Panjab was clear after the great storm. British repute stood high, consequent on the achievements of the European troops in the wars of 1846 and 1848, to whom alone the Sikhs attributed the British victories, somewhat despising the Native troops. Now these Native troops had mutinied in the most formidable manner, and were yet overcome by their foreign masters. The backbone of the rebellion had indeed been broken by the recapture of Delhi; but Lucknow and the greater part of Oudh still held out; now, however, Lucknow also had fallen to the British. Thus the Sikhs were in their first thoughts disposed to be more loyally obedient than ever. But in their second thoughts, this fair view soon became clouded over; for they began to think that after all they had largely assisted the British in the recapture of Delhi, and afterwards in the siege of Lucknow. In Oudh indeed much use had been made of the Panjabi troops, raised by John Lawrence during the crisis of the mutiny. These measures had been carried to the very verge of imprudence. One of the errors which led to the mutinies had been the employment in excessive proportion of Native troops drawn from the North-western Provinces and Oudh. Yet something like the same error was near being repeated with the Panjabi troops. For the Sikhs began to say ominously, "We have been the means of restoring the kingdom to the British; why should we not set up a kingdom for ourselves?" This rising sentiment, too, expanded, as the news came of campaigning in Central India. Sir Hugh Rose had indeed with a small force fought his way from the Bombay Presidency to the North-western Provinces, reducing many rebels as he passed along. But around Gwalior, the capital of Sindhia's State, the rebellion still surged; and Sindhia, as an ally of the British, could hardly maintain his position. This trouble was soon overcome by Sir Hugh Rose's operations, which were followed by some brilliant movements under Sir Robert Napier. The chequered events, however, affected the minds of the Sikhs, causing them to think that the great rebellion was not surely ended.

Some aggravation, also, came from the quarter of Nepal, which State was in dangerous proximity to Oudh, the focus of rebellion. The best of all the Native troops in the British service had indeed been drawn from Nepal, and had recently added much to their previously high repute. Some troops, however, of the Nepalese State co-operated with the British in the Lucknow campaign and failed to be of much use, mainly, it was thought, by reason of the doubtful attitude of the Nepal Government itself. Nepal, in the heart of the Himalayas, was situated differently from the loyal Native States of India proper; and during the mutinies was restrained by its able minister Jang Behadur, who had visited England and knew her power. The widow of old Ranjit Sing, a remarkable woman and a veteran intriguer, had taken refuge in Nepal after escaping from a British state-prison. She was believed to be fomenting mischief among the Panjabi troops quartered in Oudh and the Sikhs in the Panjab itself.

Thus in 1858 there was an uneasy feeling among the Panjabi troops stationed at many places throughout northern India from Nepal in the east to the Trans-Indus frontier in the west. These troops consisted not only of Sikhs, but also of Muhammadans drawn from the Afghan frontier. The Afghans, too, were believed to have been held back from participation in mischief only by the Amir Dost Muhammad, who, though retaining his capacity and resolution, was much advanced in years, and had no heir-apparent of equal ability. It was never ascertained, that this incipient disloyalty among the Panjabi troops reached the stage of specific or definite design. But there was every reason to believe that much conversation of a dangerous, though perhaps indefinite, kind was secretly going on; and the names were known of the probable Sikh leaders in event of a disturbance breaking out.

There were certain chiefs among the Sikhs in whose fidelity John Lawrence placed confidence and whose opinion he valued. Nihal Sing Chachi was a typical Sikh of the intelligent class, not at all educated in the Western manner, but thoroughly instructed in the public affairs of his day. His loyal frankness, in apprising us of everything likely to cause discontent among his countrymen, was most useful. I never met any Native who had a more judicious understanding of the strong and weak points in the British position politically. He was one of the few men who would speak confidentially and unreservedly on these subjects to Europeans in authority. Kanh Sing Rohsa was a Sikh of a different type, blunt untutored and out-spoken, but wise and loyal; his social weight, too, gave additional value to his advice. Raja Sahib-dyal was the most refined man of the old school then living, and had been a member of the council of regency before the annexation. He was somewhat reticent, though self-possessed, hesitating to argue any point with Europeans, whom he perhaps regarded as a somewhat violent race. But he was by experience and natural discrimination capable of giving sound opinions on political affairs. Raja Tej Sing was a historic character, having commanded a part of the Sikh army in the Satlej campaign of 1846. The political and military position he once had held naturally imposed upon him some reserve, though he was evidently well-disposed and sensible. His manager and secretary was Rai Mûl Sing, a very acute and well-informed man, who understood better perhaps than any non-official Native the condition of the Panjab as modified by British rule. These were men whose minds had not been at all affected by Western education, and whose thoughts ran in the old channels. There was one eminent character of that generation, however, who had considerable knowledge of English literature and ideas, namely, Pandit Manphul, a Brahmin of Cashmir. He was a trustworthy man of business-like ability, and subsequently served in important capacities.

As the year 1858 drew towards its end John Lawrence crossed the Indus for the last time, to visit Peshawar once more, and I was in attendance on him. As we crossed the Indus at Attock, where a grand old fortress overlooks the swiftly rushing river, he repeated his oft-expressed admiration for that position, on account of its classic interest, picturesque beauty and political importance. Recently the great river, having been in its upper course amidst the Himalayas dammed up by a landslip for some weeks, at length burst its barrier and then rushed downwards past Attock with a terrific flood, rising in a very few hours twenty feet above high-water mark. The Caubul river joins the Indus at a short distance above Attock; this flood banked up the Caubul river and the refluent water inundated the military station of Naoshera, twenty miles above the junction. As we descended from some high ground towards the valley of Peshawar and commanded a full view of the place, John Lawrence drew attention to the difficulties of the situation. "Look," he said, "at the fertile and populous plain environed on all sides by rugged hills from which implacable foes can at any moment emerge to ravage and to slay." We ascended a neighbouring mountain where it had been proposed to establish a sanitarium for fever-stricken Europeans from Peshawar; but he set his face against the project, declaring that sooner or later the helpless invalids would be attacked and slain by the blood-thirsty mountaineers. Arriving at Peshawar, we marvelled at the crowded markets and diversified wares, the mixture of Indian and Central Asian costumes, the clear-running brooks and watercourses, the blooming gardens and irrigated fields. We went as near to the mouth of the Khyber Pass as was permissible, to gaze into its gloomy recesses, rode through the Kohat Pass, with a strong escort lest the Afridi marauders should rush upon us, examined the defensive posts on the Eusufzye, and accompanied Harry Lumsden with a party of his Guide troopers on a hawking expedition.

It was at Peshawar that John Lawrence on horseback read aloud to the troops paraded for the purpose, the proclamation whereby the Queen announced her gracious assumption of the Indian administration.

His mind now reverted to a question which he had previously agitated regarding the expediency of retaining Peshawar and its valley in the British dominions. He thought that it would be better to abandon than to keep that military station and its dependent territory. This idea of his was decried by most of his critics, regretted by many of his friends, and ran counter to the prevailing current of public opinion. He seemed to be aware that his view would be unpopular with the majority of his countrymen, still he adhered to it through more of evil than of good report. During the crisis of 1857 he had broached the question of evacuating Peshawar in order that the European troops, which were then there, might be employed elsewhere for the protection of the Panjab. He did not actually insist on the step being taken, and referred for instructions to Lord Canning, who decided to hold Peshawar to the last.

Since then further experience had been gained of what might be considered the preponderating disadvantages of Peshawar, and John Lawrence again discussed the question of its abandonment. Though acknowledging the political influence and importance of the place, he did not rate these so highly as most other authorities. But he deemed that the sacrifices required for its occupation were out of proportion to its value. It was an advanced outpost surrounded by persistent foes, and needed three European battalions for its adequate maintenance and support, a force which the Government could not in his opinion properly spare for this purpose. But this was not all; the place was insalubrious to a degree apparently beyond remedy, for every corps arriving there became within a twelvemonth prostrated by autumnal fever. The regiments, then, had to be relieved at short intervals of two years, and thus the military arrangements of the whole country were disturbed. John Lawrence had a tender heart for the European soldiers, and would visit the hospitals where they lay sick with cholera or fever. So he deplored the abnormal wear and tear of British life and strength at Peshawar. Our men and money were needed for countless purposes of unquestionable importance; there was little, he thought, in Peshawar to justify the waste not only of money, but of life and strength more precious than treasure. If Peshawar were relinquished, he held that the British frontier might well rest on the Indus, and he was fond of riding along the left bank of that river and pointing out the many positions there which were defensible against an invading army. If, however, Peshawar should be wanted under certain conceivable circumstances, it could at pleasure be occupied temporarily by a British force advancing from the Indus.

The counter arguments, asserting the political importance of Peshawar—as being quite worth the sacrifices involved—continued to prevail, and the objections grew less as the salubrity of the place improved. Nowadays nothing is further from the thoughts of the Government than the relinquishment of this most valuable position.

At this time a noteworthy memorial was being transmitted to the Government by the members of the Covenanted Civil Service in reference to the consequences of the late war. By the original constitution of the service, a fund for widows and orphans had been formed by subscriptions levied from the Civil Servants. Recently, however, they had been exposed to the very brunt of danger, and bore an honourable share in encountering the calamities of the time. Consequently so many of them had been killed in the execution of their duty that the number of widows and orphans claiming provision greatly exceeded the resources of the fund, which had never been calculated to meet such contingencies as these. The Government was therefore asked to take upon itself the payment of the allowances to claimants in excess of the average number for which the fund was estimated ordinarily to provide.

John Lawrence now deemed that the time had come when he might leave the Panjab in security and repair to England. The affection in his head (already mentioned) had grown gradually worse from mental labour, and was injuring his health and strength generally. He resolved to depart before he should be incapacitated by illness, notwithstanding the dissuasion of Lord Canning. The Chief Commissionership of the Panjab being advanced to a Lieutenant-Governorship, he was appointed to be Lieutenant-Governor shortly before he departed. He was made a Privy Councillor and a Baronet by the Queen, the Court of Directors had before the extinction of the Company granted him a special pension on his retirement, and he was appointed a member of the new Council of India which had been established in London to assist the Secretary of State. Before his departure he received a valedictory address from the principal European gentlemen engaged in the administration of the Panjab. In his reply he attributed the successes, which were commemorated, mainly to the fact that he had, without fear favour or partiality, persisted in choosing the best ablest and fittest men to do whatever work was prescribed.

He was succeeded by Sir Robert Montgomery, who left the Chief Commissionership of Oudh in order to take up the Lieutenant-Governorship of the Panjab, and whose antecedents marked him out as the fittest man for the succession. Montgomery assumed office at a moment when the Panjab had in the main become quieted and free from any general danger. Still there remained the swell with which the political sea heaves after a long-protracted storm. Some traitorous designs of Sikh origin having been discovered at or near Lahore, the requisite steps were promptly taken.

Though there were many Sikhs in the city of Lahore, yet the Muhammadan element was very considerable there. As usual, the forerunner of treasonable agitation was an announcement of the speedy advent of one of the prophets who are yet to appear before the world comes to an end. The idea was to enlist the Native civil officials secretly in the cause, and procure the murder of the principal European officers, in the hope that then the people would rise *en masse* and the Native army mutiny once more. The very absurdity of such notions proved the fitful state in which the Muhammadan mind then was, swayed by every silly impulse, and rocked by every gust,

> "Vain as the leaf upon the stream
> And fickle as a changeful dream,
> Fantastic as a woman's mood
> And fierce as frenzy's fevered blood."

The priests in the mosques were preaching sermons which contained more of politics than of religion; indeed the sacred cloisters and arcades were trysting-places where the faithful gathered in knots to hear exhortations on the duty of rebellion.

Our information on this head being specific and deemed by us to be authentic, I one morning assembled the Muhammadan priests from all quarters of the city in the courtyard of the principal mosque. After reminding them that these buildings had been erected by the piety of former rulers for divine worship and the instruction of youth in the faith of Islam, and that in the exercise of these functions perfect freedom was enjoyed under British rule,—I warned them that we would not suffer the use of the mosques to be perverted for the profane purposes of sedition. The scene was interesting as these men sat in a large circle around me on the tesselated pavement, with their refined features, their venerable beards, their countenances indicating culture yet bearing traces of suppressed passion—while over us the marble domes cast their long shadows, and in front of us the minarets with enamelled colouring stood out brightly in the sunlight.

Soon afterwards there occurred the festival when the Shiah sect among the Muhammadans celebrate the martyrdom of their saints Hasan and Husen, to the great annoyance of the Sunni sect. One night I went to the upper gallery of a palace whence I could see and hear the Shiahs at their devotions in the spacious courtyard below. From a pulpit the reader recited, in pathetic tones and with studied elocution, Persian verses setting forth the fortitude charity and fidelity of the martyrs. At some moments the audience would be swayed by genuine emotion, and sobs of sincere sorrow or pity were audible. Again some devotees, evidently appointed and commissioned, would rise chanting lamentations in a dolorous but exactly measured cadence, and beating themselves severely with chains. Though their grief was artificial in its inception, they worked their minds by bodily exertion into a real frenzy. Next morning I watched the procession, as the riderless horses were led, their trappings transfixed with arrows and their flanks sprinkled with carmine in imitation of blood, indicating the death of the warrior saints in battle. Sounds of grief, either formal or heartfelt, came from the multitude, and even Hindu women were at times moved to tears. As the funeral car gaudy with tinsel was being consigned to its resting-place, stones began to fly thickly—doubtless flung by Sunni hands—and it was only through the exertions of us European officers that a collision was prevented.

The most noteworthy event of this time, however, was the mutiny of a part of the European forces of the late East India Company, or "the local European troops," as they were then styled. It had been determined by the English Government after the abolition of the East India Company, that the Indian armies, both European and Native, should be amalgamated with the Royal army. The measure passed off quite well so far as the Native armies were concerned. But with the European forces the amalgamation produced troubles which assumed the gravest complexion, requiring the most careful and judicious treatment in order to avert perilous results. These forces consisted partly of artillery, which bore on its colours the motto of "ubique," intimating that whereas other regiments might bear the names of many victories, this regiment of artillery had been engaged in every action that had ever been fought in India. Indeed it was not until the exigencies of the mutinies arose that the Royal artillery began to be employed in India. The infantry consisted of nine regiments in all, of which some had sustained the honour of English arms in many battles since the latter half of the eighteenth century. The men of the artillery and infantry had been enlisted in English recruiting grounds indeed, but the recruits were usually found in classes different from those which furnished soldiers to the Royal army. The physique of the Company's European soldiers, especially of the artillerymen, was fine, and, on the whole, the troops, though said to be not so strictly disciplined as the Royal army, were fit for any service that could be demanded of them. The cavalry had been newly raised during the crisis of the mutinies in 1857, without the proper admixture of seasoned or experienced soldiers, and consequently these troops were in a raw and unsatisfactory condition.

On the amalgamation being settled, the authorities held that no fresh oath and no new re-enlistment would be required, because all the men had, on their enlistment, sworn to serve the Crown as well as the Company; and this view legally and technically was quite correct. The men however had never realized the fact that they had taken the twofold oath, but were under the impression that they had sworn to serve the Company and no other authority. If, then, they were now to serve the Crown, they expected to be re-enlisted, thereupon receiving some bounty, and to be allowed the option of taking their discharge. Most of them however were willing, indeed desirous, to continue their service, as they had become accustomed to India and liked the country, provided that they were invited to serve with an offer of bounty. On finding that they would be regarded as servants of the Crown, without any new conditions being offered, they thought they were being treated without due consideration, and this idea aroused resentment in their minds. That they should have mistaken their legal status and laid such stress upon the formality of re-enlistment, may be deemed extraordinary, but the fact illustrates the oft-repeated lesson of grave events arising from apparently trivial causes. The mischief began with the artillery, and spread to the infantry; the movement was then taken up by the cavalry, who having been so recently raised, had only the flimsiest pretext for moving. Mutinous acts ensued at several of the most important military stations in northern India; I shall here relate only those which came under my own observation.

I was then Commissioner of the civil Division comprising districts around Lahore, that is, head of the local administration including (among many other things) the police and the magistracy. Instruction came to me from the Lieutenant-Governor (Sir Robert Montgomery) that mutinous messages and despatches were likely to be sent from the late Company's European troops in the North-western Provinces to their comrades at Lahore, and that such communications were, if possible, to be intercepted. In the course of a few days several despatches of this nature were intercepted, one of which was remarkable. It purported to come, and certainly came, from the artillery at Meerut to the address of their comrades at Lahore. It set forth that they were being arbitrarily and unjustly transferred from the Company to another master, and that they were resolved "to make a fine gale of it in order not to serve the Crown." It enumerated all the batteries of artillery in northern India which might be expected to join the movement. It also stated that the artillery would break away from Meerut and march upon Delhi (less than thirty miles) in the hope that the other, or Royal, European troops "would not fire a shot" against their countrymen. I took this letter to General Windham (of Crimean celebrity), who then commanded the Lahore Division, and he requested me to accompany him on his visit to the barracks on the evening of that day, as a witness in the event of serious circumstances suddenly arising. Before we reached the barracks, reports came that the artillerymen had refused to turn out for ordinary duty, and that the cavalry were following their example. On entering the barracks in company with the regimental commandants, we found the men in somewhat wild disorder; they began to salute us with cries like those which sometimes come from the gallery of a theatre. General Windham evidently desired to bring them back to the semblance of order without applying force. When he raised his voice they instinctively gathered round him in silence. He began by simply saying they were all English, Scotch or Irish, on which cries arose of "so we be"; whatever name they might be called by, they were to fight for old England in this foreign country; while obedience would be commanded and enforced, justice would be done; it was, as they all knew, the practice of general officers to enquire for complaints or grievances, therefore a certain number of them were to come with him outside and state what they meant by refusing to obey their officers, while the rest must stay inside the barracks. The men then became quiet, and a few were selected by the regimental officers to attend the General outside. Upon being required to explain themselves, they said in effect that the conditions of their service were being broken by their transfer to the Crown. Their meaning was set forth by such words as "we ought not to be turned over from the Company to any one else without being first asked," or "we are being handed like cattle from one owner to another," and many other similar expressions. Their tone and manner shewed excitement from a genuine sense of injury. The General said that they must see that this was a point which could be considered, not by him or by their officers, but by the Government alone, that they would the next morning be required one by one to state whatever grievance was felt, and that meanwhile they must obey their officers. They separated quietly, and the next morning every man presented himself as ordered. Thus they were for the moment led gently back to the path of obedience, and remained orderly. We also went to the cavalry barracks; the men there were reported to be verging on insubordination, though they had not refused to obey orders. They were inclined to be noisy and boisterous when the General spoke to them, but they did not declare themselves aggrieved. The next day their insubordination increased, and they ended by refusing to do duty. The authorities, however, managed to avoid the necessity of applying force; and no violent outbreak occurred. General Windham behaved with coolness of temper and presence of mind in trying moments, when even the slightest indiscretion might have rendered an appeal to force inevitable.

The anxiety of the military authorities and the Government was at this time strained to a high degree of tension. What would happen, they inwardly thought, if with many hundreds of armed Europeans in this excited state, any acts of violence were to be committed, or some of the men were to break loose and move off, or, worse still, if the dire necessity were to arise of shedding English blood by English hands on Indian soil? What too, they wondered, would the effect be upon the Native army and people of the Panjab, a province but recently freed from the agitation consequent on the war of the mutinies? As tidings came of mutinous conduct on the part of the late Company's European troops at Cawnpore, Allahabad, Patna, and elsewhere, the anxiety at Lahore was quickened lest the men, who were quiescent with a suppressed agitation, should lose the power of self-restraint. By the mercy of Providence, however, nothing of consequence happened in the Panjab. The counsels of the Government of India depended on Canning and Clyde, two men in whom temper, firmness and judgment were happily combined. Severity was exercised as little as possible, and a wise clemency was displayed towards soldiers who after many years of splendid service had fallen into a temporary aberration. Their thoughtless misconduct was, indeed, fraught with peril to the State; but it is incredible that they ever dreamt of striking at British rule in India. They doubtless meant, by raising a storm, to assert their supposed rights. The Government, then, desired to rid itself quietly of discontented soldiers from among its European forces in India, and those men who proved unwilling to remain in the public service were allowed to take their discharge.

The effect of these events on the Native mind, though in a certain degree mischievous, was neither great nor lasting. Many Natives feared that the mutinous European soldiery would plunder the neighbouring country. Some, also, began to say significantly that the English were setting fire to their own house; but such sayings did not convey any serious import. For the Natives were unable to realize the possibility of disruption really occurring among the English in India, and felt convinced that the cohesion which had always imparted stability to British rule would somehow be maintained.

When this conjuncture had safely passed, I took a brief journey to Cashmir, marching thither over the crest known as that of the Pîr Panjâl, the route by which the Mogul emperors used to pass to and fro on the journey between their empire in northern India and their summer retreat in the happy valley. Consequently the imperial line of march—it could not be called a road—was found to be marked at each stage by the remains of some caravanserai or mosque, recalling scenes when all the pomp and pageantry of the east were set off by the wildness of mountain scenery. No Englishman, with all the Western culture of modern times, could love Cashmir more than the Mogul emperors loved it. They enriched, with the products of their art and architecture, a valley already pre-eminent for beauty.

Entering Cashmir, traversing the plain by means of the navigable channel of the Jhelam and crossing the lakes decked with water-lilies we ascended "Solomon's throne," a hill jutting out into the valley.

From the summit of this hill was beheld the finest panorama in the whole Himalayan region. Deep beneath our feet lay the city with its highways consisting of canals, the rocky citadel, the poplar avenues, the lake and its floating gardens, the Mogul fountains and summer-houses on its margin, the wooded isle of plane-trees. Beyond there ran the river meandering in streaks of light through villages and orchards, here or there spanned by quaint wooden bridges and sometimes flowing under the ruins left by ancient Hindu dynasties. In the distance stood the snowy range bounding the entire circumference of the horizon. To whatever direction our gaze was turned, whether north toward Ladakh, or south towards India, or east towards the main Himalayas, or west towards the Indus, we saw the unbroken boundary of glistening white. The circumvallation of snow was not uniform, being diversified by many peaks which the Muhammadans dignify as "Pirs," or saints, in varying shapes, cones, domes, pyramids or spires. These are celebrated, some as shrines of pilgrimage, some as fastnesses of untameable tribes, some as stations for scientific surveys. With a prospect seen from so great an altitude and extending over so wide an area as this, atmospheric phenomena in the utmost variety were visible from sunrise to sunset. One part of the plains, lakes or mountains in the vast landscape would be in stormy shadow, another in sunshine, another in driving vapour. The eye glanced from the lake reposing in murky gloom to the summits glittering against the azure, from the gleams of light across the city groves meads and saffron fields to the hillside with its shining glaciers and darkling cedars half shrouded in mist. Fair as was the earth below the sky above was fairer still. At morn the clouds gathered in rolling volumes of grey tipped with red. At midday they were white as masses of wool scattered over the blue empyrean, here and there melting into showers or arched with iridescent colours. At eventide they caught every hue of crimson and orange, becoming more and more luminous each moment. Up to this time the glory of the earth had held its own against that of the heaven. But near sunset the earth seemed quite submerged and lost to view, we had eyes only for the resplendent ether, or for the summits to which the sun was bidding a bright farewell for the night. Then after we had watched the changeful moods of Cashmir all through the long summer's day, there rose to our minds the Persian couplet which declares that if paradise exists on the face of the earth, it is here, it is here!

CHAPTER VIII.

(1856–1859.)

CANNING THE JUST.

Contrast between Canning and his predecessor Dalhousie—Canning undertakes war with Persia—His conduct after the outburst of the mutinies in northern India—His policy towards the Natives in disturbed districts—His temporary unpopularity at Calcutta and elsewhere—His management of military affairs—His relations with Sir Hugh Rose (now Lord Strathnairn), Commander-in-Chief—His support accorded to George Balfour and the Military Finance department—He proceeds with the re-organization of the police for India—His civil and political administration—His principal advisers and Councillors—His departure from India—Death of Lady Canning at Calcutta.

I FIRST met Lord Canning at Calcutta on my way from the Panjab to England in the autumn of 1856; and stayed with him for a few days at Barrackpur, the country seat of the Governors-General on the banks of the Hughli river, some fourteen miles from the capital. In several respects his aspect presented a contrast to that which we so vividly recollected in Dalhousie his predecessor. Canning seemed calm, grave, reflective, disposed to enquire deeply and broadly; but he was more than ordinarily deliberate in forming a definite conclusion, and cautious in taking action upon such conclusion when formed. This mental attitude was, indeed, natural and appropriate in a ruler newly arrived on a scene so vast and strange as India. But it was surprising at first to those who had grown accustomed to the positive policy, incisive dicta and vigorous action which Dalhousie felt justified in adopting upon the information and experience gathered during a long tenure of his high office. At the outset Dalhousie had evinced a disposition to enquire and ponder with comprehensive circumspection, and to stay conclusive action for a while. But it was evident that he would, after adequate enquiry, yet with due promptitude, satisfy himself even respecting the most complex affairs, and, having done so, would take effective action. Now, Canning would be ready enough to take up every intricate subject that suggested itself, and to look at it all round, but there was doubt whether he would see such a way through its intricacies, as might satisfy the requirements of his judgment. Consequently, after several years of administrative activity under Dalhousie, India enjoyed quiescence during the first year and a half of Canning's administration. The numerous schemes which had been originated and launched into operation were allowed to produce their legitimate results; and the current business of an empire, daily presenting numerous points for immediate decision, was duly performed. Whether Canning, after having passed through this preliminary course, and served, as it were, the apprenticeship for supreme command, would proceed onwards and carve out an administrative policy for himself, cannot now be determined. For urgent circumstances arose which, gathering strength as they passed, drove him imperatively into action in numerous directions and, when their force was spent, left him in the midst of changed conditions.

Like every other Governor-General elect, he had left England full of protestations that the preservation of peace was the foremost object of his policy. Nevertheless, in common with several of his predecessors, he was shortly after his arrival compelled to prepare for war. One morning John Lawrence was surprised to receive a letter from the new Governor-General explaining that his Government was likely to come to blows with the Shah of Persia. The aggressive conduct of the Persian authorities in respect of Herat, caused the speedy despatch of a British expedition up the Persian Gulf. This expedition not only averted aggression from Herat, but also shewed how easily the British Government could control at least the southern part of Persia.

The brief campaign in southern Persia was scarcely concluded when the first symptoms of mutiny appeared in the Native army of Bengal. As the mischief spread with startling rapidity and the insufficiency of the European forces became manifest, the public justly regarded the temporary withdrawal of some of the European troops from India for the Persian expedition as one of the many causes which had conduced to place the Indian Government in a critical position. At the time when that expedition sailed from India for the Persian Gulf, there was not indeed the faintest indication of disloyalty in the Native army. Still, on an impartial retrospect, it must be admitted that a consideration of the recent additions to British dominion in India—the latest of which, namely, the province of Oudh, abounded in elements of danger—ought to have convinced the Government that the European troops needed for service in Persia must be supplied, not from India, but from elsewhere. The responsibility in this respect must, however, be shared by other authorities besides Canning the newly arrived Governor-General.

When in May 1857 the Sepoys were successful in their insurrection at Meerut, despite the presence of European troops there, and proceeded to seize Delhi, public opinion in northern India and at Calcutta swayed hither and thither in wild excitement. Most men were at first unwilling to believe that the sepoys would or could rebel in a mass, many adhered to their faith in the general loyalty of soldiers who had served long and faithfully, some authorities still hoped that extreme consequences might be averted. Soon, however, Canning with his penetrating judgment saw that a national crisis had arisen, which must be encountered without hesitation. When he was thus aroused, his doubting temperament disappeared, and was replaced by a prompt and positive disposition. He acted with instantaneous decision in despatching every available European to the scene of disaster or of danger, summoning English troops from Burma and Ceylon, recalling the men who could be spared after the Persian expedition, suggesting to Lord Elgin the temporary diversion to India of the expedition then on its way to China. His reports to the Government in England explaining the conjuncture and demanding reinforcements, his public utterances and proclamations in India, were temperate resolute and dignified. Before the Native army and people he vindicated the justice of the British Government. While evincing an immovable determination to suppress rebellion, he displayed a generous consideration to those who might have been temporarily misled, and a forgiving temper towards all who might return to their allegiance. Matters rapidly grew worse, no hope remained of stamping out the fire, and it was but too clear that the mutiny would embrace nearly the whole Native army of Bengal, communicating a dangerous excitement to the Native armies of Madras and Bombay. There would be extensive insurrections in many parts of the country and a paralysis of British authority, in the North-western Provinces at least. Then the hearts of many began to sink, even in the Anglo-Indian community which is habituated to the contemplation of danger. Still many strong Englishmen in every part of the threatened country kept their knees firm and steady in the midst of the whirling torrent. And Canning was foremost among the brave and the staunch. In those trying moments it was truly said of him that his eye quailed not, neither did his cheek pale.

As the Anglo-Indian community nerved itself to cope with the astounding situation, a sort of vindictiveness began to get possession of the public mind. This feeling is not, indeed, to be justified; but it was natural to men excited by tremendous events. There had been no time for schooling the thoughts so that stern severity might be evinced where necessary, and mercy shewn when called for. The mutinies had occurred with startling suddenness, and were accompanied by every aggravation of unfaithfulness, by cruelty, even by barbarity. British officers were required most unexpectedly to deal with a conjuncture demanding on their part, not only unflinching decision of character, but also a judicious self-restraint under ardent excitement. Any one who knows the working of the human heart under such circumstances, will hardly be surprised to find that they exhibited more of decisiveness than of self-restraint. Moreover they all had an abiding sense of the fact that their power rested on opinion quite as much as on force; and this consideration was now brought into striking prominence. The enmity and animosity evinced by comparatively few, might spread like wild-fire among the countless many; and then the scattered groups of Europeans would be helpless amidst raging multitudes. Thus it was held that almost the only chance for safety lay in the adoption of such masterful measures as should strike the Native mind with terror; just as a tiger is sometimes cowed by the steady human eye. If this policy caused bloodshed, the conscience was momentarily quieted by the reflection that "it is a question of their lives against ours," or, "either they or we must die, we'll kill them to save ourselves." Impelled by such sentiments, many will act at the outset with a severity which beats down the rising mischief, and proves to be really merciful in the end; some blood of the guilty is shed at first inevitably, in order that further blood-shedding may be averted. But the tendency is to carry this severity to undue extremes; to multiply executions with less and less of discrimination regarding the degree of guilt. As the crisis waxes and lasts, the prolonged tension of the mind, the wearing anxiety during the days, the sleep broken by the apprehension of nocturnal attacks, unfit men for the exercise of considerateness in weighing evidence or adjudging punishment. Even when the worst of the crisis is overpast, they are too apt to continue a severity which was justifiable only while the dangers were at their height. Thus much happened which morally is to be regretted and of which the continuance might ultimately have provoked retaliation from the other side, and led to an internecine conflict between the European and Native races. As a point of national honour, it was to be earnestly wished that the escutcheon of British valour and constancy, which was splendidly displayed, should not be disfigured by sanguinary deeds.

Canning then took his stand on the plain principles that justice must be tempered with mercy, and that extreme severity might be tolerated so long as it was absolutely necessary, but not a moment longer. Thoughtful persons everywhere approved this policy, as consistent with the almost paternal attitude which the British Government had at all times assumed towards the people of India. Many others, however, by misapprehension, took it to mean that the arm of British authority was to be shortened when blows had to be struck, and that a halter of undue responsibility was to be hung round the necks of those who were battling with bloodthirsty foes. Thus there arose in many quarters an angry feeling against the Governor-General, who was hailed by the name of "Clemency Canning." Then appeared the first clouds of unpopularity on his horizon.

At that time the newspaper press in India generally, and at Calcutta especially, teemed with statements and comments which were considered by the Government to be detrimental to the public safety. Canning resolved to establish temporarily a moderate censorship in respect of matters relating to the war the mutinies and the rebellion. Although it was not ordinarily the practice for the Governor-General to preside at meetings of the Legislative Council, he exercised on that occasion his legal function of President, and made a speech explaining the need for this temporary restraint of the press for a special purpose. He doubtless thought that this invidious duty should be discharged with all the weight attaching to himself and his office. The law was passed as he desired, but, as might be expected, this aroused against him the jealousy with which Englishmen everywhere regard any interference with the liberty of the press.

While Canning himself preserved a dauntless demeanour, the European community at Calcutta considered that he was not sufficiently alive to the local dangers which threatened this capital city. There were sepoy regiments close by which might mutiny and march upon an almost defenceless town. It was thought that there had been unnecessary delay in disarming them. The Native quarters were densely inhabited by a population in part at least affected by fanaticism. The European garrison was reduced to its lowest ebb by the despatch of troops to the many seats of war. At that time no system of volunteering had been organized, and the civil members of the European community were unarmed and untrained. The Government was thought to be tardy in accepting the patriotic offers made by the European inhabitants to arm and organize themselves. At times alarm would seize the public mind, and people actually contemplated leaving their houses and living for awhile on board the mercantile ships lying in the river. This alarm was probably not altogether without reason, though by many it was denounced as needless panic. The regulations regarding the importation and possession of arms were applied in a manner at which the non-official Europeans took offence. In these various affairs many Europeans, official and non-official, failed to recognize in Canning a ruler to their liking, and withdrew from him their confidence. Nor did they regard with favour the advisers, councillors, secretaries and others by whom he was surrounded. In several ways the community grew dissatisfied with the Government, and with Canning as its head. Some people even were highly incensed, and by all accounts, in daily conversation, used language of which the heat and vehemence would seem amazing if considered in quieter moments. These feelings ultimately caused the preparation of a memorial from the non-official community of Calcutta to Her Majesty's Government praying for the recall of Canning from the office of Governor-General. When this document was transmitted to him by the Government in England for any remarks which might seem requisite, he reviewed every argument and allegation with judicial calmness. None could tell from his impassive demeanour whether he was sensitive or not to the disapproval manifested by his countrymen dwelling around his headquarters. He probably regarded this as one of the many trials which had to be sustained with calmness and fortitude at a time of unexampled danger and excitement. He must, however, have looked back on it with astonishment when, four years later, the same community, taking a juster retrospect of his conduct at this time, and generously appreciating his subsequent acts, presented valedictory addresses on his departure from India, and raised funds for the erection at Calcutta of a statue in remembrance of him.

Much attention was attracted to a publication summarizing the events of the mutinies and commonly called "the red pamphlet." The author was known to be Captain (now Colonel) George Bruce Malleson, a very talented writer. In this narrative, Canning's management of affairs was gravely impugned and his principal advisers, namely the Councillors and Secretaries, were particularly assailed. They failed, it was said, to give him sound advice in respect to allaying the fear undoubtedly felt by the sepoys for their caste or religion, and dealing with the premonitory symptoms of the insurrectionary storm. They possessed competent experience, indeed, but it was not of the right sort. There was a want of special knowledge relating to northern India where the scenes of trouble and danger lay. The most important post in the secretariat was held by George Edmonstone, already mentioned in chapter V., who certainly was highly qualified in this respect, and among the Councillors John Peter Grant was a man of commanding talent. Still, on the whole, there was hardly at Calcutta a display of that genius in emergency which might have been expected, and which actually appeared in many parts of India during those most troublous months. In fact Calcutta is not a place favourably situated for feeling the pulse, as it were, of the political classes in the country, or for understanding the spirit of rebellion whenever it may be abroad. To this disadvantage Calcutta was inevitably subject, as a drawback to its many advantages in other respects. Doubtless Canning's counsels must have suffered from this cause at the beginning.

Having remained at Calcutta during the summer and autumn of 1857, Canning proceeded at the close of the year to Allahabad. His purpose was to supervise personally the affairs of those provinces which had been disturbed, afford to the Commander-in-Chief, Lord Clyde, such support as might be required for terminating the rebellion which still lasted in Oudh and Central India, and deal promptly with the political questions which would arise when victory had been won in the field. In all affairs of military urgency he acted with due quickness, and did all that could be done by the Government for despatching troops to Lord Clyde from every quarter for the several campaigns which were in progress, and furnishing the commanders with all the resources needed for conducting their operations successfully. But he soon became unable to despatch with equal efficiency the countless affairs, of secondary importance or urgency, military, political and civil, which crowded upon him; and arrears of business were fast accumulating. He was attended at this time by George Edmonstone, the Foreign Secretary, a man of eminent attainments, who had a reputation for businesslike capacity and commanded public confidence. But even Edmonstone could not obtain the timely imprimatur of the over-burdened Governor-General to the numerous orders necessary for the due management of affairs. One main cause of difficulty was Canning's determination to take upon himself the administration of the North-western Provinces in addition to his duties as Governor-General. In this administration his Secretary was William Muir, who has been already mentioned, from whom all possible assistance was derived. Nevertheless, both the imperial work of India and the local administration of the North-western Provinces suffered because Canning attempted to perform the double duty. After some time, however, he restored to these provinces their Lieutenant-Governorship, appointing Edmonstone to that office and leaving him in sole charge.

It was at this time (1858) Canning issued his famous proclamation to the landowners of Oudh, declaring that they had as a body incurred the penalty of forfeiture by reason of rebellion, but offering full and immediate restitution to all who should by a certain date present themselves and tender submission, excepting always those who had been concerned in the murder of European British subjects. He intended that the substance of this proclamation, while maintaining the dignity of the British Government and marking the character of the rebellion, should yet be moderate and reasonable, and leave wide open a door for repentance. The wording, however, was by many in India thought likely to be misconstrued, and cause alarm in the minds of the Natives generally.

There had recently been a change of Government in England, and the new Secretary of State, Lord Ellenborough, addressed to the Government of India a despatch criticizing in severe terms the proclamation and the policy which had led to it. This despatch became public, and the publication produced a grave effect in India, both among Europeans and Natives. Speculation became rife as to whether Canning would resign in consequence; but sympathy was generally felt for him when this fresh embarrassment was piled upon his already oppressive load of care. It soon became understood, however, that he would not quit his post for any reason of this sort, and having piloted the ship so far would persevere till the harbour should be reached. Then news came from England to the effect that there would be no interference with the policy already announced by the Governor-General respecting Oudh.

The proclamation answered its object, and most of the landowners of Oudh having duly submitted and presented themselves, were acknowledged by the Government as being in full possession of all their rights. Afterwards, in January 1859, Canning proceeded to Lucknow, the capital of Oudh, to meet the principal landowners styled "Talukdars," in ceremonial durbar, or levee. He there addressed to them an impressive speech setting forth both their position and its duties, which speech is regarded by them as one of the great charters of their rights.

He then set himself to reassure the Native chiefs throughout India, lest they should imagine that after the great rebellion the heart of the British Government would be turned against them all. He knew that one of the sentiments abiding in their minds was the fear lest they should not be permitted to adopt heirs on failure of issue. In an able and dignified Minute he argued that a declaration of their right to make such adoption would be the happiest of all boons which could be conceded to them. Accordingly he obtained the sanction of Her Majesty's Government to issue a formal patent (sanad) in these terms to all Native princes and chiefs who were governing their own territories. This measure produced a good effect on the Native aristocracy, and caused him to be gratefully remembered by them.

In order to re-establish public confidence, he made tours of state throughout northern India, holding receptions not only for the Native princes, but also for the lesser chiefs and the upper classes among the Natives. Never in the history of

British rule had there been more real significance in the signs of public rejoicing—the brilliant cavalcades—the processions of elephants—the streets lined with multitudes, eager-gazing silent almost voiceless and rapt in attention—the housetops crowded with spectators—the illuminations, with the spray of fountains and the flash of light, or the forms of mosques minarets temples marked by luminous lines against the black sky. Many traitors at heart who had vainly imagined that the British power was burnt down almost to ashes, now saw it rising, Phœnix-like, grander than ever and flaunting its hated symbols in the breeze of victory. Some thoughtful men, knowing the political failings of their fatherland, thanked the various deities of their respective faiths that it had not been made the sport of revolution or the prey of anarchy, and that the British had prevailed as being the only power having a just will together with an invincible arm. The larger number, however, simply congratulated themselves on having bided quietly for some decisive issue of events, and being now enabled to declare themselves on the winning side. Never had the Natives, princes noblemen gentry, been more anxious to be presented to the British Representative than they were to make their obeisance to Canning the Viceroy. In his public speeches, which were carefully translated into the vernacular languages, suitable allusion was made to the recent disturbances, while assurances were given regarding the gracious intentions of the Queen and the sympathetic benevolence of the British people towards all their loyal fellow-subjects in the East. On these occasions his fine head, handsome face, sonorous voice and dignified mien were admired by all present; he appeared also to be in good health after his labours and anxieties. Loyalty and fidelity, wherever they had been evinced, were acknowledged, merciful assurances were given, and the resolve of the Government to persevere in maintaining order was declared. Thus a special significance was imparted to these formal ceremonies, and a cheerful hopefulness diffused, after the storms which had been disturbing the political atmosphere.

He had now seen the termination of the widespread war of

the mutiny and rebellion, the pacification of the disturbed districts, the adjudication of forfeiture or other penalties against those whose misconduct had been unpardonable, the extension of mercy to all who had any claim to consideration, and the restoration of public confidence. He had settled in conjunction with the Commander-in-Chief, Lord Clyde, the threatening affair with the European troops of the late East India Company already mentioned in chapter VII. He had welcomed the arrival of James Wilson, who was despatched from England by Her Majesty's Government as Financial Member of the Governor-General's Council. He then applied himself at Calcutta to the heavy task of reorganizing the public establishments which had been thrown into confusion by the convulsions of the two past years, and rehabilitating, in such manner as might be immediately practicable, the finances which had been disordered by these grave events.

The primary matter was the revision of the military forces, with the view of returning to a peace footing, and reducing the subsidiary establishments which had grown so largely during the war. Sir Hugh Rose (already mentioned in chapter VII.) succeeded Lord Clyde as Commander-in-Chief. The outgoing Commander Lord Clyde, though not always able to satisfy the impatient expectations of the public during a time of excitement, was at the end of his Indian career regarded by all men as a safe, wise and successful man, in a word, as a good old soldier. The incoming Commander, Sir Hugh Rose (now Lord Strathnairn), entered on the duties of his high office with the repute of having shewn both promptitude and persistency in the achievement of large results by comparatively slender forces. He forthwith applied his zeal and talent to all that concerned the welfare and discipline of the troops both European and Native. The condition of the European soldiers received his special attention, inasmuch as often their lodgings were defective and their surroundings insanitary. When additional reinforcements poured into the country, barracks had been hastily and temporarily constructed at many stations. Sir Hugh Rose strove with considerable success to establish camps and quarters for the soldiers in salubrious places beyond the reach of the extreme heat and fever-breeding malaria. Various changes were at that time being made in the drill and armament of the troops European and Native, and to these affairs he devoted his skill, having first mastered personally, often with laborious study, all the details of that which he had to impress upon others. I saw much of him in those days, having been, at the instance of James Wilson, appointed by Lord Canning to be a member of the newly constituted Commission for Military Finance.

This Commission consisted of several military officers besides myself; amongst its members the most eminent was Colonel (now Sir George) Balfour; one of its secretaries was Colonel G. B. Malleson, already mentioned, and subsequently well known as an historian. It afterwards merged into the Military Finance Department, and exercised for full three years a decisive influence on the fortunes of Indian finance. It strove to reduce to tolerable proportions a military outlay which, amounting to millions annually at the culminating point, threatened to become financially intolerable. It proposed many savings in the charges on account of the European forces, the strength of which had been somewhat lessened by the Government and brought down to a little more than double that which existed before the war of the mutinies. It pressed with much detailed argument for a revision of the three Native armies in order to obtain a judicious reduction, and for the disbandment of the Native levies which had been raised in many districts. It recommended as a subsidiary measure, the better organization of the Police, which might then perform many civil duties wherein a considerable part of the army was being employed. It reviewed the expenditure of the Commissariat and Ordnance, and expedited the discharge of those enormous transport establishments which had been collected during the several campaigns. George Balfour brought to this work complete professional knowledge of military matters, and a remarkable aptitude for finance. His eminent services in procuring reduction of military expenditure were highly appreciated by James Wilson, and publicly acknowledged by the succeeding finance minister, Samuel Laing. Through the exertions of all departments together, and with the support of Lord Canning and Sir Hugh Rose, the military expenditure was reduced from 21 sterling millions to 12½ millions annually.

In connexion with these measures relating to the army, the reorganization of the police was undertaken throughout the empire. One cause of the Native army being maintained at an excessive strength was the employment of the soldiers in guarding jails, treasuries, court-houses and civil buildings, or in furnishing escorts for prisoners and for every sort of state property while in transit from one place to another. The police being unarmed and undrilled were not suited for the performance of such work. But they might fulfil these duties, if properly trained, thus relieving the army to a certain extent and enabling the Government to dispense with some of the Native soldiery. This consideration led to the question of improving the police establishment, which had long been regarded as inefficient, and below the general standard of British administration. Foremost among the means of such improvement would be the employment of European officers to supervise the department in its work and proceedings. An example had been set in the Madras Presidency when Lord Harris was Governor, and the newly organized police there was being ably superintended by Mr. (afterwards Sir William) Robinson. A commission was then appointed at Calcutta, consisting of representatives from every division of the empire, to revise the police department throughout British India. The reorganization which they recommended was gradually carried into effect, and sanctioned by legislation. The measure has not perhaps produced all the reforms which were expected, but it has resulted in the augmentation of the emoluments of policemen, the elevation of the status of Native police-officers, and an infusion of European energy into the department.

Simultaneously, a wide and searching enquiry was made into the expenditure in all other branches of the administration, including the Indian Navy and Marine, the courts of justice and the several departments of revenue. For this purpose a Civil Finance Commission was appointed, by whom were made frequent recommendations in the direction of economy. It was about this time that several important measures were taken in hand, such as the abolition of the Indian Navy, and the substitution in Bengal of imported English salt for salts locally manufactured.

In these days Canning bestowed much thought on the constitution of his Council, especially attending to that part of it which was mainly concerned in legislation. Already one Legislative Council had been appointed (in 1854), consisting solely of official persons selected by the Governor-General from different parts of India. It sat at Calcutta under the able and distinguished presidency of Sir Barnes Peacock, then Chief Justice of Bengal. But it was now deemed inadequate for legislating in respect of all the local interests existing in a widely extended empire. After full discussion with the Government in England, four Legislative Councils were constituted in India, namely, one, that of the Governor-General, to sit wherever he might appoint, and three pertaining to the provincial Governments of Madras Bombay and Bengal, to sit within the respective jurisdictions of those Governments. Non-official gentlemen were appointed members of these Councils to serve together with the official members. At first men wondered whether the local Councils would maintain the decorum and gravity becoming their functions; and it was jocularly said that the legitimate drama would be enacted in the Governor-General's Council, and comedy or farce in the other Councils. In practice, however, the proceedings of the local Councils have been perfectly decorous.

As the interior of the empire quieted itself after the political storms, commercial and agricultural prosperity bounded forwards. Among other things, the rice and other products of Bengal rose in price while one article, in the production of which many European firms were concerned, namely indigo, remained stationary. Consequently there arose serious disputes between the Native cultivators of indigo and their European employers, styled Indigo planters. The Europeans held that the Natives were bound to continue the cultivation of indigo under long-standing agreements. The Natives wished to escape from these agreements, declaring that it was more profitable for them to devote their fields to rice and other products than to cultivate indigo. Inasmuch as the European planters were landlords on a large scale, and the Natives were tenants, these disputes regarding indigo rapidly acquired an agrarian character, leading to much excitement in many districts, and in some places to actual rioting. A commission was appointed to investigate the subject under the presidency of Walter Scott Seton-Karr, one of the most eminent Civil Servants in Bengal. He was afterwards a Judge of the High Court, Foreign Secretary to the Government of India and Vice-Chancellor of the Calcutta University; for some time also he was one of the most brilliant contributors to the *Calcutta Review.* The report of this Commission was promptly considered by the Lieutenant-Governor of Bengal, Sir John Peter Grant (afterwards Governor of Jamaica), one of the ablest men that the Bengal Civil Service has ever produced. The indigo planters did their best under misfortunes arising from no fault of theirs, but indigo planting in Bengal inevitably succumbed to the fact that the plant could no longer be produced with profit to the cultivator.

While some old products declined, several new products fast rose to prominence; foremost among these were tea and coffee. The planting of tea among the Himalayas in the north and of coffee among the Nilgiri mountains in the south, all under European agency or supervision, led immediately to questions regarding the title and tenure of land in those regions. The land there was technically "waste," and the absolute property of the State. It could therefore be granted to individuals, in what the Anglo-Indians loved to call "fee simple." After careful consideration, Canning's Government issued the "waste land rules," which have since become famous, and of which the effect was to grant to Europeans or others waste lands as absolute property for ever free of land tax, on the payment of fixed sums in very moderate amounts. A great impulse was thus given to the settlement of Europeans in the mountainous regions of the Himalayas of eastern Bengal and of the Nilgiris. Thus, too, the outlay of European capital on tea-gardens and coffee-plantations was facilitated. Some imprudent expenditure and reckless management ensued; consequently at the outset fortunes were lost rather than made. The enterprises being, however, substantially sound, righted themselves after a season, though not until much loss had been incurred by individuals. There were hopes that Europeans might under these rules be able to settle as proprietors or managers of estates in other parts of India besides the mountains in the north and south; no such result, however, has actually ensued.

Municipal improvement which had been interrupted by the war of the mutinies was vigorously resumed throughout the country; and it necessarily conduced to sanitation, although the sanitary departments had not yet been fully constituted. This improvement involved local taxation in various shapes, and fear soon arose lest dissatisfaction should be caused by the imposition of a new burden even for the sake of good effected under the eye of the tax-payer.

Some important steps were taken in respect of high education. The machinery which had lasted for one generation was superseded by the establishment of three universities for Calcutta Madras and Bombay respectively. Much attention was bestowed upon the legislation undertaken for this important object, the intention being to vest the governance of these institutions in a senate comprising all the highest talent, learning and experience to be found in the country.

It was about this time that the difference between the old school and the new school of Natives became clearly perceptible. The men of the former had the more restricted vision and the more punctilious manners. Those of the latter had naturally wider ideas and sympathies, and a more open or frank manner. Some Europeans liked the former as being pleasant and polite. Others preferred the latter as being willing to express their real sentiments without reserve.

Many other measures were considered, taken in hand or carried into effect by Canning's Government. Having been a member of the several commissions which sat upon military finance, civil finance, police organization, and indigo planting, and having also been employed on the staff of the Financial member of the Governor-General's Council, I am able to write from personal knowledge.

In most affairs of that time, considerations of finance were uppermost; the finances during the latter years of Canning's Government were supervised by two English financiers, first James Wilson, then Samuel Laing; and the financial policy pursued by both these statesmen will be mentioned in future chapters. But it is well here to state briefly the part which Canning took respecting this main branch of the public service. Besides allowing an augmentation of the stamp-duties, which was judicious, he assented to the doubling of the most important among the customs duties, in the hope that there would be a corresponding increase of revenue, and this part of his financial policy is not altogether to be commended. He supported Wilson in the production of a budget which comprised proposals for an income-tax, a tobacco-tax, and a system of licences on trades and professions. He was most unwilling to impose new taxes which he deemed likely to provoke a dangerous discontent; still he accepted Wilson's proposals in the belief of their absolute necessity. After the publication of the budget there ensued at first an apparent approbation, but afterwards a gradually swelling murmur, which confirmed Canning's fears regarding the probability of popular discontent. He resolved, however, to uphold the income-tax because it fell upon classes which flourished especially under British rule and had previously escaped taxation. But he asked Wilson to forego pressing the tobacco-tax and the licence-duties, and the proposals for these imposts were accordingly stayed. It was then that he uttered his well-known dictum that, danger for danger, he would rather see even the European forces reduced than unpopular taxes imposed on the people at large.

Apart from his high qualities in dealing with affairs of the gravest moment, Canning's ability as a practical administrator remains to be sketched. He possessed, in a fair and average degree, the constructive and organizing aptitude which his predecessor Dalhousie had manifested in the highest degree. He inherited his father's mastery of classical English diction. But his cultured taste led him to spend much time in polishing the language of official papers—precious time needed for more important affairs. His excellent handwriting indicated strength of will and refinement of mind. His oratory both as regards matter and manner was very impressive. Intellectually his critical faculty was so acute and strong that in practice it overmastered his other faculties. He saw quickly and completely all the sides of complicated questions, the merits and demerits of each of the several courses suggested as possible; but he did not see equally well which side should be taken and which course preferred. He balanced conflicting opinions accurately and, for a while at least, halted between them. He went on weighing and re-weighing, but hesitated to strike the balance. He had caution in an admirable degree, because his cautiousness arose from a highly cultivated intelligence which appreciated perfectly all the facts and considerations bearing upon the matter in hand. But he carried this caution to an extreme, because doubting and debating what course should be pursued, he occasionally ended in doing nothing when something one way or other was necessary or desirable to be done. He would seem in some difficult case to have all but made up his mind, and then just stopping short of decision, let it lie over for a while; but sooner or later it would have to be resumed, whereupon the labour of consideration must be repeated. The proverb that many questions if left unanswered for a certain time will answer themselves, found application during one part of his administration. He would devote conscientious and patient care to the controversial correspondence referred to him whenever disagreements arose between high authorities as is often the case during periods of turmoil. Such cases, however, scarcely deserved the portion which he allotted to them out of his heavily taxed time. If a matter was politically emergent, or involved moral considerations of gravity, then he cast away his over-caution. Having considered the circumstances with all his judicial impartiality, he promptly pronounced his decree and vigorously enforced it. But matters of administrative organization, however important, are seldom of this urgent character, and can be put off till the morrow; it was with these that he sometimes allowed procrastination. This tendency to delay occurred at a time when measures remodelling and reconstructing were required after such commotions as those which had shaken the empire: and it seemed likely to impair the otherwise excellent effect of his administration. His bark righted itself, however, because he acquired a discriminating perception as to what he could supervise for himself, and what he should entrust to others who were competent to deal with it under his general control. Having committed a large matter to able and trustworthy men, he supported them generously. Thus he gathered round him many persons who suggested the necessary measures after due enquiry, the scope of which he mastered for himself and sanctioned, leaving the details to them. He learnt to do this, without abnegating any of his proper functions or at all derogating from his authority. The tide of progress began to flow again, under his eye, and once his Government had embarked upon measures of improvement, it guided them judiciously and skilfully to the end. In these ways his administration, which at first hardly promised to be fruitful, became ultimately abundant in results.

Among Canning's advisers the foremost was Sir Bartle Frere, who after having managed the province of Sind with remarkable ability during the troubles of 1857 and 1858, was appointed member of the Governor-General's Council. Frere's influence was felt in the adoption of a progressive policy and of conciliatory measures towards the Natives. His presence helped to surround the Government with an atmosphere of cheerfulness and popularity. The military member of Council was first Sir James Outram, esteemed to be among the boldest of soldiers and the most chivalrous of men, and next Sir Robert Napier, who, after brave deeds during the war of the mutinies, had returned with fresh laurels from the war in China; in having two such advisers Canning was very fortunate.

The important office of Private Secretary to the Governor-General was held by Lewin Bowring of the Civil Service, son of Sir John Bowring, the British minister in China. He rendered much service to Canning in all civil or political affairs, being greatly respected by the community; after the departure of his chief from India, he became Commissioner of Mysore.

Among the non-official community the most influential and popular character was John O'Brien Saunders, the proprietor of the *Englishman* newspaper at Calcutta. He was called "the Nestor of Anglo-Indian journalism," and his wise genial wit endeared him to the community.

The well-known quarterly periodical the *Calcutta Review* was at that time in danger of extinction. With the help of Dr. George Smith, the editor of the *Friend of India*, I took it up and for several months sustained the publication. Our reason for so doing was the consideration that this periodical had been for twenty years the best contemporary record of Anglo-Indian thought, and reckoned among its contributors some of the most renowned men of this generation, Henry Lawrence, Alexander Duff, W. S. Seton Karr, William Mackay, John Macdonald, Baird Smith and others.

During these busy years Canning appeared to be physically well and strong. His habits were, however, hardly suited to the preservation of health in a hot climate, for he did not ride much except on particular occasions, and took walking exercise but little. Thus the conditions of Indian life were insidiously making inroads on his naturally fine constitution.

The last months of his time in India were clouded by a domestic bereavement; Lady Canning died after a few days' illness in Government House at Calcutta from a malarious fever caught while travelling in the eastern Himalayas. He composed the touching and beautiful inscription which was set up over her grave on the bank of the Hughli at Barrackpur near Calcutta. No English lady in India ever gained a wider respect and popularity. She had evinced the highest moral courage throughout the darkest days of the mutiny; in all the miseries and distresses which came within her reach or cognizance she displayed a solicitous and assiduous charity; and in many cases she promoted actively the ministrations of relief. Her grace, talent and accomplishments had won general admiration; her good deeds added fresh dignity to the British name; her loss was lamented as a general calamity; and a useful charity was by public subscription founded in remembrance of her.

As the time for his departure approached the public sentiments gathered affectionately around him. The non-official European community at Calcutta generously forgot the differences which had previously induced them to petition for his recall. They remembered only the national victory which had been won, the peace which had been secured, the moral and material progress which had followed. The Native community were, as might have been anticipated, earnest in their grateful commendations. An address was voted to him at a public meeting of the inhabitants of Calcutta; and subscriptions were raised for the erection of a statue in his memory. I was standing near and able to note his demeanour when he was receiving and replying to the address as it was presented to him by a deputation at Government House. His lip slightly trembled with emotion when he recalled the past, acknowledging thankfully their kind words, declaring that he had done his best on behalf of the interests which they represented, and had striven to secure justice for all alike whether European or Native.

The wonderful and tremendous events with which his name is associated will secure to him historic fame. In one sense it was suitable for him to be plunged into the midst of tempestuous waves, and exposed to cutting blasts; for thus were evoked and displayed those qualities which he possessed in the grandest degree. Had he ruled during a peaceful period when national progress was above all things demanded, his administrative capacity, though sound and good, might scarcely have equalled that of the greatest among his predecessors or his successors. But under a dire pressure of circumstances the hour came demanding equable calmness, unshakeable firmness, equity tempered with mercy; for that hour he was eminently the man. As the Greeks associated justice with the name of Aristides, so men regarded the departing Viceroy as Canning the Just.

CHAPTER IX.

(1860.)

JAMES WILSON THE ECONOMIST.

James Wilson arrives in India as Finance Minister—His tour in northern India—His financial budget produced at Calcutta—His measures of taxation—His project of a Government paper currency—His influence in the reduction of civil and military expenditure—In the re-organization of the police—In the inquiry into the indigo riots in Bengal—His untimely death at Calcutta—Summary of his policy in India.

IT will readily be understood that after the events and under the circumstances which have been mentioned in the preceding chapter, the finances of India caused grave anxiety both to the Government and the public. The collection of revenue remained for some time in abeyance throughout extensive tracts which were scenes of disturbance. On the other hand an enormous expense had been involved in the despatch, from England to India round the Cape of Good Hope, of English forces equal in strength to an army corps. There was a vast military transport within India itself by road and river, the operations of war having been spread over whole districts and provinces. Loans were being raised, chiefly in England, for the service of the Indian Government, augmenting the public debt of India by more than one-third. The old Native army of Bengal had, indeed, by mutinying effaced itself and the expenses incurred on its account. But it was more than replaced by Native troops specially enlisted and by local levies hastily raised in the disturbed districts. Thus, notwithstanding that the cost of European troops had been doubled, the charges for Native forces were not diminished. Extraordinary outlay was being incurred for the pacification of territories where society had been convulsed. The time, then, had come for bestowing on Indian finance a consideration which should include all manner of administrative affairs; otherwise the financial ship must soon become, as it were, waterlogged.

In those days there was little or none of the distribution of work which now exists between the Governor-General and the Members of his Council, whereby the Government of India works somewhat after the manner of an English cabinet; each Councillor taking a department of which he is virtually the minister, the whole being supervised by the Governor-General. On the contrary, with some exceptions in the departments of war and legislation, the whole work of the Government was brought before the Governor-General and all his Councillors. Consequently, finance was the business, not of any one member of the Government, but of all members alike. It was then determined in England that a Financial Member of Council should be appointed to whom, upon a division of labour or a distribution of business among the several Councillors, would be assigned the charge of the Financial department. The Financial Member would have individuality and particular responsibility. Still the Governor-General would retain his supreme control, the other members of Council remaining generally responsible for finance as for all other branches of the Government.

The selection fell upon the Right Honourable James Wilson, who had been formerly Under Secretary of State to the Board of Control for India, then Financial Secretary to the Treasury, and was at that time Vice-President of the Board of Trade. His appointment was regarded in India as a sign that the English Government deemed the situation of Indian finance to be serious; for he had long enjoyed the reputation of being one of the first economists of his day. It was remarked also that he must have esteemed highly the importance of India when he interrupted his political and parliamentary career in order to superintend her finances.

James Wilson arrived in Calcutta at the end of November 1859, and shortly afterwards proceeded on a rapid tour, through the North-western Provinces to the Panjab as far as Lahore, and then returned to Calcutta, establishing his head-quarters there. I met him for the first time, on his arrival at Lahore early in January 1860. John Lawrence had quitted the Lieutenant-Governorship of the Panjab, to which Robert Montgomery succeeded. I had resigned the Secretaryship and become Commissioner of the districts around Lahore. Wilson required an officer of Indian experience to assist him in economizing expenditure, introducing a new paper currency, devising fiscal improvement, and generally in his work as Finance Minister. This officer was to be on his personal staff in addition to the ordinary financial secretariat of the Government. He chose me for that appointment, and the choice was ratified by Lord Canning. I immediately joined him on his return to Calcutta, and thenceforward was on intimate terms of official association with him. I became much attached to him, and whether as master, teacher or friend, he made on my mind an impression which time cannot weaken.

He was of the middle height, with considerable breadth of chest and shoulder, his physical frame indicating strength and endurance. His age was fifty-four years, rather late perhaps for a man who proceeds to India for the first time; still he seemed to bring with him an abundant stock of freshness and vigour. His complexion was light, and the broad prominent brow, over-shadowing the eyes, gave an intellectual cast to the face. He had a keen perception of every object that met his view, a habit of casting observant looks in all directions, and an extraordinarily retentive memory of what he saw heard or read. His manner and conversation, though grave while he was intent on work, were bright and vivacious in society. He delighted in India as a country, and regarded her resources with hopeful interest, her people with sympathy, her scenery with admiration, her antiquities with curiosity. Nothing, he said, could be imagined more intensely interesting than India; with the ancient cities, the relics of decayed dynasties, the thronging population, the bustle of trade at every corner, the expansive plains bounded by alpine ranges affording a climate for new varieties of production, the large rivers, the magnificent canals irrigating the country, the careful agriculture with cultivation up to the roadside, the thrifty and economical habits of the people bent on active and profitable pursuits. These descriptive expressions are his own, being taken straight from his sayings and writings. It was instructive as well as amusing to accompany him in his walks during the early morning hours amidst the suburbs of Calcutta. He would observe every Native garden that we passed, talking about the natural habitat, culture and uses of the trees or plants. He would often stop at the wayside booths or shops, discussing the manufacture, prices and style of the wares. He would note the carts, drawn by bullocks and laden with produce, on their way to the capital, also the men and women carrying head-loads of articles to market. Then he would ever and anon exclaim that the country seemed bursting, as it were, with vitality and industry. The fairs which were held almost daily in various places, and more especially the central market of Calcutta, offered to him an extensive scope for economic reflection. He would watch the piece-goods and fancy-wares from Europe, the Oriental stuffs made in far-off cities, the flowers and vegetables brought by railway from gardens distant hundreds of miles, the game snared or shot in forests and marshes. He regarded all these goods, indeed, with the eye of an economist, in reference to their uses, but having a lively imagination he recognized their beauty also. If a thing seemed beautiful he felt all the more zealous in promoting its usefulness; if a thing was useful he appreciated it the better from its being beautiful also. Having been from the first imbued with the principles of unrestricted freedom in trade, he loved to speculate upon the moral advantages arising from the interchange of produce, which were in their way as great as the material advantages. Trade, he would say, is a great agency for securing peace and charity among men in all parts of the earth, enlarging the minds of diverse nations, raising their thoughts beyond petty jealousy, softening their mutual animosities, and uniting them by the bonds of goodwill and of common interest. I once heard him press strongly this view regarding commerce upon the Scotch missionary Alexander Duff, who had one morning paid a formal visit, and was adverting to the importance of cultivating kindly relations with the Natives.

Wilson's intellect was essentially methodical in its habits, ever searching for first principles or fundamental axioms, and then applying them to practice and to actual circumstances. He was fond of trying practical dicta by the test of principle; if principle and practice failed to agree, he would deem that there must be some error in one or other of them, or perhaps in the application of one to the other. A principle, he thought, which is sound in one country must be equally sound in another; if after having succeeded in one place it is found to fail elsewhere, the failure does not prove its unsoundness, but only shews that it must have been erroneously applied to unsuitable circumstances. He apprehended that there was danger of administrative science, as established in the most civilized countries, being disregarded in India because Indian conditions are strange. While he was, to this extent, theoretical, he was far from being unpractical; on the contrary, he was eminently practical. His principles lay deep in his mind, but in respect to practice he was ever studying the variety of circumstances, keeping his imagination open for the reception of the new ideas to be derived from the facts as recently learnt, and from the phenomena as freshly perceived. He was most anxious to understand India not as she had been supposed to be, or as she ought to have become, but as she actually was. While keeping in recollection the broad traits of human nature, as common to mankind in all times and places, he was especially desirous to realize to himself the idiosyncrasies aptitudes and tendencies, even the prejudices, of the Natives. Although the people had to be led gently towards the paths of economic science, yet he wished to shew the tenderest consideration towards the thoughts and sentiments springing from their historic antecedents. He hoped also to evince that moderation and self-restraint which befitted the peculiar position of the British as foreign masters of an eastern empire.

Such in brief was Wilson, the first scientific economist who had ever visited India. He probably learnt more of the country in a very short time, than any person who ever landed on its shores; and his general information extended daily, though it was not, of course, comparable to the knowledge possessed by those who have resided long in the East. His hopes of success in his financial policy were as high as his sense of the gravity and difficulty of his task. As weeks and months wore on, bringing with them their load of toil trouble and anxiety, his character shewed itself in a stronger light. Despite the depression from great heat, to which he had not been accustomed, his spirits were buoyant, and disposition elastic, while his bearing was genial and animated. His temper, though not destitute of warmth and impetuosity in pursuit of great objects, was yet steady and equable under disappointments. Though desirous of entering into the views of his opponents, he was yet very self-reliant, never doubting that if his plans were defeated for a time he would surely rectify them, and that they would come right in the end if only his eye should be upon them and his hand remain at the helm. He kept before his imagination a goal from which his thoughts were never diverted; if he could not win it at once he would be content with some progress, and pause with the full intention of starting again some day from the point where he had then stopped. His mind was fertile in expedients, and whenever obstacles threatened him with failure he would forthwith contrive remedies, in the conviction that his policy was good for the public interests and must ultimately prevail.

In February 1860 he produced his financial budget before the Legislative Council at Calcutta, carefully explaining that his proposals had the concurrence of his colleagues and the approval of Lord Canning. His speech on that occasion was the most able and eloquent statement that had ever up to that time been made orally in India. Remarkable minutes and reports had been frequent in India, but not speeches; and since that day the proceedings of the Indian legislature have often been animated by oratory. But the novelty of Wilson's oratorical effort, enlivening so grave a subject as finance, charmed as well as astonished both those who heard the statement and those who read the verbatim report of it. The warmth confidence and enthusiasm of his words, also the solidity of his arguments founded on a financial experience far larger than that possessed by any one in India, seemed to take, as it were, the public mind by storm. All men believed that the State having passed successfully through its political and military trials, was drifting into another danger, which, if less pressing, was more abiding, namely, that of certain disorder and possible disaster financially. As matters grew worse a state of urgency appeared to be approaching; the time was full and, in public estimation, here was Wilson, the man to cope with it.

His budget embraced proposals for three taxes, first an income-tax on all incomes above a certain amount, secondly a licence-duty on trades and professions, thirdly an excise on home-grown tobacco. The necessity for his proposals was maintained by the demonstration of a deficit of 21 millions sterling for the two years of the mutiny war, 1857–8, and 1858–9, of 9 millions for the year then closing, 1859–60, and of 6 millions expected for the coming year 1860–1. The sum of these deficits, amounting to 36 millions on an annual income, as it then stood, of 37 millions, exceeded anything which had happened in former times of misfortune, and startled even those who were prepared to face a serious crisis. Men felt that some remedy must be applied, and were prepared to support the man who proposed a definite policy. The European members of the community both official and non-official were, indeed, jealous of being "taxed without representation," that is, taxed under a Government which had no representative institutions. Still they loyally accepted a necessity which had been proved to their satisfaction, and patriotically acquiesced in the sacrifices demanded from them. The Anglo-Indian newspaper press strongly and cordially supported the budget. The Natives generally were silent; and the organs of Native opinion seemed to yield to the current of approbation which had set in.

Thus it happened that Wilson was at the outset greeted with a chorus of public approval. Though he relied much on the spirit and patriotism of his countrymen in India, he was agreeably surprised at the more than favourable reception accorded to his budget statement. And as congratulations continued to pour in from many quarters, he used to declare himself to be "the most fortunate of tax-gatherers." To complete his contentment, he received friendly support from the then Secretary of State, Sir Charles Wood (afterwards Lord Halifax).

Soon, however, clouds began to rise on this clear horizon, as was indeed to be expected by all who knew the changeableness of the "popularis aura." It transpired that one important functionary, Sir Charles Trevelyan, Governor of Madras, disapproved the budget, describing its main provisions as "three tremendous taxes." He was then in the full swing of his administration, and was deemed to be one of the most competent and energetic Governors that had ever ruled over the Madras Presidency. His unfavourable view in respect to the budget, besides exercising great influence with his colleagues at Madras and his principal officers, affected public opinion throughout southern India. He then allowed the local newspapers to publish the protest which he had deemed it his duty to record against the proposed taxation. This publication caused excitement at Calcutta and other centres of opinion in India, and was thought to constitute an official collision between the Government of Madras and the Supreme Government. Lord Canning, who was then absent in northern India, returned to Calcutta, in order that he might better arrange measures for vindicating his authority. Sir Charles Trevelyan shortly left Madras (having been recalled by the Government in England) amidst the regrets of the whole community European and Native in the Madras Presidency. The necessity of his recall under the circumstances seemed to be recognized, still all earnest and zealous men were sorry that a career of administrative usefulness should be suddenly interrupted.

Next the Native press of Bengal, consisting of many newspapers published daily or weekly in the Bengali vernacular, began to criticize the budget generally and the income-tax particularly. Some of these newspapers reflected the views of the great landholders (zemindars) who were much disappointed at finding that they were not to be exempted from the income-tax. The zemindars had hoped that the Permanent Settlement, which fixed for ever the demand of the land-tax, would save their landed income from the operation of the income-tax. But Wilson shewed that income from land must, in respect of general taxation, be treated in the same manner as all other kinds of income. This was the first time that the question had been brought to a decisive issue, and the zemindars felt that this decision would govern other questions of a like nature which might arise. If their income were to be thus taxed for imperial purposes, it might, they foresaw, be taxed for local or municipal objects. They feared that their Permanent Settlement would be, not indeed subverted or openly invaded, but undermined and gradually rendered nugatory. They doubtless became reassured subsequently on this point, but at that time they felt genuine alarm and communicated their dissatisfaction to the organs of Native opinion. The middle classes receiving fixed incomes, were among the main supporters of the vernacular press, and the income-tax would fall on them with accurate incidence without leaving any chance for evasion. Thus there arose from the Bengali press a chorus of bitter animadversion. The sarcasm and invective were conveyed under various forms of Oriental imagery, and often were set forth in a humorous and entertaining manner. This press did not indeed represent the people, but it did in a considerable degree represent the limited classes whom the income-tax would affect. On that account only did Wilson deem the vernacular newspapers to deserve the careful attention which he gave to their utterances, though his judgment was not thereby affected. It was to be inferred, however, that the unexpressed opinion of the tax-paying classes in other parts of the country would be the same as that which had been so loudly expressed in Bengal, and that the income-tax would, in the first instance at least, be unpopular with the Natives.

Then Lord Canning, having travelled down the country from the Himalayas towards Calcutta, was much impressed by all he heard on the way from Europeans and Natives regarding the danger of spreading direct taxation over too large an area ; in other words, of applying it to too many classes of the people simultaneously. He had sanctioned Wilson's budget with its three new taxes, namely the income-tax the licence on trades and professions and the tobacco-tax, having regard to the financial needs of the Government. The tobacco-tax indeed had the character of novelty, though tobacco was acknowledged to be a fit subject for taxation, if only under the circumstances of India a suitable method of taxing it could be devised. But the principle of the licence-tax, though little adopted by the British Government in recent times, had an ancient origin in India, and was commonly applied in the Native States. Shortly before Wilson's arrival, a bill for imposing licence-duties had been introduced into the Legislative Council by Mr. (afterwards Sir Henry) Harington on behalf of the Government, with the approval of almost all the best-informed authorities; and these duties really constituted a rough income-tax on several classes. The principle of a regularly assessed income-tax as proposed by Wilson was admitted on all hands to have one cardinal advantage, namely, this, that it taxed the rich Native traders who flourished under British rule and had heretofore escaped taxation. Thus Canning had, like Wilson, hoped for the best, when the budget was promulgated; but after its promulgation, he began to hesitate, on finding that objections of various forms were being raised in many quarters. Having with infinite difficulty guided the country into smooth and quiet ways, after turmoil and confusion, he was naturally anxious that no fresh disturbing force should be called into action. So he proposed to Wilson that the income-tax should be first taken in hand, passed through the Legislature and levied; that action should be suspended for the present regarding the licence-tax with the proviso that the measure would be subsequently undertaken should circumstances prove favourable; and that the proposed tobacco-tax should stand over on the understanding that its ultimate abandonment might be found necessary. After surveying the whole position, Wilson cheerfully acquiesced in the Governor-General's proposals, especially as they took the form of postponement only, and would not render necessary any further declaration of financial policy. As

Wilson must naturally have been elated by the wonderfully favourable reception at first accorded to his proposals, he could hardly fail to be somewhat depressed by the turn which public opinion was beginning to take, and the curtailment to which his plans were being subjected. Yet he buckled himself manfully to the task of giving effect to the general scheme of the budget, remembering that the proposed income-tax, the head and front of his policy, was still intact. While this important tax was maintained, he was prepared to sacrifice something of the full project as originally conceived. So he proceeded with the drafting of his income-tax bill on the model of the English income-tax acts, deriving great assistance in this respect from William Ritchie, then Advocate-General to the Government, and one of the best-informed English lawyers that ever practised at the Calcutta bar. He also revised the draft bill with special regard to the circumstances of Native society, and brought it before the Legislative Council for consideration. In that consideration he received cordial support from the President of the Council, Sir Barnes Peacock, from Sir Mordaunt Wells, and from Mr. (afterwards Sir Henry) Harington.

Meanwhile he had produced before the Legislative Council his measure for a Government paper currency, to which great importance was attached. His speech on that occasion was so lucid as to invest with much interest a subject not ordinarily attractive. Being the first statement of that kind made in India, it was received with admiring attention.

The Indian currency was then, as it still is, fraught with practical difficulties. The silver coins were the sole legal tender to an unlimited amount, but the gold coins issued from the Government mints were not legal tender at all. The Banks of Bengal Madras and Bombay, called the Presidency Banks, in which the Government held shares, had for many years been authorized to issue notes which were not legal tender. These notes had a circulation which though considerable was yet small for so great a country; it was, however, sustained throughout the time of political depression in 1857; even at its lowest point there were two millions sterling worth of notes in circulation. Wilson thought that if the notes of the Banks should be withdrawn and a paper currency established by the direct agency of the Government, the circulation of notes would greatly expand. This result must be specially advantageous in a country where no metallic currency except the bulky silver coinage was practicable. It would also be a source of large and legitimate profit to the Government, the Treasury being enabled to hold a large amount of its own securities against a part of the notes which were issued. He rejoiced in anticipating this profit, and said that it would be as good as if a mine of silver had been discovered beneath the great plain which lies in front of Calcutta. He founded his scheme on what he regarded as the principle whereby the notes are issued in London by the Bank of England; though there may be doubt whether he followed that model exactly. The Government, according to his plan, was to issue notes in return for coin; it was to invest in its own securities a portion not exceeding two-thirds of the coin thus received; the interest would be held in abeyance on the securities thus bought in, and the amount by these means annually saved to the Government would constitute the profit, less the slight expense incurred in managing the department of issue. In other words, of the total amount of notes issued, two-thirds might be held against Government securities and one-third against coin; both the securities and the coin were to be held by the department of issue, on behalf of the Government which guaranteed the absolute and immediate convertibility of the notes. For instance, if the issue of notes should fortunately amount to 30 millions sterling, then there would be in the possession of the department at least 10 millions of coin and perhaps 20 millions-worth of securities, on which the interest (at 5 per cent., the then rate) would be 1 million, constituting the annual profit of the Government; if the issue should amount to only 15 millions, then the profit would be half a million. Wilson did not undertake to predict the future amount of the issue, but he hoped that it might reach to something between 15 and 30 millions, say 20 millions, and that consequently the profit would range from half a million to a million sterling. He seemed to expect an expansion of the issue by an early date to the amount of 15 millions, and thereafter a gradual increase. This expectation of his would indeed have hardly been fulfilled, for in practice the issue has seldom exceeded 13 millions, an amount somewhat small for so great a country. Still, had he lived he might have stimulated the circulation by improving the facilities for cashing the notes. For, although the notes are absolutely convertible at the place of issue or the presidency town, yet there has been some delay or difficulty in cashing them under certain circumstances at a distance from the place of issue. At the least, however, there has been a profit which though less than half a million sterling annually, is yet considerable, and for which the Government is indebted to his suggestive and enterprising mind. He arrived at the proportion of two-thirds to be held in securities from a review of the experience of the Bank of England. The securities held by the Bank against the notes, under legal sanction, amounted to 14 millions and the circulation averaged 21 millions. Therefore according to the most approved practice about two-thirds of the notes were issued against securities, and one-third against coin; and he considered that a similar proportion might be safely applied to India.

This view of the principle whereby these proportions should be fixed was not, however, approved by the Secretary of State, Sir Charles Wood. He held that "the sound principle for "regulating the issue of a paper circulation is that which was "enforced on the Bank of England by the Act of 1844, namely, "that the amount of notes issued on Government securities "should be maintained at a fixed sum within the limit of the "smallest amount which experience has proved to be necessary "for the monetary transactions of the country, and that any "further amount of notes should be issued on coin or bullion. ". . . In this country (England) the smallest amount of notes "required has been ascertained by long experience, but what that "quantity may be in India can only be ascertained in like "manner." He considered that at the outset the quantity for India might be assumed on the data furnished by the note issues of the Presidency banks; those issues were generally less than four millions. These instructions did not indeed prevent the launching of Wilson's scheme, nor hinder the preparation for carrying it into effect; but they made a perceptible inroad into one of its important parts, and lowered the hopes which had been raised regarding the profits to be derived therefrom. He must doubtless have felt vexation on finding that here again his plans were abridged, and that the advantages which he hoped to secure for the Treasury would be shorn of their original dimensions. But he bore up bravely against this further disappointment, with the same buoyancy which he had displayed under the other trials already mentioned. How far he would with his consummate mastery of economic facts have managed, despite all obstacles, to carry into practice his principles of paper currency, and what degree of expansion he might have secured for the note circulation—it is impossible to say, as his death occurred too soon for him to develop his proposals under the altered conditions which had arisen.

It may be interesting, however, to consider for a moment what would have been the effect of Wilson's principle as compared with Sir Charles Wood's instructions, which have been actually followed and which probably will be approved by many authorities. In round numbers, the average Indian note circulation may be stated at 12 millions sterling, of which 6 millions are, under legal sanction, issued against securities and the rest against coin; thus while the circulation stands at 12 millions the coin reserve will amount to 6 millions. According to Wilson's principle the coin reserve would have been 4 millions, and the securities 8 millions. If the circulation should rise to 15 millions the coin reserve will be 9 millions, as no more than 6 millions can be issued against securities; whereas according to Wilson's principle the coin reserve would be 5 millions, and the securities 10 millions.

Wilson then remembered what he had said in his budget speech to the effect that although the Government hoped to restore an equilibrium between income and expenditure partly by means of the new taxes, yet reliance must largely be placed on reduction of expenditure in accordance with the maxim "magnum vectigal est parsimonia."

He first applied himself to studying the functions which were being discharged by the Military Finance Commission already mentioned in chapter VIII., of which Colonel (now Sir George) Balfour was the able President. This Commission had been appointed a short time before his arrival to investigate all branches of military expenditure and suggest reductions or savings; he now procured an enlargement of its powers, so that it might be entrusted with the supervision of the audit for all military accounts. He thus made its position very authoritative in relation to the great executive and spending departments of the army, namely, the Pay office, the Commissariat, the Ordnance, the Medical branch; while to it the Audit and account department were directly subordinate. The Commission was in constant and direct communication with him, also with the Governor-General and the Military member of Council; and its duties related to the three armies of Bengal Madras and Bombay alike. It was regarded by him as a special and extraordinary instrument outside and above all the other departments of military administration, to be used by the Government as the means of effecting every possible saving or reduction of expense consistently with safety and efficiency. If these means should be deemed unusual, he would urge in justification the paramount necessity, in respect to the safety of the national finance, for diminishing the armaments and their subsidiary charges which together had swollen to a size greater than the country could permanently bear. This matter was among the most pressing questions of the moment, and he resolved, for the emergency, to make full use of the Commission by effecting such diminution in the military expenses as should produce almost immediately a sensible effect on the finances of the empire. He hoped to see the retrenchments amount to two millions sterling annually within a very short time, and carried further afterwards to the extent of three or even four millions. He gave to the Commission the benefit not only of his support, but also of his advice in numerous particulars. He encouraged it to freely communicate with the Commander-in-Chief personally, upon whose co-operation the efficiency of its work largely depended. Sir Hugh Rose, then the Commander-in-Chief, received its representations with the utmost readiness and frankness, explaining his own views in reply and stating how far he could support particular retrenchments. Thus it was able to frame its proposals with more of confidence and precision than would otherwise have been practicable. The retrenchments first fell upon the overgrown transport establishments, large numbers of elephants, camels, bullocks, wagons, carts, and their attendant employés being discharged. The stores under the several categories of commissariat, ordnance, medical, miscellaneous, were revised, the despatch of these costly articles from England was diminished, and the purchase of them on the spot in India checked. Some moderate reduction of the European forces was cautiously ordered by the Government, but the principle was upheld that these forces must for the future be maintained in sufficient strength to overawe the Native army and to constitute the basis of British power.

In connexion with the military expenditure Wilson saw that the organization and functions of the Police must be reconsidered. It has been stated in a previous chapter that one cause of the Native army having been maintained at an excessive strength was the burden of civil duties imposed on the sepoys; and that the guards for treasuries, court-houses, prisons, as well as the escorts for prisoners, treasure, public stores in transit, were furnished by the Native army. This system was detrimental to military efficiency and discipline; it was expensive also as causing soldiers to do what should be more cheaply done by police. But its justification was this: that the police were so imperfectly organized and so slightly drilled that they could not be trusted with work of this nature. The Madras Presidency had in the time of Lord Harris and afterwards during the incumbency of Sir Charles Trevelyan organized their police in a fitting manner, Wilson, seeing this, caused the head of the Madras police, Mr. (now Sir William) Robinson, to be summoned to Calcutta for consultation as to the best way of extending that organization to the police in the other parts of the empire. A Police commission was then appointed, partly at Wilson's instance, consisting of representative men from every province, to devise an organization which would be suitable for all India.

Next Wilson began to consider the position and duties of the Indian Navy, which had indeed done much gallant service in many quarters and laid the foundation of a marine survey for several coasts, but was no longer effective for defensive purposes, as its vessels were not suited for the new requirements of naval warfare. The expenses of this Navy might be saved if its duties could be taken by the Royal Navy.

Then he induced the Government to appoint a Civil Finance Commission, of which I was appointed President, for the purpose of examining all branches of civil expenditure. He held that the number of offices and appointments should be diminished as much as possible by the abolition of superfluous employments; but that those offices and appointments which were retained should be well remunerated. He was opposed to any general reduction of salaries, believing that such a measure would injure efficiency, give birth to discontent, and therefore fail in conducing to ultimate economy. Before his arrival various proposals had been made for reducing the pay of the Covenanted Civil Service; but to these he was opposed. By the simplification of work and the abridgment of labour, he hoped to see many establishments pared down or even cut off. The Civil Finance Commission proceeded to review the expenses of each department, judicial fiscal administrative, in conjunction with the principal officers concerned. There was no scope for any large reduction; but after a comprehensive yet minute survey, small savings were made in many different directions, so that the aggregate result became considerable. Among many other things this Commission had its attention drawn to the expensive establishments entertained for the manufacture of salt in Bengal, all which might be abolished if arrangements could be made for importing this article in sufficient quantities from England.

He occupied himself much in plans for the improvement of the existing system of audit and account, which was in several respects antiquated and no longer suited to the altered requirements of the administration. His general ideas were indeed fixed, but time and study were needed to mature details.

It was during his time that there arose in Bengal the indigo riots already mentioned in the previous chapter VIII. These disputes involved many economic questions regarding which reference was made to Wilson. He paid much attention to the subject and took a large share in the deliberations which led to the appointment of a Commission of enquiry.

Shortly before his illness he began to consider public works and roads with a view to increase the production of cotton flax, wool and other raw materials needed for European manufactures. Had his life been prolonged he would have guided the discussions regarding the application of State capital to these works, whether roads railways or canals. To few branches was his premature loss more lamentable than to the department of material improvement.

Besides attending to the specific measures mentioned above, he discharged all the duties pertaining to the financial portfolio of a large empire, and to his position as a member of the Government generally.

Thus the short winter of the Calcutta climate, the spring and the hot season of 1860 passed over his head; then the rainy season set in, about the middle of June. At first his health seemed to be quite good, but failed slightly as the heat waxed fiercer and fiercer. Still he maintained his vivacity of temperament and alacrity of bearing, while his mental activity suffered no abatement. He was at one time disposed to adhere to the English habit of reading late at night and resting in the morning hours. But he soon perceived the incompatibility of this habit with health in a climate like that of India, and adopted the Indian practice of retiring to rest before midnight and taking outdoor exercise in the morning ere the sun had ascended the heavens. By degrees, however, the early rising became more and more intermittent, and as the rains of June descended steadily day after day, with a high temperature depressing atmosphere and exhalations from the humid ground, his physical strength waned visibly. It was then understood that he had for some little time been suffering from a dysenteric ailment, which, perhaps but little noticed at first, grew stealthily upon him, fixing its hold upon his constitution. He continued, however, to discharge all his public and official duties, though he went less frequently out of doors or into general society. At the end of July, dysentery of a normal type declared itself, and he was confined to his bed. Before that time Mrs. Wilson had repaired for the benefit of her health to the Nilgiri hills in southern India, leaving him in apparently fair health and not at all apprehending any danger being in store for him. William Halsey, his son-in-law and private Secretary, and two of his daughters remained with him. At first his illness excited no alarm in his family or among the public, and the general impression regarding his vigour and vitality remained undisturbed. He continued to read official papers, giving general attention to public affairs without performing much actual business. But he was soon obliged to accede to the request of his physician, Dr. Alexander Macrae, of Calcutta, that he should call in a second medical adviser, and cease reading or thinking; then warnings of danger began to be whispered abroad. As the dysentery developed more and more of its formidable symptoms day after day, he asked for a categorical statement of his condition from Dr. Macrae, in whose judgment and devotion he placed much confidence. The physician's reply, without absolutely shutting out hope, led him to prepare for a speedy end. He immediately sent to ask the Governor-General, Lord Canning, to come for a last interview. During that conversation he commended the services of several who had worked with him, and mentioned some arrangements he had intended to propose, evincing thoughtfulness for others to the last. His countenance had become emaciated in the extreme; he looked as if he had been starved to death by the illness, as Lord Canning thus described his aspect to me afterwards. He then wrote a letter to his wife in the Nilgiri hills, also dictated various messages on public and private affairs with steady coolness and entire self-possession. A few hours later, he sank under dysentery in its most fatal form on the evening of Saturday, August 11th. The following evening he was buried in the principal cemetery of Calcutta, and as his coffin was lowered, there stood around his grave one of the most important and varied assemblages that had ever been seen in that place—an assemblage comprising representatives of every class of the European community whether official or non-official. The strings of carriages, carrying sorrowful spectators, covered more than two miles of the road leading to the burial-ground. That sabbath was a day of mourning, and in every church of the city allusion was made from the pulpit to the solemn lesson conveyed to the community by the sudden demise of one among the foremost citizens of the empire.

On a retrospect of that stirring and eventful time, the mind at first hardly realizes that these broadly laid plans embracing, with a comprehensive policy, vast affairs and varied subjects, were all crowded by Wilson into the brief space of eight months. A review of these proceedings will help us to imagine what great things a man, who did so much in a few months, would have accomplished had he been spared for a few years. Between December and July, he introduced for the first time in India a financial budget framed upon the English model—inspired the public mind with fresh confidence — brought together the threads of finance which had been broken and scattered by a military and political convulsion—proposed to the legislature three new taxes and carried one of them, the income-tax, through several stages in the Legislative Council—devised a scheme for the Government paper currency—stimulated the operations of the Military Finance Commission over the entire range of army expenditure for both the European and Native forces—procured the appointment of a commission to review the numerous branches of civil expenditure—caused arrangements to be begun for reorganizing the whole police of the empire—reviewed the existing system of audit and account—besides discharging the multifarious duties devolving on a finance minister and a member of the general Government. All this was compassed by him immediately on landing in an utterly strange country amidst an alien people, and further was carried on with unabated vigour despite the depression caused by a tropical climate.

CHAPTER X.

(1861–1862.)

SAMUEL LAING THE FINANCIER.

Interval between death of Wilson and arrival of his successor—My deputation to Pegu—City of Rangûn—Sir Arthur Phayre Commissioner—River Irawaddy and city of Prome—View at Moulmein—Chief Commissionership of British Burma—Samuel Laing arrives at Calcutta as successor to Wilson—Contrast between the two statesmen—Laing produces financial budget—Introduces a modified scheme of Government paper currency—Prosecutes reduction of civil and military expenditure—Assists in abolition of the Indian Navy—Produces second budget—My deputation to Hyderabad in the Deccan, to Nagpur and Jabalpur.

THE death of James Wilson in July 1860, in the heyday of his financial career and the midst of administrative operations which he had either originated or promoted, struck the Government of India as a heavy sea strikes a vessel in stormy weather. But the political ship, heeling over momentarily after his sudden loss, righted itself; thereby proving the fundamental excellence of his work. No temporary appointment was made by the Government of India, on the spot, to manage the financial helm which had fallen from his hands; and the arrival of a successor from England was awaited. Nevertheless the Governor-General, Lord Canning, and his Councillors took up the various threads of work left by their lamented colleague. The legislative and executive measures for introducing and collecting the income-tax were adopted, and the licence-tax law was prepared in detail for enactment. The enquiries with a view to reduction of military and civil expenditure were prosecuted; much also was actually done in that direction. Still there was necessarily a *vis inertiæ* opposed to such measures, many interests being arrayed against them. Thus it was difficult to ensure anything approaching to full success in the absence of a Finance Minister personally answerable for the result and therefore resolute to infuse energy into the proceedings.

As it became known in the autumn of 1860 that Wilson's successor would not arrive for some little time, and as there was a pending question as to whether the several Burmese provinces should or should not be combined under one administration—Lord Canning despatched me in company with Colonel Herbert Bruce to Burma. We had instructions to examine into and report on that question and return to Calcutta by January in 1861 in order to meet the new Finance Minister, who would by that time have arrived from England.

Colonel Bruce was in every respect an excellent colleague in affairs of this nature; he had organized the police of Oudh in 1858 immediately after Sir Colin Campbell had restored order by military operations. He had taken an active part in the work of the Commission mentioned in the last two chapters as having been formed for the reorganization of the police throughout India. He was afterwards employed with the army in the Bhotan war of 1864, and became the British Commissioner appointed in conjunction with the Bhotan delegates to conclude the terms of peace as approved by the Government of India. He died prematurely from fever caught during those operations, and in him the Government lost an able servant.

After sailing from Calcutta we neared the coast of Arracan, and were enveloped in a dense mist with rain. For two days the commander of the vessel could not make the necessary observations, and was obliged to anchor for fear of being carried by the oceanic currents towards the reefs on that dangerous shore. Suddenly as rain and mist cleared, we found ourselves opposite Akyab with its tropical landscape. It seemed as if we had emerged from cloud-land and passed into an earthly paradise. Akyab, the seaport of the maritime province of Arracan, was then rising towards the importance it has since attained as a place for the exportation of rice to Europe. We landed in order to confer with the authorities regarding the cost of the public establishments and the like, and then sailed for Rangûn, the capital of

Pegu and the principal seaport of Burma. Rangûn somewhat resembles Calcutta, in that it is situated inland at some distance from the seashore; the approach to it consists of a broad river navigable for ocean-going vessels. As we steamed up the river, the banks on either side were low and wooded, and the great Pagoda was to us a shining landmark from afar, as the afternoon sunlight rested on its gilded spire.

Rangûn was then an active rising place, but had quite an unfinished air; new streets were being marked out in all directions, the foundations of houses in rows were laid, quays and wharves were in course of erection. The city has subsequently grown so much that probably few traces of its former self could now be recognized. Its chief glory was then and must ever be the Shwe Dagôn pagoda. Out of the plain there rises abruptly a steep and lofty mound from the top of which the pagoda springs. The terraces round the basement of the pagoda are fortified; the gateway at the bottom of the flight of steps leading up the sides of the mound is as the entrance to a fortress. Thus, although the structure was sacred, its subsidiary buildings had been so arranged by the Burmese as to render it the principal fort of the country. In the last war it was stormed by the British troops, and upon its capture the dominion over the surrounding territory, indeed over the whole province of Pegu, passed to the victors. There is no architectural term in English whereby this pagoda may be described; its form is somewhat that of an obelisk surmounted by a spire; and the upper part is encased in copper which is gilt. It rises to a height of 300 feet from its base on the summit of the mound. The gilding under the glare of sunlight has a resplendent effect against the azure of the sky. Around its basement are masonry images of griffins, utterly grotesque and bizarre, contrasted strangely with the Buddhistic images which symbolize eternal quietude. Near one side of the mound was a lake, on the other were groves clothing the surface of the mound, so that the burnished obelisk seemed to rise up straight from amidst the foliage.

The Burmese having the flat Indo-Chinese face, and being

small in stature, did not make much impression on us whose eyes had been accustomed to the varied and picturesque aspect of an Indian crowd. In their manner and bearing they seemed to be a light-hearted laughter-loving people.

At Rangûn we met Colonel (now Sir Arthur) Phayre, the Commissioner of Pegu which was the maritime province of the old Burmese kingdom and comprised the delta of the Irawaddy. It had been annexed on Lord Dalhousie's recommendation after the conclusion of the second Burmese war. Phayre had been at the head of that mission to Ava graphically described by Henry Yule. He became afterwards the first Chief Commissioner of British Burma, and ultimately Governor of the Mauritius. He was at this time bringing the administration of Pegu to an advanced stage. His knowledge of the language, history and customs of the Burmese people was very considerable; he had also devoted much study to the Buddhist religion which the Burmese profess. Though a man of gentle manners courteous address and discriminating judgment, he was yet full of energy and resolution, and as a ruler was popular and respected. We now started with him in a river steamer on a short voyage up the Irawaddy, to see the upper part of Pegu, also the border between that province and the kingdom of Ava which is all that now remains to the Burmese dynasty out of the old Burmese empire.

On leaving Rangûn our vessel for the first two days passed through the deltaic creeks and channels of the Irawaddy; the flat banks being continuously clothed with low forest. At eventide the scene would consist of gorgeous clouds mirrored in an expanse of water; the splendour of the sky being parted from that of the water by the dark horizontal line of the low wooded bank. Then we passed under the solitary and precipitous cliff of which the scarped side is carved with Buddhist images in bas-relief, and from which the Burmese authorities in former days used to collect toll on the laden boats plying up and down the river. After a time the group of detached hills came into sight in the midst of which is situated the city of Prome. One of these hills was covered and crowned with pagodas;

and as each pagoda had its spire the hill seemed to us a forest of spires and pinnacles. The masses of elaborate wood carving about these pagodas excite wonder, when the great quantity of the work and the minuteness of its detail are considered. In juxtaposition with the dark-coloured woodwork was seen the verdure of the luxuriant vegetation. In the foreground as a relief against this mass of sombre and rich colour there stood out groups of priests in their bright saffron robes.

Arrived at the frontier near Meeaday, we ascended some hills whence a view was obtained of the broad Irawaddy then flowing through a region of apparently interminable forests. It is probable that since those days large inroads into those forests have been made by advancing cultivation.

Having discussed with Phayre the military charges, the strength of the police, the cost of the civil administration and the finances of the Pegu province, we returned to Rangûn.

I there met for the first time Dr. Dietrich Brandis, of Berlin, the Conservator of Forests. The teak forests of Burma being perhaps the best in the world, and their timber being required for the British Admiralty, it was important to preserve them, both for use and for reproduction, by means of scientific forestry. On the other hand, the timber trade being very profitable, the traders were anxious to do many things which the Conservator would not allow; and they were presenting remonstrances on the subject to Phayre as the superior over the Conservator. I was struck by the patience and argumentative skill with which Brandis met these objections.

From Rangûn we crossed in a steamer the bay which lies between the mouth of the Irawaddy and Moulmein the capital of the Tenasserim province. Having seen three views which would never be effaced from the memory, namely, that of the Akyab harbour, that of the Rangûn pagoda, and that of the temple-crowned hill of Prome—we were destined yet to see at Moulmein a fourth more beautiful still. Behind the city of Moulmein there rises a wooded mount on the summit of which are several pagodas. These, though not remarkable as separate structures, yet massed together form a good foreground. It is the distant view which delights the spectator, inasmuch as three rivers, the Gyne, the Attaran, and the Salwîn, are descried winding through the vast plain to unite near Moulmein before flowing onwards to the sea; and one of these, the Salwîn, is a mighty stream. The plain covered with rice crops is broken here and there abruptly by masses of granite, and in the distance the horizon is bounded by the mountains of Siam. Opposite the traveller there is the town of Martaban, and down low at his feet lie the station, the villas, and the city of Moulmein. Pictorially and geographically this view is one of the finest in the eastern empire.

After carefully examining the finances of the Tenasserim province with the assistance of the Commissioner, Colonel Hopkinson, we returned to Calcutta and submitted our report.

The substance of our recommendations was this: that the three kindred provinces, namely Arracan under the Bengal Government, Pegu and Tenasserim under separate administrations of their own, should be formed into one jurisdiction to be called the Chief Commissionership of British Burma. We proposed that several local battalions be disbanded and a new police organized, also that the Native portion of the military forces be reduced. It was shewn that with the adoption of such measures the revenues of these territories would more than suffice to meet the expenses properly chargeable to them. These recommendations were in the main approved by Lord Canning, who shortly afterwards published his Resolution constituting the administration of British Burma as a separate Chief Commissionership. British Burma has since that time been blessed with a marvellous prosperity, increasing in cultivation trade wealth and revenue, thus more than fulfilling any anticipations which we ventured to form.

I then awaited at Calcutta the arrival of my new master, namely, the financier appointed to succeed Wilson.

The choice of the English Government fell upon Samuel Laing, as Minister of Finance for India, who arrived at Calcutta towards the end of 1860. I fell into a position on his staff similar to that which I had occupied under his predecessor. He was as an official superior most kind, pleasant and satisfactory.

He was the son of Samuel Laing known in literature and science as a traveller and an author. He had sat in Parliament for many years, thereby acquiring practical acquaintance with public business, together with a power of facile and expressive speech. He possessed much financial experience, having been connected with enterprises industrial and commercial. In general knowledge, intellectual grasp, penetrative insight, capacity for gauging the probable direction of fluctuating circumstances and estimating the net result of conflicting considerations, he was nearly equal to Wilson, his great predecessor. In other respects, however, he was quite different from Wilson, with reference at least to the financial circumstances of India. Without at all despising theory or abstract principle, he apparently desired to ascertain and measure the practical needs of the hour, to deal with them adequately up to their existing limits and no more; to note considerately the strange peculiarities of Oriental life and society, and to avoid raising questions which though derived from the best analogies of Europe might, if inopportunely pressed, do more harm than good in the East. Thus he dwelt much less than Wilson upon fundamental axioms as established by European statesmanship or economic science; and was more disposed to take views similar to those ordinarily held by men whose experience lay entirely in India.

Immediately after his arrival in Calcutta, Laing was, during January 1861, much pressed by requisitions from the Indian treasury for the supply of funds. For the cash balances, which had been satisfactorily high twelve months before, now suffered depletion, because the expenses of military and police establishments were not yet reduced to a normal standard. He used to say under these emergent conditions that he was required, in nautical analogy, to cry now "starboard," and now "port," before he had time to fully examine his charts or to properly take his bearings. His next anxiety was to ensure judicious moderation in levying the income-tax, introducing such modifications in detail as might remove or at least mitigate any causes of reasonable discontent. He heard much on this subject from Europeans official and non-official, and used to converse with Natives of status loyalty and intelligence, concerning direct taxation. From their replies he became imbued with a sense of the political disadvantages attending fiscal measures of this nature among the people of India. He took to heart the dictum of Lord Canning, as already mentioned, that even the danger from having too small a force of European troops was of less moment than the danger from imposing too heavy a burden of taxation upon large classes of the people.

Soon he proceeded with the inchoate legislation for the new paper currency. He held that the principles, on which Wilson had founded the first proposals for this currency, would, if carried to their extreme, produce a system inadequate to sustain the shock of a political or commercial crisis. He adopted unreservedly the views set forth in the instructions of the Secretary of State, Sir Charles Wood, as already described in chapter IX.; and a bill, revised accordingly, was passed by the Indian legislature at Calcutta. He thereby arranged that the department of issue should be connected with the mint, the master of the mint becoming the head commissioner of paper currency. Power was taken to issue notes against Government securities up to the amount of four millions sterling; that being the amount below which, as shewn by experience, the note circulation could not possibly go; and all notes beyond this amount were to be issued against cash only. There were three circles of issue established, namely those of Calcutta, Madras and Bombay. The notes of a circle were payable at the note-office or offices of that circle, but not of other circles. It was not thought safe to undertake the cashing of notes in circles other than those in which they were issued. In any circle, however, sub-circles might be established; and the notes of a sub-circle would be payable at its own note-office, and at the note-office of the circle; but not in other circles. The new note circulation immediately exceeded the amount of four millions, and rose steadily from time to time. The old note circulation of the three Presidency banks, as already mentioned, was abolished.

Turning to administrative affairs he gave a strong support to the measures then in progress for diminishing expenditure. He earnestly attended to the disbanding of military police and of quasi-military levies, the reorganizing of the new police in their stead, the discharging of establishments connected with transport and other subsidiary departments of war, the better regulating of expenses connected with the European forces, and the reducing of the strength of Native troops. He declared his belief that there was hardly a man of weight and authority in India who did not feel that the Government in reducing the Native army as it then stood, were following the path not only of financial reform, but of political prudence. He gave every encouragement to the two Commissions, already mentioned in chapter IX., for the revision of military and civil finance respectively; and he cordially acknowledged the aid afforded by the most important of the two, namely, the Military Finance Commission, in the reduction of military expenditure generally.

He then in March (1861) introduced his budget before the Legislative Council at Calcutta by a speech replete with stirring and graphic metaphors. Though he pointedly disclaimed the character of an orator, yet there was actually much eloquence of a certain kind in his utterances. But his oratory was quite different from Wilson's measured and sonorous periods which still seemed to resound in our ears. It was generally of a familiar type, borrowing similes from every-day life, especially from the hunting field, applying them appositely and felicitously to the financial point in hand, and so illustrating the particular policy of the Government on matters which, however important, would usually seem dull and obscure. In his conversation he commonly used expressive figures of speech, and it was with such images that in his first budget statement he communicated to the audience the same vivid impressions which he had in his own mind. At the moment, however, his hearers, accustomed to the gravity of official speakers, received the speech with a good-humoured surprise, while acknowledging its vigour and cogency.

Still, in this speech he sometimes rose to higher flights, and produced one passage which is worth quoting. After reminding his audience that India is not altogether devoid of that spirit of self-government which characterizes the Anglo-Saxon, he spoke thus:—

"India has never, within the period of history, been a nation. It has been an aggregate of various tribes, distinct communities, and petty despotisms, of which now one, now the other, shot up into ephemeral importance or decayed, with the accident of the hour, with the success of some military adventurer, and the degeneracy of his heir. . . . I have a vision of an India—where the science of the West has removed impediments to communication; where the consequent increase of trade has diffused material prosperity; where English energy and capital stimulate improvement in every district; and where the Native population, with expanding ideas and improving intelligence, are taught by the education of schools and of events, of books and railways, to know us and to know one another; and are gradually trained in the management of their own local affairs for those of a wider area; so that India may at length have what it has never yet had—a political life, and at length be, what it has never yet been—a nation."

Like Wilson, he was much impressed by the indications of India's vitality and resources and of her ability to overcome the financial difficulties of the hour, grave as they were. He anticipated much benefit from material improvement, especially the construction of canals for irrigation. Respecting the canals he used these emphatic words: "Colonel Cotton has truly said that water is gold in India. It is more than gold, it is life; and amongst the most lamentable consequences of our financial embarrassments had been the necessity of starving works which convert famine into plenty."

Like Wilson again, while anxious to check extravagance and enforce a wise economy, he thought that such economy could be attained only in conjunction with efficiency. He said that "a Government to be well served and generally respected must never do a sharp, mean or illiberal act, for depend upon it the paltry saving of to-day will come back with tenfold expense and a hundred-fold discredit on the morrow."

He declared himself in favour of the principle which subsequently under Lord Mayo was developed into the scheme of provincial services. He proposed to augment the financial responsibilities of the provincial Governments, to give them budgets of their own for several heads of income and expenditure, and accord them certain powers to raise taxes for themselves. In his own words he wished to say to them, "Take what we are able to give you; and for the residue take certain powers of local taxation and raise it for yourselves." Immediate effect was not given to these ideas, and when forming them he was somewhat in advance of the time; but being sound, they were, in their essentials, adopted during after years.

The financial situation with which he had to cope when producing his first budget, was in this wise. Of the new taxation devised by Wilson a part had been relinquished, and the remainder was but partially imposed. The tobacco-tax had been abandoned the licence-tax, though prepared fully and ready for enactment, was not actually enacted. The collection of the income-tax was only in progress, and its management, as might have been feared, had suffered considerably from the death of its author. Thus the expected augmentation of income was far from being realized. On the other hand the measures for reducing the vast expense of the national defences, of the army the military police and the like, which had been begun before Wilson's arrival and prosecuted during his time, had not taken full effect. The measures were discussed elaborated and in some respects executed; all which constituted a real gain to progress. Still the carrying out of them had not yet been ordered in that complete manner which alone can ensure a good result financially. Consequently the expenditure still remained intolerably high; and the current deficit of more than six millions annually which Wilson intended to avert, threatened to last. As no loan had been raised recently, the continuance of deficit had drained the cash balance of the Government to a very low ebb.

He proposed to make the most of the income-tax as it had been already imposed, but to refrain from levying the licence-tax; on the other hand he arranged to augment the salt-duties; and so a goodly amount of new income, about 2 millions sterling, would be realized. Then he hoped to see effect really given to the proposals which had been matured for reducing the expenses of the national defence, that is, of the army the armed police and the Indian navy. If the orders which had been or were being issued should be put into execution, then he estimated that a saving of 3½ millions sterling annually would be obtained. Thus with 2 millions of fresh income and an economy in expenditure of 3½ millions, he expected to meet 5½ out of 6 millions of the deficit, leaving ½ million to be made up.

This half million he proposed to make up by what was then regarded as an unusual plan, but which is in principle recognized abundantly nowadays. The scheme was to deduct this amount from the imperial grants for material improvement in the various provinces of the empire, and to inform the several provincial Governments that they would be at liberty to recoup themselves by levying special taxes for material improvement within their respective jurisdictions. The imperial finance would *pro tanto* experience relief, and the burden would be transferred to the provincial Governments. This plan was sanctioned by the Government of India at the time, but was not carried into effect, because as the year wore on the necessity of executing it disappeared or was thought to disappear. It involved the principle of the scheme for Provincial Services which was brought forward some years later in Lord Mayo's time and is now in operation.

Laing saw that the new income, included in his estimate, was in the main secure, and that the success or failure of his estimate really depended on the reduction of expenditure. The saving of so large an amount as 3½ millions sterling might arouse indirect opposition, and there would always be a *vis inertiæ* militating against reforms of this nature. He therefore felt that an active support must be given to those who were charged with the execution of these measures of economy, that is, to Colonel Balfour and his colleagues in the Military Finance Department. They would have been the first to acknowledge that their success was largely due to the strenuous support which he afforded. Indeed his adroitness in piloting proposals through the shoals of opposition and avoiding the reefs of disappointment was remarkable. After a time he had the pleasure of reviewing the results accomplished within a very few years, and shewing that the cost of the army defrayed in India stood at

£20,909,307 in 1859–60,
£15,838,980 in 1860–1,
£12,800,000 in 1861–2,
£12,200,000 in 1862–3.

When adverting to this satisfactory topic he invariably commended the signal services of Colonel Balfour already mentioned. The Native armed force, including military police, had been reduced in two years from 350,000 men to less than 130,000, and the European army from 90,000 to less than 70,000 men.

The expenditure on the Indian Navy and the Indian marine fell within the sphere of the Civil Finance Commission, and to them he gave the same vigorous support in carrying out reduction. He held that the Indian Navy cost one million sterling annually, without affording any real naval protection. He then succeeded in reducing this charge to less than half a million, by the abolition of the naval establishment altogether and by dispensing with half the marine; a small and inexpensive force being obtained instead from the Royal Navy. He further, by following up the recommendations of the Commission, obtained savings in the civil administration to an amount of £500,000 yearly.

In these affairs he evinced much dexterity, displaying this quality in a degree not surpassed by any man in India within this generation. To it he added unfailing tact and good-humour, besides a ready skill in bringing matters to the desired conclusion.

Having witnessed the favourable reception accorded to his budget by all classes of the community, he became violently ill with dysentery, the same disease which had carried off his predecessor. He bore up bravely against this ominous attack, and proceeded on a short sea voyage to the Straits of Malacca, whence he returned in a few weeks, much improved in health and able to work, though somewhat shaken. Warned thereby of the necessity for reinvigorating by European air a constitution that had once been affected by tropical disease, he proceeded on short leave to England, and soon came back to resume his financial portfolio.

He produced his second budget in April 1862, and by it shewed that the anticipations set forth in his first budget had been mainly realized, that the orders for reducing the expenditure had really been carried into effect, that the taxes had been fairly productive, and that the revenue was flourishing. The army charges had reached their culminating point in 1859–60, when they stood at 21 millions; they had since fallen first to 16 millions, then to 13 millions, and were expected to fall further still to nearly 12 millions. He then thought that the time had come when the duty on English piece-goods imported into India, which had been raised to 10 per cent. during the time of the utmost financial depression, might be lowered to 5 per cent. He discussed the question whether such a duty operated as a protection to the manufactures then springing up in India; a duty of 10 per cent. might have this effect, but a duty of 5 per cent. under the existing circumstances would not. Still if a protective effect should become apparent, he would be prepared to reconsider the question, declaring that he was "anxious not to bestow on Indian manufactures the fatal boon of a temporary and precarious protection."

His first budget (for 1861–2) had ended with the anticipation of a small surplus, which was not actually realized—there was indeed a small deficit; essentially, however, during that year an equilibrium was maintained between income and expenditure. This his second budget (for 1862–3) comprised the estimate again of a small surplus; but ultimately a large surplus was realized.

In both of his budget speeches he virtually pronounced against the scientific income-tax in the form which it had assumed under Wilson's direction. While admitting its merit in bringing untaxed yet wealthy classes under taxation, he deemed it unsuitable to the circumstances of India, and financially unsuccessful. He did his best to lighten it by lowering its rate, by waiving the claim to revise assessments, and by exempting the lower incomes altogether. But he was in favour of a rough income-tax in the shape of licence-duties according to the plan which had been superseded by Wilson's regular income-tax. It is remarkable that the Government have in the most recent years reverted to this very plan since the remission of the income-tax in 1873.

He carefully considered the opium revenue in all its bearings, and declared himself thus: "I can see no reason why the revenue derived by India from opium should be considered more precarious than that derived by England from gin and tobacco."

Lastly, before his departure he thus spoke of the resources of India: "I came out here under the impression of the gloomy, almost despairing views of Indian finance which were prevalent, and it is only by degrees, and as the result of close enquiry, that the conviction has forced itself on my mind that the revenue of India is really buoyant and elastic in an extraordinary degree."

While Laing was absent in England I was deputed by Lord Canning to several important places in the interior of the country for the purpose of investigating, in conjunction with the local authorities, various matters concerning finance.

At that time the military expenditure incurred by the British Government at Hyderabad, the capital of the Nizam of the

Deccan, was attracting attention. By treaty the British Government was bound to maintain a body of troops there styled "the Subsidiary Force"—quite apart from another body of troops known as "the Hyderabad Contingent." In consideration of the Subsidiary Force being stationed near Hyderabad for his support and protection, the Nizam had in the beginning of this century ceded to the British Government certain territories which now form the Ceded districts of the Madras Presidency. It was estimated at the time that the revenues of these districts would be about equal to the cost of the Subsidiary Force. For a long time the Force was maintained at the strength specified in the treaty and no more. But during the war of the mutinies the European part of the force had been largely augmented. It was then alleged by financiers that the British Government was maintaining, at a heavy cost, a force certainly larger than that required by the treaty, and possibly beyond the actual needs of the time. I was accordingly instructed to proceed to Hyderabad by the Madras route, to confer with the Governor of Madras regarding the present value of the Ceded districts, and with the Resident of Hyderabad regarding the cost and strength of the Subsidiary Force.

Arrived at Madras I had several interviews with the Governor, Sir William Denison, who had recently come there from his Governorship in Australia. He was fast acquiring popularity at Madras, having the tastes and ways of an English squire, and being essentially a man of masculine common-sense. He was not likely to acquire that insight into the wants of the country which his predecessor, Sir Charles Trevelyan had evinced as the result of old experience, but being an officer of Engineers he had much knowledge that would come into play for the benefit of an Indian administration.

I there met Colonel Sir Arthur Cotton of the Madras Engineers, who had rendered splendid services to the cause of irrigation and navigation by canals in southern India. He was anxious to see projects for the same purposes undertaken in the central territories which I was about to visit. In his characteristic manner he took a large map and marked with different colours the basins of the rivers in the centre of India, denoting the several water-systems which might be utilized by means of engineering works. He also explained to me the merits of the Godavery scheme which will be mentioned hereafter.

In those days there had been only one railway opened in the Madras Presidency, namely that which ran from Madras on the Coromandel coast across the peninsula to Beypur on the Malabar coast. This railway passed near the base of the Mysore plateau, and I determined to visit Mysore and thence proceed to Bellary in the ceded districts already mentioned.

Bangalore was the European station on the Mysore plateau where the troops were cantoned. It was also the residence of the Commissioner (then Mr. C. B. Saunders) who was managing the territory on behalf of the Raja. Many years previously internal troubles, caused by misrule, had compelled the British Government to assume charge of the administration. Adequate allowances from the treasury of the State were made to maintain the household and court of the Raja, who lived at Mysore, some sixty miles from Bangalore. I went in company with Mr. Saunders to pay my respects to His Highness. Arrived at the palace we passed through a noble hall of audience with the pillars and arches which are shewn in the background of the historic picture representing the youthful Raja as he received investiture from the British delegates when being placed on the throne of his ancestors after the capture of Seringapatam and the death of Tippoo Saib. That scene must have appealed most forcibly to the sentiments of Hindus, who regarded Tippoo the Muhammadan iconoclast and his sacrilegious myrmidons with that sort of fear which villagers feel for the man-eating tiger. The East India Company, having, vanquished Tippoo by operations redounding to its fame as a military power, sought out the heir of the ancient dynasty which the Muhammadans had displaced, in order to set him on the ancestral throne. Seldom has a fairer prospect presented itself to an Indian youth than that which opened out before the Raja on the auspicious day of his enthronement. But though fairly educated, courteous and free from evil intention, he was unstable as water and a hopelessly incompetent ruler. His kingdom became a scene of anarchy, and when the British Government interposed to restore order he subsided into the position of a pensioner in his own palace. There he was still residing in his old age, and we were about to see him. He received us very courteously in an apartment decorated with Oriental colouring and brightened with mirrors. He was more ready to engage in conversation than is usual with Native princes on a first interview. He spoke of the past without any awkwardness or reserve, and reminded us that he was the very man whom the British Government had placed upon the throne in 1799.

On our way back to Bangalore we visited Seringapatam, noting the encampment of the British besiegers, the points where the breaching batteries were mounted and the storming parties made good their ingress. We also stood upon the spot where the beaten Sultan, Tippoo, died fighting sword in hand. The city with its walls, gateways, streets, houses, were still standing, and some few inhabitants were there. But the houses were for the most part empty, the streets vacant, the stone pavement grass-grown. This desertion of a well-built city still standing, and, as it were, proclaiming its own overthrow, impressed the mind more than the desolation of a town marked by masses of ruins; and made me realize the force of such a title as "the city of the dead."

From Bangalore I journeyed to Bellary, and thence by Karnûl to Hyderabad. The aspect of the country is ordinarily arid, with brown grass, black soil, grey rocks, and trees at intervals far apart. At that season, however, the end of June, the periodical rains had begun to fall, and the whole surface of the earth was decked with verdure. Jolting tediously over stony roads in a van drawn by bullocks at the rate of two miles an hour, I reached Hyderabad, and was hospitably received by the Resident, Colonel Cuthbert Davidson. My colleague in the financial enquiry already mentioned, Colonel Browne, had also come from Madras, and we proceeded with our work.

We found that the British Government was maintaining the Subsidiary Force at a strength much beyond that specified in the treaty. The European part of the force was strong, and consequently very expensive; still it was essential for the safety of the Nizam and of Hyderabad after the dangers which had menaced the Deccan during the war of the mutinies. Without the presence of European troops revolution would have occurred, and might still occur, at Hyderabad; such an event would be injurious to the empire, and cause trouble to the neighbouring British territories. The British Government therefore in the discharge of its imperial duty must bear the cost of maintaining, in excess of its obligations by treaty, such additional force as might be required at Hyderabad for the public safety in central and southern India. We were, however, able to recommend some reduction in the Native part of the force, and suggest economy in several directions.

During this time I made the acquaintance of Salar Jang, already famous as the able Minister on whose shoulders the Nizam's government rested. I was destined to have close relations with him officially at a subsequent time, as will be explained in a future chapter.

Next after the Minister was the Muhammadan nobleman who bore the title of Amîr-i-Kabîr; he was then advanced in years and had the most picturesque and interesting aspect that I ever saw in any Native of India—the features being manly though delicate, their expression calm yet vigorous.

In company with Colonel Davidson I went to pay my respects to the Nizam. We were received with the self-possession and reserve so characteristic of His Highness, who though polite after the Oriental fashion, sat quite apart, serene and almost motionless, as if he were a statue to be gazed at with reverence.

Colonel Davidson invited me to a farewell party at Golconda on one of those surpassingly lovely days which occur during the intervals between the bursts of rain at that season in the Deccan. The entertainment took place at Golconda in tents pitched amidst palm-trees and granite rocks, near the base of a frowning citadel and almost in the shadow of the ruined mausolea of the kings belonging to an extinct dynasty.

I then left Hyderabad *en route* for those districts in the centre of India which were about to be formed into the Central Provinces and placed under a new administration. For I had been instructed to examine the various financial points affecting this arrangement, with a view to economy.

The summer rains had fallen abundantly, the rivers were swollen, in many places the floods were out, there were no railways and very few roads: so the journey, however interesting, promised to be difficult. Shortly after leaving Hyderabad in a van drawn by bullocks, I diverged from the main road in order to visit the ruins of Beder, formerly the seat of one of the independent Muhammadan kingdoms which were absorbed into the empire of the Great Mogul. The bastions of the fortress had a rich colouring subdued by age, being built of the red laterite of which the hills are there formed. The style of the mosque was grand and severe, quite different from the polished and graceful manner of the Mogul architects in later times. The chief object of beauty in the place was the college which had been founded for the encouragement of learning in relation to the Muhammadan faith. The exterior of the building had once been covered with exquisitely coloured glazing in floral devices, of which there was still much remaining to delight the spectator. This building is perhaps the finest of its kind surviving in India; and the visitor may well feel wonder on reflecting that so refined a structure should have been erected in times of war violence and rapine. It was necessary to be prompt in examining and sketching these remains, for the clouds were fast gathering in dark masses and soon the rain descended, flooding the country and rendering it difficult for me to regain the highroad.

Shortly afterwards the hills of Naldrûg came into view presenting features quite different geologically; instead of the red laterite there was the black trap-rock. A stream had been dammed up with massive masonry so as to form first a fine tank amidst the rocks, and then a sparkling cascade as the surplus water escaped over the dam. This place is situated near the border between the Nizam's dominions and the Bombay Presidency.

Then the railway was reached at Sholapur on the frontier of the Bombay Presidency, whence I proceeded smoothly and rapidly to Poona. The smoothness and rapidity afforded new sensations to one who had been plodding for several days and nights consecutively at the rate of 1½ mile an hour through wet black loam.

At Poona I met Sir George Clerk, who was then Governor of Bombay for the second time. After playing a distinguished, indeed a historic, part in the politics of the North-west frontier, he had some time before the war of the mutinies been appointed Governor of Bombay; since the war he had recently been re-appointed to the Governorship in succession to Lord Elphinstone. He was then occupied in making the arrangements consequent on the financial and administrative changes ordered by Lord Canning's Government, as already mentioned in the previous chapter VIII. Besides the many pacific measures necessarily required after a time of general trouble, he was reorganizing the police, completing the reduction of the Native forces, and preparing for the abolition of the Indian Navy. No man living possessed so great a knowledge as he of the Native princes, chiefs and upper classes generally. He thought much of their power for good or for evil, and felt doubt whether this powerful influence had always been so conciliated by the British that it might be ranged on the side of loyalty and public order. Yet in the hope that such conciliation would be found possible, he desired to see endeavours directed towards this object.

From Poona I journeyed to Ahmednagar, a famed Muhammadan fort, which the Mahrattas surrendered to the Duke of Wellington, then General Arthur Wellesley. Thence I re-entered the Nizam's dominions and proceeded to Aurangabad, another city of historic fame, its neighbourhood being replete with more notable associations than any other place in the central part of India. It is near the old fortress of Deogarh, afterwards styled Daolatabad, where the invading Muhammadans first compelled a Hindu sovereign in the Deccan to surrender, from which event there commenced a series of "woes unnumbered," conquests and re-conquests, defeats retrieved after desperate struggles, empires raised on the ruin of kingdoms and then in their turn subverted. The hill fortress consists of a magnificent mass of scarped trap-rock, rising black and precipitous out of a flat plain to the height of a thousand feet. There are many such hill forts in central and southern India, all very fine, but Daolatabad is the most impressive of them all. A few miles distant is that long-stretching hill-side which is literally honey-combed with the caves of the Ellora group. The rock-cut temples, so numerous in western India, become like many other wonderful things familiar after long experience, but to me on the first sight of them they were awe-inspiring. The light penetrated the cavernous recesses with uncertain ray, displaying in dim outline the sculptured columns, the carved figures, the chiselled features. The gloom was intensified by the colour of the stone, for the trap-rock, naturally grey, had become jet black from the all-pervading moisture at this time in the midst of the rainy season. From every crevice the water was exuding or trickling and broke the profound silence of the caves as it dropped with a pattering sound. Immediately opposite the entrance of one cave, the water tumbling over the ledge of a rock-wall formed a vista of gleaming cascades to the spectator as he stood inside the dark recess.

Close to these marvellous records of the dynasties subverted by his ancestors, the Mogul Emperor Aurangzêb reposes, the last of the emperors who could claim the title of Great Mogul. His tomb is of the simplest character, not covered by any stately dome or even humble canopy, but exposed, according to the most rigid Muhammadan doctrine, to the wind and rain of heaven. After all his crimes and disastrous wars, the old tiger almost bereft of teeth and claws retired to this neighbourhood, saying as he alighted that he had made his last march and fought his final campaign.

From Aurangabad my road lay through Berar, which province I traversed slowly in a palanquin in order to reach Nagpur. Some days were spent there by me conferring with the Commissioner, Colonel Edward King Elliot, regarding the finances of the Nagpur province. I then crossed the Satpura mountains, travelling still by palanquin to Jabalpur; the road which has since been scientifically bridged and metalled was then rugged and difficult. The summer rains were over, the bright autumn had set in, the foliage of the Satpura forest was gorgeous; but the landscape had a treacherous beauty, as it was the season when malarious exhalations rose from the moist ground under the sunny skies. Then crossing the Nerbadda, the most picturesque of all Indian rivers, I reached Jabalpur, where the finance of the Nerbadda territories was duly examined in concert with the local authorities.

Thence I proceeded to the Governor-General's camp which was at Lucknow, in order to explain to Lord Canning the result of my enquiries. He was then about to hold a ceremonial reception for the Native chiefs of Oudh. Such a reception has been aptly termed by an able writer "an Oriental edition of the Field of the Cloth of gold," with marquees, pavilions, lustrous displays of jewelry, "bellicose aspect of motley followers" and the "fanfare of martial music." Near at hand was the "Bailey" guard, a battered ruin attesting British heroism, and the shattered chamber where Henry Lawrence received his death-wound. The river Gumti flowed close by, with a bridge of boats across it, and from the opposite bank we saw an imposing line of tall though tasteless structures. These were erected by the Muhammadan sovereigns in their pride, but had recently become celebrated in relation to the defence whereby the small British garrison held their own against a vast body of besiegers. I then submitted to the Government of India my report on the financial results of combining the province of Nagpur and the Nerbadda districts into one jurisdiction to be called the Central Provinces, and returned to my post in attendance on the Finance Minister, Mr. Laing. Shortly afterwards Lord Canning issued the necessary orders regarding the revenues to be realized from the new administration of the Central Provinces and the expenses to be allowed for it, Colonel Elliot, already mentioned, being appointed to be the first Chief Commissioner.

Colonel Elliot organized the new administration, but was soon afterwards obliged by ill-health to proceed to Europe; and Lord Canning offered me the post of Chief Commissioner of the Central Provinces, which I accepted. My financial chief Mr. Laing was at that time intending to return to England immediately after the production of his second budget. When I consulted him as to the expediency of giving up finance for the present and returning to the administrative line he advised me to do so; with the characteristic remark that I had learnt the lesson to be gathered from the rough experience of financial difficulties and that the heroics of Indian finance were now over. In after years I had much reason to rejoice at having followed his wise advice.

CHAPTER XI.

(1862–1866.)

THE CENTRAL PROVINCES.

Beginning of Lord Elgin's administration—Chief Commissionership of the Central Provinces—Scenery of the Satpura mountains—Disbandment of the Nagpur force—The Mahrattas of Nagpur—Their landed tenures—Visit of Bishop Cotton—Education of the people—Scottish mission—Aboriginal races—Forests and forestry—Wild beasts—Roads and railways—Project for navigating the Godavery—Desolate country near the Mahanaddy river—General administration of the Provinces.

JAMES BRUCE, Earl of Elgin and Kincardine, arrived at Calcutta, as successor to Lord Canning, in January 1861. As the outgoing statesman met the in-coming Governor-General on the steps of the Government House, the somewhat saddening, though inevitable, contrast was presented. Canning looked pale wan toil-worn and grief-stricken; the brow and forehead had, indeed, their inseparable dignity; but the complexion had become sallow, losing those hues which had so often lighted up his aspect on occasions of state ceremony. Men attributed the change in his appearance to supreme efforts in winding up the affairs of his imperial stewardship, and to his recent bereavement by the decease of Lady Canning. None suspected that the real cause was the approach of death, which had begun already to cast its shadow over him before striking the last blow. Elgin, on the other hand, came up gaily, ruddy in face, massive and square in forehead, buoyant in manner, and stalwart in frame, though of short stature. Respecting him, also, we little thought that his remaining years were to be so very few. He landed on the shores of Bengal after having won a reputation in fields of action similar to those presented by Indian politics, and possessing antecedents peculiarly fitting him for the Vice-regal office in an eastern empire. He was highly esteemed by the Anglo-Indian community for the self-denying readiness with which he had diverted to India the European force destined to support him in China, postponing important schemes in the execution of which he was specially interested, and for the success of which he was answerable, in order to succour the Indian Government in its moment of need.

Five months afterwards, the Calcutta Gazette announced to all India, in befitting terms, that Canning had died in London after a brief illness. It soon became known that shortly after his arrival in England he had fallen sick unto death. When warned by the physicians of his impending end, he said, "What, so soon!" and then quietly turned his face towards the wall to die.

Entering upon his duties Lord Elgin remained for nearly a year at Calcutta, making his preliminary study of the strange country under his care, learning all that could be learnt at the capital in respect to those wide dominions, and discovering that this knowledge is but a small part of the great lesson which has sooner or later to be mastered. Being naturally a man of social tastes and cheery disposition, he became very popular at Calcutta. He wisely endeavoured to conciliate European opinion there, perhaps remembering how hostile it had once been towards his predecessor. He possessed a manner which pleased and attracted the leading classes at Calcutta, to a degree seldom attained by any Governor-General. When he was departing thence on his journey to the north, the European inhabitants gave a public entertainment in his honour at the Town Hall and testified their regard for him in the most emphatic manner.

I had the advantage of interviews with him several times, without doing much work under his immediate orders, because, as already mentioned in chapter X., I had been appointed by Lord Canning, shortly before his departure from India, to act as Chief Commissioner of the Central Provinces.

These Provinces were, as their name implies, situate in the

very middle of the Indian continent, and their boundaries touched upon all the three Presidencies of Bengal, Bombay and Madras. They were made up of several pieces; one piece being taken from the North-western Provinces, another from Bengal, while the third and most important consisted of the Nagpur province; the several portions being thus combined into an administrative whole by one of the latest acts of Lord Canning's Government. Geographically they comprised a part of the two parallel ranges of mountains, namely, those of the Vindhya and the Satpura, together with the intermediate valleys and submontane tracts adjacent to the hills. Consequently their scenery is more diversified than that of any Indian province south of the Himalayas. The mountain ranges stretch for hundreds of miles, and have in some places a height of four thousand feet above sea-level; their rocks are fine specimens of trap and sandstone formations; their sides are often clothed with forests; and they give birth to many rivers. It is at Amar Kantak, the culminating point of the Satpura range, that the river Nerbadda rises, in a verdant plateau environed by forests of Sâl (*Shorea robusta*), and for several months of the year deluged by ceaseless rainfall. There the dense fogs, clouds and mists of midsummer and autumn give place to the beauties of a bright and sunny, though cold, winter and a delicious spring. The Nerbadda, at first a tiny babbling brook, falls after a short distance in a flashing line of light over a black precipice of trap. Then, after meandering for many miles between the steep hillsides, it forces its passage through a mass of marble, before entering the plains near Jabalpur. The brilliant white walls, by which the river is here hemmed in, are the celebrated marble rocks, justly esteemed as forming the gem of all the natural beauties in India. In another part of the Satpura range, mighty sandstone rocks at Pachmari rise up abruptly to a height of 4500 feet (above sea-level) in the midst of the great trap formation. This place has been made a sanitarium and summer resort for Europeans. The precipices, magnificently scarped and coloured with all the tints of red, afford a grand contrast to the sombre hues of the prevailing trap. The cavernous fissures, descending to a seemingly unfathomable depth in the bowels of the mountain, add features of wonder to the glories of the landscape. As is usual with spots of great beauty in Hindu lands, Pachmari has sacred shrines whither pilgrims used to resort in vast numbers. On one occasion, when many thousands were thus huddled together in a rude encampment on the mountain summit, the hapless multitude was seized with deadly cholera. Then ensued a miserable scene, as the shrine was crowded with people dead or dying, and the fugitives rushed and stumbled in wild terror down the precipitous paths of the mountain.

The forests of the Satpura range though displaying rich verdure, yet lack the variety imparted by the coniferæ, cedars firs or cypresses, to the Himalayan forests. These Satpura forests, however, have the teak, the sâl, and several species of the terminalia, in great abundance. In some places they possess the finest bamboos I ever saw, clustering in splendid clumps 70 to 80 feet in height, and gracefully overhanging the pellucid water in which their images are reflected. These hills in their uplands and upper valleys comprise large areas of luscious and succulent pasturage, into which herds of cattle are driven from distant plains during the early spring. The animals, having worked hard on scanty fare during the winter months of brisk traffic, know instinctively when the season approaches for their being released to graze in the hills. Sometimes they will rush off, without any guidance from their drivers, in mad excitement towards those Elysian fields.

Immediately after joining the Chief Commissionership, I was required to undertake the reorganization of the police on the lines laid down by the Police Commission as already explained in chapter VIII. This comprised the disbandment of the Nagpur Irregular Force, which had been raised from among the remains of the Mahratta army after the annexation of the province in Lord Dalhousie's time, and was now to be amalgamated with the police. Gratuities and pensions on retirement, or employment in the new police as an alternative, were offered to the men who had remained faithful throughout the dangers of 1857. These men liked their military service and resented disbandment; the moment was a trying one, and the spirit of mutiny arose among them. Despite the terrible example set by the recent suppression of the great mutiny, they seemed to imagine that upon their shewing signs of resistance, the Government would desist from discharging them. It became necessary to overawe them by a slight display of force with regular troops, and the disbandment then proceeded quietly.

Several portions of the Central Provinces had been for many years under British rule; one important portion, however, the Nagpur territory, had been annexed only a few years previously, and shewed many traces, not yet obliterated, of the preceding Native rule.

Mahratta rule in Nagpur differed in several respects from the Mahratta sway in the Deccan, which was the original home and the proper country of Mahratta nationality. There the State assigned some villages or tracts to chiefs who collected the land revenue in place of the Government; in all other tracts the State collected its land-revenue directly from the yeomanry and peasantry without the intervention of any farmer or middleman. There were few or no landlords, and peasant proprietorship was an essential characteristic of Mahratta rule. In fact the State and the people were homogeneous, all owning the same nationality.

In the Nagpur territory the Mahrattas were invaders and conquerors; the population was of a different race, made up of aboriginal tribes, with which Rajputs and other of the upper Hindu castes had commingled during many previous generations. There the Mahratta State instead of collecting the land-revenue directly from the villagers as peasant proprietors, farmed it out to Mahrattas or Muhammadans. These farmers gradually acquired the position of landlords, and during three generations had firmly fixed their hold upon the villages. They collected rents from the peasantry out of which was paid the land-revenue. The peasants became accustomed to paying rent to the landlord instead of revenue to the State, and most, though not all, of them lost any sense of peasant proprietorship which they may have ever had. These Mahratta landlords were not generally harsh or oppressive; and any evil tendencies they may have had were repressed when the State fell for several years under British management during the minority of the Prince. The manager at that time was Sir Richard Jenkins, who gained great distinction in frustrating an attempted revolution that ended with the fight at Sitabaldi; and whose fame for just and considerate administration was still remembered by the people.

At Nagpur the remains of the Mahratta court and camp were still to be seen. The widows of the late Raja were there, also the young man who had been adopted, not by the ruler but by the family after his death, and whose succession to the throne was not allowed by the British Government, as explained in chapter VI. The family and relations of the late ruler belonged to the Bhonslas, one of the highest of the Mahratta clans. They were stout manly-looking men, and good riders; but they had externally none of those high-born characteristics commonly found in the princely families of India. The most useful man of this family was Nana Ahirao, the father of the youth whom the Raja's widow had adopted. Being an active horseman he had acquired much knowledge of the country and people, and he loyally placed his unpaid services at the disposal of the British authorities. As a rule refinement of aspect and nobility of mien are not observable in the chiefs of pure Mahratta blood, who invariably belong to the humble castes. The members of the Mahratta nationality, whose imposing aspect is so well known, are not real Mahrattas, but are Mahratta Brahmins; the Peshwas or hereditary heads of the Mahratta federation belonged to the Brahmin caste. There were then but few Mahratta Brahmins at Nagpur, and they followed the money-lending profession. The largest money-lender there, however, was a Marwari from Marwar in Rajputana. This was an instance of the manner in which the enterprising Marwaris spread throughout India, and form that money-lending class which, notwithstanding its many merits, has often drawn down odium upon itself. There was also at Nagpur the Gond Raja, the lineal descendant of the ancient kings of the aboriginal tribe of Gonds in the Satpura mountains. He was flat-faced, with the semi-Tartar look characteristic of several among the aboriginal races. In religion he was a zealous Muhammadan, his ancestors having been by force or influence converted to the faith of Islam by the Mogul emperors. His dynasty had been supplanted by the Mahrattas, and he was then a state pensioner.

The city of Nagpur was ill-built and uninteresting, but in it was situate the palace, having a stately hall of audience supported by noble pillars which consisted of the trunks of teak trees finely carved and polished, the roof and galleries being also of the same wood. While this palace was occupied by the Bhonsla family, an accidental fire broke out, and the woodwork—being saturated with the oil which had been during so many years spread over and rubbed into it for ornament—burned like tinder. Thus unluckily perished one of the finest chambers in India, and the most characteristic structure ever raised by Mahratta hands. In the environs of the city were orange gardens, of which the black soil produced trees with matchless fruit; since the opening of the railway these oranges are exported to distant parts of India. A square mass of black-coloured trap rock formed the natural fortress of Sitabaldi overlooking the city. In the neighbourhood were several tanks of great dimensions, wherefrom water was conducted by massive pipes of stone masonry with siphons; these works constituted creditable monuments of Mahratta skill.

The Mahratta nobles were pleasant companions on long rides and in all field sports; they were especially fond of the sport which is to be had with the hunting cheeta; and we used to accompany them occasionally. In the spring season, when the green wheat crops were beginning to stand high, we would watch the unsuspecting herd of deer feeding, as the cheeta sprang upon them. Often we used to attend the Mahratta festivals when in summer-time the plough bullocks were gaily caparisoned, their flanks smeared with pigments and their horns decorated with tinsel; or when in autumn the balconies were illuminated and the tanks lit up with lamps arranged in rows on the water's edge.

The settlement of the land-revenue was the first matter claiming attention. Surveys of all the villages, field by field, similar to those already described in chapters IV. and V., and comprising topographical details, had been for some time in progress. The revenue was assessed for long terms of twenty to thirty years in the same manner as in northern India, but relatively at somewhat lighter rates; nowhere in India were the landholders more contented with the assessment than here. Questions indeed arose as to whether the assessment was not being made too light, but it was maintained intact, on being seen to operate favourably in regard to popular contentment. The country was blessed with unfailing seasons, receiving the early and latter rains in abundance. The neighbouring Satpura mountains attracted and condensed the masses of vapour coursing over the Deccan. Thus, the districts at their base were among the very few Indian tracts which enjoyed immunity from drought and famine.

After some discussion the tenure, already described as having been established by the Mahrattas, was recognized and confirmed by this settlement. It differed from what was probably the original tenure of these Provinces, and certainly the existing tenure in neighbouring Mahratta territories. As just explained, the peasant proprietors had been here reduced from their proprietary status by the Mahrattas, and landlords had been placed in all the villages. But the landlords had been established for some generations, and the peasantry did not for the most part seek for or expect a position higher than that of tenants. The tenure had thus become in essentials Zemindari as in Bengal. Here, however, the estates, instead of being as in Bengal large, were generally small, and so the tenures might be described as petty Zemindari. It was usual for the landlord to keep a few fields under his own management, a sort of home farm near the dwelling-places, and to leave in the hands of tenants the remaining fields of the village. Of the landlords many resided on their estates, while some lived apart, visiting their villages from time to time; a few only were absentees altogether.

Under these arrangements the question of tenant-right became very important, especially as no such right had, in these districts, been recognized under Mahratta rule. Not indeed that the tenantry had been oppressed, because there were hardly hands enough to cultivate the lands in a fertile and sparsely peopled country, and thus a sort of competition arose among landlords for tenants. Now, however, that proprietary right, heritable, transferable, marketable, was being conferred upon the landlords great and small, or rather recognized formally as belonging to them, it was consonant with Indian practice that tenant-right should be in the same degree recognized and protected. In this matter the same principles as those already described in chapters IV. and V. were adopted. All tenants, who had been for some time in occupation of their fields, were registered as being entitled to have their rents judicially fixed and to be free from liability to ejectment so long as they paid that rent. Some classes of tenants were after special enquiry placed in the position of inferior proprietors. These provisions on behalf of tenant-right were far advanced during the time when I was Chief Commissioner. They were taken up again by my successor, Mr. (afterwards Sir George) Campbell, and were rendered still more favourable to the tenantry.

There was always much intercommunication between the peasantry of Nagpur and their neighbours of Berar in the Nizam's dominions. While Nagpur, under the management of Sir Richard Jenkins, was comparatively well administered, Berar was harassed by misrule under the Nizam, so Berar cultivators migrated largely into Nagpur. Now, however, Berar had come under British administration also, and was being settled under conditions more favourable to the peasantry even than those in Nagpur, for in effect the occupants were being made peasant proprietors as no landlord class was found in existence. Then Nagpur cultivators returned to their old fields in Berar, with that tenacious regard for ancestral lands which so often characterizes an Indian peasantry. They found also much virgin soil, of uncommon fertility, to be had under secure and satisfactory tenures. This turn in the tide of migration back towards Berar affected for a time the prosperity of Nagpur.

At this time the American Civil War caused an extraordinary demand for the cotton of these Provinces. This staple was produced both in the valley of the Nerbadda and the plains of Nagpur. The stimulus, thereby afforded to trade and enterprise generally, raised the prices of all agricultural produce. This movement filled the pockets of all the landed classes, and raised the wages of labour both skilled and unskilled, while it distressed all those classes who were living on fixed incomes. The numerous persons drawing small pensions, the relics of Mahratta rule, were really straitened for the necessaries of life, and used to complain that in the midst of plenty and prosperity, food was being sold at famine prices. This difficulty became mitigated when prices fell after the slackening of demand in consequence of the restoration of peace within the United States and the cessation of the commercial disturbances caused by the war.

While food grains were dear in most districts, an extraordinary cheapness prevailed in the eastern region called Chatisgarh. There a populous and fertile plain, blessed with an unfailing rainfall, was surrounded by hills and forests, whence the surplus produce could not find an outlet. Formerly the local markets were glutted with grain in excess of the local consumption. Our hope was to open out communications by which this grain might be conveyed to many places where it was sorely needed.

In a new province like that of Nagpur the building of churches was one of those matters which had to be undertaken *ab initio.* Our first care was to finish the new church at Nagpur itself, in time for it to be consecrated when the Bishop should arrive. Dr. George Cotton, the Bishop of Calcutta, was then on his tour of visitation, and his episcopal inspection was awaited with much pleasurable interest. Nowhere do the ordinances of religion exercise a more decisive effect upon the mind, than in a remote land amidst alien circumstances. Besides the comparatively large church at Nagpur, small chapels were in course of erection at the civil stations in the interior of the province where a few Europeans had been gathered together, and Christian cemeteries were being enclosed in suitable places. The founding of schools was in progress for the children of middle-class Europeans and East Indians who were scattered over the district; one of these was called the Bishop's School in memory of this visitation. Dr. Cotton's presence awakened recollection of the days when I sat under him, as he was one of the Masters at Rugby. He left a happy impression upon the minds of the Christian community of Nagpur, and much grief was felt by them when, a few months afterwards, the intelligence was received of his sudden and accidental death.

One of the matters claiming early attention was education; accordingly a Director of Public Instruction was appointed for the whole country. Captain (now Colonel) Dods, an accomplished officer of the Bombay service, was chosen for this post, because we desired to introduce some new blood into the Provinces by employing men from western India. North of the Satpura mountains, the vernacular taught in the schools was the same as that of the North-western Provinces, and the upper students worked towards the standard prescribed by the Calcutta University. South of the Satpura mountains, the Mahratta language was for the most part used, and the upper students aimed at fulfilling the requirements of the Bombay University.

Besides the ordinary machinery of education, two large exhibitions of art and industry were organized, one at Nagpur the other at Jabalpur. To these great displays the Natives of all classes high and humble flocked in tens of thousands. Before their wondering gaze were shewn not only the products from distant parts of their own country, but also specimens of the manufactures in western lands. The ornamental work from Europe would, it was fondly, perhaps vainly, supposed, inform their minds with fresh ideas of the Beautiful, while the machinery and implements might give them an impression of powers and forces unknown before, and so fill them with reflections regarding the Useful. The objects which we thus set before ourselves were but imperfectly realized. The exhibitions were wonders for a short time only, though it may be hoped that some educational result was produced by all the labour which we bestowed on their preparation. One effect at least they had, namely this, that the civil officers and the merchants gained a far more accurate knowledge than they would otherwise have possessed regarding the resources and manufactures of these remote provinces, and thus some stimulus was given to trade.

At Nagpur the best schools then existing belonged to the mission established many years previously by the Free Church of Scotland, under the leadership of the Reverend Stephen Hislop. Indeed the mission establishment had been for many years a little focus of enlightenment in an isolated and uncivilized part of the empire. Hislop was among the most gifted and accomplished missionaries whom this generation has seen in India. Besides having much ability for organization and education generally, for philology and antiquarian research, he had a taste and aptitude for physical science—especially botany and geology. His varied talents were all brought to bear on the work of his sacred profession as an evangelist. He was a good teacher and preacher in the Mahratta language, and had much knowledge of Hindu philosophy. He also perceived that the aboriginal tribes formed a not inconsiderable part of the population, and were as yet free from any preconceived notions, having minds quite open to the reception of Christianity, unless, owing to tardiness in missionary work on the part of the Christian Church, they should fall under the proselytizing influences of Hinduism. He therefore specially studied the unwritten languages or dialects of these aboriginal tribes, collecting carefully their ballads legends proverbs, and gathering information of much value and originality. He acquired an insight into the geology and botany of the province, as affecting the soil products and climate. He had also a predilection for observing the prehistoric remains scattered about the country, and pertaining to the so-called Scythian era before the coming of the Hindus to India. It was this zeal for research that led to his sudden and accidental death. He was staying with me in camp near Nagpur at the beginning of autumn, a season which is cool after the rains and still showery. We had been during the day excavating some of these Scythian remains. In the evening I rode back to my encampment, leaving him to follow on horseback after arranging the curiosities which had been exhumed and examining a village school. About nightfall I was shocked at seeing his horse gallop into camp riderless, with a wet saddle which had evidently passed through water. This directed our instant search by torchlight to a neighbouring streamlet which had just been flushed by a shower of rain; and there his body was found, life being extinct. He had evidently been drowned in trying to cross the flood. This most lamentable accident deprived Nagpur of a man who could ill be spared, who while still in his prime had become a shining light, a power for good, and who, had he lived, would have become, under Providence, an instrument of incalculable benefit to the people. It is sad to think what holy aspirations, what lofty hopes, what bright promises, were buried in his grave.

The Gonds, as a tribe, deserve and will repay attentive care. Originally leading an arboreal life, they had their home in the forests of the Satpura mountains. They felled trees for their scanty clearances, and raised crops with the minimum of cultivation upon bits of soil here and there among the valleys and uplands. Battling with wild beasts, they became first skilled marksmen or sturdy warriors with the spear and the bow, and organized themselves under chiefs. Emboldened by the success of their organization, they issued forth to the lowlands which they could overlook from their mountains, to the valley of the Nerbadda and the plains of Nagpur. Their worship was primitive, while these lowlands were occupied by a population of the Hindu faith. They thus established a considerable dominion, divided into at least three, perhaps four, principalities. They confined themselves mainly to fighting or collecting revenue, and settled but little as dwellers in the plains over which they held sway. They borrowed their civilization from their conquered subjects, and on a lesser scale the history was repeated of "Grecia capta ferum victorem cepit." It is probable that their dominion was of some size, extending over three millions of souls, though from the magnitude of their ruined forts and palaces the enquirer would infer that their jurisdiction must have been of still larger extent. Their forts were built either in commanding situations near the plains, or else right in the heart of the hills. Their architecture had some characteristics of its own, but was mainly an imitation of the Hindu Rajput style, the Mahrattas not having then risen to fame. In building their palaces they equalled the most advanced Hindus, and surpassed any Hindu structures to be found within hundreds of miles. One of their ruined palaces near Mandla in the upper valley of the Nerbadda may indeed be placed in the first rank among the remains of that class in India. As their rule became established in the champaign country of Nagpur, they turned their minds to more useful things, and began to construct works of irrigation, selecting open valleys whence the drainage escaped by narrow gorges—the valley being like a bottle of which the neck was formed by the gorge. They stopped up the gorges by dams of massive masonry, the valleys then filling with water and becoming reservoirs, some five some ten some even twenty miles in circumference, worthy to be called artificial lakes. They must have employed Hindu builders, but still they commanded or controlled the operations, and may claim credit for the results. Subsequently they became vassals of the Muhammadan empire as it spread over central India, and some of their chiefs adopted the Muhammadan faith. But their tribesmen in the mass adhered to the primitive worship, though evincing a tendency to adopt Hindu ideas and manners, and engraft some Hindu tenets upon their rude religion. They succumbed to the rising tide of Mahratta aggression about the middle of the eighteenth century, and thus lost all hold upon the plains. As they ceased to draw revenue from the champaign territory their forts and palaces fell into decay and ruin, though their works of irrigation remained for the benefit of succeeding generations. They then remained among their Native hills and forests, and are still to be seen in considerable numbers, though widely scattered.

Their national vice is intemperance, to which the humid and chilly climate of their hills offers special temptations. It was found that the then existing system of British excise on spirituous liquors, though designed to tax the liquor and so to check intemperance, was really confirming them in this evil habit. The system was therefore revised so that the tax might operate as an obstacle to their drinking in excess, by rendering liquor dear and scarce for them. Some improvement was wrought in their habits; but drunkenness on social occasions, marriages, festivals, and the like, continued to be the bane of their life. Here as elsewhere, most of the crimes and offences among brave, sturdy and truth-telling tribes were directly traceable to drink.

The forests, already mentioned, were very extensive and well stocked with timber trees; being comparatively remote from the centres of Mahratta rule, and from British public works, they had for the most part escaped destruction. At this time the Government had begun to act with some degree of vigour and resolution, on the principle that forests ought to be preserved as forming a part of the national resources. A department of forest conservancy was constituted for the Central Provinces in common with all other provinces of the empire. The first Conservator was Captain (now Colonel) Pearson, who has recently been employed in the supervision of the English students at the French school of forestry at Nancy. He was succeeded by Captain Forsyth, the author of a charming and graphic volume entitled 'The Highlands of Central India.' These officers and their European associates in the work, loved the forest for the sake of its diversified vegetation and spreading trees, with an affection transcending even official zeal. For them the wildness the perennial novelty and the unfailing freshness of camp life amidst the woods and dells, had a peculiar attraction.

This charm sustained moral resolution and helped to support even physical strength under the depression arising from that malarious fever which lurks in the loveliest verdure, and from which no European forester escapes. We then had the advantage of a visit from Dr. Dietrich Brandis, already mentioned in the last chapter as having been Conservator in British Burma. He had become Inspector-General of Forests to the Government of India, and it devolved upon him to travel about and see whether the Government or Administration in each province was duly giving effect to the system of forestry as prescribed for the empire at large.

The chief enemies of the forester were the fires, partly accidental but chiefly intentional. The system whereby the hill people and aboriginal tribes burn the forest for the sake of its fertilizing ashes, in order to save themselves the trouble of tillage, is but too well known in many parts of India. Nowhere was this pernicious practice more rife than in these Provinces, for nowhere were the aborigines more numerous. We could not interdict it altogether, for the inhabitants partly lived by its means; but we gradually checked it, and as an alternative, some arable lands and even loans of money were granted to the people in order that they might support themselves by rational methods of cultivation.

In the extensive forests there dwelt numbers of wild animals, of which some were timid and harmless such as the deer, while others were fierce and carnivorous such as the tiger. The deer lived on the vegetation of the forest and the tiger lived upon the deer. The tiger and his kindred panther and leopard, however, found the deer difficult to catch, and were doubtless glad to have another source of food supply, namely, the cattle and other animals domesticated by man. The peculiarity of the country was this, that tracts well populated, highly cultivated, and abounding in cattle, were interspersed among forests which furnished a home to the wild beasts. Therefore at some seasons of the year the tiger had to subsist on deer scantily and precariously; at other seasons he fed more easily and luxuriously on the cattle in the fields and near the homesteads. He thus not only laid a heavy tax on the property of the village folk, but also inspired them with fear and anxiety for their lives. Thus when such and such a village was infested by a plague of tigers, its dwellings would gradually become deserted and its fields left fallow unless the plague could be stayed. The policy of the Government provided wisely that the people should be without arms altogether or very slightly armed. Thus the villagers had but little means of resisting their feline enemy, and very properly looked to the British sportsman, or still more to the Government, to rid them of the pest. With so many inducements offered in this way, the sporting tastes of the resident English were much cultivated; and almost every military officer, magistrate, revenue collector, or other official, took part in field sports tending to the destruction of wild animals. Among them were several men whose names will be commemorated by the chroniclers of sport in the East. The destruction thus effected, however, would not alone have sufficed, and the Government offered rewards graduated on a scale proportionable to the mischief of which each kind of animal was considered to be capable, so much for the destruction of a tiger, so much for that of a leopard, so much for that of a wolf, and so on. Some of these animals occasionally preyed upon man, and a "man-eater" soon acquired an infamy which rendered his destruction necessary at the earliest possible moment—so a greatly enhanced reward was set upon his head by the Government schedule of rewards. "Man-eaters" were as a rule intensely cunning and stealthy, but sometimes they shewed audacity. For instance, one of them dashed into a marriage procession and carried off his victim. A servant of mine was seized on the line of march; and again, a man was killed thus in my encampment.

Native huntsmen called "Shikaris" had always existed in these Provinces; and this useful class set themselves more systematically than ever to their business, deriving good wages from it in the shape of rewards for animals killed. So large was the number shewn in the returns of the animals thus destroyed, that once the Government of

India expressed a hope that due precautions were taken for attestation. The answer was that in every instance the carcase or the head had been produced before a responsible authority. Besides the professional huntsmen many individual villagers having obtained shooting licences from the magistrate, and sometimes even the firearms, took to tiger-killing, not so much from the love of sport, as from the hope of reward. The expense incurred by Government for rewards was considerable, but was actually well laid out; indeed without it, the prosperity of some parts of the country could hardly have been maintained.

Among our hills a herd of wild elephants was roaming; these were the descendants of some elephants which had escaped from the custody of the Commissariat. Deeming these animals to be too valuable for ordinary sport, we employed a trained establishment for their capture. They used to be surrounded by fences gradually narrowing to a point towards which they were driven by the beaters; when thus hemmed in they would be secured after a stout struggle.

In provinces wherein the most highly cultivated tracts were separated from each other by intervening mountains, and whereof the whole area was isolated by long distances from the seaports and other centres of trade, roads and communications became of the utmost importance. Rich districts were divided from each other by intervening ranges of hills, and these ranges had to be penetrated in every direction. The trunk line between Nagpur and Jabalpur, which crossed the dorsal ridge of the continent, is one of the many monuments of British engineering. In many places lesser works were made to suffice; the object being to smooth the roughest parts of the route so as to make them passable for wheeled traffic. The local carts were curiously adapted for a rugged track, as their wheels consisted of stone disks, which could not be broken by even the most violent jolting. These carts would bear severe inequalities in the track, and were only stopped by such irregularity in the ground as might be called precipitous. Thus by a little engineering in a desperately steep place here and there, we were often able to throw open whole lines of communication to the carts. As the roads improved from year to year, so carts of civilized build, with wheels having spokes tires and the like, came into use, and the stone disks went out of fashion.

Meanwhile much of the traffic was carried by pack-bullocks in thousands belonging to a gipsy tribe, commonly called Brinjaras. These people were once common throughout the empire, but their occupation has passed away with the introduction of British roads or railways, and they have "marched into darkness," disappearing as those people always do disappear whose functions in the world have ceased. Their habits were always nomadic, sometimes respectable and at other times predatory. Though destitute of habitations, they carried their "lares and penates" with them in rude but substantial comfort. It was most amusing to watch their encampments in the heart of the mountains, with rocks and forests rising around. A compact though extensive square was formed, the inner compartment or centre being filled with women, children, and the most valuable goods; next the outer line consisted of the cattle and bulky baggage, then outside of all a number of men stayed keeping watch against wild beasts and robbers. The watch-fires would after sun-down lighten the scene with ruddy glare, breaking through the thick misty air of the forest. Sometimes these people looking upon us as the emissaries of a new civilization would enquire what was to become of them and their business when the roads and railways took up all the traffic. We could only warn them against what they probably thought the most obvious alternative, namely, plundering, and suggest that they must perforce seek the employment which was so abundantly offering itself in the public works and elsewhere; they did not, however, seem to relish the inevitable.

As the Provinces lay further inland than any other portion of the empire, their distance from the coast was the greatest drawback to their progress. Therefore the completion of the railways then in progress was the primary desideratum. At this time there were no railways open, but shortly afterwards the line from Allahabad to Bombay was completed which ran right through the upper portion of the Provinces, and the line was opened from Bombay to Nagpur which afforded communication by rail to the lower portion. In some districts the railway passed near the base of the Satpura range, and after heavy rain the floods would descend with terrific force and often destroy the viaducts. It was said that during a wild night masonry piers would be snapped asunder as if they had been sticks of sealing-wax. The engineers had to gain experience and modify the designs, making greater allowance for the velocity and volume of the waters. The repairing of damage, restoration of broken bridges, modification of designs, and other difficulties incidental to work of a novel character in a strange country, caused considerable delay. Still the railway authorities and the engineers evinced a perseverance worthy of the great cause in hand. Thus at length the lines were completed, not in a temporary style, but after a durable manner fitted to permanently withstand the floods.

As the line was opened to each important place such as Nagpur and Jabalpur, the occasion used to be celebrated with festivities in which real joy mingled with the convivialities. For the local residents rejoiced at being able to fly away for recreation or in quest of health when sick, the engineers were light-hearted at the remembrance of anxieties dissipated and toils ended, the administrators were exhilarated by the thought of material resources augmented and opportunities enlarged.

There was an additional railway project which we endeavoured to promote, namely, that for the line which should run from Nagpur due east towards Calcutta, and should "tap," as the phrase ran, the surplus produce of the Chatisgarh region already described, which was overstocked with grain. After a protracted discussion, this project was included in the system of State railways, and was thus in due course undertaken.

In those days we were anxious to utilize for purposes of communication the two great rivers, the Godavery and the Mahanaddy, which run from these Provinces to the eastern coast, that is, to the Bay of Bengal. As already mentioned in chapter X., I had, while at Madras, heard much on this subject from Sir Arthur Cotton.

The Godavery was generally navigable except at three points where it crossed formations of rock. Obstruction to navigation was caused by the rocks, which were therefore called barriers. The intention was by engineering operations to remove these barriers, and so enable boats to pass up and down for hundreds of miles. Operations were actually begun on the first of the three barriers, and much progress was made towards the removal of the rocky obstacles. But subsequently, in Lord Mayo's time, the work was stopped, because the outlay was thought too great in proportion to any result in boat traffic which might be reasonably anticipated. The opening of the railways to the west coast diverted the interest which had been felt in communications with the east coast, and so an end was put to this remarkable project, originated by Sir Arthur Cotton, and carried on by one among the best men of his school, Colonel Haig of the Madras Engineers. I protested, though in vain, against the stoppage of this project, as the outlay already incurred was rendered nearly valueless, because but little use could be made of the incomplete works. If the entire scheme for all the barriers was found too expensive, still the first and second barriers might at least be opened at a moderate cost in addition to the sums already spent, and this with great advantage to the surrounding country.

Had the Godavery project succeeded, we intended to recommend a similar scheme for the Mahanaddy, of which the circumstances are similar, that is to say, a fine river navigable for the most part, but obstructed at certain points by rocky barriers.

Such schemes, if successfully executed, would develop and civilize extensive regions which have a fine soil with an abundance of natural resources, and which, though scantily inhabited now, would become capable of sustaining a large population hereafter. These regions are kept in a wild and semi-barbarous state by their segregation and seclusion. Being to a large extent abandoned to savagery, they are overgrown with tangled brushwood as well as valuable forest. Malaria and fever are rife, and the population is thus prevented from increasing. This insalubrity would gradually disappear if, while the useful forests were preserved, the jungle were to be cleared for cultivation. The condition of the country would be entirely altered were the projects relating to the Godavery and Mahanaddy duly executed. But these beneficent schemes must be considered in reference to capital outlay and prospective returns. Since those days, as the empire has advanced in prosperity, the power of the Government has naturally been directed towards regions which, though improvable, are already populous and will rapidly repay improvement. This is so far well; still it is to be remembered that here exists a territory which is now partially destitute of human habitation, but which has inherent and spontaneous resources. This natural wealth may be indefinitely developed by such public works as can be constructed by Government, but by Government only.

In order to investigate these projects, I voyaged up and down these rivers, taking due precautions against malaria, though with all our care it was impossible to avoid fever. The scenery of the great zone of jungle is in itself fine, but becomes monotonous and depressing from its unvarying extent. The spirits of the traveller gradually sink when he moves along day by day and sees nothing from sunrise to sunset but forest, scrub, bushes, or thick underwood, covering hill and dale. The ascent of a hill scarcely affords a prospect, for the view is obstructed by foliage or branches. The rocks produce some variety, but they, too, assume a melancholy aspect. The clusters of huts and the rice plots seem like forlorn oases in the wilderness. Sometimes indeed a wide clearance appears where the hill people have been preparing the ground for seed-time after their barbarous fashion by setting fire to the vegetation. This variety, however, affords something the very reverse of relief; for to the eye of an administrator the blackened trunks, charred branches, shrivelled leaves, and ground strewed wastefully with the ashes of valuable wood—make up a horrid spectacle. He is, however, rudely awakened from reflections of this nature by the fact that the forest is still on fire. Riding on he finds the smoke becoming thicker and thicker, and the crackling louder than before, until, right and left, he perceives the woods to be ablaze. Once during very hot weather we were marching at night, and our way was for many miles lighted fitfully by the burning forest, the flames spreading as they listed among the dry grass and curling idly among the vegetation.

A real variety to the scene was afforded whenever the great river came in sight, for then the still waters caught the golden colours of the eastern sky, the rapids made a merry noise as they hurried along, the effect of the rocks was doubled by the reflections, and teak trees, laden with their yellow blossoms, hung over the margin of the stream. We were one day on horseback, another day in boats; and it was from the midstream that the best views presented themselves. When the river was winding through mountain gorges, the hillsides widely parted would allow the water to broaden itself into a small lake; the voyager issuing from it by the river passage, would turn a corner and find himself in a fresh lake, whence he might enter another and yet another—each lake differing from its neighbour. Certainly, both the Godavery and the Mahanaddy for many miles of their respective courses have what, according to the highest standard of judgment, would be considered fine river-scenery.

As year after year glided by, while we were all engaged in welding the administration of these diverse territories into a homogeneous whole, the European officers, drawn as they were from distant parts of the empire, were by degrees formed into a school of their own for the Central Provinces. They thus took a pride in their work, believing in the future of the country and people under their charge. The judicial administration had in the first instance the great advantage of being supervised by Mr. (now Sir John) Strachey, who had already afforded proofs of the high capacity which he has subsequently evinced. Much valuable support was received from John Scarlett Campbell (brother of Sir George Campbell), Mr., now Sir Robert,

Egerton, who afterwards became Lieutenant-Governor of the Panjab, and Mr. (now Sir Alfred) Lyall. The Secretaries rendered most valuable aid; they were first Colonel Hector Mackenzie, who possessed administrative experience gained in the Panjab, and then Mr. Charles Bernard (a nephew of John Lawrence), who has subsequently acted as Chief Commissioner in British Burma and Assam.

Having served for four years in the Central Provinces, and endeavoured to bring them up to the high-water mark, so to speak, of Indian administration by adapting, as much as possible, the experience of the more advanced and civilized parts of the empire, I was appointed Resident at Hyderabad. The administration of these Provinces afterwards fell into the very competent hands of Mr. John Henry Morris, who had for some time supervised the operations of the land revenue settlement. In our younger days he and I served together in the settlement department of the Panjab and were brought up in the same official school. He has for several years retained his important charge, and perfected the administration gradually and steadily, so that at the present time there is probably no part of the empire better managed than the Provinces under his care.

CHAPTER XII.

(1862–1866.)

SIR BARTLE FRERE AND WESTERN INDIA.

Beginning of Sir Bartle Frere's Government—Principal members of the European community of Bombay—Of the Native community—Public works—Railways—Native chiefs—Education—Legislative Council—Land revenue settlement—Effect on Bombay of the American civil war—Unwise speculation—Commercial failure—Native munificence—Public buildings in Bombay—Instruction in Art—Departure of Sir Bartle Frere—Summary of his public character.

THE Central Provinces, though forming an intermediate space between the three Presidencies of Bengal Madras and Bombay, are more closely connected with the Bombay Presidency than with any other. Much of their external trade is with Bombay and its dependencies; many of their exports are despatched to Bombay for shipment to foreign countries; and through Bombay they receive the imports of European goods which are sent in return. In some of their districts, too, the Mahratta language of Western India is current. During 1864 and 1865 the railway from Bombay to Nagpur, the capital of the Central Provinces, was being constructed; Mahratta officials were being selected in Bombay for service in the territory around Nagpur; comparisons were being instituted between the landed settlements in progress in the Bombay Presidency and in the Nagpur districts. These and other affairs caused me to visit Bombay several times, and renew my familiar intercourse with Sir Bartle Frere, who had been recently appointed Governor of Bombay.

Sir Bartle Frere assumed the Governorship of Bombay with extraordinary advantages, such as hardly any other Governor has possessed during this century. As a young man he had entered the Bombay Civil Service, and thoroughly served an apprenticeship in the Mahratta districts, which constitute the most important divisions of the Bombay Presidency. When British Resident at the Court of Sattara, he had become versed in the ways of the Native States which form one of the most interesting parts of western India. He had been for several years Private Secretary to Sir George Arthur when Governor of Bombay. He was appointed by Lord Falkland, the then Governor, to be Commissioner in the province of Sind. As Commissioner he set his mark upon that province, applied its resources with remarkable zeal and energy to help in suppressing disturbance in northern India during 1857, and bequeathed to his successors a heritage of moral material and administrative progress, when he was transferred to Calcutta as a member of the Governor-General's Council in 1858. The community erected in his memory a spacious hall and library at Karachi, the capital of Sind. His past career therefore afforded a promise that he would prove one of the best Governors that Bombay ever had, which promise he actually fulfilled in many essential respects.

On the occasion of my first visit to him the journey from Nagpur caused me to ascend the Bhore Ghat railway incline, whereby the line rises from the coast region of Bombay to the Deccan uplands, two thousand feet above sea-level. The rainy season was at its height, and the greatest rainfall occurs on the crest of the Western Ghat range. When we neared the foot of the mountains the weather was hot and bright, the sunshine bursting through masses of white cloud. As we began our ascent the clouds grew thicker, until they enveloped us in mists which could be felt. Then as the altitude increased the temperature fell; and as the vapour condensed, rain came down, not in drops, but sheets of water. The forest-clad hillsides trickled with countless rills; every ravine became a roaring torrent bed; the surface of the rocks exuded and their crevices distilled moisture. Few objects, distant more than a few yards, could be seen; there was neither wind nor sound from the air, nothing was heard save the sounds of the fast-moving train, and of water falling, pattering, dripping, rushing in every direction. As we arrived near the crest of the range the clouds gradually parted, like curtains being drawn back, and then was disclosed a landscape which travellers at that season see repeatedly, yet never tire of seeing. The trap-rock rose in domes and towers piercing the sky; the geological formations ranged themselves in precipices like mighty walls. Over these steep sides there tumbled numerous cascades, hundreds of feet from top to bottom, so that the dark escarpment was marked with lines of glittering white. All around us the forest and the lesser vegetation had that luxuriance which is produced when rainfall, measured not in inches but in feet, is followed by sunlight shining strongly through a hot atmosphere.

By reason of several visits on official business connected with the Central Provinces, I was able to observe the manner in which Sir Bartle Frere was administering the Government of Bombay. I also became acquainted with the principal persons, European and Native, who were prominent in society or influential in public affairs.

Sir William Mansfield (afterwards Lord Sandhurst) was then Commander-in-Chief of the Bombay Army and ex-officio a Member of the Governor's Council. He had served with much efficiency as Chief of the Staff to Sir Colin Campbell, afterwards Lord Clyde, during the war of the mutinies, and thus carried great weight in all military affairs. His experience had not, however, been confined to the army, for he had formerly obtained diplomatic employment in Europe. Also he had from his early years applied himself to all manner of questions concerning currency, banking and general finance, for which he possessed naturally an extraordinary aptitude. Indeed it was understood that he had at one time deliberated on the expediency of resigning the command of his regiment in order to direct the management of a bank. Though much occupied by his proper duties as Commander-in-Chief, he retained his liking for economic studies. He also took a keen interest in the commercial affairs of Bombay, which interest grew keener as these affairs were forced by the urgency of events into sharper and yet sharper prominence.

Among the other members of the Governor's Council, Mr. Ellis (now Sir Barrow Ellis) was eminent. He had served with much success under Sir Bartle Frere in Sind, and was a great support to his old chief. He thoroughly understood the affairs of the Presidency in each and all of its parts; and his opinion carried weight both in official and non-official circles. His ability in the public service was all the more useful in that he was a very popular member of society.

Outside the Government circle, the most influential person was the Reverend John Wilson, D.D., missionary of the Free Church of Scotland. He was to Bombay what Alexander Duff had been to Calcutta, and worked on the same lines, namely, those of giving Christian instruction to the more intelligent Natives of the capital, and affording high education as a means of paving the way for the reception of religious truth. The Free Church Institution at Bombay under his guidance became one of the best colleges in the country, and sent up yearly many successful students to the University. He was afterwards appointed by Government to be Vice-Chancellor of the Bombay University; and this is the only instance of a missionary being nominated to that dignity. He was an effective speaker, but had not such a gift of eloquence as that which distinguished Alexander Duff. In scholarly acquirements he was superior to Duff; his work upon Hindu castes is a monument of learning judiciously applied to a subject of practical importance. He studied especially the religion of the Parsis, a class becoming very important in Bombay. He analyzed the doctrines of Zoroaster in order to shew that they were defective, and that there must be truths above or beyond them. He was one of the principal supporters of the Bombay branch of the Royal Asiatic Society; and was always among the foremost in respect of every good work which could be promoted by persuasive speaking or writing. For many years he exercised a moral power at Bombay equally great whether in

European or Native society; and his death left a blank which has not yet been filled up by time.

Dr. Murray Mitchell, also belonging to the Free Church mission, was a missionary of much fervour ability and influence. He subsequently held a position of importance in the Institution at Calcutta, and having thus been in contact with the intellectual Natives in both the west and east of India, possesses probably a wider experience than any of his fellow-labourers.

In the European section of the mercantile community the two foremost men were Michael Scott and John Fleming. They became involved in misfortune afterwards, but at that time their influence was considerable. During the period of speculation which soon followed, Michael Scott's action, though undertaken at the moment with the best intentions, did indirectly stimulate the excitement then springing up in the public mind. The errors committed by a man of such enterprising talent and of so high a character, should serve as a warning to those whose lot it may be to guide commercial opinion during future crises. Fleming's conduct at that time was steady and cautious, and he was regarded as a breakwater by which the floods of speculation might be stemmed. So highly was he esteemed that he had the honour of being appointed a Companion of the Order of the Star of India. His subsequent misfortunes should not cause his services rendered at this time to be forgotten.

Among the Natives engaged in trade, two men were particularly distinguished, one a Parsi, the other a Hindu. The Parsi was Rustamji, son of the Jamsetji Jijibhoy who received a Baronetcy, being the first Native of India upon whom that dignity had been bestowed. The Parsis of Bombay are famed for skill, energy and enterprise in commercial affairs and for munificent benevolence in the disposal of their wealth. Among them Rustamji was placed in the first rank; and his social position afforded him additional opportunity of employing adequately his means of doing good. But he became involved in the commercial speculations of this time, though his honour was not compromised he lost the status previously enjoyed by him, and of the many failures which occurred none caused more regret than his. The Hindu was Premchand Roychand, an experienced manager of the money market, with a genius and a passion for that particular business. His bark rode on the crest of the wave, and he was the acknowledged leader among the knot of speculators from whom many financial associations had their origin. He and his friends had capital, resources, experience, and there was some method in their proceedings; they understood the business, and their intentions may have been quite legitimate. But his example had an exciting effect upon hundreds who had but little means and were predisposed to imprudent speculation. Doubtless he did not intend to produce any injurious effect upon his countrymen; but it often becomes impossible for a man to moderate influences once set in motion by him. He acquired vast nominal wealth, though none could say whether it was realizable: and he fell for a time, though he partially recovered himself. During his prosperity he strove to make the best use of his money, and gave several of the noblest benefactions for the service of education and of charity that have ever been given by a Native of India. For these his name will be remembered in future generations when the troubles of 1864–5 are forgotten.

There were many other Native gentlemen conspicuous for good works or for talents and accomplishments. Among these was Jaganath Shankarset, a man of general culture and social influence, all which he devoted to the cause of education. Mangaldas Nathubai made a fortune in trade, and being a well-educated man, acquired a large knowledge of the country, the results of which he would communicate with more frankness than is usual, often uttering homely criticism on British policy. Vishwanath Narain Mandlik, a Brahmin of the Concan, was an eminent member of the Native bar, probably surpassing his contemporaries in sagacity of discernment and solidity of judgment. He held enlightened views regarding education and had a large knowledge of public affairs. Cowasji Jehangir, again, was a rich Parsi and kept his fortune unimpaired in essentials; he perhaps did more for charity and for the public good in various ways than any of his contemporaries, though in culture he may have been hardly equal to some of those already mentioned. There was much public satisfaction when he received the honour of knighthood. Bhao Daji was a man belonging to a different class of society, and his fame had reference to learning. He had that passion for antiquarian research which though not unknown among the Natives is yet comparatively rare with them, and is more generally found among studious Europeans. He not only studied the classical languages of his country, but also visited the antique remains and strove to read the lessons which they present to succeeding generations. Further his knowledge extended to some branches of science, and on the whole he was the most eminent Native intellectually of that time in western India.

It is remarkable that while the Mahratta Brahmins were chiefly observable in politics and administration, the men most prominent in works of public usefulness were either Parsis or else Gujeratis belonging to the Jain religion and to the commercial profession.

Prominent among those possessing original character was David Sassoon, a Jew. His native place was Bagdad, but his family had left Turkish Arabia many years previously and were naturalized in Bombay. He amassed a large fortune in trade, and his firm became one of the wealthiest in British India. At this time he was bestowing a munificent gift on the foundation of a hospital and dispensary at Poona for Europeans and Natives. When laying the foundation stone Sir Bartle Frere addressed him in suitable terms, to which he replied by reading a short address in Arabic. He was then advanced in years, and his grave countenance, commanding figure, rich turban and flowing robes, made up a picture worth beholding. His family have subsequently won much esteem in Bombay for works of public usefulness, and set a good example by building synagogues and schools for their own people. His eldest son became Sir Albert Sassoon, and is now residing in England.

The man whom Frere himself would probably have chosen as the most truly noteworthy character of that æra, was Karsundas

Mulji, a member of the Bhattia tribe of traders. Among these was a sect whose tenets, under cover of devotion to its priests, styled Maharajas, caused the foulest and meanest immorality to be practised. Karsundas exposed this fell plague-spot before the public, with a persistency and moral courage which can be fully appreciated only by those who know what moral coercion and social torments can in a Hindu community be brought to bear upon a recalcitrant individual. The wrath of the priests and their followers culminated in an action for libel against Karsundas in the High Court of Bombay in 1862, when neither expense nor trouble was spared, as regards legal advice and array of evidence, in order to crush him. He met his formidable accusers quite undaunted, and pleaded as his justification the truth of his allegations. His counsel was the well-known Chisholm Anstey, and after a protracted trial, the decision was pronounced entirely in his favour by the Judge, Sir Joseph Arnould. Indeed he was declared, by one of the most remarkable judgments ever delivered from the bench of the High Court, to be not only blameless in his proceedings but also a public benefactor. His writings in vindication of domestic morality, against furtive invasion by detestable doctrines, redound not only to his honour but also to that of his race, as proving that conscience asserts her sway even among those who have been nurtured under corrupt influences, and that the eternal principles of right shed their rays even amidst degrading associations. Despite the triumphs and successes, which to a man of his mental constitution must have been the dearest imaginable—he remained unselfish and unassuming to the end of his life, which was probably shortened by the agitation of controversy. He was one of the most virtuous men that the Hindu nation ever produced, and few Native characters would better repay exact study than his. However hateful may be the details of the immorality which he bravely combated, his career forms an episode deserving the best attention of moralists and reformers.

Another marked figure in Native society was a Persian, Aga Khan, the chief of the veritable and lineal descendants of the band of assassins who owned allegiance to the famous Old Man of the Mountain in the middle ages. He derived a large income from the offerings of his sect, the Khojas, who were among the most enterprising and wealthy traders in western India. His early life was spent in the Persian province of Kerman, where he once raised a rebellion; afterwards he raised and commanded a body of irregular horse on the British side at Candahar during the first Afghan war; next he rendered service to the British in the conquest of Sind. Subsequently certain disputes regarding the income derived by him from the Khojas formed the subject of serious litigation in the High Court of Bombay, and the Judge, Sir Joseph Arnould, decided in his favour. Thenceforward he dwelt in western India as a private gentleman, after having run a romantic and adventurous career. But while externally devoting himself to sport, especially horse-racing, and keeping some of the best blood of Arabia in his stables, he kept his eye upon every move on the political chess-board of Central Asia, and loyally exerted on the British side his influence over widely extended communities.

In short the Bombay Presidency was teeming with active and spirited men of all sorts, both European and Native, so that Sir Bartle Frere may well have felt himself to be at the head of a community which he was proud to lead.

Underneath a gentle and composed demeanour Frere had an ever-welling spring of enthusiasm. Just then also western India, that is, the Bombay Presidency, was bursting into new life; for in that year (1862) the civil war in America was beginning. The blockade of the ports in the Southern States was cutting short the cotton supply of England, and that was affecting the exportation of cotton from Bombay. Then whatever concerned Bombay would act powerfully on western India. If the Government were to march with the good time, it must improve the communications; so Frere immediately turned his thoughts towards the roads. Road-making in western India was more than ordinarily difficult, for behind the Bombay city at a distance of forty miles there rises the range of the Western Ghât mountains stretching from north to south for hundreds of miles, and throwing out long spurs, or subsidiary lines of hill in every direction. How Frere contrived to obtain from the Government of India the grants of money necessary for all the engineering operations then undertaken on the roads, may indeed excite wonder; but his Government commanded the confidence of the then Governor-General, Lord Elgin, and the means were found. The operations were not confined to large works, for material improvements of all sorts, great and small, were forwarded in every district throughout the country.

The principal engineers were Europeans, but soon the want of Native assistants and subordinates began to be felt. So the College of civil engineering at Poona was developed; young Natives of some education were attracted to its class-rooms, a building of handsome and suitable dimensions was erected for it, and workshops were attached to the institution.

As might be expected, Frere took the most lively interest in the progress of railways within his jurisdiction. The line from Bombay to Madras was nearly completed, but the line from Bombay ascending the Western Ghât mountains on the way towards Calcutta, and that from Bombay passing up the coast of Guzerat towards Rajputana, were in full progress. These lines were being constructed by Guaranteed Companies under the general control of the provincial Government. Thus Frere's influence in promoting progress was strongly felt; his hope being that portions at least of the lines might be opened soon enough to carry the traffic which was likely to arise in consequence of the rising tide of trade.

The railways from Bombay to Madras and Calcutta ascend the Western Ghât mountains to a height of 2000 feet above sea-level at two places known as the Bhore Ghât and the Thall Ghât. The Bhore Ghât Incline, with which the name of the engineer James Berkley is most honourably associated, had just been completed, Frere having with due official ceremony declared it open for traffic. But the works of the Thall Ghât Incline were in full progress, and involved great engineering difficulties. The railway had to pass through an insalubrious and malarious forest, which spread itself along the base of the mountains. Here the European engineers engaged in the surveys and designs were often struck down by fever, but despite this they were full of zeal for the progress of the line. The admiring interest which men take in a project of this nature seems always to sustain them in their labours and distresses, the imagination adding moral force to physical energy. Many engineers suffered permanently in health, and some few lost their lives in the discharge of their duty. The railway from Bombay running northwards to Guzerat was being constructed; it passed through a flat country, but had to encounter difficulties worse even than those presented by mountains. For it must cross near the mouths of several rivers, all liable to inundations rising rapidly, and rushing with an accelerated speed consequent on the proximity of mountains. When the torrents of rain on the hill-tops are remembered, the accumulation of drainage in the valleys beneath can be understood. The scouring of the water, too, tears up the alluvial soil of the river-bed, rendering it difficult to establish foundations for the piers of the viaducts. The piers were being founded with piles driven deep into the ground and fixed there by screws. The structures, though looking very strong, as they really were, yet had a light and airy appearance which made them highly picturesque. The viaduct then being raised across the Nerbadda opposite Broach had an imposing appearance. The Nerbadda, however, scorned the earlier attempts to span her broad current, and uprooted the screw-piles. The engineers, nothing daunted, drove stronger piles still deeper into the ground, but the river again extirpated the structure. It was only after a third trial that this river was safely bridged, if even now the viaduct can be deemed permanently secure. On this railway the names of French and Mathew were always mentioned with praise on account of efforts directed with enthusiasm and yet with skill and judgment.

Besides communications, many other public works claimed attention. There, as elsewhere in India, the housing and lodging of the additional European troops retained after the war of the mutinies had to be reconsidered. The result was that most of the old barracks were condemned, and the construction of many new barracks was begun. There were also numerous structures undertaken for civil purposes, and of these buildings some will be mentioned presently.

From his antecedents and by the political situations which he had held, Frere was well fitted to deal successfully with the Native States and Chiefs of the Deccan. Indeed he was more highly qualified in that respect than any Governor since the days of Mountstuart Elphinstone. This great territorial class, comprising many members of different ranks, from the head of a considerable principality to the petty chieftain with a few acres, has not yet been, and perhaps never will be, in a satisfactory condition. The lesser nobility still look back wistfully towards the departed splendour of Mahratta rule. As a man of this class rides over the Deccan and thinks of all that his ancestors enjoyed there, contrasting it with the narrow opportunities of the present, he begins to

> "Feel like one who treads alone
> Some banquet hall deserted,
> Whose lights are fled, whose glories dead."

Such moody reflections, over decay which cannot be arrested must lead to discontent. But even in the Native States of the South Mahratta country which are well preserved, the embers of trouble are always smouldering. Still some good can be done among them all by a popular Governor, and that was thoroughly effected by Frere. They fully recognized the kindliness of his dealings and the benevolence of his aims. On his departure they presented to him an address, which without any flattery, or any attempt to ascribe to the British Government merits which could hardly be evinced under the circumstances, exactly stated the measures which he had taken or striven to take for their benefit. They specially adverted to his efforts to provide suitable instruction for their sons, and as a memorial of him they endowed twenty scholarships in an institution established for the education of young Native noblemen.

Education was a subject in which Frere took a liberal and

enlightened interest. Some administrators have thought that, for the Government at least, primary education is the most important object, and that high education may be left to private effort. This may, indeed, prove to be true ultimately, and at all events such is the goal to which our policy ought to be directed. But in the first instance it was important that the Government should take the initiative with high education. Without such initiative the Natives had neither the means nor the inclination to begin the movement. The establishment of high education was essential in order to set up a moral and intellectual standard among the people, and supply means for conducting the secondary and primary education. Those who deprecate the maintenance of colleges and high schools by Government, seem hardly to remember that, without such institutions, there would not be the means of training masters for the village schools. Moreover, one legitimate object of State education is to prepare Natives for the public service in its various grades and branches. Now Frere understood that, in the earlier stages at least, the Government must support all kinds of education alike, whether superior or middle-class or primary. He was ex-officio Chancellor of the University of Bombay, and delivered at its convocations several addresses framed with much care. He strove to develop the colleges affiliated to it; and next after them the middle-class schools. But being well acquainted with the peasantry, he appreciated the importance of primary education, and in his time much was done to establish the village schools, so that they might diffuse knowledge among the agricultural classes which form the backbone of the population. He doubtless hoped that as the settlements had secured a proprietary title to the peasants with the land-tax moderately fixed for long terms of years, the sense of status prosperity and security would excite a desire for elementary knowledge. There, as elsewhere in India, this hope has either been disappointed or its realization is seen to be but very gradual.

A decided impulse was given at this time to female education, both among the higher and humbler classes of the Native community. The Parsis had always taken a more liberal and enlightened view of this important subject, and shaken themselves free of any prejudice which may have ever existed among them. Mr. Manockji Cursetji, a Parsi gentleman who had travelled in Europe and seen much of society there, was a leader in this good cause; and the ladies of his family by culture and learning set an excellent example. Some Hindus followed this example cautiously and tentatively, and so the movement spread. Lady Frere herself afforded hearty encouragement, and by much graceful ministration won her way to the hearts of many Native families as a power for good. Miss Frere evinced sympathy with her Asiatic sisters by collecting the popular legends current in southern India and presenting them to the public in an English garb under the title of 'Old Deccan Days.'

Shortly before Frere's arrival, the several local legislatures had been constituted, and Bombay thus had a Legislative Council of its own, the members being limited in number, and consisting of Europeans and Natives, official and non-official. He presided regularly at the sittings, took part largely in the deliberations, and strove to inspire it with high ideas of its uses and functions. He also caused a handsome building to be erected for its accommodation. He was careful in selecting as its members Native gentlemen of social and territorial rank, of liberal views, or of signal acquirements, who should be good representatives of the best elements in the community. The personal history of the men, whose unpaid services he thus secured, would illustrate the moral forces which were then pervading Native society.

The term of years, for which the land revenue had been assessed, was expiring, and a revised assessment was being made. To this matter Frere devoted much attention, and deeming that the rules and regulations upon so important a matter should rest on something more than executive authority, he caused them all to be embodied in one comprehensive law, which was passed by his Legislative Council and is now the charter of the land settlement. The work of the assessment proceeded very happily and successfully in the hands of many able men under the supervision of Colonel Francis and Colonel W. C. Anderson, both very experienced officers, whose names will long be remembered in that part of the country. The seasons were propitious for some years in a region which ordinarily is somewhat liable to visitations of drought. The prices of agricultural produce were remunerative to the peasantry as producers. The labour market was brisk in consequence of the employment afforded by the public works then in progress, the roads, the buildings, and especially the railways. The population had within the last generation grown considerably; the cultivation had been increasing for many years, and was then approaching its utmost limit. All lands which would repay culture were being cultivated, and even some lands, hardly worth cultivating, were brought under the plough. Under these circumstances, although the rates of assessment were judiciously kept low, the revenue increased spontaneously by reason of the expanding cultivation and the improvement of the crops. Frere was naturally pleased by all this success, and the fame of the Bombay settlements grew apace.

The prevailing tenure was that known as "Ryot-wari," which there meant the status of peasant proprietors. With these "Ryot" proprietors the land revenue was assessed for thirty years, and within that term they were to have the benefit of their own improvements, and of the "unearned increment" from any rise in the value of their produce.

They very soon found the value of their produce rising to a height beyond any expectations they could have formed. For the American Civil War, as it lasted from month to month, wrought its full effect upon India by causing an unexampled exportation of cotton. The produce of all the great cotton-fields of India, Nagpur, Berar, Guzerat, the South Mahratta country, found its way to Bombay in order to be exported to England, with all possible despatch while the high prices ruled and the blockade of the South American ports lasted. So sudden was the demand, so high the range of price, so vast the profits, that an economic disturbance set in. Money seemed to lose its purchasing power, the prices of almost all articles rose simultaneously, and the wages of labour were enhanced in proportion. In some places, despite good harvests, the food grains were sold at rates so dear as almost to be tantamount to famine prices, and yet the people seemed to thrive, doubtless because of their prosperity in other ways. The peasant proprietors were foremost in the race of temporary prosperity; and made use of their collateral advantages. They engaged largely in the carrying business, employing their carts and draught cattle for that purpose. They gained good wages on the public works at every season when they were not busy in their fields. Then it was that the popular saying told how the tires of their cart-wheels were made of silver instead of iron, and that their bullocks also were being shod with the precious metal.

This sunshine was, as might have been anticipated, too bright to last; after blazing for a time it was succeeded by some chilling reverses; and during its continuance the peasantry acquired some habits of extravagance which they rued in after years.

The effect upon the city of Bombay, and all the vast interests connected with it, was still more electrical. An enormous quantity of cotton having been exported within two years at unprecedentedly high prices, great fortunes were rapidly made by many firms and individuals. Thus money was saved and accumulated much faster than safe or reasonable investments for it could be found. Then all sorts of unsafe and unreasonable investments began to be invented. The economic history of most commercial countries has shewn that when money in vast quantities seeks for, and fails to find, sound investments it will be wasted. The wastage takes the form of unwise or insane speculation. It was to such speculation that Bombay fell a victim at this time. Instances of a like kind are to be found in the annals of almost every commercial centre in the world, and a strong example was furnished by all that now occurred at Bombay. Financial associations formed for various purposes sprung up like mushrooms; companies expanded with an inflation as that of bubbles; projects blossomed only to decay. Not only were baseless schemes put forth, but also schemes, which originally had a sound foundation, were pushed forward so imprudently that they ended in becoming unsound and involving in loss or ruin those who were concerned in them. The case of the Back Bay Reclamation Company afforded a striking case. This was a scheme for reclaiming a large quantity of land from the sea; it proved ultimately to be in excess of the local needs, still in its inception it was so well framed that the Government had shares in it. This was before any economic disturbance had been anticipated. But under the circumstances of the time, the Bombay Government judiciously decided to dispose of its shares in order to become free from the project. The shares, on being sold by auction, brought extraordinarily high prices, and the sale-proceeds were straightway invested by the Company in a new bank which had lately been founded and which lasted for two years till the general crash came. The shares of the Company rose extraordinarily in value; and for some time the owner of a single "Back Bay" share was deemed fortunate. But the sums, paid in open market for these shares, were so high that no conceivable returns from the works could afford to the holders interest on the money they were thus paying. This being so, the ultimate holders must be losers. Even summary calculation shewed this, nevertheless the public buying and selling of the shares went on. The collapse was only a question of time, and when it occurred the loss and distress were widespread. A portion of the project had been carried out and much land reclaimed; the remaining works were stopped. Over the land thus reclaimed there runs now a railway and a road generally crowded with vehicles. Those who pass by little reflect, perhaps, that they are really riding or driving over the wreck of many fortunes.

One reclamation company held its ground throughout the crisis, namely, "the Elphinstone," formed for reclaiming land along the foreshore of the harbour. Its property was afterwards transferred to Government, and has since been developed into a Port Trust.

Of the enterprises then undertaken, some were well founded and honourably carried out. But many of the new schemes suddenly launched and floated, proved to be nothing more than the fabrics of a vision. The minds of men were confused, their judgment blinded, their senses dazzled. The impetuosity of the hour would hardly be imagined by any save those who have witnessed such scenes there or elsewhere. The Europeans, accustomed to lead in all good ways, took but too often the leadership of this folly also. The Natives proved to be very apt followers, and once having given their thoughts to speculation, they became greater adepts in it than the Europeans. Numbers of them regarded speculating in the shares of these companies as a means of livelihood. When the day of retribution came they were often frank in their professions of repentance. One of them said to me: "What madness it was that we should want to win land at an enormous cost from the sea in front of us, when we had plenty of land in the continent behind us."

Nevertheless a mass of real wealth, to be reckoned by many millions sterling, had been poured into the lap of Bombay, already a wealthy place. This was quite enough to justify a large expansion of legitimate enterprise. Had the prosperity come by degrees, all might have gone well; but the suddenness of its accession upset the balance of judgment in the minds of men. Still, despite all the errors which were committed, the fabric of general prosperity would have been maintained if the exportation of cotton in vast quantities at a high price had continued. There was no doubt that it would endure while the American civil war lasted; but it was thought likely to continue even after the termination of the war, whether victory should be with the North or with the South. In either case the institution of slavery was doomed, without which it was believed the cultivation of cotton in the Southern States could not be kept up. This belief has, indeed, proved to be quite erroneous, but there was much apparent reason for it at the time. On the other hand, it was thought that Bombay had obtained a firm hold on the cotton trade with England.

A belief gained ground to the effect that this hold could not be shaken, and that Indian cottons would never be displaced from their recent vantage ground in the English markets. It was not indeed forgotten that England wanted the long staple cotton, which America could produce and India could not. Efforts had indeed been made with some success, under the auspices of Sir Bartle Frere's Government, to produce long staple cotton in parts of western India, still the mass of the recent exports of cotton had been of the short staple, which was accepted in England for want of anything better. Manifestly, then, if the long staple cotton should again be produced it must displace the Indian short staple. But it was anticipated that on the abolition of slavery the production of long staple cotton in the Southern States would cease, and that the Indian cottons would retain their position. The short staple cotton would not suit the English machinery; but that machinery would, it was supposed, have to be modified and adapted to the new staple. These ideas have been dissipated by subsequent experience, still many people besides the Bombay men believed that England, no longer depending on the Southern States for cotton, would have to seek her supplies in other countries. In Manchester itself the "Cotton Supply Association" was formed, and soon had its correspondents in Bombay.

Thus during the height of the speculation, those who reflected at all on the commercial prospect, found reasonable ground for anticipating a continuance of prosperity. But it is to be feared that many, in the excitement of the hour, failed to exercise any careful thought.

While Bombay for a while lay in sack-cloth, the public was but too ready to point its finger. Calcutta, it was said, proved wiser, avoiding these quick-sands or discountenancing speculation. The Bank of Bengal, too, being well managed, was a rock immovable, instead of falling like the Bombay bank together with the general ruin. The fact is that Calcutta, not being a great port for cotton, never was subjected to the same temptation as Bombay. It is true, however, that even if speculation had set in, the Bank of Bengal would in truth have proved a safeguard. Nevertheless at Calcutta an affair had arisen, comparable in respect of sanguine enterprise with some of the affairs which occurred at Bombay. The project was to found on the Matla river a second capital, at first to be the handmaid but ultimately the rival of Calcutta; the Hughli was spurned as a river which had seen its day, and would be replaced by the Matla. A company was formed, under the undoubtedly able auspices of Mr. Ferdinand Schiller, a German gentleman and member of a mercantile firm at Calcutta. The Government encouraged the plan, a short line of railway was made to the place, which was named Port Canning after the Governor-General. But the scheme, though conceived with much talent, was much in advance of any want really felt by the country, therefore after a very few years the proceedings collapsed, the establishments were discharged and the disused railway broken up.

When in the spring of 1865 the long-protracted resistance of the Southern States collapsed with startling rapidity, the blockade ended and a mass of American cotton entered the English markets. Then the price of the Bombay cotton fell fast, property in produce estimated at many millions sterling declined in a few weeks to less than half that value. The enterprises, which had been founded on the expectation that this value would be sustained, began crumbling to pieces. I passed through Bombay on my way to England in the spring of 1865, and saw the depression beginning to be felt. Returning to India in the following autumn, I again passed through Bombay, and found the city in the very throes of trouble, her leading merchants ruined, many of her old-established firms in peril, her banking corporations in liquidation, her enterprises suspended. Never had I witnessed in any place a ruin so widely distributed, nor such distress following so quickly on the heels of such prosperity.

The Native merchants were as important as, and much more numerous than, the Europeans, and upon both alike had swift retribution descended. As is usual in disastrous times, recrimination and mutual reproach were rife, and accusations of mercantile misconduct were bandied about. Happily the instances of misbehaviour on the part of Europeans, or on the part of Natives of rank or status, were rare. But many Natives of lesser education and position were drawn into the vortex of the speculation which verges upon gambling and leads to paths heaped with temptations to questionable actions. Soon the courts of justice became overloaded with cases in which misguided Natives were figuring as defendants. At this time, a temporary vacancy occurring in the bench of the High Court, Sir Bartle Frere appointed the well-known Mr. Chisholm Anstey, then a prominent member of the Bombay Bar, to fill the post. Anstey passed severe orders in the numerous cases of mercantile misconduct wherein Natives were concerned; and frequently made stringent comments on the manner in which morality had in his opinion been sacrificed. The Native community took umbrage at these proceedings, and memorialized Sir Bartle Frere, praying that Anstey, after the expiration of the time for which he had temporarily been appointed, might not be reappointed to the bench. Frere, however, believing that Anstey was striving to do his judicial duty in circumstances which required a severe example, vindicated the proceedings which had been taken, and gave the moral weight of his authority in support of the judge.

Amidst the crash of companies, firms and individuals, all ruined, the failure of the Bank of Bombay was announced. The Government held shares in this bank and had directors sitting at the board of management; there also the public funds needed for current expenses were deposited. The rule in this bank, as in the other banks in India with which the Government was connected, had been that advances should not be made on any securities except those of the Government. But unfortunately by some recent legislation on a renewal of the Bank's charter, some provisions had been inserted whereby the Bank was empowered to make advances on certain kinds of securities other than those of the Government. In virtue of this power the Bank had made advances to companies during the time of prosperity, on the security of their shares, to such an extent that when the companies became insolvent amidst the general ruin, the Bank also failed. This failure was noticed with sharp animadversion by the public, and especially by those who had become shareholders in the Bank on the faith of its being supervised by the Government. Indignation rose high against the Government Director (since deceased) who, as financial adviser of the Government in this matter, was specially bound to see that the Bank steered clear of the threatening shoals. It was felt also that the Government itself could not be exempted from responsibility for not having more effectually watched and corrected the conduct of the Directors. Subsequently this grave affair became the subject of discussion in Parliament, and was investigated by a Commission which sat in England.

During the season of prosperity, many native gentlemen, having made much money, desired to give out of their abundance large contributions towards objects of public usefulness and charity. Sir Bartle Frere was ready and earnest to encourage them in such munificence; indeed there never was a Governor endowed with greater aptitude than he for inspiring Natives with feelings of generosity and ambition for doing good in their generation. More hospitals, schools and other public institutions were founded by private benevolence at that time than at any other before or since. Ceremonial meetings were often held to commemorate the founding or the opening of these institutions. Frere was most willing to accept invitations to attend on these occasions, and to deliver speeches of the kind which the Natives ever love to hear from the mouths of their rulers. His utterances, proceeding from long and intimate knowledge of the Natives, were judiciously calculated to develop the best parts of their character, stimulate all their noblest sentiments, and raise their ideas to the highest attainable standard. He appealed skilfully to the noblest promptings of their nature, and while touching with a gentle finger all the faults in their conduct kept their uplifted gaze turned towards the highest standard attainable.

The addresses delivered by him on many occasions have since been collected and republished by a Native, Balkrishna Pitale, and form a volume interesting to the Indian student. Prosperity, Frere would tell the Natives, carries with it infinite responsibilities, and should be signalized by charitable efforts. I remember hearing him warn them that many observers apprehended a speedy decline of prosperity in Bombay, but be the prosperity short-lived or permanent, he urged them to make good use of it during its continuance, and reminded them that the best of all possible uses was the provision of resources for good works. He desired that the accession of wealth should be made memorable by deeds done for the benefit of posterity; and certainly that time is well remembered for the sake of the many charities then instituted.

The old European fort of Bombay was standing in those days, and within its walls was the populous British settlement founded two centuries previously; a broad plain separated this town within fortifications from the great Native city. As lands for building purposes were very much needed and would command a high price, a project was formed for throwing down the walls of the fort, taking up a portion of the plain, and making allotments of ground available for building. Sir Bartle Frere took up this project with his accustomed zeal, and obtained large sums in purchase-money from those who bid for the allotments. The means thus acquired, together with grants from the Government, were collected and formed into a Special Fund for the construction of public offices and buildings for Bombay. The formation and management of this Fund caused much correspondence with the Government of India; but the scheme held good, and was duly carried into effect. Previously these buildings had been found unsuitable for the growing needs of a capital city, being cramped in space, badly situated and imperfectly ventilated; they were erected at a time when civilization was but little advanced in the settlements of the East India Company, and when architectural taste was almost unknown in British India. The opportunity was to be taken of giving Bombay a series of structures worthy of her wealth her populousness and her geographical situation. The designs were to be of the highest character architecturally, therefore architects were obtained from England to frame them elaborately, and due thought was given to artistic effect. The operations were planned deliberately, and well begun while Frere was still in Bombay. Their completion has been arranged by his successors very much on the lines which he had laid down. They comprise the Government Secretariat, the University Library, the Convocation Hall, the High Court, the Electric Telegraph Department, the Post Office, all in one grand line facing the sea. Other Buildings in a similar style were built in other parts of the city, such as the Elphinstone College, the Victoria Museum, the Elphinstone High School, the School of Art, the Goculdass Hospital, the Sailors' Home, and others. Few cities in the world can shew a finer series of structures; and those who admire the buildings after a lapse of fifteen years from the beginning of the work, may well be reminded that it is to Sir Bartle Frere that Bombay owes the origination and inception of this comprehensive project. It would be a mistake to attribute too much to individual Governors, for when work is demanded by the spirit of the age it will be done in some shape or other, whoever may be in power. But in justice it must be said that Frere deserves the lion's share in the credit of this undertaking, and that without him the work would never have reached that magnitude which is now beheld by all English spectators with a feeling of national pride.

No less remarkable was the advance of municipal improvement in the city of Bombay under Sir Bartle Frere's administration. The artificial lake, wherefrom water is conducted for the use of the urban population, was constructed under his predecessors. But it was under him that many new streets were opened out or metalled, and the magnificent markets constructed. These are called "the Crawford markets," after Arthur Crawford of the Civil Service, the Municipal Commissioner, who had a genius for works of this nature, who effected so many external improvements that it would be difficult to enumerate them all, and who left his beneficent mark on the face of this great city.

In many departments of progress, Sir Bartle Frere found a worthy coadjutor in Dr. (now Sir George) Birdwood of the Medical Service, an officer of scientific literary and artistic culture. As registrar of the University, as Director of the Victoria Museum and Gardens, as a prominent member of the Bombay branch of the Royal Asiatic Society, and in several other capacities, Birdwood displayed an enthusiasm which aroused a responsive sentiment among the Natives. Having made them feel that he sincerely cared for their welfare as a friend, he then, as an instructor, guided their intellects in the ways of European science, and towards those principles which belong to true art, whether in Europe or in Asia. They lamented his departure from Bombay as the loss of one among their heartiest well-wishers.

Besides Bombay almost all other towns and stations, in the interior of the Presidency, witnessed the erection of public structures in good architectural style. It may almost be said, indeed, that architecture for civil buildings, in western India, dates from Frere's time. At Poona especially the many fine buildings, the Government House, the Deccan College, the Civil Engineering College, the Sassoon Hospital, the Legislative Council House, were designed and built in his time, though some of them may have been completed under his successors.

About the same time a School of Art was founded at Bombay for Native students, which bears the name of Sir Jamsetji Jijibhoy, its munificent benefactor. It was not meant that European instruction should suppress the ideas of indigenous art in the minds of the Native students. On the contrary, the many sound principles, which pervade the ancient art of India, were to be affectionately and reverently preserved. But it was thought that European instruction could shew the Native youth many things not found in their own art, respecting both form and colour, could teach them at least, how to draw from nature correctly and artistically, and could at all events make sure that the beauties of the works, produced in olden times, should be duly observed by the present generation. Competent instructors were employed;

and the class-rooms became filled. The students were made to sketch not only objects modelled in the European style, but also the finest portions of the antique ruins.

I was not present to witness Sir Bartle Frere's departure from Bombay, but the occasion was often mentioned in after years by Europeans and Natives, who recounted how troops of friends from all nationalities crowded the place of embarkation, how kind messages and utterances innumerable greeted the departing ruler.

In respect to principles of policy, much resemblance will be observed between Bartle Frere and James Thomason, whose character has been described in chapter III. Both administrators set before themselves certain cardinal objects to be pursued with perseverance, namely, the perfecting of the land revenue settlements, the promotion of public works, the instruction of the Natives in civil engineering, and the advancement of education generally. Both felt enthusiasm for the cause of general improvement, and were hopeful regarding the character of the people and its future development. Both were men of much culture in all general knowledge relating to the East. There were also points of dissimilarity between them, or rather several matters in which the one excelled more particularly than the other. Thomason was superior to Frere in the systematizing of public business and the management of fiscal details; he did the most for primary education, for irrigation by canals, and for tenant-right. Frere on the other hand was superior to Thomason in dealing with the chiefs and upper classes among the Natives, and in promoting high education; it was only in Sind that he had an opportunity of supporting tenant-right, or promoting irrigation on a large scale. Thomason was not tried in times of public peril or in emergencies of war and politics, and it is impossible to tell how far he would have succeeded in such spheres of duty. But experience proved that Frere was eminently fitted to cope with critical danger—the greater the emergency the higher did his spirit soar—and he would rise to the height of each occasion with a moral courage tempered like the finest steel.

CHAPTER XIII.

(1867-1868.)

THE INDIAN FOREIGN SECRETARYSHIP.

The political or diplomatic department of the Indian service—The dominions of the Nizam—The British Resident at his court—Character of the Nizam—Salar Jang his Minister—The Arab chiefs and troops—The Nizam's army—The finances of his government—The interior of his country—Life at his capital—The province of Berar—Project of a railway—My departure from Hyderabad—Visit to Madras—I take charge of the Indian Foreign Secretaryship—Affairs of Afghanistan—Eminent Native princes in India—Native statesmen and administrators.

The political or diplomatic department has always been a separate branch of the Indian administration; and the term "Political" is its technical or official designation. It is engaged in conducting the relations of the Indian Government with the Native States, of which most are within the borders of British India, while some lie on those borders or even beyond. It is also concerned in the international affairs between India and the other Asiatic countries. For these duties a separate body of European officers is organized and trained, of whom most are drawn from the Staff Corps of the army, and some from the Civil Service. The work, however, being very extensive and varied, is not entirely performed by them. Portions of it are often entrusted to high civil functionaries in addition to their other duties. Indeed there is scarcely any civil administrator on a large scale who has not some diplomatic or political functions attached to his office. Each of the several provincial Governments has some political work of its own to perform, and under the Bombay Government this work is very considerable. For all the larger Native States, and for Asiatic countries beyond Indian limits, the political business is under the direct management of the Government of India, that is, the Governor-General in Council. For the transaction of this business there is, and always has been, in the secretariat of the Government of India, a separate secretary, whose official designation is that of "Foreign Secretary." One section of his work is external, and truly foreign, concerning countries outside India. Another part is, in a strict sense, internal, relating to Native States inside India, which are under the control, though not the direct administration, of the Indian Government. Much of prestige interest and popularity amongst the public service, has always attached to the Political Department, and the Foreign Secretaryship is regarded as the choicest post in the Indian secretariat.

When an offer of the Foreign Secretaryship came to me from the Governor-General, I was Resident at Hyderabad, or in official language British Resident at the Court of His Highness the Nizam of the Deccan. This post of Resident at Hyderabad is the highest of the political or diplomatic appointments under the Government of India. When it was offered to me, I was Chief Commissioner of the Central Provinces, as already explained in chapter XI., and felt some reluctance in moving to Hyderabad. But the then Resident, Sir George Yule, was being promoted to a seat in the Governor-General's Council, and at that moment one of the periodical crises between the Nizam and his Minister was going on, therefore in the event of any trouble arising the new Resident would have important duties to discharge. So I quitted the Central Provinces, with hearty regret for the people among whom I had worked so hard, but with happy anticipations of a career in pastures new. Having served some time at Hyderabad, and learnt to regard the Residentship as the pleasantest appointment that could be found, I was to undergo another change, this time to a still higher post in the same line. So I departed from Hyderabad, sorry to part from those left behind, but hopeful regarding all that might be before me.

As the Residentship of Hyderabad may be considered to constitute a preparation for the Foreign Secretaryship, and as it furnishes the best example of the diplomatic and political duties which fall to the lot of British officers in India, I will here attempt some description of its surroundings as they then were.

The dominions of the Nizam, including Berar, comprise an area of 80,000 square miles with a population of nine millions, and are diversified in an extraordinary degree, as regards geology, products, race and language. They are surrounded by British territories, the Madras Presidency lying on the south and east of them, the Bombay Presidency on the west, and the Central Provinces on the north. In one part of them there are trap-rock formations, rich black soil and cotton cultivation; in another granite rocks, light soil and rice fields. In some tracts the laterite formations affect the soil and the cultivation. Many tracts are destitute of artificial irrigation; in the eastern quarter, however, full use is made of natural advantages, after the manner already described in chapter XI., to form artificial lakes as reservoirs for small canals. The facilities presented by nature in this region for the construction of such reservoirs are greater than in any other part of India. These tanks, or, as they should often be designated, lakes, are common in several provinces or districts of the empire, but nowhere are they so numerous as here; and one of them is the largest of its kind in the empire. They are memorials of the early Hindu kings of the Telugu race whom the Muhammadans displaced. A lake of this description is always picturesque, because hills hollows ravines and torrent beds are essential to its successful construction. Above and around it there will be rocks woods and lairs of wild beasts, and below it the irrigated fields with their rich crops.

The Nizam's subjects are in the mass Hindus, speaking in the north and west the Mahratta language, in the east and south the Telugu, and in the south-west the Canarese. The Nizam and his nobles are Muhammadan, so also is a large part of his army; but the Muhammadans dwell in the Deccan as rulers priests landlords soldiers, and have not any hold upon the land as agriculturists.

The position of the British Resident was in those days very influential, but necessarily undefined; it has during recent years been rendered more directly potential by reason of the Nizam being a minor. At that time, however, there was a real Nizam of the old school on the throne, very tenacious, indeed not unreasonably jealous, of his position in relation to that of the Resident. During the early days and the political struggles of the East India Company, the Nizam was in treaties regarded as an ally or an equal, and though he soon became its dependant, still the form or style of equality was preserved. His obligation to govern his territories according to the advice of the Resident was quite vague or slight, nevertheless in practice it had come into real existence. Formally he was not bound to seek the counsel of the Resident, but practically he was, because his predecessors had allowed the State to drift into violent disorders from which extrication was impossible without British assistance. Nothing but British power, represented by armed force, prevented his State from being torn to pieces by factions, and saved him from becoming a prisoner in his palace to his own guards. Thus although the Resident had not, either in the wording of treaties or the terms of his credentials, any declared right of interfering, yet he was the Atlas on whose shoulders rested the government of the State. He must interpose when actual disturbance threatened; then indeed his aid would probably be invoked. Otherwise he would as much as possible avoid the semblance of interfering; and leave the Native Government to manage for itself without being weakened by over-much supervision, on the understanding always that it must keep the general course of affairs tolerably straight.

One portion of the Nizam's dominions, namely Berar, was, as has already been mentioned in chapter VI., under British administration according to treaty. For this territory the Resident represented the local government, subject to the general control of the Governor-General in Council. Though regulating under British authority the income and expenses of this territory, he presented periodically to the Nizam a statement of its finances, giving up to His Highness any surplus revenue which might be left, and in my time a considerable sum was thus paid. He also managed, quite independently of the Nizam, all affairs relating to the Hyderabad Contingent, a force which the British Government was bound by treaty to maintain for the preservation of order in His Highness's dominions. If the services of these troops should in any case be required, he was to be the judge as to whether they might be employed or not. Formerly they were frequently engaged thus, but in my time the policy of the Nizam's government was to maintain order with its own troops and avoid the necessity of applying to the Resident for the services of the Contingent. The Nizam's Minister naturally took pride in the improvement of affairs, whereby he was enabled to answer for order without in every instance seeking British aid.

The Residency is the house in which the Resident resides officially; it was built half a century ago by the Nizam, for the accommodation of the British representative, on a liberal and handsome scale, and in a fine architectural style according to European notions. Though not appearing to be adapted for defence, it is to some extent defensible, and its enclosure is surrounded by a strong wall, with small bastions on that side which faces towards the city. This moderate amount of fortification is necessary, as may be proved by the fact that during the time of public danger in 1857, consequent on the war of the mutinies, an infuriated mob rushed towards the Residency to destroy every person and thing there. Salar Jang, the Minister, though unable to restrain them, contrived to send timely intelligence to the Resident, Colonel Davidson, of their approach. So they were received with cannon-shot and musketry from the bastions of the Residency enclosure. They pressed on however with much resolution, and were repulsed, but only after some loss of life. The Resident had indeed been prepared long beforehand, and the attack had no chance of success; had it succeeded, however, the moral effect on the surrounding country would have been disastrous.

On my arrival at Hyderabad in April 1867, Sir George Yule informed me fully regarding the differences which had arisen between the Nizam and his Minister, Sir Salar Jang. It had been feared that they would lead to the Minister's resignation, and on such an event grave troubles in the Nizam's dominions were likely to ensue. But the Nizam had conferred with the chief among his nobles, who advised him to retain the services of his indispensable Minister. My first official business was to transmit to His Highness a letter from the Governor-General giving firm but friendly monition on the same subject. His Highness being hedged round with ceremonies, the essence of which was delay, some days elapsed before I was allowed to wait upon him.

The visit of the Resident to the Nizam used to be made an occasion of pomp and circumstance. Our procession inside the city was formed with elephants, and it proceeded through streets lined with His Highness's troops. We then saw in the cavalcade the insignia and ornaments of which poets have read, —"The feathers of the egret in the turbans, the costly armour "of the cavaliers, the gilt pine-apples on the tops of the palan-"quins, the embroidered trappings of the elephants bearing on "their backs small turrets in the shape of antique temples." Approaching the heart of the city we passed underneath the great gateway with the four towers, a structure unique of its kind in India. Then we had on our right hand the Nizam's mosque, built on the model of the great mosque at Mecca, and presenting an architectural style quite different from that of the Indian Muhammadans. On our way we glanced at the marble tombs of successive Nizams within its consecrated enclosure. So far we saw sights worthy of the renown of Hyderabad, but on entering the Nizam's palace we were surprised by the plainness of its style, than which indeed nothing could be more common-place. It consisted of a cluster of modern houses, built mainly in the European fashion, without the least attempt at architectural design. The cause is this that originally, in the days of the Mogul empire, the Nizam was technically considered to be encamped in the Deccan and not established in any permanent palace. His successors cling still to that tradition and never erect any palatial structures. All the way from the Residency to the Nizam's summer-house, for it could not be called palace, the eager-gazing multitude were kept back by the troops, as a matter of real precaution. On one of these occasions in my predecessor's time, shots had been heard almost within the precincts of the Nizam's dwelling; and were fired in the street on another occasion shortly after my departure from Hyderabad. The crowd, however, could be seen quite well by us from our raised seats on the elephants, and certainly it excelled in pictorial effect even the proverbially picturesque crowds of India. For in addition to the ordinary Oriental dress and paraphernalia the men wore arms and accoutrements obtained from distant parts of Asia. Among them some looked cheerful and contented, some being retainers of the Minister seemed positively friendly, some were scowling fanatics, some were smooth-faced villains who at that moment appeared smiling and joyous, but had only the other day committed outrages under the very walls of the city when they heard that the Minister's fall from power would relax the bonds of order.

The Nizam received us with a demeanour not haughty perhaps, but calm, almost impassible, as if to imply that he dwelt on serene altitudes and we were creatures struggling with mundane affairs; so that we hesitated to break the ice of ceremony. The Minister Salar Jang accompanied us, and was made to feel thoroughly subdued in the presence of His Highness; the term "presence" was to his ear an awe-inspiring sound, and for him his master had a quiet look of ineffable hauteur. After a chilling pause, the conversation began in the Hindustani language, and touched upon inevitable topics such as the health of the Governor-General, the season and the like. Then in order to say something especially civil and polite I congratulated His Highness on the order and good government patent everywhere in his dominions. He replied, in a tone of slight displeasure, that as there had during past times been good government in his dominions so there was still. Herein he was manifestly in error, for formerly there had been much misrule. He had however interpreted my compliment to be an indirect recommendation of his Minister and his susceptibility was aroused. This incident prepared me for finding him sensitively jealous in everything that concerned Salar Jang.

The Nizam afforded an example of the effect which the enervating conditions of India produced in the course of a few generations upon the conquering tribes that came from Central Asia. A Muhammadan of the best Mogul blood, and born of a stock which had sent forth men of courage, capacity and perseverance, he had never learnt even the rudiments of government, had received but slight education, and was not actually competent for conducting any important business. He had a tall and massive figure, a handsome countenance, and the dark-blue eye characteristic of his race. In his youth he had been trained to some manly sports and pursuits; but he had long led a secluded life in his palace and gardens, associating chiefly with humble dependants. His health had been enfeebled and his constitution impaired by his own imprudence. He was addicted to superstition, and soothsayers or astrologers had power over his impressionable mind. If there was any idea in politics on which his thoughts fixed themselves it was this, that whatever thing had novelty must be evil, and that any so-called reform which the British Resident might suggest should be regarded with circumspection. He desired if possible to keep his people aloof from all European notions, social as well as political. Such notions might act upon their minds, he would say, as a whirligig and cause their thoughts to spin round and round. For all that, he was loyal to the British Government which he felt to be his sole support. Only he wished that it would leave him to his own devices, and never interfere save to throw its ægis over him if he were threatened with insurrection, or to rescue him from his financial difficulties, should they prove otherwise insurmountable. He had some power of humorous sarcasm; though ordinarily apathetic, he had an "unbounded stomach," and was quickly susceptible of anger. Such was the man whom the Muhammadans of the Deccan venerated as the embodiment of authority. He must have been endued with generosity and other cognate qualities in order to attract and retain the chivalrous affection of his people.

The business of the Government was performed by the Minister Salar Jang, then in the prime of life. He had been from his earliest years educated under European supervision and trained especially for this high office, into which he had been inducted when a very young man. He was therefore qualified in an unprecedented degree for his public and official duties. He discharged them with unwearying assiduity, entire integrity and an efficiency unprecedented in the Deccan. He was a gentleman in the highest sense of the term; the quality of his mind was indicated in his discreet manner and refined aspect. He came from the family which had usually during several generations furnished ministers to the State; some of his relations had been great in that capacity, but none so good as he. In those days I regarded him the most among all the Natives of India I had ever met. Humanly speaking, his life was likely to last long; but if he should unfortunately be removed there was no man of his rank in the country who could take up the work which then devolved on him.

Yet he was kept by the Nizam in a state of thraldom; he was almost a prisoner in his own house, and could not move beyond the outer gates of his courtyard without his master's permission. If he wished to give a social entertainment in his summer-house outside the city, or attend a parade of British troops or have an interview with the Resident, he must ask leave, not as a mere formality, but as a request which might be refused, or if allowed would be granted grudgingly. I had much business with him, and its transaction was difficult; to see him often would renew the Nizam's jealousy, to send him papers in despatch-boxes would be open to the same objection, for that also became known to His Highness. Salar Jang did not seem to regard this in the light of a personal grievance; he shared the reverence which his countrymen felt for their master. He seldom was admitted to the Nizam's presence; when he was, however, he would be almost pale from agitation.

He must have been quite hopeless of conciliating his master's regard, yet he was perfectly loyal, and would have undergone any labour for the welfare of his liege.

The reason of the Nizam's strange conduct was this, that Salar Jang, being an enlightened man, was anxious to introduce good government into a distracted and well-nigh ruined state. In that policy he was consistently supported by the British Government. The Nizam therefore felt himself to be really under the control of his Minister in all state affairs; then chafing and fretting at this he revenged himself by punctiliously enforcing a supervision in social matters.

Salar Jang had never up to that time seen any place excepting Hyderabad, and his being thus confined to one spot was disadvantageous to him as an administrator. Indeed, considering how restricted was his actual vision, I was surprised to find that he had so much liberality and comprehensiveness of view. Still, no administration in India can prosper unless it be inspected by its chief from time to time. Hence the public interest demanded that he should make tours through the country, see his officers at their work, observe the needs for works of public improvement and hear the grievances of the people. The Nizam would never allow this unless moral pressure were applied to him by the British Government; even then he would yield only after a lengthened, perhaps an embittered, argument. I was willing, however, to make the attempt, considering the administrative benefit that would result therefrom, and the manifest absurdity of the objections. The Governor-General, however, feared that our relations with the Nizam would be compromised thereby, and so the project dropped.

As Minister, Salar Jang had charge of the civil and military administration of all the territories directly administered by the Nizam's Government, and these formed the greater part of the country. But there were some nobles to whom territory was assigned in consideration of their maintaining troops or otherwise performing service for the state. Among these the first was the Amîr-i-Kabîr, hereditary commandant of the Pagah or bodyguard of the Nizam, a considerable number of troops. The Amîr-i-Kabîr maintained his troops and governed the districts assigned to him under the general control of the Nizam to be exercised through the Minister; this control however was quite nominal.

The Amîr-i-Kabîr was a high-born Muhammadan of the old school, refined dignified and judicious, though somewhat enfeebled by age. He was the son of the handsome father mentioned in chapter X. His face aspect and figure would have made a fine subject for the portrait-painter. His inner thoughts probably clung to the old ways, and he never lent himself to promote reforms. Still he realized the progress which was going on in the outer world, and desired that the Nizam's government should march with the age, and maintain good relations with the British. He was so placed that he wanted nothing for himself or his friends, and felt no jealousy of the Minister or any one else; thus he acquired the position of consulting physician to the state. Though possessing firmness and courage, he loved tranquillity, and seemed to regard violence or lawlessness as essentially vulgar. His opinions had much weight with the Nizam, indeed he was the only man at that time who had any influence over His Highness for good. It was mainly through his friendly offices that the recent dispute between the Nizam, and the Minister had been composed.

Similarly, some districts were retained by the Nizam under his own direct management, and from their revenue were defrayed the expenses of his palace and household. These were governed by men whom the Nizam appointed without the intervention of the Minister.

There were also tracts and territories of various sizes, large and small, occupied by Muhammadan noblemen, often relatives of the Nizam. Some of these were men of capacity and activity, but many lived in a state of vacuity and listlessness, almost of lethargy.

Notwithstanding these abatements from his power, the Minister had a great position, controlling the regular army, the revenues, and the civil administration generally. He was also the channel of official communication between the British Resident and the Nizam's government.

In the army the most important men were the Arab chiefs and their Arab troops; these men had in spirit cohesion and physical strength so great a superiority over the population of the Deccan that they were likened to wolves among sheep. Like other Indian princes, Hindu and Muhammadan, during the eighteenth century, the Nizams had employed Arab soldiery; and when the State became more and more a prey to disorder, the employment of Arabs increased. As drastic remedies often aggravate the disease they are meant to cure, so the Arabs made confusion worse confounded, till at length the British Government under Lord Dalhousie were obliged to interfere. The Arabs then became quiescent but remained powerful, and when I visited Hyderabad in 1861, several Arab commanders were pointed out to me as men who would in 1857 have caused a revolution and set up an Arab State in the Deccan, had the British power been subverted. These chiefs were then aged men, and had by this time (1867) passed away, but their sons being born of Deccani mothers had only half the native Arabian fire or spirit. Their troops however were constantly recruited from Hadramaut, near the southern coast of Arabia; and the phalanx remained unbroken. At that time (1867) there was nothing save the English troops near Hyderabad to prevent the Arabs from beating down the Nizam's Indian troops, immuring His Highness in his own palace and seizing the government of the Deccan. Successive Nizams, too, had allowed the organization of the Arab troops to grow in a manner which endowed the leaders with great wealth and established them in a territorial position. An Arab chief contracted for supplying a certain number of men and for paying them; he would also invest some capital in this business. After a time the Nizam's treasury fell into arrears of pay due to the men. Then came the chief's opportunity—instead of cash he would take a mortgage of the land revenue of a district; whereupon that district was made over to him and he garrisoned it with his men. The power hence acquired was dangerous, but still worse was the misrule which unscrupulous adventurers thus inflicted upon many tracts of the Deccan. Some Arab chiefs, however, were regularly paid in cash, and the fortunes made by them out of their military contracts, which extended to the payment armament equipment and lodgment of some thousand soldiers, can be readily imagined. At that time several of these chiefs had invested their savings largely in general business, and not only controlled the armed forces of the country, but actually possessed much influence over its money markets. Nevertheless the Arabs as a class, though ready for any violence which their chiefs might command, were not addicted to plundering without orders, or to lawless crime of any sort; when off duty they were like lordly tigers not condescending to common prey.

It was the Rohilla tribe that furnished the incorrigible robbers and miscreants, the common enemies of the Deccan people. The name "Rohilla," which belongs to a noble clan of Muhammadans in the north, had been appropriated by these southern plunderers, and included every sort of free-lance. These men used to prowl about the country in bands like hungry wolves; the government deemed it prudent to keep them out of mischief by employment, and the Deccani nobles adopted the same course. Indeed Rohilla guards afforded the best protection against Rohilla outrage. Then their chiefs contracted for the payment and equipment of the men, and sometimes obtained mortgages of lands in the same manner as the Arabs, though to a much less extent.

The Nizam's government had in those days begun to act on the policy of organizing a new body of men which received the name of "the reformed troops." It wished thereby to prepare itself for coping with elements of trouble without applying to the Resident for assistance. In so far as any addition was thereby made to the numbers of the Nizam's army, the movement was to be deprecated; because that army, being already in excess of real acquirements, was a severe burden to the finances, and might even prove an embarrassment to the British government. The commandant of "the reformed troops" was an Englishman; and in virtue of his office he wore the sword of Raymond, a Frenchman who was in the Nizam's service towards the end of the eighteenth century, and whose memory was so much revered by Native soldiers that lights were, as they probably still are, kept burning at his tomb.

Shortly after my arrival on the occasion of a great Muhammadan festival, there was held before the Minister, acting on behalf of the Nizam, a general parade of his master's troops. I sat for several hours on a broiling day in May with the Minister in a balcony of his house in the city watching the troops as they defiled before us along the narrow street. The "reformed troops" came first, having among their officers many Europeans; next the other Deccani troops, for the most part dressed in uniform after the European model; then followed the Arabs in the plainest white costume, with nothing martial save their matchlocks, pouches and daggers, the Rohillas much more showy with their Indian dress and accoutrements, and some Abyssinians lending variety to the long line; lastly the contingent of the Amîr-i-Kabîr, whose troops chiefly wore the European uniform, closed the procession. The strength to which these forces had grown during several generations suggested thoughts of political danger. But any diminution in the army of a Native State must be gradual, and can only be effected by ceasing to recruit. As the men do not enlist for a time, but regard the military service of the State as a life-long profession, an attempt on the part of a ruler to discharge them is more likely to produce revolutionary movement than any other cause that could be imagined.

A long chain of circumstances had gradually strengthened the Minister's position, and rendered it proof against the intrigues of his opponents. The innate virtue of his disposition and the excellence of his character have been already mentioned. He was not answerable for the utter mismanagement which had caused to the Nizam the loss of power in Berar, when that province was brought under British management. He had since that time striven manfully to reform every part of the administration, the land revenue, the dispensing of justice, the police, and, above all, the finances. Without evincing forceful energy of the highest kind, he was yet full of activity and promptitude. Though his temperament was nervous and susceptible of agitation, still he was resolute, capable of maintaining self-command in danger, and animated by the spirit which might be expected in a man of high birth. His sensitive disposition, harassed by many trials and troubles, would probably have worn out his body had it been feeble; but his frame though not robust was wiry. As an administrator he certainly was not superior, by many he would be thought hardly equal, to the two best Hindu Ministers of his day, Dinkar Rao of Gwalior and Madhava Rao of Baroda. But as a man of business, especially in finance, he has not been surpassed by any Native in this century. His official assiduity and mastery of details left nothing to be desired. It was difficult to discern whether he possessed original ability of the Oriental type because his mind was modelled very much by European influences. At all events he was an excellent imitator; whatever improvement the British Government introduced he would sooner or later adopt, *longo intervallo* perhaps, but still with some effect. Thus, roads caravanserais medical schools drains and conservancy, besides many miscellaneous improvements, all had a share of his attention. He exercised his vast patronage well, appointing competent and respectable men to civil offices, and endeavouring to infuse an honest fidelity into the whole service of the State. That he fully succeeded in these efforts is more than can be affirmed, especially when it is remembered that the British Government itself cannot command entire success. At all events, British rulers have no overt opposition to contend with, whereas he had many enemies open or concealed, much hostile opinion and a jealous master, all arrayed against him. Upon a retrospect of the circumstances under which he had to act, it seems wonderful that so much was accomplished by him.

The Nizam's government was oppressed by its debts, which had been incurred in many quarters at many rates of interest, all more or less ruinous. Salar Jang attempted something like an unification of the debts, the object being to establish such confidence that with its improved credit his government might raise fresh loans at moderate rates, thereby paying off some of the old loans which bore the usurious rates; and this he effected to a considerable extent. Among the old creditors to be thus repaid, the foremost were the Arab chiefs who had mortgages on the revenues of districts, as already described. The redemption of a district from mortgage meant rescuing a considerable population from Arab misrule and bringing it under civilized administration. The operation was a critical one, as the Arab chief did not care to have his principal repaid and give up the district, nor did his armed men wish to leave their quarters. However it was known to all men that this was a case in which the Resident might, if required, employ force to put down resistance to the righteous action of the Nizam's Minister. Thus several tracts of country had been redeemed without overt opposition, and some were in course of redemption at this time. One Arab chief of consequence in those days accepted repayment with apparent alacrity, and surrendered the mortgaged territory. His mother being Deccani, he had a character milder than that of his father, who was of Arabian blood by both sides, and would never have given up a mortgage without a fight. One morning, in order to pay him a compliment, I breakfasted with him in his summer-house, and praised his loyal and wise conduct in complying with the Minister's wishes. If not actually ashamed, however, he did not seem to be proud of his conduct, nor did he appreciate my thanks.

In order to master the history which had a practical bearing on the present, I studied the official correspondence of Sir Charles Metcalfe, afterwards Lord Metcalfe, which related to his incumbency as Resident at Hyderabad, and which was to be seen among the records of the Residency. The struggle in which he was then engaged had reference to the Nizam's debt; his policy was to prevent the necessity of the Nizam's government borrowing money at usurious rates from an European firm, Messrs. Palmer and Rumbold, and mortgaging to them the revenues of certain districts by way of security. He was threatened with formidable opposition, but he persisted, and, for a time at least, checked a practice which must otherwise have destroyed the Nizam's State. The transactions are well set forth in Kaye's Life of Metcalfe, and a perusal of the official papers together with enquiry on the spot fully bore out the biographer's conclusions. Indeed Metcalfe's conduct under trying circumstances was an example to all of us who followed him in the Residency, and the public servants who study those affairs may thereby gain strength and courage for the performance of duty. The firm of Messrs. Palmer, after flourishing for a time, broke up; the Mr. Palmer who gave Metcalfe so much trouble was an East Indian of good birth on his father's and his mother's side. He was then still living, though feeble from old age, a pensioner on the Nizam's government; he died shortly afterwards, and I was present at his funeral.

Despite occasional anxiety, my work at the Residency proceeded smoothly and pleasantly. The First Assistant, Mr. J. G. Cordery, was busily occupying such leisure as his official duties might allow him in completing his translation in verse of the Iliad; the Second Assistant, Major Tweedie, was translating Hafiz. Thus I used daily to hear literary discussions regarding Greek and Persian poetry.

I heard of an European officer who had mingled in disguise with a Muhammadan congregation when a political sermon was being preached in one of the mosques. The point of the discourse consisted of an allegory, aimed at the British, which was somewhat in this wise. A she-wolf in feeble health once came before the Nizam and begged for a shed to shelter her till she recovered, which was granted. After a time His Highness sent a servant to say that if she had recovered it was time for her to quit. But meanwhile several cubs had been born, and she begged yet a little time and grace for herself and her young, in order to gain strength for moving; this also was granted. In due course another messenger was sent to say that the term already allowed was expiring. But now the she-wolf was herself again, the cubs had grown strong, and they all, both mother and offspring, began to shew their teeth, refusing to move; accordingly they never have moved from that day forward!

As the Minister could not inspect the interior of the country, it was desirable that I should do so according as opportunity served. It was also necessary for me to visit Berar, which province, as already mentioned, was under British administration.

In the Nizam's dominions there are many antique remains, of which the picturesque beauty vies with historic interest in exciting the imagination. Some of these have been already mentioned in the previous chapter X.; and they were all worthy of a more leisurely examination than I, busied with official cares, was ever able to bestow. Nothing could be more exhilarating to mind and body than rapid rides such as I had to take from one end of the Deccan to the other. Few parts of the country are uninteresting, and the varied scenes when recalled to memory seem like a picture gallery in the chambers of the mind, in

> "The dome of thought, the palace of the soul."

Such scenes are the groups of mausolea, each cupola, in solitary dignity, denoting a king—the deserted mosques, their stately aisles, once thronged with warriors returning thanks after victory, now the homes of bats and jackals—the ruined colleges, with cattle stabled where doctors once taught the precepts of Islam—the spiral staircase crumbling away, by which the Muezzin used to ascend the minaret whence he called aloud to the faithful—the hall of audience blocked up with rubbish, the dry fountain, the broken cistern—the frowning fortress of black rock, its unscaleable flanks escarped by nature—the great gun once deemed "the monarch of the battle-field," now rusting in the midst of long grass—the gloomy cave-temples with their gigantic figures, some representing the faith of Brahma and some of Buddh—the frescos on rock, though half defaced, still presenting the very life of eld with its forms and colours—the lakes brilliant under an eastern sun, with their massive stone dykes—the forest where the tiger has his lair, the cavern where the bear makes his den, the sugar-cane plantation where the boar regales himself at the expense of man—the granite masses rising abruptly from the cultivated plain with clusters of palm-trees at their base.

In Berar, however, there was little of beauty to be seen except the fortress of Gawilgarh standing aloft on the finely stratified rock of the southern Sâtpura slope. This stronghold had been for several centuries deemed impregnable by successive dynasties, and so it was under the conditions of uncivilized warfare. But General Arthur Wellesley by a scientific attack took it within a single hour. Few provinces in India would furnish less material for the poet or the painter, and here the interest centred in economic and political concerns. The territory happened to be brought under British management shortly before the time when the demand for cotton and the construction of the railway began to produce their effects. These two causes, combined with an equitable settlement of the land revenue, gave a marvellous impulse to the country and caused it to burst into new life. Instead of being land-locked in the centre of the continent and remote from sea-ports, it had a railway just opened to the western coast, and was frequented by traders European and Native from Bombay. The spread of cultivation, often in virgin soil, the abundant harvests, the unfailing rainfall, and the spontaneous growth of the land revenue, were all subjects of congratulation.

The principal officer there was Mr. (now Sir Alfred) Lyall; he had served with me in the Central Provinces, and I was thankful to entrust to him the revenue and finance of Berar. Besides official and administrative ability he was endowed with many mental gifts. He has written poetical pieces describing with pathetic power the sentiments of Indians who, having grown grey in wars and revolutions, find themselves fixed in the procrustean grooves of British civilization.

Returning to Hyderabad about Christmas-time, I heard many reports of changes for the worse in the Nizam's health. During an interview which I had with him, his manner was less frigid than before, though he seemed to be labouring under physical distress. His ailments, though serious, were understood to be curable by European remedies surgical and medical; he was attended, however, by unscientific practitioners and but too often listened to the advice of quacks. Our object was to induce him to accept the professional aid of Muhammadan surgeons and physicians, educated in the medical school at Hyderabad under European supervision, some of whom were highly qualified men; but he was almost superstitiously averse. It was known that unless he allowed himself this chance for recovery, his days were numbered; and such soon afterwards proved to be the case.

About this time the races at Hyderabad used to be held; these sports, though conducted in the European fashion, excited much interest among the Natives, especially the Muhammadans, who are essentially equestrian in their tastes. To the ordinary circumstances and accessories of a racecourse were added all the pomp and glitter of the Muhammadan nobles with their prancing steeds and their gay equipages. Sometimes "the chivalry of the Deccan," as they were called, would issue forth, and clouds of horsemen in every variety of costume would be careering over the plain. These sports constituted quite a local institution, promoting friendliness and good fellowship between the European officers and the Native gentry.

After Christmas I began to prepare for my departure, but in the brief time remaining to me there was one diplomatic transaction to be completed. It was desired that there should be a branch railway made to Hyderabad, starting from the nearest point on the trunk line which runs from Bombay to Madras. This branch would pass entirely through the Nizam's dominions, and without the consent of His Highness the project could not be entertained. Such consent was however difficult to obtain, for the Nizam regarded the project with an undefined horror, as being likely to upset all orthodox notions. He said that it would make the popular mind gyrate or swing backwards and forwards, with a movement like that of children at a fair. He doubtless thought also that the measure would augment British influence within his dominions, and would bring him more than ever within the attraction of the British system. There was also a question as to whether the scheme would be remunerative or whether it might not on the other hand involve financial loss. But to the financial part of the case His Highness gave not one moment's thought, so insignificant did he regard it in comparison with the two cardinal evils of upsetting the minds of his subjects and adding to British influence in his dominions. He allowed but little scope for persuasion, as he would close discussion by an abrupt negative. It seemed probable that I should have to depart *re infectâ;* for even at my farewell interview with him he did not say he would consent. Afterwards, at the last moment, just before I left the Residency his permission was received. Though loyal at heart, he dreaded the British Government and disliked its civilization, yet he felt that it was the only strong tower where he could in extremity take refuge. So he reluctantly accepted its railway as a crowning evil.

At the farewell interview, the Nizam seemed more distant and haughty than ever towards the Minister, whose nervousness was accordingly increased. I addressed to His Highness as many kind and respectful words as could be compressed into a few sentences of Hindustani, and he relaxed so far as to give quite a gracious answer. As we left His Highness's presence, the Minister expressed his satisfaction at my having spoken so respectfully to the Nizam. It was clear from the conversation that, despite the treatment he had so long been receiving from his master, Salar Jang felt to the full that affectionate veneration which all Muhammadans of the Deccan feel for the hereditary chief of their State.

The Nizam and his Minister did all in their power to impart brightness to the farewell entertainments which, according to custom, were given to me as a departing Resident. On these occasions the pyrotechnic displays preserved their Oriental character, but were improved by European art under the direction of French artists who had been for generations in the Nizam's service. The devices were varied and ingenious, chiefly in imitation of natural objects. Fountains of fire were produced, from which the sparkling light bubbled up and, overflowing, glided along like real water. From the descending rain of the rockets there issued serpents, wreathing themselves in bright coils against the dark sky. Large masses would explode, shooting forth luminous balls or globes as of silver ruby amethyst emerald. Solid bodies, like squares of infantry, maintained a rattling fusillade for several minutes. Miniature forts burst forth in a sham cannonade and at last blew up with an explosion that shook the ground. As the display took place on the margin of a small lake, all these effects were doubled by the reflections on the still water.

I felt sorry on leaving Hyderabad, although the sphere opening before me was the very one which of all others an ambitious officer would have desired. At Calcutta, there would be the Secretariat precincts, the Council chamber, the State departments, the bustle of European life and daily contact with affairs affecting the whole empire. These things, however interesting in themselves, would not be so pleasant as the rides in the Deccan, the parties at the Minister's palace, the receptions at the Residency, and the visits to the Native nobles.

Moreover, the Deccani Muhammadans had much ingratiated themselves with me, and I felt a real regard for them. They differ from the Muhammadans of the trans-Indus frontier and from those of southern India. According to the European standard they are Native gentlemen in manner and address, having refinement without the least effeminacy, and manliness without a trace of roughness or impetuosity.

Shortly after leaving Hyderabad I heard that the Nizam's ailment took the fatal turn that had been apprehended ; he died leaving a very young boy as his heir. Therefore a regency was established in which Salar Jang had a prominent part. Then the political conditions described in this chapter immediately changed. Salar Jang, being no longer in thraldom, began to travel about, the Resident had more direct influence and the general aspect of affairs became brighter.

Afterwards Salar Jang engaged in a correspondence with the Governor-General regarding Berar, perhaps to his own detriment. But I need not allude to that matter, being without official knowledge of its latest phases.

Early in 1868 Salar Jang had the narrowest escape from death; he was in a procession similar to that described in this chapter when two shots were fired, one of which grazed his turban and the other killed a man at his side. The motives of the assassin never were discovered, but it is possible that the attempt was prompted by revenge on the part of some among the many men who had lost their places when districts, as already explained, were redeemed from mortgage.

Leaving Hyderabad I proceeded to Madras on my way to Calcutta; the Madras route would nowadays be thought quite circuitous, but at that time it was the best, as the railway system was incomplete.

At Madras I met for the first time the Governor, Lord Napier (now Lord Napier and Ettrick). He had recently been occupied in supervising with much success the operations for the relief of famine on the east coast, and was generally considered to have shewn energy and promptitude on that occasion. The principles of Native art and architecture were justly the subjects of his admiration, and he was causing them to be applied to the designs for all large structures then in course of erection at Madras under Mr. Chisholm the Government architect. The Governor's example was leading public opinion in the direction of true culture.

From Madras the journey to Calcutta was performed by steamer; and among our passengers was Dr. Norman M'Leod who had come from England to pay a short visit to India. He won his way very rapidly among the community of Calcutta, by the genial heartiness of his address. Breadth of sympathy, masculine power of thought, an insight into the sentiments which move masses of men, a desire to shew that the paths of religion are truly pleasant—these seemed his most salient characteristics. He preached often, and his eloquence in the pulpit acted as a spell upon large congregations. On secular occasions he was an effective and popular speaker; and it was thought that on his return to England his voice would always be raised on behalf of India. One day at Calcutta I went with him to hear an address delivered by Keshab Chander Sen the

Brahmo preacher, whose oratory was then becoming famous. He seemed to be much impressed with the merits of the Brahmo address, in respect of its English style, command of language, persuasive argument, and, above all, its religious spirit. He was delighted with his visit to India, and seemed to have much capacity for enjoyment. But manifestly his constitution was not one calculated to withstand the disadvantages of the Bengal climate. When afterwards the report of his death in Scotland reached India, we all felt that a friend had been lost to us.

At Calcutta I waited immediately on the Governor-General, Sir John Lawrence; friendly and cordial words passed between us on finding ourselves once more, after the lapse of ten eventful years, in our old relative positions of principal and secretary.

I then received charge of the Foreign Secretaryship from my old friend Sir William Muir, who having served as Foreign Secretary for some time was now to take his seat for a short time in the Governor-General's Council, before being appointed Lieutenant-Governor of the North-western Provinces. He had been of great service to John Lawrence in the serious controversies which had arisen regarding tenant-right in Oudh, and to these he brought unequalled acumen and experience.

The Under-Secretary in the Foreign department had been John Wyllie, a brilliant member of the Covenanted Civil Service and an excellent writer. His literary talent had been evinced by several able articles in the *Edinburgh Review*, and in some of the London magazines, regarding the foreign policy of India. He had lately proceeded to England and had been succeeded by Henry Le Poer Wynne, an officer of much promise, evidently destined to rise to a high position—should he live—but, alas! his life was not long spared.

The Foreign Office had to deal with many diverse affairs pertaining to the independent States bordering on India, the Native States within India, and several large provinces under the direct administration of the Governor-General in Council.

At that time however, as indeed at most other times, the foremost subject was Afghanistan. The Amir Shir Ali was then establishing his power at all the three points of Caubul Candahar and Herat. It was considered good for British interests that there should be one ruler in that country who really could be held responsible for its foreign relations. The distractions, lasting there for several years, were supposed to present chinks and openings in the political armour through which Russian influences might enter. At that moment the reports always more or less current, regarding Russian intrigue, were very rife, without however having more foundation than that which may always be thought to exist. The prevalence of such rumours was accounted for by the movements which Russia was understood to be making from Bokhara towards the Oxus, some of her outposts having appeared on the north bank of that river. It became my business to note and collate all available information regarding these movements, which were not however really serious.

The affairs of the principal among the Native princes of India came under the cognizance of the Foreign Office, and this may be a suitable place for stating some points of interest which I knew regarding them, though the knowledge may in some instances have been acquired somewhat earlier or somewhat later than the year 1868.

The best of the Native princes of that day was the Maharaja of Jyepur, and by his death recently the country has suffered a loss. Though a Rajput of the highest birth, descended from the sun and moon, he possessed none of those physical characteristics for which his race is famed; instead of having a tall and erect figure he was short of stature and had a stooping gait; instead of the proud fiery look of his ancestors, he cast shy timid glances around him, being half blinded by cataract from which he had been partially relieved through European skill. Still he was not deficient in nerve and decision, and while good-tempered in the main, had pride and generosity. He was loyal and well-disposed, probably there was not among all the Indian princes a truer friend to the British Government, and his ambition was turned into good channels. He wished to be thought a wise ruler and to be esteemed as the head of a prosperous State. He co-operated with the British Government in modifying the system for the collection of the salt-duties, though at some sacrifice of his own susceptibilities. He rendered much assistance in establishing the college for educating the young chiefs of Rajputana. Once I visited him at his capital of Jyepur when a festival was being held; he was issuing forth from his palace to pass through the streets upon an elephant by torchlight to receive the greetings of his people. He drove us to Ambair the ancient capital before the modern Jyepur was built, and shewed us the castle, the town, the lake, all nestling amidst the hills.

The Maharaja Sindhia was prominent at that time; his fidelity had been proved in trials and dangers. His disposition was understood to be wayward and fitful, sometimes even prone to melancholy; he had a hesitation in speech with a good-natured bluffness of manner. He was anxious that the British garrison should be removed from his fortress of Gwalior; against such removal, however, there were obvious objections as the position was one of political importance and renown. He had been unable to hold it efficiently or securely during the war of the mutinies, and if it were ever to fall into hostile hands, the moral effect would be bad. On visiting Gwalior, I could not but be struck by the grandeur of the vast oblong rock rising abruptly out of the cultivated plain. Sindhia had much chequered experience of war during the troubles which followed the mutinies; his military taste was thus cultivated, and he always gave his chief attention to the management of his army. For the civil administration he had wisely trusted to his Minister Dinkar Rao: and when that able minister resigned a competent successor was fortunately found. Unlike the Nizam, he greatly favoured the cause of railway extension, and under the auspices of the British Government, invested a large sum of money in the construction of a railroad to Gwalior.

Sindhia like most other Mahrattas was of a humble caste, therefore it was customary and proper that he should have a Mahratta Brahmin to be his minister. Dinkar Rao was a Mahratta Brahmin and an excellent specimen of his caste. He was slight in figure, his features were delicate, his brow lofty;

he had polished manners, his speech was soft, gentle and persuasive; his mien indicated that quiet pride which, transmitted through many generations, is characteristic of the Brahmins. Beneath this smooth exterior there lay a masterful temper and an immovable will. He did not learn English, and never assimilated European ideas into his mental constitution. Indeed in some matters pertaining to social improvement, such as female education, he would probably be found, in heart at least, retrogressive. But in plain matters of administration he was a man of original thought and commanding ability. As Minister he served for a comparatively short time, but during that time he acquired a reputation as high as that of any other Hindu during this generation. His integrity was unquestioned, and he retired into private life with a very moderate competency.

Next after Dinkar Rao, the most notable Hindu administrator of the time is Madhava Rao, the Minister of the Baroda State, also a Brahmin, but a man of a totally different type. His conduct in private and public life is exemplary, while his ability is of a high order. By reason of his excellent attainments in English, his comprehensive experience and his large acquaintance with public affairs, he is, on the whole, the best-informed Native in India. He is enlightened in respect to all matters of improvement; but perhaps in his heart he hardly approves of some among the social reforms which are now advocated. He first won fame as the Minister of Travancore; then for a time he was in Holkar's service, and lastly became Minister of Baroda. He found that State seriously disordered by the late Gaekwar Mulhar Rao, an infamous ruler, but he brought it within a few years into a condition of much prosperity.

Next after Sindhia the most important Mahratta prince is the Maharaja Holkar, whose manner of ruling affords but little scope for an able Minister. Holkar is probably the best man of business among Native princes whom this generation has seen. He received, when young, a sound practical education under European supervision, and acquired early a fondness for public affairs. His attention is given not so much to statesman-like reforms as to the despatch of business. His diligence in auditing the accounts of his government and regulating his finances is remarkable for a Native prince; therefore he justly prides himself on this assiduity.

The Begum of Bhopal affords an example which may cheer the advocate of female education in India, as shewing the standard which a woman may reach. For here is a Princess known to be effectively loyal, and to govern well by her own high capacity without leaning on any Minister. It devolved on me as a knight of the Order to accompany Her Highness when she was invested with the insignia of the Star of India. She seemed slight in figure, and from external appearance it was difficult to judge of her ability.

The kingdom of Jammu and Cashmir has been already mentioned in chapter VII. in reference to the first visit I paid to it in 1859, when it had recently recovered from a pestilence of cholera. I was able to visit it again ten years later, and found it much improved; the famines which have subsequently desolated that fair region had not then appeared. Until he failed to cope with these visitations of famine, the Maharaja Rambhir Sing was thought to be a fairly good ruler, and certainly a very competent man in public business. His kindness, consideration and hospitality to travellers have made him deservedly popular with the European community. But he is not thought by the public to have adequately developed the resources of the valley, or to have made the most of the advantages with which nature has so bounteously endowed it. He set up a judicial establishment and introduced various administrative improvements. Still the land revenue system, which was of more consequence than anything else, remained without essential alteration. The fact of the northern provinces of this State being conterminous with territories in which the Russians have been operating politically, causes constant anxiety to the British Government. Sinister reports thence arise which may seldom be believed, but are yet not put out of mind. Thus, too, temptation presents itself to the evil-disposed within this State.

The personal influence of the present Maharaja and of his

father, Golab Sing, has always been so potential in the State as to leave but little scope for their subordinates. Still there was one very competent Minister, Kirpa Ram, belonging to the Khatri or writer caste of the Panjab, a man of the best education according to the Oriental style only, and one of the ablest natives in India next after those who had received a Western education. He had a high-born aspect and a refined manner, with some resemblance to Salar Jang in general appearance.

In the Cis-Satlej territories the chiefs of Pattiala and Jhind, who personally were so well remembered for their conduct during the war of the mutinies, and whose characters have been described in chapter VII., had passed away. The chief of Jhind had a worthy successor in his son; in Pattiala the demise of the good and able chief was followed by a regency composed of faithful men, and the heritage was transmitted in good condition to the young chief, who despite all the advantages of education died prematurely from his own imprudence.

In those days the Native princes or nobles in the North-western Provinces and Oudh who bore the best repute for loyalty and high-mindedness were the Maharaja of Benares, the Maharaja of Balrampur, the Nawab of Rampur and Deo Narain Sing of Benares. The conversation of Deo Narain Sing was instructive and interesting to those Europeans who were most concerned in understanding the sentiments and wishes of the people.

The kingdom of Nepal suffered what seemed to be an irreparable loss by the death of its Minister Jang Behadur; but the dissensions expected to arise after his death have fortunately not arisen. In his case, as in that of some other great workers, the results of his work have survived him. At this time he was in the zenith of his fame and power, and after having passed through evil and good report was now esteemed universally. I saw something of him at a later time, and his conversation confirmed the opinion previously formed by me in common with most people regarding his ability and other high qualities. In his youth he must have been fiercely barbarous, and even in his old age he retained perhaps a semi-barbaric character. When remembrance is borne of the associations in which his youth must have been passed, the awful scenes he witnessed, the massacres in which he participated, the blood he shed—then there is wonder at the moderation and self-control afterwards displayed by him, the discipline enforced by his system, and the public order secured by his stern yet just rule. What his feelings may have originally been towards the British no man can now say; but he visited England and returned to Nepal with a conviction from which he never swerved, that it would be well to adhere to the English side, as that was sure to be ultimately victorious. The conduct of the Nepal State during the war of the mutinies was unsatisfactory on the whole; whether the Nepalese were ripe for revolt against the British is doubtful; but there were reasons for fearing that they might have joined the rebellion had it not been for the dissuading voice and restraining hand of Jang Behadur.

It was one of these Native statesmen who warned us that, however excellent the conduct of the British Government may be, many influential classes will yet labour under an uneasy feeling and an indefinable restlessness. There might, he said, be no rational cause for discontent, still a desire for political change would supervene; and he illustrated the feeling thus. On a sultry night in an Indian summer a sleeper, lying on one side of his couch, is distressed by the stifling heat; he then seeks relief in turning to the other side. So it often is with the sentiments of some among the Natives; under British rule the very stillness of the political atmosphere becomes oppressive to them, and they inwardly sigh for the breeze even though it should ultimately freshen into a gale.

CHAPTER XIV.

(1864–68.)

JOHN LAWRENCE AS VICEROY.

Arrival of John Lawrence at Calcutta as Viceroy—The North-west frontier—The Bhotan war—Barracks for the European soldiery—The Sanitary Department—Summer residence at Simla for the Government of India—Tenant-right in Oudh—Proposals for extending the permanent settlement—The famine in Orissa—Canals of irrigation—Development of the railway system—The Bishopric of Calcutta, George Cotton and Robert Milman—Progress of legislation—Henry Sumner Maine—Leave and furlough rules for the civil and military services—Financial management—Relations with Afghanistan—Affairs of Central Asia—John Lawrence's departure from India.

In the autumn of 1863 Lord Elgin was understood to be entering upon the course of his administration, in nautical phrase, at full speed. He had been nearly two years in India, and had become acquainted with all the central departments of the State during a residence of several months at Calcutta. He travelled thence to the north, holding levées and receptions on the way, thus making the acquaintance of the principal European officers and of the Native princes, also seeing something of the Indian population. He spent a summer at Simla in the Himalayas arranging his thoughts and considering his plans. By staying one season at Calcutta and another in the hills, he measured the advantages or disadvantages of the climate, together with his own capabilities of labour. He intended to spend Christmas and perhaps the greater part of the winter in the Panjab; he was to hold large receptions for the Native chiefs at Lahore, the capital of that province; and he summoned thither his executive and legislative councils to meet for a session which might last several weeks. He had a special reason, also, for proceeding towards the North-west quarter of the empire. For after consultation with the Lieutenant-Governor of the Panjab, he determined to apply armed force against certain tribes dwelling in the hills which overhang the Indus a little to the north of Attock. The operations proceeded not so favourably for the British arms as might have been anticipated, and the area of disturbance seemed likely to extend itself. Still after his experience of grave conjunctures in other countries he had a just confidence in his own capacity for dealing with this affair, however serious it might become.

On his way to Lahore he desired to traverse some of the hill districts which lie between Simla and the Panjab, so he began his journey by daily marches. One morning he was crossing a stream by a suspension-bridge made of canes and bamboos, by which only one person could pass at a time, as it swung and oscillated considerably. During this passage he was seized with giddiness and faintness, and it shortly after became apparent that his heart was fatally affected. He arrived in the course of a very few days, though with some difficulty, at Dharmsala in the Kangra district, telegraphed to England his resignation of the Governor-Generalship, and prepared himself to die. He summoned to his bedside Dr. Macrae from Calcutta, the same physician who had attended James Wilson in his last illness. Dharmsala is the capital of a Himalayan valley lying above the well-known fort of Kangra. From it the spectator looks up towards forest-clad hillsides, and thence to snowy heights which seem to tower right over his head, while below him there is a fair prospect over the rice-fields threaded with the rivulets and watercourses which supply the artificial irrigation; and the November season is the finest in the year. Altogether the place had an exceeding loveliness which cheered Lord Elgin during the distressful depression of his last days. He rallied slightly at times, and would turn his thoughts towards the prospects of war on the frontier and the programme of the assemblage at Lahore. He was, however, hopelessly lingering, and sank after protracted suffering borne with Christian resignation. He was buried in the picturesque churchyard of

Dharmsala; but the monument with the entablature commemorating his great deeds in various countries is in the cathedral of Calcutta. There was much public sorrow over a great career suddenly and prematurely closed. The arrangements for the meeting of the Council at Lahore, and the other proceedings intended to be held there, were countermanded.

Lord Elgin died in November 1863, and no person appointed to be his successor being present in India, Sir William Denison, the Governor of Madras, became by law acting Governor-General, as he was the senior of the two Presidency Governors. Sir William proceeded to Calcutta to meet the members of the Council there, and conducted efficiently the current affairs of the general government. He intended, however, to move northwards very soon, because he was vigorously dealing with the military and political affairs on the Indus frontier, and it was thought that warlike events might, perhaps, develop themselves. But he suspended this intention on receiving the announcement that Sir John Lawrence had been appointed Governor-General and was starting immediately for India.

Nowadays the news of a Governor-General being nominated in England, to fill a vacancy suddenly created, would be flashed by electric telegraph throughout the East quite a month before he could land upon Indian shores. The telegraphic communication not having been, as yet, established between England and India in 1863, the new Governor-General arrived almost as soon as the notification of his appointment. When the steamship carrying him touched at Ceylon, the men on the first boat from the shore asked, "Who is to be the Governor-General of India?" the answer came, "John Lawrence, and he is on board."

A feeling of confidence and satisfaction arose in the public mind, when John Lawrence entered Government House at Calcutta, on January 12th, 1864, just sixteen years after the arrival of his great master, Dalhousie. All classes believed that he had been the means not only of saving the Panjab during the war of the mutinies in 1857, but also of directing its resources towards the recapture of Delhi and pacification of the

North-western Provinces. The mercantile and professional community regarded him as a ruler thoroughly understanding, from arduous experience, the many needs of the country. The official classes rejoiced that, as one was to be chosen from among their ranks for the supreme command, the choice had fallen upon a really able and competent man, who would do justice to the selection, and acquit himself well, whatever might betide, in his lofty though difficult sphere. The heart throbbed and the pulse beat high with those ambitious men, happily numerous in India, who expected to carve out their career by the force of will and intellect, and knew that their new ruler would impartially discern merit and demerit. Other Governors-General had possessed personal capacity and an insight into human character, but could gain only by degrees that Indian experience of which they were necessarily destitute. Here was one who to at least an equal ability joined a long acquaintance with both the work and the men who were to perform it. Soon, however, the envious few began to say that he would hardly receive full support from the Government in England during the conjunctures and controversies incidental to Indian administration, not having been conspicuous in any of the English political parties. It was sometimes added, in disparaging tones, that he had been appointed only because war was at that moment deemed likely to spread along the Indus frontier, and he was the fittest man to cope with such emergencies. In so far as this reason, among others, may have weighed with the English authorities, it constituted, not any disparagement, but, on the contrary, the best tribute to his fame.

I had just made over the charge of the Central Provinces to Colonel Elliot, when John Lawrence arrived at Calcutta; and he summoned me to meet him there. I stayed with him at Government House for a short time before returning to the Central Provinces, on Colonel Elliot being appointed Governor-General's Agent in Rajputana. Thus, I became acquainted with the views, policy and intentions in regard to the coming administration, of one who was the new Governor-General and my old master.

John Lawrence's first appearance in public at Calcutta was for the purpose of opening the agricultural exhibition which had been prepared on a large scale by Sir Cecil Beadon, then Lieutenant-Governor of Bengal. In his speech on that occasion the Governor-General reminded his audience that Indian agriculture, despite its many merits, was still backward, and that all persons interested in it should educate themselves by studying the results achieved in more advanced countries. Even he, cautious as he was in forming expectations, seemed to hope that the public would learn much practically from this great exhibition. The show, indeed, with all its paraphernalia was elaborately prepared; most of the machines and implements, to be seen at an agricultural exhibition in England, were paraded before a vast concourse of Bengali Natives, several experiments with steam-ploughs were displayed, and indigenous products in great variety from the remotest parts of vast provinces were spread before the crowd. There was a general awakening, for the country was recovering fast after the war of the mutinies; the civil contest in America, then at its height, was stimulating the Indian trade; resources no longer required for indigo culture, were being transferred to Himalayan tea-gardens; and the waste land rules mentioned in chapter VIII. were causing an additional influx of British capital. Men were disposed to be sanguine, and seeing this exhibition began to exclaim that two blades of cereals would be made to grow where one had grown before. Sir Cecil Beadon, having taken the most laudable trouble in arranging the show, seemed to catch the enthusiasm of the moment. Doubtless the exhibition had some educational effect upon the Natives, but its influence in improving their agriculture was inappreciable. The moral to be gathered is this, that an impulse to the industry of a nation cannot be artificially imparted by even the most powerful rulers.

John Lawrence next appeared publicly in the uniform of the Calcutta Volunteers, which he donned in order to inspect that corps. His experience during the war of the mutinies led him to attach much political importance to the Volunteer movement in India. The European inhabitants might at any moment be required to stand to their arms. If organized and drilled they would all the better evince the national qualities which during the late disturbances had been so conspicuous. He dwelt much on the public services which such a corps as that then before him might have rendered had it existed in Calcutta during the critical months of 1857.

One of his first official acts was the publication of a Government Gazette to thank the officers and men for their gallantry and endurance during the recent operations on the Indus frontier, which have been already mentioned. The expedition against certain hill tribes of the mountains overhanging the Indus had begun as a little war, but soon grew into a serious affair. The tribes had shewn much prowess in several actions, the issue of which was not quite satisfactory to the British troops and commanders. Much apprehension was felt lest these particular tribes should combine with those of the neighbouring hills and a general movement arise all along the trans-Indus border, although previous experience shewed that one of the fortunate peculiarities of these tribes was their incapacity for combination. The authorities, however, deemed it advisable to make extensive preparations for any ulterior operations which might become necessary. The hostile junction, as anticipated by some, failed to occur, and the resistance of the tribes after a short time ceased or collapsed. The result though victorious was hardly proportionate to the means employed, and less successful than that of the previous expeditions on the trans-Indus frontier already mentioned in chapter V.

This was not the only occurrence causing John Lawrence's thoughts to revert to that frontier with which in former years he had been familiar. A despatch had recently been received from the Bombay Government, of which Sir Bartle Frere was the head, comparing the management of that portion of the trans-Indus frontier which was under the Bombay Government with the administration of that section which was under the Panjab, and naturally drawing conclusions very favourable to the Bombay authorities. The Bombay section of the frontier was represented by the province of Sind, of which Sir Bartle had been so long the distinguished head. The gravamen of the allegation amounted to this, that the Sind method of dealing with the hill tribes had been mild and yet successful, whereas the Panjab method was severe and yet had a lesser degree of success. John Lawrence, however, soon shewed that the Panjab hill tribes were much more fierce and unruly than the Sind hill tribes, and consequently required sharper and more frequent chastisement. If outrages are committed, warning and every other alternative short of armed force may be judiciously tried. If they are persistently continued, then as a last resort armed force must be applied. This was the short and plain justification of the Panjab proceedings on the frontier; and on a similar provocation, or tissue of provocations, the Sind authorities must perforce have adopted equally stringent remedies. Charles Napier and John Jacob had commanded on the Sind frontier; they were not the men to allow repeated incursions to pass with impunity, but employed their troops as occasion might demand for the vindication of British authority. It was the good fortune of the Sind authorities that, having less turbulent characters to deal with, they had not to draw the sword so often as their comrades in the Panjab.

After a short time John Lawrence had to undertake hostilities against Bhotan in order to punish that semi-barbarous state for the insults offered by it to the mission which had been despatched in Lord Elgin's time. He entered upon the war with a heavy heart, believing that the British troops would encounter formidable obstacles in forests favouring ambuscades, stockades protected by impervious thickets, malarious valleys and a deluging rainfall.

Having disposed of the immediate questions relating to military operations, he turned his attention to matters concerning the physical and moral welfare of the European troops in India. During his earlier years he had been shocked by the drunkenness seen to prevail among them. His feeling in respect to the value of these soldiers had been intensified by the experience of 1857 and of the war which ensued. He was impressed by the waste of life, the wear and tear of precious strength, the loss of public resources, which arose from defective accommodation and faulty sanitation in an Eastern climate. He had shared his brother Henry's enthusiasm in the cause of improving the condition and the surroundings of the British soldier in India. Imbued with these ideas, he had, before starting from England conferred earnestly with Florence Nightingale on this subject, and consulted the Army Sanitary Commission. On his arrival at Calcutta, he forthwith set about establishing a sanitary department for each of the three armies of India, and selected officers of high ability as sanitary commissioners, some drawn from the medical and others from the civil or military service. He had in the Military member of Council, Sir Robert Napier (now Lord Napier of Magdala), and in the Commander-in-Chief, Sir Hugh Rose (now Lord Strathnairn), two colleagues believing equally with himself in the need of sanitary improvement, and eminently qualified by experience and special knowledge to afford co-operation. He found public opinion quickened in this respect by the occurrence during recent years of epidemic cholera at some of the largest military stations. Those frightful outbreaks were understood to have been at least partly due to preventible causes.

But sanitation, however scientific and well-conducted, would be of little avail if the barracks were faulty and insalubrious. Some of the Indian barracks begun by Sir Charles Napier or undertaken by Lord Dalhousie comprised all, or nearly all, that could be reasonably desired. Others, however, were old, and their style obsolete; many, too, were of a temporary character, having been hastily erected in consequence of the rapid influx of European reinforcements from England during the war of the mutinies. Of these temporary barracks, again, some had been built at stations which were needed for the special purposes of the pending campaigns, but which were being abandoned after the final pacification of the country. The policy was to determine the distribution of the European forces for the future among the various stations, to consider what stations had, and what had not, barracks of a good style, and then to construct suitable buildings at those stations which were destitute of proper accommodation. Next, the dimensions of the structures were reconsidered; and the intention was to improve even upon the style introduced under Lord Dalhousie. Double-storied barracks were to be built, it being intended that the men should dine downstairs, and sleep upstairs beyond the reach of the malarious exhalations from the ground in a hot climate. The expense would be considerable, far beyond the ordinary means of the Government. But John Lawrence and his advisers deemed the importance of the matter to be paramount; and decided that, while devoting as much as possible from the current revenues to this purpose, they would borrow such sums as might be required from time to time for completing the work. The total sum to be furnished from current revenues and loan funds together, amounted to the large sum of ten millions sterling.

In connexion with army sanitation, John Lawrence developed the sanitary department as it now exists throughout India. A Sanitary Commissioner was appointed to serve as the professional adviser of each of the several provincial Governments; under him were many sanitary assistants, all medical men; and under them again were sub-assistants, of lesser grades. There was a Sanitary Commissioner of the highest grade attached to the Government of India who acted as professional adviser to the supreme authority. Annual sanitary reports were ordered to be prepared by the various provincial Governments; these were reviewed by the Government of India and ultimately sent to be examined by a Commission of experts in England. The results of these measures were not indeed immediate, but the benefit has after the lapse of some time, proved considerable, and will be greater in the future if only the people themselves can be induced to afford a more intelligent co-operation. At all events John Lawrence laid the foundation and may almost be called the father of Indian sanitation.

When Sir Hugh Rose (Lord Strathnairn) returned to England,

his successor was Sir William Mansfield (Lord Sandhurst), who has been mentioned in the previous chapters VIII. and XII. as an eminent commander and military administrator. The Military Secretary to the Government was Colonel (now Sir Henry) Norman, a very able and distinguished officer who had served as Adjutant-General during the siege of Delhi and the Oudh campaign. He enjoyed the entire confidence of Colin Campbell, Lord Clyde, and now had great weight with John Lawrence in all military affairs; indeed there was none whose advice was valued more than his.

John Lawrence then considered the questions relating to the localities where the head-quarters of the Government of India might be best established. He knew that an idea was set afloat in those days to the effect that Calcutta was out of date as a capital, and the head-quarters of the Government of India might well be fixed elsewhere. Indeed he told me that during his farewell interview with the Prime Minister (Lord Palmerston) before departing from England, allusion was made to this topic. But manifestly to move the local habitation of a vast establishment like that of the Government of India would involve an enormous expense; and he failed to see that the change would produce any corresponding benefit. On the contrary he thought that any change of this sort would be for the worse. Calcutta had in his judgment unequalled advantages as the head-quarters of the Supreme Government of India. Though it may be called a sea-port, yet it has a position defended by nature against hostile attacks from the sea. Its situation nearly a hundred miles inland can be approached only by navigating the intricate and dangerous channels of the Hughli river, for which skilled pilots are necessary; the passage of an enemy can be thus barred with but slight expense. The trade is already very great, and seems likely to grow as much as that of any other place in India. The wealth and populousness of the surrounding territory are unrivalled; and the disposition of the inhabitants is wonderfully peaceful and quiet. While half of India was disturbed during 1857, demanding immense sacrifices yet yielding no revenue, Bengal was for the most part undisturbed and paid its millions into the Government treasury. While the limbs of the body politic were racked with pain, the vital organs in the centre remained intact, and the pulsation near the heart was generally, if not always, steady. Although the welfare of the Natives is the primary consideration in the mind of the Government, yet it is practically impossible to manage the country without listening to the sentiments and noting the views of the resident European community. Therefore it is essential that during a part of the year the Government of India should reside in some centre of English opinion; and Calcutta is the largest of existing centres. Regarding the climate opinions may differ, but those who are acquainted with the whole of India, know that Calcutta having the sea-breezes and some winter cold to be set against the heat of other seasons, presents as many climatic advantages as would be presented by any other place of equal magnitude in the plains of India. Thus John Lawrence gave his voice without hesitation for holding fast to Calcutta; resolving that his Government should be settled there for at least a part of every year, or during the winter season, when trade and industry are at the highest point of activity, and when the cold weather is favourable to European health.

But he thought that the Government of India, having duly arranged its sojourn at Calcutta, might with propriety and advantage reside for another part of the year in the cool and refreshing climate of the Himalayas during the summer season when the heat is severe in the plains. He was unwilling to proceed thither alone, and decided that his Council should accompany him. He noted that in former times the frequent and lengthened separation of the Governor-General from his Council had caused dissatisfaction and complaint, also that the growing bulk variety and intricacy of the public business must render the despatch of affairs difficult unless the head of the Government and his principal advisers were together. Thus he virtually for the first time established the practice whereby the Government of India, including the Governor-General the Councillors the principal Secretaries, and some of the departmental chiefs, reside through the summer months at Simla in the Himalayas. The current business of all the executive branches is there despatched, and also some part of the legislative business. The law empowers the Governor-General to summon his legislative Council to any place in British India; legally therefore the Legislature may sit at Simla. In practice, however, at its sittings there the Council takes up only such bills or projects of law as affect the interior of the country, or some special interests of the Natives. But it reserves for its sittings at Calcutta those bills which concern the whole empire, and in respect to which the contact with independent English opinion is desirable. Simla was chosen for the summer residence because it was by far the largest of the many English settlements in the Indian mountains, whether the Himalayas, the Nilgiris or others. It was the only hill station which could furnish house accommodation for so large an influx of residents and visitors. It was easily accessible by rail and road, even in the height of the rainy season. It also had the most commanding situation, politically, in the whole Himalayan region, overlooking the North-western Provinces, close to the Panjab proper, comparatively within reach of the Indus frontier, yet not in too great proximity to points which might be threatened with danger. The Government of India, while sojourning in the mountains, should be near enough to positions of political importance, in order to feel the pulse of the empire, without being exposed to actual risk, as the spectacle of the supreme authority being surrounded with danger has a bad effect on the public mind. Simla alone fulfilled all these essential conditions, while some hill stations would have been too small, some too near to troublous localities, others, again, too remote. Succeeding Governors-General have tried to find, but have never succeeded in finding, better situations than Simla, either at Ranikhet near Almora in the Himalayas, at Utacamand in the Nilgiris, or elsewhere; and experience has fully ratified the choice made by John Lawrence respecting his summer residence.

The establishment of the Government at Simla as a summer resort seemed at first to be unpopular, or at least to be disliked by the European community at Calcutta. Apprehension was felt by the Anglo-Indian press lest the absence of the State departments from the capital should lessen the opportunities of obtaining accurate knowledge on political and economic subjects, and so shut off the access to official information. But the dissatisfaction proved to be temporary and transient, and it was soon recognized that the country would pe the gainer if the Government should for a part of the year escape from the disadvantages of a tropical climate, especially as its members would be at the capital during the brisk season, when there is most to be seen heard and learnt. The provincial Government of the Panjab, too, could be summoned to Simla, and thus the Governor-General and his Council would be "en rapport" with one of the most important among the provinces. Simla itself has not, indeed, such important accessories as those possessed by some of the Indian sanitaria. It has no great industries close at hand like the tea cultivation near Darjiling in the eastern Himalayas, or the coffee plantations in the Nilgiris. It is not surrounded with very important political associations like Mahableshwar in the Deccan. But it is in the midst of the protected Hill States inhabited sparsely by a population not to be surpassed in the whole empire for loyalty and contentment. Its scenery is not only attractive to the artist, but also interesting to every man of thought and culture. Its situation is upon a ridge which divides the drainage of the Jamna and the Satlej, and actually constitutes the water-parting for two great seas, namely, the Bay of Bengal and the Indian Ocean. From its summits is to be seen the great view of the Satlej separating the Panjab from the rest of India and passing through a territory marked by decisive events from the days of the early Hindus, the Greek invaders and the Muhammadan conquerors. The imposing aspect of the place and of its neighbourhood elevates the imagination, braces the faculties, and assists the mind in forming large conceptions. The natural beauty is not of an enervating character; on the contrary, the weather is often severe and the atmospheric phenomena are impressive. Few places so beautiful as Simla have seen such great schemes evolved, such grave conjunctures considered, such problems of statesmanship solved.

Having settled his Government at Simla for the summer and autumn, John Lawrence proceeded with measures for the general good. Foremost among these in his estimation was a revision of the proceedings relating to tenant-right in Oudh. It has been stated in the previous chapter VIII. that Canning had re-established the landed aristocracy of this province, locally styled the Talukdars, in their rights and status. It was intended that the rights of the occupants and cultivators subordinate to the Talukdars should also be preserved; the belief prevailed in 1859 that in this respect adequate security had been provided; and Mr. (now Sir Charles) Wingfield was left, as Chief Commissioner, in charge of the administration. Five years having since elapsed, and considerable experience being thus gained, John Lawrence considered that the status of important classes among the cultivators was not being sufficiently protected, and that subsidiary measures for such protection were therefore necessary. Mr. Wingfield, who was still Chief Commissioner, objected to this view; nevertheless John Lawrence insisted on his measures being carried into effect, and accordingly the rights of these cultivators were secured by arrangements which have subsequently been embodied in a legislative enactment. These measures, however, aroused keen opposition in the Governor-General's own Council, and among many influential quarters the question was regarded as one of tenant *versus* landlord. At that time the landlord's interest, which was dominant in Bengal, made common cause with the Oudh Talukdars; in this interest also the mercantile community of Calcutta had much concern. Perhaps as an outcome of the war of the mutinies, an opinion had temporarily settled itself in the public mind to the effect that the Government by unduly supporting subordinate classes had alienated the Native aristocracy. From these and other causes the Anglo-Indian papers warmly espoused the side of the landlords and assailed the Governor-General as the destroyer of property and the breaker of compacts. Then for the first time after landing in India as Governor-General, almost for the first time during his long and prosperous career, John Lawrence felt the cold blast of unpopularity alternating with the heat of violent invective. There were also signs to shew that the controversy, if settled in India, would be revived in England, and that there the position taken up by the Governor-General might be menaced. I met John Lawrence about that time, and he seemed to think that the outlook of the affair was doubtful. He trusted that the Secretary of State (then Sir Charles Wood) would support him, and he was thankful for the confidence reposed in his policy. But if he should not be sustained in his measures regarding Oudh, he was prepared to resign his high office rather than yield the points under discussion. He held that the question was one of justice or injustice towards some of the industrious and deserving, though humble, classes of British subjects; that if he were prevented from giving effect to what he knew to be right, he would prefer to retire. In the sequel he was, despite the controversial excitement of the hour, generously sustained by the Secretary of State. Without resuscitating the arguments of the time on either side, it must be held that experience has justified the steps then taken regarding tenant-right on behalf of certain classes. The only question nowadays remaining is not whether those steps went too far, but whether they went far enough. If a revision were now to take place, additional classes would be included in the privileges then conceded; and the benefits would be extended in a manner which might have gladdened the heart of John Lawrence if he could, under the circumstances of his day, have adopted it.

Subsequently he found that the rights secured to several classes of cultivators in the Panjab during the settlement of that province, as explained in chapters IV. and V., were being seriously threatened. Again he came forward as a protector, and after a long discussion procured the passing of a law through the Legislative Council for the preservation of tenant-right in the Panjab under legal definitions. Having, as a member of the Legislature, been placed in charge of the bill for this purpose during its passage through the Council, I am able to attest the earnestness of his convictions on this point.

He desired, however, to be the friend not only of the tenants, but also of land-owners of all grades, from the peasant proprietor to the large landlord. During his residence in England, when serving in the Council of the Secretary of State, he had become impressed with a conviction of the advantages secured to the country by that part of the Bengal Permanent Settlement which limited for ever the Government demand on account of the land-tax. This view was doubtless in consonance with the English ideas which he may have gathered, but that he should have entertained it may appear strange to many on a consideration of his antecedents. He did not adopt the policy without grave reasons. He would adduce as arguments, the augmentation in the value of landed property consequent on the limitation of the land-tax for ever,—the confidence thereby infused into the minds of the great land-holding class in India, and the stability accruing in consequence to British rule,—the strong conservative element thus created and rendered by the strongest interest inimical to any revolution or change in the ruling power. Under a Permanent Settlement there was nothing, in his opinion, to prevent the conservation of all the subordinate rights of which some had been sacrificed when the Bengal settlement was first made. The fiscal errors of that settlement were not forgotten by him, for indeed he knew that many large tracts assessed for ever with a small sum, because they were then but little cultivated, have since become entirely cultivated. Thus on such tracts the land revenue is so relatively light as to be almost nominal, whereby injustice arises both to the national interests and to the fully assessed taxpayers in other places. Such errors, he hoped, could in future be avoided by extending the perpetual assessment only to those tracts in which the agricultural resources are fully developed, and by granting the boon of a permanent settlement solely on the condition of the agriculture having attained to that degree of excellence which could fairly be expected. With this condition he was ready to propose the extension of the Permanent Settlement to the best cultivated districts in the empire. This very condition, however, proved to be the rock upon which the proposal split. For the question arose, what are the tracts or what the villages where the agriculture can be said to have reached that degree of excellence which may fairly be expected. The average yield of produce in India is small as compared with that of European countries, and will, as all men hope, be augmented hereafter, though the prospect of such augmentation is not at this moment visible. Besides all ordinary means of improvement resulting from the outlay of capital on the land, there are the special means arising from irrigation. Now this irrigation is fast expanding in India and may yet indefinitely expand. Thus its effects upon the condition of whole provinces may prove greater than anything which is now foreseen. Then a difficult discussion arose as to what districts or tracts could reasonably be pronounced ripe for a Permanent Settlement; and the proposal was held in abeyance. Meanwhile adverse opinions sprang up in many quarters, so the idea failed to take any practical shape. But the episode is remarkable as shewing how broad were John Lawrence's sympathies and how receptive was his mind for suggestions of future improvement.

About this time, 1865, the treaty made with the Bhotan State after the termination of the hostilities already mentioned, became the theme of acrimonious discussion. It was thought by many influential sections of the Anglo-Indian community to involve a sacrifice of the just interests which the British Government had acquired after troublesome operations rendered necessary by barbaric misbehaviour. The newspaper press clamoured against John Lawrence, as having failed to sustain the national cause entrusted to him for vindication. He was not insensible to the sting inflicted by these reproaches, and strove to give all the explanation which public opinion could reasonably require, but without much avail so far as the popularity of the Government was concerned. I was present when the dissatisfaction was at its height, without having full means of judging for myself. Subsequently, however, when conducting the Government of Bengal, I had the best possible opportunity of seeing the merits of the case on the spot, and I can affirm that the terms exacted by John Lawrence from

Bhotan, so far from being inadequate, were ample for the maintenance of British interests in that quarter. As a punishment for misdeeds the Bhotan State had to cede the sub-Himalayan tracts, the finest in all its territory—tracts which are now being fast dotted with European tea-gardens—and to receive in return a cash subsidy from the British treasury. Under the altered conditions of Bhotan, these payments constitute an important item in its income, so that this State is to some extent depending on a pensionary maintenance.

John Lawrence's next trouble was the famine in Orissa, which probably caused him more grief than any other event during his rule. I was not present with him at the time, but meeting him afterwards I heard fully his views regarding that grave misfortune. The drought occurred one year and the people bore it; but it continued during the second and also the third year; then towards the end of the third year heavy rains in the neighbouring hills caused inundation to submerge the remnant of the crops; thus in his own expressive words, "that which the drought spared the floods drowned." At an early period of the drought he had been uneasy lest famine should supervene; but he was assured by the Lieutenant-Governor, Sir Cecil Beadon, who had gone to the spot in order to make personal enquiries, that the danger would pass away, and he accepted though with hesitation the assurance from so responsible a functionary. He thus deferred for a while the remedial measures which he would otherwise have adopted; indeed he afterwards took blame to himself on this account. Soon famine appeared unmistakeably in its worst form, and then the Government put forth strenuous efforts, which proved however too late to save life. The famishing people were either dead, or past recovery, before the succour reached them. The elements also warred against the relieving forces of the State and grain-laden ships were kept tossing about within sight of shore unable to land their cargoes.

This misfortune gave an impulse to the policy which John Lawrence had desired from the outset to pursue, namely, that of hastening the construction of railways and canals. If the Government was to assume the responsibility, never fully assumed during former times in India, for saving the lives of a large population threatened with death from famine, there must be railways to carry the surplus grain from productive tracts, for replenishing the gaps which drought might cause in the supplies of other tracts. There must also be canals to utilize the available waters for the irrigation of the land in a climate where the rainfall is in some years abundant, but in other years scanty or unseasonable. It would have been easy, however, to pronounce that the progress of railways and canals ought to be promoted; the real difficulty was to provide the financial means for carrying on such works. There had been no let or hindrance in this respect with the railways for which the capital had been found by certain Companies under a State guarantee of interest, as explained in the previous chapter VI. on Dalhousie's administration. But for all other works of public utility the principle had been followed of funds being furnished from ordinary revenue. This principle was justly applied to buildings civil and military, and to roads upon which no tolls were levied. But it was never properly applicable to canals which would yield returns in water-rent, and for which the ordinary revenues could never supply the funds, however necessary the works might be. Nevertheless, the cost of even the grandest canals had been defrayed from current revenue, and whenever, on depletion of the Treasury, money had been unavoidably borrowed in order to prosecute the works, the amount had been reckoned as financial deficit. If, again, the State desired, as it reasonably might desire, to construct some of the future railways, through its own agency direct instead of through the medium of guaranteed railway companies, the funds could not be provided from the ordinary revenues.

John Lawrence then held that the example of all the most civilized countries justified India in raising loans for the permanent improvement of the country by canals of irrigation and by railways to be constructed under State agency. The ordinary revenues were to defray the interest on the loans thus raised, and to be credited with the net receipts of the works after the working expenses had been defrayed. But the capital expenditure from the loan funds was to be treated as extraordinary and separate from the yearly budget of ordinary expenditure. A careful forecast was made of the amount required to be laid out on canals and State railways during a cycle of coming years. It was for this amount that loans were to be raised. Thus John Lawrence introduced this principle into Indian finances and established it with firmness. It was further developed by his successors, and though often assailed by some financial critics, it has held and will doubtless continue to hold its ground. When properly applied, it proves as safe in India as in all other civilized countries, and is essential to the improvement of the national estate committed to the charge of the British Government.

In all matters relating to the finance of public works and the progress of material improvement he derived professional assistance of the utmost value from Colonel Richard Strachey of the Corps of Engineers, an officer of great capacity for the comprehensive grasp of such affairs.

As affecting the economic condition of the country, the results of the American civil war gave a violent stimulus to the production of cotton, especially in the centre and west of the empire, already shewn by the previous chapter XII. on western India. This event, combined with the construction of railways, the influx of European capital and the general movement of affairs since the war of the mutinies, caused a remarkable rise in the prices of agricultural produce and other staples, the like of which had never been seen before in India. Money seemed to lose its purchasing power, and in many districts the necessaries of life were obtainable only at famine prices, despite abundance of harvests. The poor were in some respects pinched thereby, but for the most part recouped themselves by augmented wages; and for all industrial and trading classes, high or lowly, there was brisk business and plenty of employment. But all classes, that had fixed incomes, suffered unavoidably; and foremost among these were the servants of Government in various grades, except those who received ample salaries. An augmentation of the pay and allowances of all grades save the highest throughout the country became necessary; the task was difficult, as the number and variety of classes and departments must always be extraordinarily great in such an empire as this. It was performed by John Lawrence's Government with patient assiduity, with much consideration towards those concerned, and yet with faithful regard to public economy.

The rapid increase in the value of cotton, and the extraordinary exportation of that staple in consequence, gave birth to a hydra-headed speculation, which has been explained in the previous chapter XII. on western India. The ruin which usually follows in such cases, came in this case swiftly, on the cessation of war in America. For a climax to the misfortune, the Bank of Bombay became involved in danger; and as this institution was connected with the State, its condition caused the liveliest concern not only to the Government of Bombay, but to the Government of India. John Lawrence and his advisers did what they could to arrest the downward course and avert the catastrophe. After all, the Bank fell, causing loss more or less severe to many constituents who, relying on the Government connection, justly thought themselves safe when resorting to the Bank. Consequently much excitement arose in India, which extended to England, and formed the subject of a discussion in the House of Commons. Then a commission of enquiry was formed, which, after making full enquiries and distributing blame amongst many authorities, remarked upon the steadiness and carefulness displayed by the Government of India under John Lawrence during that troublous time.

In respect to moral progress, John Lawrence pursued the same policy regarding education as that already described in chapter V. relating to the Panjab. For high education he allowed the universities which had been established by law to work out their views tending towards instruction in classics and literature rather than in physical science. He interested himself much regarding primary education for the humbler classes, and the extension of village schools. This sort of education made considerable progress during his time in all parts of the empire save Bengal.

He rejoiced to mark the progress of Christian missions belonging to all Protestant denominations. This progress he deemed to be very considerable, and to be fraught with results that ought to stimulate the zeal of the Church in Great Britain. He placed a high value on the labours of the missionaries as bringing about the conversion of large numbers among tribes that had not yet fallen under any one of the dominant religions in the East, and diffusing by means of education the leaven of Christian morality among the masses of the rising generation. He held also that the existence of the missions, and the example set by the lives of the missionaries, produced a good effect politically, by raising the national repute of Englishmen in the esteem of the Natives. His private munificence was ever flowing in this direction; and though he was most guarded and discreet in his public utterances and his official conduct, yet the knowledge that the cause of missions had the heartiest of friends in the head of the Government did inflame the zeal of the benevolent, and cheer the missionaries in their work.

By his life and conversation he gave a never-failing support to the Bishops and clergy in the discharge of their sacred functions; and his example was a rallying-point around which all influences for good would gather. The Bishop of Calcutta and Metropolitan in India at that time was George Edward Lynch Cotton, who had been one of the masters at Rugby under Arnold, and afterwards head-master of Marlborough school. Since his arrival in India the Bishop had made a lasting impression upon the minds of the Anglo-Indian community, and fully sustained the moral influence which is accorded to the episcopal office in British India as much as anywhere in Christendom. His work had extended to many spheres of action; but there was one object for which he thought much remained to be done, and with which he accordingly identified himself. This was the provision of educational means in the Himalayas for European and East Indian children. Since the introduction of railways, and the general progress of affairs after the war of the mutinies, the number of these children had increased greatly. The old existing institutions in the plains were inadequate, and Bishop Cotton wished to found fresh or additional ones in the hills. The climate of the Himalayas seemed to him very suitable for this purpose, and he procured the establishment of several schools at the Himalayan stations, which institutions were called after him "the Bishop's schools." He was snatched away in the midst of his usefulness in October 1866 by a lamentable accident, while making a tour in northern Bengal. Having consecrated a cemetery, and given to the few persons gathered together an address with allusions to death and the future life, he was about to cross the Ganges in a steamer. Accordingly he went to the river-side where the steamer was moored, and while walking along a plank, which had been thrown across from the bank to the deck, he stumbled and fell into the water. The stream with its under-currents sucked him in so that he never was seen again. He was mourned as a gifted prelate whose vacant place it would be difficult to refill. His successor was Robert Milman, who brought to his high position much experience gained as a parish priest in England.

The work of scientific legislation made more progress during John Lawrence's time than at any previous epoch. The Legislative Councils, as already seen in chapter VIII., had been constituted several years previously, and were in full working order. When they had been constituted it was decided to have a member of the Government of India, who should be charged specially with the business of legislation. Accordingly in 1861, William Ritchie was appointed Legislative Member. He died soon afterwards, and his funeral was one of the first occasions on which Lord Elgin appeared in public at Calcutta.

To him succeeded Henry Sumner Maine (now Sir Henry) who served throughout the incumbency of Lord Elgin, and also of John Lawrence. The reputation which Maine had won as the author of several works which had made their mark on the literature of the age, secured for him public respect and favour from the day he landed. He will always be remembered as one of the most intellectually accomplished men that ever assisted in the counsels of India. His experience as a jurist, and the wide scope of his studies regarding the origin of laws and the structure of society, qualified him in the highest degree for the work of an Indian legislator at this time. Some notable laws, such as the Penal Code, had indeed been already enacted; but a mass of important subjects remained to be brought under scientific legislation. For some little time (that is since 1861) a Commission had been sitting in England to prepare drafts of law for the assistance of the legislature in India. It was accordingly engaged in preparing drafts of important Acts, such as the Civil Procedure, the Criminal Procedure, the Contract Act, the Evidence Act, the Negotiable Securities Bill, and the Transfer of Property Bill. These drafts used to be transmitted to India from time to time, and Maine then had to consider them in principle and detail, consulting the members of the Legislative Council and other well-informed persons on all points where the peculiar customs or circumstances of India might be concerned. He gave useful advice to the Governor-General regarding the composition of the Legislative Council, by the appointment of really representative men to be members of it. For its staff he obtained the services of Whitley Stokes, who soon proved himself to possess a talent for drafting laws, and to whose skill and technical knowledge the Indian legislature is greatly indebted. John Lawrence gave consistent help to this work, and presided regularly at the sittings of the Legislative Council of the Governor-General.

Besides his special work of legislation Maine took part in the general business of the administration as a member of the Government of India. He was not expected to give more than a cursory attention to such departments as war, finance, or public works; but every question that involved considerations of law, of rights or privileges, of general principle affecting either British territories or Native States, was referred to him for opinion. Further, he rendered assistance in respect of high education; for several years he served as Vice-Chancellor of the Calcutta University, and at the annual convocations delivered orations which were long remembered for their graceful eloquence and literary culture.

A revision of the rules regarding leave in India and furlough to Europe, for the three great classes of the Government, namely, the Indian Army, the Covenanted Civil Service, and the Uncovenanted Service, had been pending for some time before John Lawrence's arrival. Knowing well the bearings of this many-sided question, he resolved to settle it in a manner befitting the merits of the public servants whose labours and efforts he had witnessed in so many fields of action. He accordingly appointed the most competent persons in India to frame suitable sets of rules which he induced the Government in England to sanction with but slight modification. The simple record of this great fact affords no idea of the attention he personally gave to the multiform and often complex details which involved many conflicting considerations. The rules were demanded by the requirements of the age and would sooner or later have been passed, at least in their essentials, whoever had been Governor-General. But it is to the sympathy, the trained intelligence, the knowledge and experience of John Lawrence, that these great branches of the public service owe the speedy concession, in so acceptable a manner, of the boons which these rules bestow.

The finances caused anxiety to John Lawrence from the first, even to the last day of his incumbency. Such anxiety has been common to every Governor-General, and to its pressure is partly owing that substantial success which, despite many vicissitudes and occasional failures, has crowned the efforts of Indian financiers. Sir Charles Trevelyan was then Finance Minister in succession to Samuel Laing. He had, while Governor of Madras, as already mentioned, strenuously opposed Wilson's income-tax, and had quitted India in consequence. Returning to the country in a financial capacity he found the tax in full operation for a five years' term, of which a portion had yet to run. With due prudence and considerateness, he refrained from urging any radical change respecting the tax; but he could hardly be expected to recommend its prolongation or re-imposition on the expiry of its term in 1865. John Lawrence meanwhile had determined to raise loans if necessary for the completion of the barracks. He foresaw that money must be borrowed for carrying into effect the general schemes of canals and state railways, whereby the annual charges for interest defrayable from ordinary revenues would be much augmented. He therefore anticipated with regret the cessation of the income-tax, and would gladly have on its expiry renewed it for another term. His colleagues were, however, opposed to the renewal, and under the circumstances he found himself unable to insist upon it. He then assented to a proposal of Sir Charles Trevelyan in 1865 for imposing duties on certain articles exported from India. Though doubtless aware of the objections that would be raised against such duties, he yielded to the argument that the articles to be thus taxed, jute, wool, tea, coffee, were well able to bear the impost. When the duties were imposed by him, the measure aroused opposition and was disallowed by the Secretary of State. Thus his Government was deprived of a fiscal resource at a time when the finances were temporarily in deficit. He felt the force of the reasons which induced the Secretary of State to prohibit the levy of these duties. Still he said that in one matter, that of the income-tax, he had been opposed by his colleagues in India, and in another matter, that of the export duties, he had failed to obtain the support of his superior in England.

Sir Charles Trevelyan was succeeded in 1866 by the Right Honourable William Massey, who had been well known in Parliament as the Chairman of Committees, and in literature as the historian of the reign of George the Third. For that year no fresh measure for raising additional taxation was attempted. But during the next year, 1867, Massey introduced a measure for imposing a license-tax on trades and professions, mainly on the ground that the returns of the late income-tax shewed what large classes of persons there were who, though engaged in lucrative occupations, contributed little or nothing to the revenue. The principle of the measure comprised nothing new; as shewn in previous chapters it had been embodied in an Act before Wilson's time, was brought forward by Wilson himself, and reproduced by Laing. The European community that had paid the income-tax so cheerfully would, it was hoped, acquiesce in a license-duty which is an income-tax though in a rough shape and with very light incidence. At Calcutta, however, violent opposition arose; a public meeting was held in the Town Hall, and the cheers which greeted the orators were, it was said, loud enough to be heard in Government House close by. John Lawrence, however, held firm, and this time was supported by the Secretary of State; so the license-tax was collected during that year, 1867–8, and the following year, 1868–9, that is up to the close of his administration.

As regards the general result financially, during the five years of John Lawrence's incumbency there were 5¼ millions sterling of deficit and 2¾ millions of surplus, leaving a net deficit of 2½ millions. This net deficit arose from his outlay already mentioned, upon European barracks, and by the increased expenditure upon irrigation or other works of material improvement. He caused nearly 5 millions to be spent on the barracks out of the total sum of 10 millions estimated for the completion of the scheme. Out of the expenditure which he sanctioned for irrigation works a portion would, according to present rules, be charged in the "extraordinary" account, and not appear in the net deficit at all. But this net deficit as stated above, is taken from the public accounts which have become historical. He himself always insisted that there really was financial deficit in his time, assigning this as a reason why he ought to be better supported in imposing the necessary taxation. He was zealously determined to house and lodge the European troops properly, as well as to promote works of irrigation and State railways. For these purposes he was prepared to impose taxation if the ordinary revenue should prove insufficient, otherwise there was no alternative but to provide the funds by loan, or, what is the same thing, to incur deficit on this account, which deficit has to be made up by borrowing. During his time accordingly the public debt was augmented by 6½ millions sterling, which is fully explained by the barracks and canals. He was a hard man of business in respect to finance, for which indeed he had a more than ordinary aptitude, and if he could have pursued his own way untrammelled, he would have allowed no deficit, notwithstanding the large outlay on material improvement. But although frugal thrifty and economical in respect to public expenditure, he was neither niggardly nor short-sighted. No man ever understood better than he did the manifold needs of India and the financial means whereby alone they can be supplied. In order to afford these means he thought that the income-tax ought to have been maintained for a time, and the fact of his thus thinking affords additional proof of the wisdom of Wilson in proposing the income-tax in 1860. The great economist from England and the great Anglo-Indian statesman thought the same in this matter, and the presumption was strong that a financial maxim upon which John Lawrence and James Wilson were agreed, must be right for their time at least.

During the last few months of John Lawrence's incumbency I became Financial Member of Council. He was himself about to depart, and he enjoined me to cause the income-tax to be reimposed if that should be found possible. Otherwise he anticipated trouble for Indian financiers; the deficit would continue; the country absolutely needed improvement, and yet it was difficult to induce the wealthier classes to undergo the necessary sacrifices. These views sometimes gave a gloomy tinge to his conversation regarding finance. I promised him, however, that no effort should be spared in the pursuit of his principles, declaring that if possible deficit should be overcome and surplus secured. The next chapter will show how this promise was fulfilled during the succeeding years.

The close of his administration was brightened by the successful issue of the expedition against Magdâla, the capital and stronghold of King Theodorus in Abyssinia. He rejoiced at his old friend Sir Robert Napier (now Lord Napier of Magdâla), the Commander-in-Chief of the Bombay Army, being appointed by Her Majesty to command the expeditionary force, and he willingly placed at Napier's disposal the troops, the matériel and other resources belonging to India.

During these years he saw as much of the Natives as his preoccupation with state affairs would allow, being ever desirous to refresh his knowledge by conversing with them. He was the only Governor-General permanently appointed since the beginning of the century who could speak with the Natives in the Hindustani and Persian languages. His ceremonial receptions and levées (durbars) had for the Natives a peculiar significance because the Governor-General's address was delivered, not as usual in English, with a translation by the Foreign Secretary, but in the vernacular.

In his relations with the Natives and indeed with all classes of the community, European and other, he received judicious aid from his able and popular Private Secretary, Mr. (now Sir James) Gordon, who became afterwards Chief Commissioner of Mysore.

He greatly encouraged Mr. (now Sir Charles) Aitchison in the compilation of that extensive work which comprises all treaties between the British Government and the Native States, together with an historical résumé for each state.

Throughout his incumbency the foreign affairs of India involved much diplomatic correspondence without requiring any decisive action except in the rupture with Bhotan.

The affairs of the Persian Gulf were in those days very ably managed by the Government of Bombay, of which Sir Bartle Frere was the head; and Colonel (now Sir Lewis) Pelly was Resident at Bushire, the principal sea-port of Persia. On the shore of the Gulf lay the territory of the Sultan of Muscat, who was an ally, and in some respects a dependant, of the British Government, and was troubled by the encroaching Wahabi power that had established itself in Arabia. The Sultan was virtually protected by some naval operations, and also by energetic diplomacy, for the sake of which Pelly himself made an enterprising journey into the heart of Arabia. John Lawrence's action tended somewhat to moderate these proceedings; in the end, however, the position of Muscat was vindicated, and the Wahabi Arabs were restrained. In succession to Frere the Right Honourable (now Sir Seymour) Fitzgerald became

Governor of Bombay, and devoted much attention to British interests in the Persian Gulf. Under him the police of the sea was maintained by naval force, piracy was stamped out wherever it appeared, the pearl-fisheries were protected, the Arab chiefs were kept in check, and Turkish encroachment was prevented. Thus was consolidated a power which, extending from Basra in Mesopotamia to the mouth of the Red Sea, gives England the command of one of the most valuable situations in Asia.

In Afghanistan after the death of Dost Muhammad the succession was only for a brief time undisputed and became afterwards desperately disputed with fratricidal contests. There were then two rulers in Afghanistan, each holding a part of the country. John Lawrence refrained from any attempt to interfere or even mediate between them, maintaining friendly communications with both, but without indicating any preference for either. He obtained the fullest information regarding the battles, plots, triumphs, flights, many of which were fraught with moving incidents. As none could foresee to which party the victory would ultimately incline, he judiciously waited until one or other should remain uppermost in the struggle and become the *de facto* ruler. He was willing to accord British support, moral or material, to the ruler who might have so far proved successful.

Never was the proverbial fitfulness of the Afghan people more manifest than at that time. Their Amir might well address them in the words of the poet:

> "Who would wish to rule
> This changeling crowd * * *
> Fantastic, fickle, fierce and vain,
> Thou many-headed monster thing;
> Oh! who would wish to be thy king!"

The proceedings of Russia in Central Asia were watched by John Lawrence with unceasing vigilance, especially as the Khan of Bokhara was striving to shake off the Russian yoke. As these vain strivings only caused the Russian power to be fastened more firmly than ever on Bokhara, he scrupulously abstained from allowing the Khan to hope for British assistance, and preserved a loyally amicable attitude towards Russia. But he felt anxiety in respect to the possible bearing of these affairs upon Afghanistan. His reply to the Khan of Bokhara, who had sent an envoy to Calcutta to beg for alliance, is a model of the frank language which should be used by the representatives of one great empire in reference to a neighbouring empire of equal rank.

In relation to Southern Afghanistan, the Governor of Bombay, Sir Bartle Frere, submitted proposals for the occupation of Quetta in the Khelat territory by a British garrison. The object was to secure the line of communication by the Bolan pass against any possible invader, this pass being the second while the Khyber near Peshawar was the first, of the two main lines by which India could be approached from Central Asia. These proposals had been originated by the late General John Jacob, whose name had become historic on the Sind frontier, and were now taken up by his successor Sir Henry Green. They were however decisively rejected by John Lawrence and his colleagues.

A revolution occurred in Chinese Tartary, including Yarkand, Kashgar and Khoten; the Muhammadans rose and overpowered the Chinese; then the Muhammadan chief sent an embassy to Calcutta to ask for an offensive and defensive alliance against Russia and China. John Lawrence sent the envoy back across the Himalayas with a polite but absolute refusal.

All this time the rapid development of Russian power in Kokand and Bokhara inspired the public mind throughout India with alarm. Sensible and reflective men did not grudge Russia any advantages she might acquire in that quarter, provided that she stopped there. They feared however that her conquest there would prove but the prelude to movements towards Afghanistan with the view of indirectly menacing India. Indeed they could not conceive why Russia, having dominions already more vast than she could manage or even adequately occupy, should persist in making these fresh acquisitions at a greater financial cost than her embarrassed treasury could afford—unless there were some ulterior object. This object must they supposed relate to India, and therefore they became uneasy. Invasion was not dreaded by them, but much of Russia's conduct seemed unfriendly and they felt themselves obliged to regard her as a possible enemy that was gradually sapping and mining towards the Indian citadel, though the assault would not be delivered yet awhile, or might perhaps be put off indefinitely. They did not suggest that the Government of India should make any counter movements in Afghanistan; for they believed that it had better stay within its own borders, and that to enter into Afghan entanglements would make matters worse. But they hoped that the Government in England would see to this, and would arrive at some understanding with Russia, to be sustained, not by vague or insufficient promises, but by definite assurances which could hardly be broken or evaded.

Others there were who thought they discerned in certain emissaries and a few soldiers who had shewn themselves at certain points on or near the Oxus, the videttes of an approaching Russian army on its march for Caubul. Information to this effect used to be disseminated in India, nobody knew how; it perhaps came from one or other of the contending factions in Afghanistan in order that the British might be stirred to interfere in the contentions. These extreme opinions were ridiculed by most people and the apprehensions founded thereon were easily shown to be futile.

Some authorities made light even of the moderate fears which were entertained regarding ulterior contingencies rather than immediate danger. They would say that in the first place Russia would probably never push her border forwards till it met the British Indian limits; and that even if she did so, such an event would not really be injurious to India. This view, however, did not commend itself even to the most sober-minded classes. The truth seemed to be that those who held such a view were really at fault (as well they might be) respecting what ought to be done to counteract the danger. They apparently sought to decry the said danger, trying to shew first that it would never happen, and that even if it happened its consequences would not prove serious. If this really were the idea, then it was a manifestly unsatisfactory recommendation for the treatment of a national difficulty.

Suggestions in various ways were constantly made to John Lawrence urging him to be up and doing, also warning him against lethargy lest some day he should wake up to find that the safety of India had been compromised. These suggestions generally took the form of proposing the despatch of officers to Afghanistan to obtain information and help the Afghan ruler to organize his forces. No impression whatever was made hereby on John Lawrence's judgment; yet he feared lest this constant stream of suggestions from India should affect public opinion, and lest he should some day be required by directions from England to take steps for which he did not see his way. There was on his part no blindness to the contingencies which might eventually arise from the position of Russia in Asia; indeed no man had a deeper insight into these things than he. Still he desired if possible to keep his countrymen quiet, because there was nothing that could be properly done from India. Here was a case wherein the maxim, when in doubt do nothing, had a peculiar significance.

I had not become the Foreign Secretary as yet, being still in the Central Provinces or in the Deccan. The officer who practically had the charge of the official papers relating to Afghanistan was Mr. John Wyllie, a very talented and accomplished man. He wrote an interesting article, subsequently avowed as his, in the *Edinburgh Review* of January, 1867, on the foreign policy of John Lawrence. In that article he stated that respecting Russia this policy tended towards "a masterly inactivity." Seldom has a phrase been so caught up for praise or blame as this was at the time, though the blame preponderated. It may have comprised something of truth and of political expediency; still it had an admixture of error, and was sure to be misconstrued by the majority of the public. As is usual with unfortunate phrases, it clung to those concerned in its production. Wyllie afterwards by an article in the *Fortnightly Review* defended his use of the expression; still the words were to be regretted, as they were likely to detract from John

Lawrence's influence with many of his countrymen, an influence which at that time it was specially desirable to maintain.

I shortly afterwards joined the Government of India as Foreign Secretary. Afghanistan was once more forcing itself upon the Governor-General's attention, because the internecine strife of several years had ended in finally confirming Shir Ali as Amir of the whole dominion handed down by Dost Muhammad to his heirs.

John Lawrence was then reviewing the whole case as it had, after some eventful years, become developed into its existing shape. He called to mind how Russia had after the Crimean War subdued the Caucasian region with a great effort, and next advanced from another direction upon Kokand or Ferghana, thence pressing on to Samarkand and Bokhara, while England and India were occupied in the war of the mutinies. He had watched her every movement, while she reduced the Khan of Bokhara to a position of vassalage. His vigilance was further sharpened when she was understood to be advancing her outposts even up to the Oxus. As explained in the previous chapter XIII., I was his Political and Foreign Secretary at that moment, and had to arrange for obtaining the information he desired regarding the proceedings of the Russians on the right bank of the Oxus. He found that though a Russian advance had really been made in that quarter, it was magnified by the prevailing rumours. His idea was that a friendly and independent Afghan State should be interposed between India and Central Asia; if Russia could not be prevented from overrunning Central Asia, she could, at all events, be kept out of Afghanistan. He thought that the Russian position in Central Asia was insecure and likely to be threatened at any moment by an outbreak on the part of the inhabitants. In reality the Russians have, by comparatively good administration, consolidated their rule there much more effectually than he then anticipated. At all events, he hoped that being embarrassed in their finances, and pre-occupied with local affairs, they would abstain from troubling Afghanistan. But as a precautionary measure, he wished that the British Government should establish a permanent influence with the Afghan ruler, taking due advantage of the contiguity of India and Afghanistan. He did not repose overmuch confidence in any Afghan ruler, because the Afghans were, in his opinion, untrustworthy, and faithful to nothing save the traditions of plunder. If an invading army, he would say, ever were to march through Afghanistan towards India, it would be joined by hordes of Afghans, indeed, by every Afghan who could afford to leave his home, notwithstanding any subsidies which the British Government might in past years have been giving. Still he thought that good would result from a friendly understanding founded in some degree on such subsidies, while his main reliance rested on the power of England, through measures to be adopted not in Asia but in Europe, for virtually compelling Russia to leave Afghanistan untouched. If, however, such an understanding were to be established, a ruler must be found who could hold his own and govern an united country.

Dost Muhammad had barely attained that position before his death at an advanced age. After his demise there broke out between his sons the long-predicted contest for the succession. The successor designate, Shir Ali, did actually enter upon the succession for a time, and with him friendly relations were established. He soon afterwards lost Caubul and retained only Candahar and Herat; the British relations with him, however were maintained. Subsequently he was deprived of Candahar also, and retired to Herat; his fortunes then seemed to be so eclipsed that it might become necessary to transfer the British recognition, from him to his successful rival, as the *de facto* ruler. Shir Ali, however, by some strokes of valour and fortune, recovered his position, and after many stirring vicissitudes consolidated a dominion over the whole of Afghanistan.

John Lawrence then judged that the time had come when he might revert to the plan of supporting a friendly and independent Afghanistan with British recognition, also with subsidies in arms and money. Having obtained for his plan the approval of the English Government, he invited the Amir Shir Ali to come to some place in British territory for a personal meeting in order to discuss the best manner in which a limited support might be accorded. He remained at or near Simla for some short time in readiness to meet the Amir, who at first accepted the invitation. He was unable to wait longer, however, as there was some delay in Shir Ali's coming. This happened in December, 1868; his stay in India was then drawing to a close, and his successor Lord Mayo was expected to relieve him in the following month, January, 1869. So he reluctantly turned his face from the frontier towards Calcutta, leaving for his successor's consideration a full record of what had been contemplated in the event of Shir Ali's coming in the course of a few weeks.

Before quitting India he sent to England an elaborate despatch recording the reasons why, in his judgment, British troops should not be despatched into Afghanistan, nor British officers sent there in any diplomatic or other capacity, also why the Government of India should still remain within its existing trans-Indus frontier.

He felt regret during the last weeks of his stay at Simla at leaving a spot of wondrous beauty, where he had for several years established his Government. In that autumnal season the place was seen at its very best, and every Sunday afternoon I used to go out for a walk with him, and talk over old times and events. Though not specially educated in art, he had naturally a keen eye for the beauties of nature, having in this respect much sensibility, which always affected him, though he seldom gave expression to it. On one of these afternoons we ascended a hill named "Prospect Point," from which the best view was to be had of the town and surroundings of Simla. There stood the alpine city on its airy height with cedars or oaks around and profound valleys beneath, a sea of hills terminated by the white wall of everlasting snow, and an unclouded sky catching the glow of the setting sun. "Think," he said, "what a blessing it is that, although we are not very far from a mountainous frontier held by fierce and murderous tribes, yet in these hills the people are mild and harmless, so that here the sick, the holiday-makers, after their hard work, the women and children, and the helpless of all sorts, are safe from bloodthirsty marauders. Were it otherwise, what mishaps might occur, what ceaseless anxiety there would be."

On his return to England he was, by the Royal favour, raised to the peerage. The community in India erected a statue of him at Calcutta. But neither "storied urn" nor "animated bust" can ever satisfy the affectionate feeling respecting him, which lives in the breasts of those who worked in his company during the labours and trials of a career in the East.

CHAPTER XV.

(1868-1873.)

THE FINANCE MINISTERSHIP.

William Massey Finance Minister of India—My appointment to succeed him —Close of John Lawrence's financial administration—Lord Mayo's financial policy—My first budget for 1869-70—The income-tax—Budget for 1870-1—Increase in rate of income-tax—Financial surplus—Budget for 1871-2—Scheme of provincial services—Continuance of surplus—Budget for 1872-3 maintaining income-tax for one year—Budget for 1873-4 and remission of income-tax—Summary of financial result—Establishment of financial surplus—Buoyancy of public funds and Government securities—Progress of trade.

THE Right Honourable William Massey was Finance Minister of India at the beginning of 1868, but had officially intimated the intention of soon resigning his portfolio; and it was known that he would in the coming spring produce his last budget.

One afternoon during this spring I was, as Foreign Secretary, in my department intent upon papers relating to Central Asia, —and especially some extract translations from the Russian newspapers regarding movements between Bokhara and the bank of the Oxus,—when I received in the ordinary way, a message requesting me to wait upon the Governor-General, Sir John Lawrence. As such messages were of common occurrence, I walked unconcernedly to Government House, which was close by. When I reached the study of the Governor-General he put into my hand a telegram from the Secretary of State in England, Sir Stafford Northcote, conveying to me the offer of the finance ministership, which I accepted. Having formerly been secretary to two finance ministers in succession, I was familiar with the work of the Financial Department; still it seemed strange to be called so soon to sit in the chair of my masters.

In April Mr. Massey transferred to me the charge of the finances, having passed successfully through the Legislative Council at Calcutta the budget for 1869, of which the principal feature was the continuation of the license-tax on trades and professions, mentioned in the last chapter. The outcry, already described, against this tax had subsided, and the opposition to it, though not expired, was no longer strong. From April to the end of December 1868, John Lawrence was still Governor-General; and during this time the following measures in my department were particularly considered by him:—

... introducing into the currency of India a gold standard after the English model, and declaring the gold pieces, already coined and issued by Government, to be legal tender, to an unlimited amount, the silver coins becoming legal tender to a limited amount only, and being so far demonetized;

... extending and developing the Government savings banks already established for the benefit of the Natives;

. . . revising the salt duties with a view towards at least approaching equalization, the high rates of duty in northern India being somewhat lowered, and the low rates in western and southern India being somewhat raised;

... conceding to the several Provincial Governments a larger control than previously over the financial administration in several branches, such as roads, buildings, schools, police and prisons;

... providing funds by loan for remunerative works, such as State railways and canals, and keeping the accounts of this extraordinary expenditure separate from the ordinary finance of Government;

... enlarging the license-tax on trades and professions, making it include official incomes, and the richer rentals in the permanently settled provinces, thus converting it gradually from a roughly assessed impost into a scientifically framed income-tax with a light rate of assessment.

Respecting the gold standard, much assistance was received from the Commander-in-Chief, Sir William Mansfield (afterwards Lord Sandhurst); some improvements in the status of the gold coins were effected; but no real success was found possible. The discussion regarding savings banks, however, bore fruit in the extension of those beneficent institutions among the Natives. The consideration of the salt duties produced no immediate result, but laid the foundation for fiscal reforms which have since been introduced. The principle of conceding to the provincial Governments an increase of their financial control in certain branches was admitted, but its application was allowed in a cautious and tentative manner only, and was ultimately postponed till the arrival of the next Governor-General. The plan of accounting for the extraordinary expenditure, on State railways and canals, was afterwards carried into effect. The proposal for converting the license-tax into a light income-tax was strenuously opposed by Sir William Mansfield (afterwards Lord Sandhurst) and Sir Henry Durand, as members of the Governor-General's council; but it paved the way for imposing the income-tax during the next year.

On relinquishing the Government, John Lawrence took a somewhat unfavourable view of the financial prospect, as already mentioned in the last preceding chapter. On that account he enjoined me to procure some augmentation of the revenue by means of an income-tax; and this I regarded as his parting instruction.

When Lord Mayo arrived at Calcutta as Governor-General in the beginning of January 1869, I rejoiced to find that he was disposed to maintain the policy of his predecessor, John Lawrence, in regard to converting the existing certificate-tax into a regular income-tax with a light rate. This certificate-tax had been imposed at the recommendation of my predecessor, Mr. Massey, on trades and professions. He described it as a rough income-tax, at the light rate of one per cent. on certain classes, namely traders and professional men, whose incomes exceeded £50 per annum. It was proposed to apply the tax to all the remaining classes of the community, which consisted mainly of the landowners and the fundholders. This proposal was supported in Council by John Strachey and accepted reluctantly by Sir William Mansfield and Sir Henry Durand.

I then produced the budget with a one per cent. income-tax, assigning as a reason for this taxation, that there had been deficits on the finance of each of the three preceding years, and that even with the tax only a bare equilibrium was obtained between income and expenditure, the surplus shewn in the estimate being but £50,000. The non-official European community had for the most part been already assessed to the certificate-tax; so their taxation was not appreciably affected by the new income-tax, and they seemed glad to find that the landowners, mainly the landlords or Zemindars of Bengal, were to be included in the assessment. No objection was raised against the budget by any class, European or Native; and there was reason to hope that a light income-tax would be accepted by the country. The tax was then estimated to yield £900,000 annually, which sum might be increased by good management to a million.

There had been doubts up to that time, whether the expenditure on the barracks for European troops which has been mentioned in the last preceding chapter should be charged to capital together with State railways and canals, or defrayed from the ordinary revenue. It was definitely stated in the budget, that this expenditure must be charged against ordinary income, and that nothing save reproductive works, such as railways and canals, would be included in extraordinary expenditure and charged against capital.

For these reproductive works 3½ millions sterling were to be borrowed during the year; and it was afterwards decided that 2 millions out of this sum should be raised in India. All recent loans having been raised in England, some time had elapsed since any demand had been made by Government upon the Calcutta money market. On this occasion the market responded cheerfully to the call, subscriptions to the new loan were largely offered, and an amount was tendered greatly in excess of the 2 millions required.

Having thus disposed of the affairs relating to the budget, I repaired to England for the summer months by medical advice to recruit my health, which had temporarily suffered from exposure to the malarious climate of the Central Provinces. In the autumn before leaving England on my return to India, I received letters from Lord Mayo informing me that the receipts from opium and customs were falling much below the sum estimated in the budget, that owing to this and other circumstances a deficit upon the finance of the current year was threatened, and that the equilibrium of revenue and expenditure must be maintained by immediately augmenting the income-tax besides reducing the expenditure on ordinary public works. On returning to Calcutta, in November, I introduced a bill into the Legislative Council for raising the income-tax rate from one to two per cent. for the latter half of the year 1869–70. The particulars of the threatened deficit were explained, it was also shewn that the expenditure on ordinary public works (that is upon civil and military buildings) had been lessened, and that the salt duties in southern and western India had been raised. The objections to altering the rate within the year were manifest to us all, but Lord Mayo was urgent upon the subject, having been much impressed by the fact that there had been deficits during the three preceding years, and the estimated deficit of the last of these years was proving larger than the anticipation. He did not at all despair of the finances, indeed he felt hopeful regarding the revenues, and confident as to the ability of the Government to reduce its expenditure. But he thought that as deficit had lasted so long any further continuance of it would affect the financial credit of the Government; and he was resolved that if possible his term of office should begin at least with equilibrium if not with surplus. The soundness of his principle in general terms was manifest; indeed I would gladly at the time of the budget have provided a large surplus by levying the income-tax at a higher rate, but in the face of public opinion adverse to any such plan, the facts were not strong enough to enable me to propose it with any chance of success. The facts had meanwhile grown much stronger, and measures would be accepted by public opinion and the Legislative Council, which could not previously have found acceptance. Lord Mayo's zeal and determination commanded our sympathetic admiration, and we all felt that the financial interest must at all sacrifice be maintained. Thus there was no difficulty in obtaining the assent of the Legislature to raising the rate of the income-tax for the remainder of the current year. Ultimately the result of the measures adopted by Lord Mayo's Government proved favourable to the finances of that year, 1869–70, for the threatened deficit was averted and a small surplus secured.

But while striving to avoid deficit for the current year, we had to consider how to avert this evil for the coming year, 1870–1. The prospects of the opium revenue continued very unfavourable; commercial depression was affecting our receipts from customs, the interest charges on the public debt rose as loans were being raised for canals and State railways; various improvements had been in progress for some time which could not be arrested without detriment. Thus there were the proverbial three courses open to us, first to allow deficit to recur, secondly to modify our system respecting material improvement, thirdly to augment the rate of the income-tax. As the first course was out of the question and the second much to be lamented, I recommended the third, and proposed that the income-tax should be levied at four per cent. for the next year at least, that being the rate of Wilson's income-tax. Lord Mayo, however, and our colleagues in Council, thought four per cent. too high, and at last we all agreed upon three per cent., John Strachey according his wonted support and co-operation. I then introduced the bill for the three per cent. income-tax, which was, after considerable opposition, passed by the Legislative Council.

With the help of this tax, of which the proceeds were estimated at more than two millions sterling for the year, the budget showed a small surplus, the result being tantamount to an equilibrium between income and expenditure. Recently the Secretary of State in England had instructed us to provide a surplus of at least half a million; but it was, however, impossible to act fully up to that instruction without a four per cent. rate of income-tax, to which the necessary assent could not be obtained.

During the year, however, trade and revenue improved, the expenditure was kept well within the estimates, and the small surplus was turned into a large one, amounting to 1½ million sterling. After the disappointments of the preceding year, this favourable result was a matter for general congratulation.

No sooner had the budget been announced than a storm of abuse arose against the Government of India generally, and against me as its Financial Member particularly. Even Lord Mayo's popularity was dimmed for a time; still the public seemed to think that so popular a man could not at heart be in favour of this obnoxious income-tax, that he must have assented to it reluctantly, and would remit it as soon as possible. On the other hand it was apparently believed that the Financial Member, being directly answerable for deficit, must naturally be the authority who insisted on the taxation, and upon him accordingly much of the animadversion fell. His position was not in fact separable from that of the Government, and his colleagues were jointly responsible with him. Still his moral responsibility, whatever its exact measure might be, was very considerable. So far from disclaiming or lessening it, I was glad to accept its full weight.

The Natives no doubt disliked the tax, and among them none dreaded it more than the Zemindars or landlord class of Bengal, who objected to any sort of direct taxation on their income from the land, as being an infringement of the Permanent Settlement. They were well able to make themselves heard, and thus they lent a voice to any Native discontent which existed, fanned the flame of agitation, and formed a solid centre of opposition. The real lead in the opposition was however taken by the European part of the community, and English utterances were the loudest. The Europeans would have willingly borne the tax had it been imposed for war expenses, as in Wilson's time, or for any emergency. But although there was a necessity of another kind in this case, they failed to recognize it. The fact was that for some years past the demands of a progressive age had caused the expenses of the country to rise to a scale which might be reduced but could not be materially altered without national detriment; on the other hand, several temporary causes had depressed the revenues below expectation. European opinion had been more disposed than any other section of public opinion to demand improvement. Despite efforts for economy, deficit had gone on for three years, and the income-tax was necessary in order to substitute equilibrium or surplus. The Europeans, however, did not perceive this; they thought that the Government, had it been so minded, might have avoided this alleged necessity. They failed indeed to show what alternative could have been wisely adopted; though remedies of all sorts were propounded. It was said that we might have made a higher estimate of the opium revenue, or made a lower estimate of some items in the expenditure or charged more of the public works to capital, or virtually transferred, under the guise of financial technicalities, some of the burdens from the present to the future; in short, we might have done anything except impose an income-tax.

From that time, however, one change for the better in public opinion began to be perceptible. Formerly Europeans had been foremost in urging the Government to improve the country and the administration. Beneficent improvement is always commended with plausible effect by those who have not to bear the expense. Now, however, public opinion came to the aid of Government in suggesting economy and in counting the cost of every suggested reform.

The treasury was full, the cash balances were high, and such facts seemed to be regarded by many as proving that the additional taxation was not necessary. It was apparently forgotten that these facts were apart from the finance of the year, and that if deficit were allowed therein, the depletion of the cash balances would soon happen. In fact, however, after the deficits which had occurred, and at a time when funds were being raised for capital outlay on reproductive works, it was desirable to show signs of capacity for duly arranging the current finances, and one among such signs was the possession of a well-filled treasury.

By degrees another reason for keeping high cash balances

became apparent. Measures were being taken to reduce the rates of interest on a portion of the public debt, whereby about one-third of a million annually of the interest charges would be saved. As the terms expired for which certain of the loans had to run, the holders of the five per cent. stock were to be informed that they would be repaid in full unless they chose to accept four per cent. stock instead. Their acceptance of this offer might partly depend on their estimate of the power of Government to repay that loan, from its available resources, without raising money otherwise. Some of them also might prefer repayment of the principal to accepting lower interest. Hence there was abundant reason for maintaining a large amount of cash in hand. The holders of the five per cent. stock naturally regretted the loss of income, thinking of this more than of the benefit to the State from the saving of interest. Thus they felt dissatisfied, and helped to swell the chorus of complaint against the financial policy of the Government. Nevertheless they accepted the new stock at the lower rate of interest.

It happened that a portion of the cash reserve of the Paper Currency department had, under a law recently enacted by the legislature, to be invested in Government securities; in other words, stock to the value of 2¾ millions sterling was to be bought in by the Paper Currency department. Then 2¾ millions of the five per cent. loan were paid off and a corresponding amount of the new four per cent. securities was issued to the Paper Currency department in exchange for the cash. All this was done in strict accordance with the terms of the law, and made as advantageous as possible to the public interest. Still those whose income was diminished by so much of the five per cent. loan being paid off, were displeased with the proceedings of the Government.

In various ways popular dissatisfaction became more and more aggravated; and the clamour against the financial conduct of the Government was sustained for many months. Our consolation was found in the fact that the symptoms of the time indicated health in the finances and growth of public confidence. The moneyed classes were more willing than before to lend money to the Government on favourable terms, and the prices of the Government securities were steadily rising. Evidently those whose experience best qualified them to judge and whose interest prompted them to examine impartially, trusted the Government and believed in the efficacy of its measures. We well knew the importance of winning and retaining public confidence as the basis of financial credit. Such confidence, however, would be declared, not by irresponsible clamour, but by the action of the money market.

As Financial Member of the Government I had before the public to bear the brunt of all this captious criticism; still, I was abundantly supported, as Lord Mayo stood by me generously. Among the members of Council Sir John Strachey had always recommended the income-tax on principle; and Sir Barrow Ellis, recently arrived from Bombay, was a tower of strength in the same cause. Lord Napier of Magdâla had then become Commander-in-Chief of the army and a member of the Government; he too recognized the expediency of the tax.

My next budget for 1871–2, was produced in 1871, by which time financial prosperity was beginning to return. The year 1870–1 was showing a considerable surplus, as already mentioned, therefore it was thought that the rate of the income-tax might be fairly reduced from 3 to 1 per cent, and that the lowest class of the incomes subjected to the tax might be exempted altogether. Thus 1½ million sterling of direct taxation was remitted, and the total number of persons assessed, 480,000, was reduced by one half or in other words 240,000 tax-payers were released altogether. These measures gave partial though not complete satisfaction to the tax-paying classes, and received only a guarded approval from the public. There still remained the one per cent. income-tax on certain classes, limited in number, well-to-do, influential, and capable of making their voices heard—who never ceased to agitate against the impost.

In this budget, after the remission of so much direct taxation, a small surplus only was anticipated. The surplus, however, became larger and larger as the months rolled on, till it reached the amount of 3 millions, the largest surplus yet known in Indian finance.

In the budget statement was included an explanation of the scheme of Provincial Services which the Government of India had recently established. On behalf of the Government I explained the principle in this wise:

"The local (or provincial) Governments are to have a fixed annual allotment for particular services—jails, registration, police, education, medical services, printing, roads other than military, and civil buildings—and are to appropriate as local income all receipts connected therewith. They are to regulate, subject to certain general rules, all the expenditure on those services. If the existing income, namely, imperial allotment plus departmental receipts, shall suffice for the requirements of that expenditure, then all is well. If it shall not suffice, then the local Governments are not to apply to the Government of India for increased grants. They must raise what they need by local taxation, or by such like means, subject to our central control, if they fairly can. But if they find that they cannot fairly manage this, then they must necessarily do without the increased expenditure."

* * * * * *

"The more we consider the constant increase of late years in these headings, the difficulty which we have in resisting demands which have so much inherent excellence to recommend them, and yet the impossibility of meeting them unless local income can be legitimately augmented—the more do we perceive the importance of the financial principle."

* * * * * *

"We have inaugurated the measure by reducing the aggregate expenditure under these heads by one third of a million. This is, *per se*, something appreciable. But greater far financially is the advantage of setting some definite bounds to the constant growth and expansion of imperial outlay on these branches." . . . . "Thus an increased degree of financial control has been accorded to the several local (or provincial) Governments in India. We hope that this concession will give them an additional interest in the study and enforcement of economy in expenditure; will afford them a just inducement to supplement their local receipts from time to time by methods either most acceptable to the people or least fraught with popular objection; will cause a more complete understanding to arise between the executive authorities and the tax-paying classes respecting the development of fiscal resources; will teach the people to take a practical share in provincial finance and lead them up gradually towards a degree of local self-government."

Towards the close of December 1871, we were considering the arrangements for the coming budget of 1872–3. The discussion turned mainly on the retention or remission of the one per cent. income-tax. I advocated the retention of it for some little time to come at least, urging that it was the anchor of our finance. The proceeds of direct taxation, including income-tax and license-tax from first to last, that is, since Wilson's time, would amount to 14 millions sterling. This taxation afforded the only means by which several wealthy classes, otherwise untaxed, could be brought under taxation. It had, indeed, proved vexatious to the humbler classes of taxpayers, but that objection had been already removed by the exemption of those classes. If still any pressure or annoyance was reasonably felt, it could be remedied without the essential parts of the tax being touched. As the limited classes subjected to it became accustomed to its operation, the discontent at first felt would gradually disappear. The rate of incidence was then very light, only one per cent; but the machinery of assessment was kept up and the returns were being perfected year by year, so as to truly show the taxable income of the country. Then in any future need or emergency the raising of the rate would give a proportionable increase of revenue. Three-quarters of a million sterling of annual revenue from an income-tax of one per cent. well assessed upon trustworthy returns, might become 1½ million, or 2¼ millions by almost a stroke of the pen in event of future necessity, by raising the rate to 2 or to 3 per cent. From such results a slight abatement only need be anticipated in virtue of the experience that the raising of a rate never does yield quite the proportionable sum. Here, then, was an engine of finance, created during times of ease and quiet, which could be effectually used to meet national difficulties. But the case would be different if the tax were once remitted; for if it were to be re-imposed, the machinery must then be formed afresh, and the measure might at first fall short of success because the people had grown unaccustomed to it. The force of habit being greater in India than in any other country, the people concerned would gradually adapt themselves to the tax, so that any inconvenience, which might have been felt at first, would gradually disappear.

Lord Mayo seriously considered all these arguments, and quite appreciated the advantages derived from the income-tax. But he seemed unwilling to sanction the continuance of the tax, if that could be avoided. The question, however, was not brought to an issue by him because his lamented death took place early in 1872.

After Lord Mayo's death, the Governor of Madras, Lord Napier (now Lord Napier and Ettrick) acted as Governor-General during the time when the budget had to be prepared and produced. He sanctioned the continuance of the tax, for the coming year, though apparently with some reluctance, believing this measure to be required in order to produce a small surplus in the estimate. Accordingly I produced the budget with a surplus of a quarter of a million sterling. Once more, however, the surplus grew as the year advanced and at length amounted to 1¾ million.

Thus ended the fourth year of surplus; and this cycle of four consecutive years was the most prosperous time yet known in Indian finance. The condition of surplus was owing partly to causes beyond the control of the Government, partly also to the principles followed in framing the estimates and in regulating the expenditure. Moderation had been carefully observed in estimating the receipts under all heads of revenue, especially that of opium. The precarious and uncertain character of the opium revenue was borne in mind; our recent experience of 1869 had indeed forcibly reminded us of this. We had on that occasion estimated the price of opium in the budget on an average of the realized prices of the past three years, which was less than that which was being received about the time of the budget. Thus the estimate was to all appearances a prudent one. Still the actual receipts proved to be less than they were estimated by one-third of a million sterling, owing to causes which arose in the interior of China, and of which we never could exactly understand the operation. We therefore became more cautious than ever in framing the estimates of the opium revenue, and they were during these years fortunately exceeded by the result.

Shortly after the production of the budget for 1872–3 as last mentioned, Lord Northbrook arrived as Governor-General in succession to Lord Mayo. In due course the question again arose as to whether the income-tax should be retained or remitted, and I still advocated its retention. Lord Northbrook, however, was much impressed with the objections which had been urged against the tax from so many quarters, and did not think its continuance necessary.

Thus I had to produce in March 1873 the budget for 1873–4 without an income-tax. The estimates, however, still showed a surplus for the year of a quarter of a million. The surplus would in this year, as in preceding years, have become a large one, had not a calamity beyond human control supervened. But as the autumn approached it became evident that famine was impending over Bengal and Behar. The Government was obliged to make preparations on a most extensive scale for the relief of the anticipated distress and for preserving the lives of the people from danger. Before the end of the year operations for the prevention of famine were begun throughout a large area. The charges on account of famine relief during the year amounted to £3,864,707, which caused a deficit in the finances of £1,807,668. Had there not been this famine, no deficit would have occurred, but on the contrary there would have been a surplus of more than 2½ millions, or £2,648,401.

This proved to be my last budget; though it was intended that I should produce one more in March 1874, for the year

1874–5, before returning to England. My ordinary term of office, five years, was expiring, but I had been requested by the Secretary of State in England, the Duke of Argyll, to retain my post for an additional year. When this year was approaching its close, Lord Northbrook nominated me to be Lieutenant-Governor of Bengal. Shortly afterwards famine became imminent in northern Bengal and Behar, and I was directed to proceed immediately to the scene of distress, and superintend the operations for relief. Thus the unfinished budget was left in my financial portfolio, and the threads of it were taken up by the Governor-General himself.

During these five years I received the utmost assistance from the Financial Secretary, Robert Barclay Chapman, in framing the civil estimates, and whatever success attended them was in a considerable degree owing to his experience, carefulness and acumen. I was also much indebted to Mr. R. Hollingberry of the Uncovenanted Service. The military estimates were framed by Mr. (now Sir George) Kellner with skill and knowledge. He had an intimate acquaintance with military accounts, and is one of the ablest men whom the Uncovenanted Service of India has produced.

The financial results of the five budgets which have been mentioned may be summarized thus: the surplus or deficit relates to income and ordinary expenditure, exclusive of the outlay on reproductive works, which has been charged to the capital account, and the figures are taken from papers presented to Parliament.

Year.	£ Surplus.	£ Deficit.
1869–70	118,669	..
1870–1	1,482,990	..
1871–2	3,124,177	..
1872–3	1,765,672	..
1873–4	———	1,807,668 (Bengal famine).

	£
Total surplus	6,491,508
Deduct deficit	1,807,668
Net surplus on the five years	4,683,840

Thus the period may be regarded as fortunate financially, especially when it is remembered that but for the Bengal famine, the last of the five years would have shewn a large surplus, instead of a deficit.

This net surplus may be regarded as more than counterbalancing the net deficit of the previous five years, as will be seen thus :—

Year.	Surplus. £	Deficit. £
1864–5	———	 193,521
1865–6	2,766,068	———
1866–7	———	 2,517,491
1867–8	———	 1,007,695
1868–9	———	 2,774,030

	£
Total deficit	6,492,737
Deduct surplus	2,766,068
Net deficit	3,726,669

This result bears out the conclusion, which has now been attained after an examination extending over the twenty years during which India has possessed a formal budget system, namely this, that she fully pays all her ordinary expenses one year taken with another, and shews a small surplus on any extended series of years which may be taken.

But it demonstrates that if national solvency was to be secured by the counterbalancing of deficit by surplus, the income-tax was absolutely essential, notwithstanding all that may have been said at the time against its necessity. During the five years, the following sums were obtained by means of this tax—net, after deducting cost of collection :—

	£
1869–70	1,068,523
1870–1	2,028,034
1871–2	795,675
1872–3	561,000
Total	4,453,232

or in round numbers $4\frac{1}{2}$ millions.

It is clear, then, that without the income-tax, the financial result so essential to the solvency of India would not, indeed could not, have been obtained. This result, too, at all times necessary, was doubly so at that time, because India, having emerged from a great war, with extensive additions to her national debt, was embarking on a course of peaceful enterprise, whereby she had to borrow in time of peace in order to provide capital for outlay in reproductive works.

Outside the ordinary budget, there was a large outlay on State railways and canals of irrigation, which was charged to the capital account, and for which funds were raised by loan. The subjoined figures relating to these affairs are taken from the papers presented to Parliament:—

Year.	Outlay on public works extraordinary.	Amount raised by loan. Net less discharged.	Net discharged.
	£	£	£
1869–70	2,599,614	5,681,431	———
1870–1	1,167,810	3,626,235	———
1871–2	1,628,474	2,544,285	———
1172–3	2,184,569	2,063,922	1,510,573
1873–4	3,553,307		
		Total 13,915,873	
	Total 11,133,774		
			13,915,873
		Less discharged	1,510,573
		Total	12,405,300

Of the total borrowed, in round numbers 12½ millions, there were 3 millions raised in India, and the rest in England.

While this borrowing was in progress year by year the public credit stood high, higher indeed than at any time before. The normal rate of interest in India had been five per cent.; but these loans were raised at four per cent. At this very time, too, we were able to take advantage of the term expiring for some of the old five per cent. loans, in order to reduce the interest. This was effected by offering the holders of five per cent. paper the option of accepting four per cent. paper instead, or of being repaid in full; and they used always to accept four per cent. paper; or, in some cases, four and a half for a time and thereafter four per cent. About twenty millions sterling of the national debt were, during the five years, subjected to this operation.

There was not the least difficulty in raising the requisite funds either in England or in India. The moneyed classes and the capitalists in India were known to be able to invest a certain sum annually, from two to three millions sterling, in Government securities at four per cent., which is for India a very low rate. This amount they were glad to tender whenever subscriptions to a Government loan were invited; and they would have tendered much larger sums had the rate of interest been higher.

The frequent borrowing might have been expected to have a depressing effect on the selling price of Government securities. But instead of suffering any depreciation, these securities steadily rose in value during the five years, and on the fifth year stood at the highest point they had ever reached. The four per cent. stock in India, called "the rupee debt" (in silver) used to be sold at 91 for 100 rupees; it gradually rose to par during these years, and in 1873 reached 105, or 5 per cent. premium. In England the Indian four per cent. stock, called "the sterling debt" (in gold) used to stand at 92 for 100; it gradually rose to 106, or 6 per cent. premium. The fact was that all men saw the efforts made by the Government of India to augment income and diminish ordinary expenditure. Indeed the very unpopularity of some among the fiscal measures proved the stern resolution of the Government to pursue its policy despite opposition. It was known that the money was being borrowed, not to meet deficit or to pay for unproductive expenditure like war, but for reproductive works railways and canals for irrigation, of all which the merits were patent to the public. It was often predicted that these works would seldom be remunerative, and would sometimes even prove to be national folly. But evidently the moneyed classes thought otherwise, relying on the Government, and the event has shewn that they were right. For now these works, both railways and canals, are in technical phrase "paying," that is, yielding a return, net after defrayal of expenses. This return on the capital outlay amounts to five per cent. on the railways and six per cent. on the canals.

During this time the treasury was kept full, as will be seen from the following figures of the cash balances on the 31st March, or the last day of each official year, both in India itself and in England on account of India:—

Year.	Cash balance on 31st March. India.	England.	Total.
	£	£	£
1869	10,175,804	3,025,982	13,201,786
1870	13,940,451	2,892,483	16,832,934
1871	16,818,743	3,305,972	20,124,715
1872	21,997,715	2,821,091	24,818,806
1873	18,787,693	2,998,444	21,786,137

The revenues during the five years were stationary, their total varying somewhat according to the imposition or remission of the income-tax; while the ordinary expenditure decreased during the first four years and rose in the fifth year, owing to the Bengal famine, as will be shown by the following figures taken from the returns presented to Parliament:—

Year.	Revenue.	Ordinary expenditure.
	£	£
1869–70	50,901,081	50,782,412
1870–1	51,413,686	49,930,696
1871–2	50,110,215	46,986,038
1872–3	50,219,489	48,453,817
1873–4	49,598,253	51,405,921 (Bengal famine)

The declared value of the foreign trade of India during the five years stood thus:—

Year.	Declared value of foreign trade of India.
	£
1869–70	100,396,056
1870–1	97,469,893
1871–2	108,351,039
1872–3	92,980,052
1873–4	96,522,443

CHAPTER XVI.

(1869–1872.)

LORD MAYO'S INDIAN CAREER.

Lord Mayo arrives at Calcutta succeeding John Lawrence—Receives visit from Shir Ali, Amir of Caubul—Boundary between Afghanistan and Central Asia —Relations with Persia—Expedition against tribes on eastern border of India—Sir Henry Durand in the Panjab—Army expenses and accommodation for European troops—Lord Mayo's internal administration—He bestows special care upon finance—Causes increased control to be entrusted to provincial Governments over certain departments—Promotes public works, railways and canals—Endeavours to establish a Department of Agriculture—Progress of legislation—Visit of H.R.H the Duke of Edinburgh—Murder of Acting Chief Justice Norman—Assassination of Lord Mayo in the Andaman Islands—Funeral ceremonies at Calcutta.

On the day in January, 1869, that Lord Mayo succeeded John Lawrence as Governor-General, at the Government House, Calcutta, the contrast, in appearance, between the two men was remarked by every bystander. John Lawrence stood near the head of the flight of steps, wearing full uniform, calm in aspect, and conscious that he had, according to his own phrase, served his time and done all he could. He was somewhat pallid and care-worn, reduced in body from protracted labour while in precarious health, and looking like a hoary weather-beaten rock, round which the elements had oft-times roared and dashed.

Lord Mayo, on the other hand, mounted the steps in plain morning dress, robust in frame, beaming with the brightness of health, buoyant in spirits, and elastic with hope. He won favour with every one at first sight, and soon began to acquire a personal popularity, which, with slight intermissions at Calcutta, grew and expanded as he became more widely known. Indeed, he possessed qualifications, for conciliating the regard of an Anglo-Saxon community in the East, such as rarely fall to the lot of those who are chosen for such a post as that of Governor-General. The English in India, though willing to make allowance for bodily weakness when combined with moral power, and ready to admire the feeble frame when struggling with difficulties, do yet delight to see physical strength and manly vigour in their rulers. Now Lord Mayo was a capital rider, a practised judge of horses, and the animals which filled his stable made a sight worth seeing. Having hunted much in England and Ireland he rapidly rose to a high rank among equestrian sportsmen in India, and began to lead the field in pursuit of the wild boar. He was fond of using the gun or the rifle and would wade through the marshes near Calcutta to shoot snipe. He occasionally attended some of the principal races, and made official journeys of great length on horseback. Having once led a somewhat hard life while engaged in Irish farming, he had a frank and sympathetic bearing towards those who were battling with difficulties, and a practical insight into all circumstances of perplexity. Yet, without being at all ostentatious he always assumed a due degree of state and dignity. Personally he was generous and much given to hospitality, which he dispensed with an urbane freedom and attentive carefulness that charmed all hearts.

He seemed to us to be different from any Governor-General we had yet seen. Hardinge had been quiet and sedate; Dalhousie had preserved retiring habits by reason of the pain against which he had to contend amidst all his imperial anxieties; Canning was naturally grave and reserved, even before he felt the oppressive sense of unexampled anxiety; Elgin had been bright and genial, without displaying any remarkable degree of physical vigour; and Lawrence never lost the care-worn weather-beaten aspect caused by a life of Indian toil. But Mayo was gay, active, and enthusiastic, without at all derogating from his proper dignity; indeed enthusiasm pervaded his whole existence, and was his distinguishing mark.

Almost his first care, after assuming office, was to gather up the threads of the negotiation with the Amir of Caubul, Shir Ali, as John Lawrence had left it. The Amir had not come to meet the Governor-General in British territory before the end of John Lawrence's incumbency. Lord Mayo soon learnt, however, that Shir Ali would cross the Panjab border, and arranged that the Amir should proceed as far as Amballa for the meeting, as it was well for the Afghan ruler and his advisers to see something of the power and civilization of the British dominions. He fixed a time during April for meeting the Amir, and was accompanied to Amballa by the members of his Council, including myself. He arranged there, for the reception of the Amir and his suite, that display of various military forces, belonging to many nationalities arrayed under one banner, and that expanse of canvas in the tented fields, which never fail to lend a strange interest to occasions of state in India.

Shir Ali was aquiline in profile, short of stature, broad in build, and seemed to be in the prime of life. He had the cast of countenance which characterizes many of the Afghan chiefs; wherein a certain sort of exterior polish conceals a fierceness of which momentary flashes could hardly be suppressed. Still he had something of frankness, even of bluffness, and looked like a man who had lived in camps, fought hard-contested fields, and by the sword cut his way to power and fortune. He accepted the subsidies of arms and money which the Governor-General gave as the balance of the £60,000 promised by John Lawrence. He received also the present of a jewelled sword, vowing that it should be drawn henceforth for the British Government alone. He did not obtain, however, the definitive assurances of support which he desired from the British Government, both in respect of foreign war and internal revolution. Then he returned to Caubul, pleased with the reception which had been accorded, and doubtless intending sincerely to act up to all the loyal words he had uttered. Lord Mayo would have rejoiced if he had been empowered to give a more positive guarantee to the Amir, at least, in respect to protection against foreign aggression. Still he continued, by exercising a personal influence, to keep the Afghan ruler in a loyal and contented frame of mind. Thus for several years the Amballa meeting produced valuable results politically, which redounded to Lord Mayo's honour.

The reception at Amballa having thus ended propitiously, the Indian public began to hope that relations had been established on the part of the British Government with a real native ruler at Caubul who, in virtue of these relations, would hold his own against all comers for himself and for England his ally. Once more the vision of a friendly and independent Afghanistan floated before the popular imagination, and great credit on this account was accorded to Lord Mayo, which he fully deserved. At the same time it was necessary to remember the share which John Lawrence had taken in originating these measures, and in preparing the way for their consummation.

Lord Mayo's cares regarding Afghanistan did not end with the completion of the Amballa arrangement.

He desired to approach what was really the root of the whole question, namely, the establishment of an understanding between England and Russia regarding their respective limits of actual possession, or political control, in Asia. He virtually advocated the plan which has since been termed the international delimitation between the two empires. He took a hopeful and friendly view of the policy and intentions of Russia respecting those Asiatic matters in which England was interested. At his instance the English Government permitted Mr. (now Sir Douglas) Forsyth to proceed to St. Petersburg and discuss the subject with the Russian Ministers. It is probable that Central Asian trade entered into these discussions; this trade may be valuable so far as it goes, and Lord Mayo took great interest in its development; the real point, however, was the political safety of Afghanistan as an outwork of India.

Shortly afterwards the arrangement was begun whereby Russia agreed that Afghanistan should be regarded as beyond the sphere of her political influence. The next point was the determination of the boundaries of Afghanistan, and Lord Mayo was rejoiced to see much progress made towards the framing of a political map whereby Afghan limits would be defined in a manner satisfactory to England. This result, so far as it went, was really sound and good. Shir Ali too preserved a loyal and comparatively cheerful demeanour. Thus the anxiety which had been growing so fast in India, as explained in the previous chapter XIV., regarding the intentions of Russia, began temporarily to subside, and fortune seemed for a moment to smile on Lord Mayo's efforts.

It was not until after Lord Mayo's death that anxiety was aroused by the Russian expedition against Khiva in 1873, and the arrangements consequent thereon, which really made the Khivan chief a vassal of the Czar. Thereupon the Amir of Caubul shewed much alarm, and wondered whether, if Russia having thus absorbed Khiva were to compass the absorption of Afghanistan, there would be anything really to stop her. It was then that he first began to swerve from the fidelity which he had promised to Lord Mayo.

Then Persia became troublesome, first by aggression upon Seistan on the Afghan border, next by a truly presumptuous claim on territory which belonged to the Khan of Khelat, an ally of the British, and actually touched the British frontier in Sind. Lord Mayo saw at once the importance of keeping Persia at arm's length from the Indian frontier, and arranged for the satisfactory disposal of this unreasonable claim. That affair is known in the diplomatic records as the settlement of the Mekran boundary. The dispute between Persia and Afghanistan soon assumed a serious aspect. Seistan may be described as one of those remarkable depressions which characterize the physical geography of Asia. Into it there flows the Helmand, which drains all central and southern Afghanistan, and finds no other outlet. It is for the most part a vast swamp, but in former ages was highly cultivated, and possesses classical associations to Persians as having been the native land of Rustam and other heroes. It has, notwithstanding its comparative desolation and insalubrity, an important position politically, as being one of the two natural highways whereby Afghanistan may be approached from the west and military communication opened from Persia to Candahar. It was now claimed almost wholly by Persia, and parts of it were seized by Persian troops. The Amir, Shir Ali, remonstrated strenuously, and claimed the good offices of the British Government, which were granted by Lord Mayo. Resort was had to arbitration, whereby a part of the disputed territory was adjudged to Persia, while the rest remained in Afghanistan. The final adjudication was not arrived at till after Lord Mayo's time. Meanwhile the Amir did not seem to appreciate at their full worth the efforts put forth by the British Government, but rather to imagine that his just interests were being unduly sacrificed.

The Muhammadan chief who had overthrown Chinese authority in Yarkand, and whose overtures were rejected by John Lawrence, again evinced anxiety for British friendship. Lord Mayo deemed the time had come for renewing negotiations, and despatched thither a mission under Sir Douglas Forsyth. The results of the mission proved satisfactory so long as the Muhammadan power lasted in that region.

So far then Lord Mayo was fortunate in diplomacy respecting Central Asia. He had seen the Afghan ruler established, in independence indeed, but still distinctly in friendship with England. He had made progress in concert with Russia toward determining the boundaries of Afghanistan as being outside the limits of Russian interference. The ambitious projects of Persia had been checked, and British influence had been established in Yarkand. The only cloud which hung over this fair horizon was the design which Russia was meditating for the expedition which she afterwards launched against Khiva.

All that was possible at the time for promoting the foreign interests of India had been done, and Lord Mayo might well feel at liberty to bend his mind towards the internal administration of the empire.

There was yet, however, one external trouble to be encountered, for complications of a threatening character arose on the North-eastern border. The extension of tea-plantations under European supervision, and the spread of Bengali cultivation among the naturally fertile and wooded valleys of the hill ranges on the eastern border of Bengal, had been proceeding apace for several years. These circumstances excited the unreasoning jealousy and cupidity of the tribes inhabiting the broad belt of mountains which overlook the British border for five hundred miles. Their outrages having become intolerable, two expeditions were despatched against the offending tribes from opposite directions: one from Assam in the north under General (now Sir George) Bourchier; the other from Chittagong on the south under General (now Sir Charles) Brownlow. The operations were quite successful, and the tribes which were then chastised have ever since behaved better than formerly. I had officially to visit a part of that frontier in after years, and found the moral effect of these expeditions to have been considerable.

The first important appointment which Lord Mayo made was that of Sir Henry Durand (then military member of the Governor-General's Council) to be Lieutenant Governor of the Panjab in succession to Sir Donald Macleod. Durand had, after a long, eventful and perhaps somewhat chequered career in peace and war, ended by becoming more popular with Europeans in India than any one of that time. He was a man of grand appearance, his figure being very tall and broad, his aspect grave resolute and commanding. He was esteemed to be a man of clear vision, calm judgment, just disposition, accurate discrimination, and to all these qualities was added an intrepid courage. Though of warm temper, he was generous, indeed without the attribute of generosity in a large degree it would have been impossible for a man to become as popular as he was. Being an officer of the Corps of Engineers, and well educated in many professional subjects, he had acquired much general culture. Altogether he was a strong man, whether in the cabinet or in the field, and his troops of friends anticipated for him fresh successes in the administrative sphere of the Panjab. But within a twelvemonth he was accidentally killed while marching along the frontier; at dusk, when mounted on an elephant, he was trying to pass under an archway which proved to be too low for so tall a beast as the one he rode. He was thrown off violently on the ground, and received a mortal injury in the spine. Men in their grief felt that a great spirit had suddenly passed away from their midst.

The next appointment of this nature made by Lord Mayo

was that of Mr. (now Sir George) Campbell to be Lieutenant-Governor of Bengal. As Campbell was known to be one of the most active-minded men in the Civil Service, many auguries were formed of progress and improvement for Bengal. It will be shewn in a future chapter how fully these hopes were realized.

From his habits of mind, Lord Mayo was fond of attending to military affairs, and formed the idea that the expense of the army in India was too heavy. Perhaps he hardly realised the efforts that had been made by some of his predecessors and advisers for diminishing that expense, and the extent to which the reduction had already been carried. That the charge was then, as it ever will be, very heavy, was undoubted; but the question was whether it could be lessened with safety, and he seemed to think that it could. Certainly he set himself laudably to the study of economy in this branch, and although additional charges were unavoidably caused by improvements in armament, he succeeded in obtaining a diminution of the total expenditure. As might be expected, he examined carefully the fine barracks for European troops which, according to the large scheme mentioned in the preceding chapter XIV., were being constructed at many stations. These also he deemed to be too costly, and strove to effect savings in the outlay. One plan of his was to place more regiments than heretofore in the Himalayas, where barracks smaller and cheaper than those to be erected in the Indian plains would prove sufficient; in this way the construction of some of the more expensive barracks might be dispensed with. He doubtless saw the political danger of keeping too large a portion of the European troops in the hills, far away from the plains where their services might be required, as has been indicated in the previous chapter VII. But he held, perhaps judiciously, that the introduction of railways had quite altered the aspect of the case—mobilizing the army to an extent hardly conceivable in past times—and that it would be both safe and economical to afford to the European soldiers, in a larger degree than formerly, the benefit of a sojourn in the cool climate of the hills.

Sir William Mansfield (afterwards Lord Sandhurst) was then Commander-in-Chief; and he was disposed to second the efforts of the Governor-General in the direction of economy. The prominent part taken by Mansfield, in the civil as well as the military business of the Government of India, has been already mentioned in chapter XIV. As he was about to resign his command and return to England, Lord Mayo entertained him at a farewell banquet in Government House, and commemorated his war services in a suitable and graceful speech.

Lord Napier of Magdâla was welcomed by the public as well as the army on succeeding to the high office of Commander-in-Chief. He was not disposed to lend the weight of his authority to proposals for economy unless they were manifestly consistent with safety and efficiency. Regarding the style and size of the new barracks for the European troops, he generally concurred in what had been done already, and was inclined to deprecate any considerable saving as being likely to cause detriment to the health of the men.

Though Lord Mayo was, as has been seen, much interested in political and military affairs, it was towards the internal administration of the empire, and the progress of moral and material improvement, that his best thoughts and highest hopes were directed. His policy has been excellently sketched in an elaborate minute, drawn up immediately after his premature and lamented death, by Sir John Strachey, who was the senior member of his Council, and had the best possible data for preparing such a description. Many facts and particulars also are furnished in the biography of him by Dr. W. W. Hunter. I shall here mention those circumstances which came under my own observation as one of the members of his government.

The financial policy of Lord Mayo has for the most part been set forth in the previous chapter XV. relating to the Finance Ministership. There remain, however, some particulars to be stated respecting his bearing towards the Financial Department of the Government. It might have been anticipated that being a progressive administrator, an ardent advocate of material improvement, an impressionable and popular statesman, a grand and conspicuous man generally—he would dislike the check imposed by finance, or at least be disposed to overlook the cost when in full view of the results attainable by beneficent measures. Such however was not the case with him; on the contrary, financial considerations were never for a moment absent from his mind. However eager he might be in the pursuit of any advantage desirable for the public weal, he paused instantly on being confronted by a financial obstacle. He would forego his most darling wish rather than incur even the slightest deficit, and submit to any trouble, even sacrificing the popularity which as a generously minded man he liked to retain, in order to secure an equilibrium between income and expenses. So far from underrating financial difficulties, he was rather inclined to over-rate them, or sometimes even to be unnecessarily disquieted on their account. He seemed to feel an absolute respect for the authority and influence of "the Treasury," as he called it, meaning in India the Financial Department; and was most unwilling to embark upon any course involving the collection or the disbursement of public money, unless his responsible advisers financially concurred. Nor did his care relate only to the plain matters of receipts and expenses; it extended also throughout the whole field of audit and account. Had his training been in the bureau of an auditor, instead of in the field and the cabinet, he could hardly have been more punctiliously anxious respecting the public accounts than he actually was. As Finance Minister I found him a most pleasant and satisfactory Governor-General to deal with. When he suddenly perished he was "flebilis" to many departments, but to none was he "flebilior" than to the Financial Department. On producing the budget for British India in April, 1872, shortly after his death, it became my duty to express the sentiment of Indian financiers in these words: "Those who were in almost daily communication with him regarding the administration of the exchequer, the work of the treasury department, the gathering in of receipts, the regulation of expenses, must necessarily know best how firm he was in the enforcement of economy, how strict in adherence to rule, how anxious that the state resources should be reserved for indispensable or beneficent purposes, how consistent in the vindication of financial considerations, and how generous in supporting those engaged in the conduct of affairs."

Concerning finance, there was one matter in which he took much personal interest, and for its successful accomplishment he deserved great credit individually, namely, the plan of augmenting the control and responsibility of the several provincial governments in India for certain branches of the civil expenditure, officially styled "the scheme of Provincial Services."

It had for several years been felt that in respect of moral and material improvement, comprised practically in education, roads and communications, hospitals and sanitation, civil buildings and prisons—the demands of a progressive age were constantly causing increase of expenditure. The objects in question, being excellent, were urged by the local authorities and provincial governments with indisputable force, but there remained the question as to how the needful money was to be found. The provincial governments were not answerable for its production, though they recommended the expending of it; the supreme authority, namely the Government of India, had to provide the funds. Consequently the Government of India used to check and curtail the proposed measures in every possible way, and, as might be expected, the provincial governments were hardly so economical in framing their recommendations as they would have been if answerable for providing the ways and means. But this detailed check on the part of the Government of India respecting matters wherein the provincial governments and local authorities were the best informed, was in its nature invidious, and produced incessant friction. The modification of this system had been carefully considered by John Lawrence, but he was anxious regarding the finances, and unwilling to relax the financial check which his Government had vigilantly exercised. So the matter rested until some time after Lord Mayo's arrival in 1869. During the discussions on the budget of April 1870, at Calcutta, he adverted several times to the advantage of relaxing the financial check heretofore exercised by the Government of India in the various branches of moral or material improvement already mentioned above, and proportionately augmenting the financial responsibility of the provincial governments. It was known that one of our colleagues, Sir John Strachey, was especially favourable to this principle. When we were all assembled at Simla, after the publication of the budget, I went one day to see Lord Mayo, and asked him to explain to me his wishes, promising that as Finance Minister I would help in giving effect to them. He then said that a yearly grant of money in a fixed amount ought to be made by the Government of India to each of the several provincial governments for the branches and departments already mentioned; that any unspent portion of the grant should be credited to the next year, and so on; also that several items of local income should be assigned to them, so that they might have the benefit of good management, or suffer the loss arising from inferior management. Thus they would have funds of their own, for the administration of which they must be answerable. From these funds they would have to provide the means for conducting the work of the departments above mentioned. If they desired more and more improvements, they might have these if only they could find the money. They would thus be placed in their proper position relatively to the Government of India, would cease to make proposals without regard to expense, and remain content with such a moderate degree of progress as the funds at their disposal might allow. The general control of the Government of India was to be maintained in these particular branches, as in all the larger branches of the public service. The plan was then matured, and assistance was received to the utmost from Sir John Strachey in passing it through the Council.

The department, however, towards which Lord Mayo's brightest thoughts turned, was that of Public Works. He delighted in roads, railways, and canals, and regarded India as an imperial estate, upon which capital was to be beneficently laid out to the utmost limit compatible with financial safety. In this cardinal respect he was on a par even with the great Dalhousie, and essentially a Governor-General for such works. He felt so keen an interest in this department that he took it under his own direct control, whereas it had previously been supervised by one of the members of the Government. Ordinarily in the division of labour between the head and the members of the Government, the Governor-General takes the Foreign department, and distributes the other departments among his colleagues. But Lord Mayo managed both the Foreign and the Public Works departments, thereby subjecting himself to an additional burden of work.

He discerned the precise extent of the need which India had for works of artificial irrigation, and appreciated the magnificence of the canal system which she already possessed. But while anxious to diffuse as widely as possible the blessings of water in season among arid lands, by the outlay of capital on the part of the State—he thought that the canals must be made to yield a profitable return, not in a more or less remote future, but within a very few years after the opening of the works. He held that however demonstrable the beneficence of these works might be, they could not be properly undertaken by the State unless some such remunerative return were, not only promised, but actually secured. With this view, he proposed that a local rate should be levied on those villages which had the opportunity of deriving irrigation from the new canals; for he apprehended that full reliance could not be placed on the sale of canal-water to the farmers and cultivators. In this proposal he was supported by the concurrent opinion of his colleagues in Council, and a bill for levying such a rate was in due course passed by the legislature in India. The measure however gave rise to an animated discussion, and was ultimately disallowed by the Secretary of State in England.

Respecting railways, Lord Mayo deemed that the cost had been excessive of the lines already made in India by the

Guaranteed Companies, that is the Companies to whom a certain rate of interest on their capital outlay had been guaranteed by the State. He therefore desired much to try some cheaper system of construction for the future. Believing that the lines remaining to be made could be constructed quite as well and more economically by the Government, he favoured the plan already initiated of forming a department for State railways. Instead of entrusting the new railways to companies with a State guarantee of interest on capital, he promoted the construction of railways by the Government through its own officers. Though he duly appreciated the great services which the Guaranteed Companies had rendered to India, he hoped to profit by their experience for the benefit of the future lines, in economy at least if not in efficiency. In respect to the saving of expense he mainly relied on a specific measure namely, the diminution of the gauge. For the existing gauge of 5 ft. 6 in. he proposed to substitute a gauge of 3 ft. 3 in. This proposal caused a battle of the gauges to be stirred up in India, and it was surprising to note how rapidly the various authorities began to range themselves on one side or the other. The opposition to the gauge of 3 ft. 3 in. proceeded in the first instance from those concerned in the Guaranteed railways who by this time had become a considerable party in the State. Their view spread largely among the mercantile community which was naturally disposed to accept a highly competent non-official authority like this in preference to the official authority of the Government. Then stress was laid on the fact that as a narrow gauge was to be introduced into a country which already possessed many railways made on a broader gauge, there would be a break of gauge in many places. Now a break of gauge is usually dreaded by military authorities in respect to army transport, so they, with Lord Napier of Magdâla at their head, arrayed themselves in argument against the proposed narrow gauge. The difference of opinion extended to Lord Mayo's own Council; upon a division there, however, he obtained a majority. The main objection was this, that the narrow gauge while causing manifold inconveniences would fail to save expense appreciably. But Lord Mayo had little difficulty in showing that a smaller thing would be less expensive than a larger. Then several of the new State railways were begun upon the gauge of 3 ft. 3 in. and a comprehensive scheme was prepared whereby the lines generally west of Delhi, namely those in the Panjab and Sind, and those running from the North-western Provinces through Rajputana and Central India towards Bombay, should be constructed on this gauge. This scheme was after Lord Mayo's death abandoned as regards the Panjab, but is in the main being carried into effect for the lines in Rajputana and Central Asia.

Lord Mayo was quite prepared to raise money by loan, about four millions sterling annually, for the construction of railways and canals, and to depend on the Government being recouped, by the net income from these useful works, for the interest on the capital laid out upon them. He acquiesced in the principle already established, to the effect that this outlay and all charges and receipts incidental to it should be kept separate from the ordinary budget of revenue and expenditure and treated as technically "extraordinary." But he was anxious that a separate audit should be set up, to be conducted with the public as witness. In these matters he continued to receive the same valuable support which his predecessor had received from Colonel Richard Strachey.

He supported all plans which were judiciously and considerately framed with a view to levying special rates in the several Provinces of the empire for purposes of local improvement. An important beginning was made in Bengal by the imposition of the road cess for schools and roads, notwithstanding the opposition raised on the score of the permanent settlement.

Some considerable impulse was given by him to the project for abolishing the inland customs line, whereby sugar and salt were taxed in transit. He induced the Native Princes in whose territory the sources of salt supply were situated to allow them to be managed by the British authorities, so that the duty might be levied at the place of production. He then arranged for the construction of railways to these sources of supply.

He strove to systematize the proceedings whereby loans were granted by the State to corporations, municipal or other, for the execution of useful works, and to individuals for the improvement of their estates. A law indeed was enacted by his Legislative Council for the purpose. Many of the municipalities largely availed themselves of the privilege he thus secured for them, as they thereby obtained from Government better terms than any they could obtain in the money market. As regards the improvement of estates, landowners now borrow but little from Government for this purpose save in times of drought, when a demand usually arises for the lesser works of irrigation; so the hopes formed in this respect have hardly been realized.

All proposals for sanitation in large towns, and for sanitary reform in the country generally, received Lord Mayo's sympathetic attention.

In respect to internal improvement he greatly set his heart upon founding what in some countries would be termed an agricultural bureau. He thought more upon the improvement of agriculture than any other Governor-General, and at first seemed to cherish a hope that he might see a path of progress opened amidst the maze of popular ignorance, though this hope must have grown weaker and weaker as he gained experience of the dead weight to be overcome. Every one had seen that Indian agriculture was backward in comparison with European countries, and might be improved, but none had known how to promote such improvement. It was admitted that instruction in scientific agriculture ought to form part of the national education in India; but, how this instruction should be given, and of what it should consist, were questions far from being solved. The experiments undertaken from time to time were desultory and fruitless. The model farms, established here and there, had failed to prove the practicability of any improvement. Now, Lord Mayo wished to set up a department of practical and scientific agriculture, which should be a part of the ordinary administration, with its head-quarters under the Government of India, and its branches under the several provincial governments. This scheme, being based on a sound and scientific idea, was with some modifications accepted by the authorities in India, and would if carried into effect have produced results, slowly at first but surely in the end, though after the lapse of a long time. But when submitted to the authorities in England for sanction it underwent alterations, and instead of being a department of Agriculture only, it became a secretariat of Revenue, Agriculture, and Commerce, which was quite a different thing. The sort of attention which could be afforded to agriculture in conjunction with revenue and commerce was already understood in India, and was in some degree bestowed, though doubtless that degree might well be increased. The supervision now wanted was specifically different, namely, a scientific attention, which could not properly be afforded by a department concerned in other branches, fiscal or commercial. Moreover the officers concerned in a department embracing three such branches as these above mentioned, must necessarily be men of general qualifications and not professional agriculturists. It would on the other hand be a waste of power to appoint purely scientific men to manage a department which, in addition to science, had charge of revenue and commerce. Thus Lord Mayo's original plan became transformed in effect, and merely improved the existing practice instead of introducing, as he intended, a new one altogether. He, however, *faute de mieux*, accepted the modified scheme and constituted the new secretariat of Revenue, Agriculture, and Commerce, appointing as the first Secretary Mr. Allan Hume, of the Covenanted Civil Service, one of the few officers then in India who with administrative ability combined an aptitude for physical science. No marked result to the country at large ensued upon this arrangement being brought into effect.

The three years of Lord Mayo's incumbency were, in respect of legislation, perhaps the busiest that have ever passed in British India. Henry Sumner Maine was, in 1869, approaching the close of a six years' tenure as legislative member of the Government, the results of which have been mentioned in the chapter XIV. on John Lawrence as Governor-General. His successor, James Fitzjames Stephen, was received in India with the deference due to the high reputation acquired by him in England as a jurist, a legal authority in criminal law especially, and as a public writer. From the beginning of 1870, Fitzjames Stephen applied himself with really splendid energy to the pending matters of Indian legislation. He found that his distinguished predecessor had not only procured the passing of several important Acts, but had prepared the way for others of importance to be enacted thereafter; that a High Commission had been sitting in England to prepare several projects of general laws for the consideration of the Government in India; andthat considerable progress had been made towards the codification of those existing in India partly through the exertions of Whitley Stokes, legislative secretary to the Government. Thus he found a large field, with a harvest ready to be reaped by a man who possessed, as he did, knowledge combined with administrative power. He perceived the constitution of the legislature to have become such that the faculty of oral exposition was almost as useful there as in a British assembly; and he speedily gave proofs of possessing that faculty in a degree quite commensurate with the importance of the many occasions which were frequently presenting themselves. Within a month after assuming office he made a speech before the Legislative Council on a bill then pending; as we walked away together, after the sitting was over, Lord Mayo remarked to me that the man who had just delivered that speech would soon make his mark on the face of Indian affairs. Without apparently attempting the polished oratory which had distinguished so many of Maine's speeches, he spoke clearly as well as with force and energy. Some of his speeches on important measures, such as the Indian Contract Act, form landmarks in the history of Indian legislation. Others, again, such as that upon the Marriage Act, for Indians not professing the Hindu or Muhammadan religion, form striking episodes in the annals of the Legislative Council. His oration too, in reply to the objections of the Bengal landlords to the imposition of the road cess, indicated the most fruitful research into the early history of the Permanent Settlement. He also took a decided part in all the deliberations of the Government on general subjects, and was during his Indian service quite a power in the State.

In these days his Royal Highness the Duke of Edinburgh, then in command of the *Galatea*, honoured India with a gracious visit. Lord Mayo received His Royal Highness at Calcutta with magnificence, befitting this the first occasion of a member of the Royal family visiting India. The Governors, the Lieutenant-Governors, the principal European officials, the Native princes and chiefs of the empire, assembled at the capital to render homage. His Royal Highness was invested with the insignia of the Star of India in the presence of one of the largest and most brilliant assemblages ever witnessed in India. The royal sojourn was deeply impressed on the hearts of the Natives, and they founded useful institutions in remembrance of it. His Royal Highness gave to the community of Calcutta an entertainment on board the *Galatea*, which was then lying in the Hughli river; and the beauty of the scene that evening will ever be remembered by all who were present.

In all political and social affairs Lord Mayo derived the utmost assistance from his Private Secretary, Colonel, now Sir Owen, Burne. The duties of the Private Secretaryship being very important, it is essential to the prestige and influence of the Governor-General that his Private Secretary should possess not only ability in business, but also courtesy, judgment, and popularity. Burne had all these qualities in a high degree, and like his chief was fast acquiring knowledge of Indian policy and of Native sentiments.

One evening near Calcutta I was riding home with Lord Mayo and our conversation adverted to the several qualities most desirable in an Englishman who rules over an Indian province. I asked him what he considered to be the most important quality of all. He at once answered, an enthusiasm which makes a man believe in the possibility of improvement and strive to attain it. He added that this single-minded zeal pervaded the public service in India.

By the end of 1871 Lord Mayo had reached the zenith of popularity in India. Every one of the many departments which make up the great entity of the government of India found that his propelling or regulating hand was under the guidance of a master-mind. Every one of the many provinces visited by him acknowledged the readiness of his perception, the genial manner whereby he entered into local questions, the cordiality and tact with which he seemed to identify himself with the sentiments and genius of the places where he stopped. The provinces as yet unvisited were looking forward with hopefulness to a visit from him. He had by many and varied tours, travelled more than twenty thousand miles since his arrival in India, of which distance much had been traversed on horseback. People were dazzled by the personal vigour thus displayed by him, when they saw that every tour was followed by some administrative result. In his thirst for ocular evidence, he was conscious that at the best he could learn only a little regarding so vast a country as India; still no man ever saw so much of India within three years as he. His public labours and anxieties never dulled the warm sunshine of his manner towards all with whom he came in contact. He had maintained a gracious, friendly and conciliatory bearing towards the Native princes and chiefs, not only at ceremonial receptions but at separate or confidential interviews. Some of them, indeed, became sincerely attached to him. A college called after his name had been founded by him at Ajmir in Rajputana for educating the scions and cadets of princely houses. He had endured cheerfully the unpopularity which had arisen from the support accorded by him to the income tax; but this shadow was but transient, especially since the diminution in the rate of the tax. There was that glowing sensation of national progress which always delights and exhilarates the Indian public, European and Native combined. The Natives are, indeed, disposed to regard a progressive epoch with timid circumspection, still even they looked upon Lord Mayo as a frank and benevolent ruler. Altogether there was a genial warmth pervading the political atmosphere.

But as so often happens in moments of almost universal brightness, some untoward clouds were appearing. Certain conspiracies on the part of Muhammadans in Calcutta and in Patna, the capital of the Behar Province had been discovered. Patna, indeed, had for many years been known to the Government as a focus of mischief; and the secret designs emanating from this centre, as well as from others in the north, had always been watched, sometimes also frustrated by the British authorities. These particular conspiracies might have been regarded as only forming an exacerbation of a chronic ailment. Recently, however, there had been in Arabia a reforming and fanatical stir among the Wahabis ; similar movements had occurred, too, in other Muhammadan countries ; and altogether there seemed to be a thrill throughout the whole body of Islam. Though generally unwilling to bring Muhammadan plots into prominence by prosecution, the Government of India deemed that the evidence which existed of these particular conspiracies ought to be produced at the criminal bar against the conspirators. Accordingly several Muhammadans of more or less note were prosecuted before the High Court of Calcutta ; the prisoners engaged in their defence the well known counsel from Bombay, Mr. Chisholm Anstey. In the course of the defence Anstey adopted a tone, style, and language which caused much remark, as being calculated to agitate the minds of the disaffected. Though unguarded in his expressions, he was loyally anxious on behalf of his clients, and the Judges felt a delicacy in checking the licence of a counsel defending men who were on trial for treason. While the trials were pending, the Acting Chief Justice, Mr. Norman, was stabbed mortally one morning in October while ascending the staircase of his courthouse, the passage being quite unprotected. Enquiry proved beyond doubt that the murderer perpetrated the deed in the vain idea of influencing the judicial proceedings. It was remarkable that the criminal chose for his crime that time and place as affording his only opportunity, so difficult was it for him otherwise to approach his victim under the circumstances of residence at Calcutta. Subsequent reflection showed the local authorities that while political trials are pending, the avenues and approaches, by which the ministers of justice must pass, should be effectually guarded. The effect of a deed like this is always serious in India, and instantly suggests a repetition of assassination to the thoughts of the evil-minded. No outbreak, however, occurred, or other immediate sequel to this grave event.

In the following January (1872) Lord Mayo proceeded to inspect the convict settlement at Port Blair of the Andaman Islands in the Bay of Bengal. The superintendent of the settlement was General Stewart (now Sir Donald Stewart, Commander-in-Chief of the army in India), who took every precaution for the safety of the Viceroy during the inspection. Guarded vigilantly at every step and turn, Lord Mayo safely completed his inspection exactly according to the official programme, comparatively early in the afternoon. Finding that there were two hours and more to spare, he suddenly decided to ascend a hill close by, though this ascent was not in the day's programme, and consequently no special arrangements for guarding him had been completed beforehand on that particular line. As he ascended and descended the hill, his course was dogged in the shadow of the surrounding forest by a ticket-of-leave man, who had previously resolved on seizing any opportunity for assassination which presented itself. He was still so surrounded by guards that no chance occurred for striking a blow. He had returned at dusk by torch-light to within a few yards of the steam-launch which was to convey him on board his ship, a man-of-war. Just at the last he walked very quickly a step or two a-head of his staff; at that moment, but not till that moment, the looked-for chance offered itself to the assassin, who instantly rushed forward, sprung like a tiger on his back, and stabbed him fatally in the chest. The man was a Muhammadan of the hills near Peshawur, who had several years previously been sentenced to transportation for complicity in a murder; he declared to the last that the thought of assassinating the Viceroy had sprung only from fanatical bravado and from a feeling of revenge against the Government which had imprisoned him. Careful enquiry was made as to whether this assassination was connected with the recent murder of the Chief Justice at Calcutta; possibly there may have been some indirect connection, though no clue to it was ever discovered.

At this time I was in Calcutta, as Financial Member in the Council of which Sir John Strachey was temporarily President, during the absence of the Governor-General. One afternoon Strachey sent me a message asking me to come and see him quickly. On entering his room, I found our other colleagues coming also; he said that a cypher telegram had just been received which was being deciphered, but which already showed that something serious had happened to Lord Mayo. We all stood round watching while the telegram was being deciphered, and word after word was spelt out completing the melancholy tale. The necessary steps were immediately taken to carry on the Government without the slightest interruption, and Strachey assumed, by law, the Governor-Generalship, until the coming of Lord Napier from Madras, who as senior Governor of a Presidency, became, under the Statute, Governor-General pending the arrival of the person who might be appointed to succeed Lord Mayo. The public grief was manifested in every form and manner; there was much excitement among several disaffected classes among the Natives of Calcutta, though no overt sign of it was allowed by them to appear. The strictest precautions were adopted to guard against any fresh attempt being made on the life of any prominent European, inasmuch as the occurrence of two very notable assassinations within four months was calculated to give rise to a murderous impulse which, if once started, might spread like an infection.

A few days afterwards the corpse of Lord Mayo arrived by ship, and was escorted from the landing-place to Government House for two miles by a long procession of all the European notables of Calcutta on foot. The concourse of Native spectators was vast, and at Government House the cortège was received by the European troops together with the Calcutta Volunteer Rifles. He was borne in his coffin up the flight of steps which he had just three years previously ascended full of strength and hope to take charge of his high office. He was then carried into the chamber where only a month before his voice had been daily heard. The burial service was there read before his widow, the members of his staff, his councillors and a few others. A more solemn and impressive scene could not be imagined for us who stood in the very place which was full of the freshest associations relating to his life and actions, where we seemed almost to breathe his presence, and hear the echo of his latest utterances. Then the coffin lay in state for several days in the throne-room, where he had held so many public and private receptions, until it was taken with due ceremony on board a ship of war to be conveyed to Ireland.

In November 1868 the Prime Minister, Mr. Disraeli, said: "Upon the Earl of Mayo, for his sagacity, for his judgment, for his fine temper and his knowledge of men, Her Majesty has been pleased to confer the office of Viceroy of India. I believe he will earn a reputation that his country will honour."

This is a complete as well as concise description of Lord Mayo's character, and the prediction with which it concludes has been abundantly realized. Besides the qualities pourtrayed above, he displayed the energy of an administrator and the capacity of a statesman. At every time and place he made fast friends, whether in the study, the council-chamber, the hunting-field, the social gathering. When sudden death overtook him, he had reached the rare height occupied by those regarding whom all men speak well.

CHAPTER XVII

(1872-1874.)

LORD NORTHBROOK AND THE BENGAL FAMINE.

State of public opinion after the death of Lord Mayo—Lord Napier acts as Governor-General—The financial budget—Riots in the Panjab—Lord Northbrook assumes charge of the Government of India—Voyages down the Indus and visits Bombay—Remission of the income-tax—Drought in Behar and northern Bengal—Importation of grain by Government—Organization of transport—Character and extent of famine—Estimate prepared beforehand of cost to be incurred in relief—Employment of distressed poor and gratuitous succour to the infirm—Reserve of Government grain—Public criticism on relief measures—Native opinion thereon.

AFTER the assassination of Lord Mayo, the administration of India went on as usual without the break of a single hour. The members of the Government, though shocked and deeply moved, felt the importance of preserving a calm front before the Native public. From the moment of Lord Mayo's death, Lord Napier (now Lord Napier and Ettrick) the Governor of Madras became by law the head of the Government of India *pro tempore.* Until his arrival at Calcutta, the senior member of the Council, Sir John Strachey, assumed, also according to law, the functions of Governor-General. A few days afterwards the King of Siam who had been visiting India, and had recently received hospitable attention from Lord Mayo at the capital, returned to Calcutta on his way home. Strachey received him at the top of the flight of stairs, and in a few well-chosen words declared that the Government of India, while mourning for its lost Head, nevertheless preserved the tenour of its course uninterrupted.

Nevertheless there was anxiety in the inner thoughts of the Government, and much agitation in the public mind. Though the excitement was suppressed it remained for some weeks, so to speak, in a sub-acute stage. The Hindu section of the population at Calcutta is trustworthy, and many excellent Muhammadans also are to be found there. Yet at that time several centres of Muhammadan disloyalty and treason existed at the capital, and whole classes of Muhammadans were ready for mischief, in a more or less aggravated form according to opportunity. There is always a fear at such times, lest one successful crime acquiring an infamous celebrity, should lead to the commission of other crimes. Accordingly the strict precautions, already mentioned in the last chapter, were maintained; providentially, however, nothing occurred.

Shortly afterwards, Lord Napier arrived from Madras, and became temporarily the head of the Government of India. At that moment, the preparations were being made for the financial budget which I had to lay before him. Thereupon he applied himself to finance with the utmost assiduity, and the result in regard to the budget has been already mentioned in the previous chapter XV.

He had to deal with one affair, the issue of which is worthy to be remembered. A disturbance, partly religious and partly political in its character, arose in the Panjab, in the districts near the river Satlej. Its originators were quite infatuated, and mad in their conception, ostensibly looking for some prophet to come, while their real design was to raise an insurrection against British rule. The fact that fanatical enthusiasts at a period of general peace should dream of braving the British Government in the plenitude of its power, was very significant to reflective statesmen. Moreover, the trouble for a brief moment seemed to spread like wildfire in a dry forest during the summer heat. It was immediately put down by the authorities with vigour and promptitude; and during the course of these repressive measures, a number of prisoners were taken *in flagrante delicto,* having been participators in the outbreak, but not otherwise proved to be guilty of heinous crime. Thereupon a civil officer belonging to the Uncovenanted Service, caused them to be executed on the spot, no doubt believing in good faith that this extreme severity was necessary, under the supposed emergency of the circumstances. His conduct was, as might be expected, immediately called into question; and the Government of the Panjab, though disapproving this action, nevertheless thought that under the circumstances it need not be visited by more than severe censure. The Government of India however, after full consideration, held that the execution was not justifiable on the ground of emergent circumstances which had actually ceased when it took place, the insurrection having been just suppressed; that good faith could not be pleaded as an excuse for an indiscriminate and unlawful execution; that the moral effect of such proceedings upon the country would be bad, unless an example were set; and that the officer must be removed from the service of the Government.

Lord Northbrook arrived at Calcutta in May, 1872, and assumed the office of Viceroy and Governor-General. He possessed a greater knowledge of finance, and the several subjects cognate to it, than any Governor-General who ever landed in India. The financial policy which he adopted, so far as it affected the budget of the following year, has been explained in chapter XV. The remission of the income-tax brought to his Government much popular approval among the European community and the middle as well as the upper classes of the Natives. After sojourning for a brief time at Simla, he proceeded on a voyage down the Indus, holding on the way a reception at Multan for the Native chiefs of the Derajat or southern Trans-Indus territory. In Sind he met the Khan of Khelat and settled many political affairs with that chief. From Karachi he went by sea to Bombay, and there held with due ceremony a levée for the princes and chiefs of western and central India.

Major Evelyn Baring, R.A., as Private Secretary to the Governor-General, displayed an ability equal to that of his most distinguished predecessors in this important office. He afterwards filled a difficult post in Egypt, and then became Finance Minister of India.

In legislative business there was a slight lull for a time, as Sir James Fitzjames Stephen, already mentioned in chapter XVI., had departed, and Mr. (now Sir Arthur) Hobhouse had succeeded him in the responsible office of legislative member of the Governor-General's Council. Hobhouse was already known as an author upon some branches of law, and had held several important public posts in England. He soon won his way in public as well as official esteem in India, and while steadily promoting the large measures begun by his predecessors, took every suitable opportunity of proposing additional laws when necessary. There never had been any valid reason for the complaints often made regarding over-legislation. But the most sensitive critics in this respect were obliged to admit that Hobhouse displayed judicious moderation as well as professional skill and statesmanlike ability.

During the autumn of 1873, reports were received from the Lieutenant-Governor of Bengal, Sir George Campbell, to the effect that the usual rains had failed, and that danger of famine threatened, though there was hope that seasonable showers might yet come at the eleventh hour to save the crops. We, the members of the Government, were then at Simla preparing to return to Calcutta for the winter. Before proceeding thither, I was about to pay, according to custom, a flying visit to some distant parts of the empire in order to master current affairs relating to finance. I had entered a railway-carriage at Amballa, and the train was about to start, when I received a telegraphic message from Lord Northbrook saying that he had just received worse news from Bengal, and requesting me to accompany him immediately to Calcutta, which I did.

After arriving at Calcutta and conferring with the Lieutenant-Governor and the local authorities, we found that in most parts of Behar and northern Bengal, the summer crop of rice had been short in yield, and the autumnal or principal crop was failing altogether, while the seed sown for the coming spring harvest was not likely to germinate by reason of the drought. This disaster affected 20 millions of people in a greater or less degree. The supply of grain was known to be scanty in these particular territories consequent on exportation in former years. In many of the remaining districts of Bengal, the yield of the harvest was poor, and in the neighbouring districts of the North-western Provinces quite deficient. The deficiency in the food supply then, for so many people could not be made good from local resources, and therefore vast quantities of grain must be brought from a distance. Still, as the distress would not set in until the spring, there was the winter before us in which to make preparations. Again, the sad experience of former occasions shewed that the first year of drought would probably be followed by a second, and that our calculations in order to be safe must go beyond the consequences of this drought, and provide for some continuance of the distress.

Lord Northbrook had, in the first place, to consider the question whether the Government should undertake the responsibility for counteracting the effects of this drought, and for averting the famine which would otherwise result. He decided that it should, although such a task had never yet been accomplished in India. During the former famines of this century, so much mortality had occurred despite the efforts put forth by the State, that loss of life had come to be regarded as inevitable. Nevertheless, it was announced in the Gazette that a widespread famine was anticipated, that much was expected of the people in the way of self-help and from the trade in respect of enterprise, but that the Government would interpose to do whatever could not otherwise be done in order that none should perish who might possibly be saved. The general instruction thus conveyed by the Governor-General to the provincial Government of Bengal was in absolute and unqualified terms.

In pursuing this policy the Governor-General received full support from the Secretary of State in England, first the Duke of Argyll, and then the Marquis of Salisbury.

The announcement of the Governor-General's intentions quieted the public mind in Bengal, and prevented any agitation arising in respect to the policy of Government. But even with this assurance there was much alarm in the Native mind throughout Bengal, and at Calcutta especially. The remembrance of the Orissa famine survived, when many famishing refugees wended their weary way to the capital and threw themselves on the bounty of the charitable there. Unofficial estimates of the probable deficiency in food supply were brought forward, and moving representations came from many quarters. The idea, which was oppressing the imaginations of men like a weight, related to the magnitude of the numbers concerned. If such sad consequences followed on the Orissa famine affecting four millions of souls, how dire would be this calamity involving twenty millions.

Having fixed the general outline of what was to be done, Lord Northbrook applied himself with the fullest precision to consider the means of doing it. Much was to be expected from the operations of trade; nevertheless, there was a consensus in the warnings which the Government had received from many quarters to the effect that private enterprise would not be able to fill the void caused by the drought. All the best information available pointed to the conclusion that a large quantity of food must be imported by the Government. The neighbouring province of British Burma had been blessed as usual with an abundant harvest, therefore Lord Northbrook determined to purchase grain there, through the very competent agency of the Chief Commissioner, the Honourable Ashley (now Sir Ashley) Eden. The quantity of grain thus to be purchased was a matter for anxious consideration, and the decision depended on the time during which the famine might be expected to last. The distress would begin in March, 1874, and should the periodical rains fall propitiously during June and the succeeding months, it would be over by the autumn. But the rains might not come in June, and meteorological experience indicated the probability that they would fail, as drought once set in generally lasts for at least two years. In that case the distress would continue right through the year 1874. If, then, the provision was to be at all complete and effectual, it must embrace the whole summer autumn and winter of 1874, and there must be a large reserve formed on that understanding. The calculations thus made pointed to an amount of 450,000 tons of grain (rice), which was almost entirely purchased in Burma.

These supplies of rice were transported from Burma to

Calcutta with entire efficiency and punctuality by the vessels of the British India Steam Navigation Company. The service of this Company had been very ably organized by Mr. Mackinnon.

It was fortunate that the Government had a treasury full beyond all precedent and a large quantity of available cash, wherewith to begin the formidable undertaking on which it was about to embark. As shown in the previous chapter XV., the finances had been in a condition of surplus for four consecutive years, and the cash balance in India stood at 16 millions sterling. Though the fall in the value of silver was beginning to threaten, it had not yet shewn itself in any marked manner, nor did it appreciably affect the rate of exchange in the remittances by Government from India to England.

In the arrangements for combating the famine, Lord Northbrook, in addition to his statesmanlike grasp of imperial affairs, evinced an admirable mastery of finance, economic facts and statistics, such as I have never seen surpassed in India, not even by such economists and financiers as Wilson or Laing.

While willing to afford sustenance during the famine to all those who could not otherwise support themselves, he desired that the able-bodied should work fully in return for what they received, and that their work should be made as useful as possible to the country. The excavation of tanks, and the construction of roads, would be undertaken by the provincial authorities. Beyond this, however, there were certain operations for which the sanction of the Government of India was requisite. Such were the works already in progress for the canal from the river Sone and the railway running from the bank of the Ganges through northern Bengal to the foot of the Himalayas near Darjiling. This railway had been previously designed, and was now to be actually begun as a means of employing the distressed people, under the able management of Colonel James G. Lindsay of the Engineers.

When adopting this positive policy and girding itself for an arduous task, the Government derived much support morally from public sentiment. The organs of Native opinion in Bengal urged the necessity of action and described the misery of widespread starvation, with entreaties that Government would stretch out its arm to save the people. The British Indian Association, consisting of the principal Zemindars or landlords of Bengal, signalized itself by its representations, supported as they were by an array of figures. The Indian correspondents of the London newspapers, especially of the *Times*, sent vivid word-pictures of the coming calamity, and set forth many considerations, the moral of which was that the English Sovereign and nation should hold the Government of India answerable for averting, to the utmost of its power, the consequences of the drought. This view was developed by the leading organs of opinion in England itself, and so far as the authorities in India could judge, English opinion was becoming strongly excited. A public meeting, under the presidency of the Lord Mayor, was held in London, and a national subscription was raised with an organization which centred in the Mansion House. Great as may have been the material help thus afforded, the moral effect was greater still, proving as it did to the Natives the sympathy of their English fellow-subjects. Similarly public meetings were held in the Town Hall of Calcutta, and again the sentiments of the community were stirred. Thus the minds of all were subjected to a severe strain, and the officers of Government began to feel that they would be impeached if any failure were to occur, or if life should be lost through any shortcoming of theirs.

The Lieutenant-Governor, Sir George Campbell, was specially qualified for giving effect to Lord Northbrook's general instructions. Campbell had been for more than two years ruling the provinces under the Government of Bengal with a vigour rarely surpassed in Anglo-Indian history, acquiring among many other things an exact knowledge of their resources. Some time before he was placed by Lord Mayo in charge of the united provinces of Bengal Behar and Orissa, he had been deputed by John Lawrence to preside over the commission of enquiry regarding the famine in Orissa, as mentioned in chapter XIV. He thus knew more of the realities of famine than any officer then in India. Orissa, indeed, was on this occasion the only one of these provinces which had an abundant harvest, but he would effectively apply the experience gained there to the calamity which, on a much larger scale, menaced Behar and northern Bengal. On receiving from Lord Northbrook the general instruction already mentioned regarding the manner in which the famine was to be encountered, he issued an admirable set of detailed directions to his local officers.

There was, however, one remedy suggested by Sir George Campbell which did not commend itself to Lord Northbrook's judgment, namely this, the stopping of the exportation of rice and other cereals from the ports of Calcutta and British Burma. This was not allowed, as it was thought injurious to trade, and as likely to affect the wealth resources and prosperity of the country, at a time when every sinew would be strained in order to encounter calamity.

Having settled matters so far, Lord Northbrook proceeded to the north of India, to keep the engagements which he had made for the reception of Native princes and chiefs at Lucknow and Agra long before any apprehensions of drought had arisen, leaving me as President in Council at Calcutta to watch the progress of the famine and the arrangements consequent thereon.

Shortly afterwards (in December 1873) Sir George Campbell's health became seriously impaired, and medical authorities warned him that he would not be able to bear up against the heat of the next spring and summer. He resolved, however, to sustain his toils despite illness until at least the spring; but it became necessary to choose a successor. At that time it had been arranged that I should resign my office of Finance Minister in the spring and return to England; but Lord Northbrook offered me the post of Lieutenant-Governor on Sir George Campbell's departure, which appointment I accepted.

By January 1874 the consignments of Government grain already mentioned began to arrive from Burma, and were being despatched from Calcutta by railway to the bank of the Ganges.

Thence the vast quantities of grain would have to be carried by local conveyance to the distressed tracts distant from 50 to 90 miles in north Behar. Anxiety was felt lest the wheeled traffic of the province should prove insufficient, and the supplies procured by Government should fail to reach their destination in time. Lord Northbrook then associated me with the Government of Bengal in order to ensure the completion of all necessary arrangements, and deputed me to Behar for this purpose. I made over to him my financial portfolio, and thenceforth was officially connected with the Bengal administration only.

On entering the northern part of Behar at the end of January 1874, I was struck by the difficulties affecting the transport of grain in large quantities during the dry season which had already begun, and would become drier still as the months rolled on. The traffic of the country was ordinarily carried by boats on the many navigable streams which flow from the Himalayas to join the Ganges; but these streams were now almost devoid of water. Wheeled carriage for commercial purposes did not exist in any considerable quantity, and thus trade was for a time paralyzed. The only persons, possessing carts and draught bullocks in large numbers, were the European indigo planters who used these vehicles for their manufacturing work. Their business was so slack, partly by reason of the famine, that they could spare their carts, which were accordingly hired by tens of thousands, and the transport of the Government grain was so far secured. The organization of this enormous amount of hired transport was placed under Colonel (now Sir Charles) Macgregor of the Quartermaster-General's department, a public servant of high capacity and unsurpassed energy, with a large staff of military officers. But as the security of the transport was vital, it was decided to construct a temporary railway from the Ganges to every one of the points where distress threatened most. This work was, under the vigorous supervision of Captain Stanton of the Engineers, constructed at the rate of a mile a day. Further, a special transport train, consisting of carts bullocks mules and ponies, was obtained from northern India, and organized by Mr. Harry Rivett Carnac of the Civil Service with much promptitude and ability. Thus the several hundred thousand tons of Government grain were, despite the burning heat and the dust-laden tracks, conveyed to the remote villages with absolute punctuality and without failure even in a single instance.

At this time special correspondents deputed by some of the London newspapers had begun to arrive upon the scene. First and foremost among these was Mr. Archibald Forbes on the part of the *Daily News*, who spared no effort of mind or body to probe the reality of the distress and to understand the measures adopted for its relief. He pourtrayed with graphic force and absolute fidelity, for the information of the English public, the mortal peril to which the people were exposed, and from which they could be rescued only by the utmost exertions of the Government. He discharged his professional duties with signal success, and also rendered much service to the general administration.

The transport for the Government grain having been secured, my object was to observe personally the physical condition of the people. For this purpose the able-bodied employed on relief works, and the infirm receiving gratuitous relief, were mustered at convenient spots for inspection. Thus tens and hundreds of thousands of poor people, at different times and places, passed under observation, whereby a check was imposed on idleness and imposture. Often, too, when marching through a village we would assemble all the men, women and children in it, so as to note any signs of emaciation or of distress. In short, no pains were intermitted to ascertain from personal observation all particulars regarding the physical condition of the people.

A system then was organized whereby, as the famine became worse, a visitation should be periodically instituted from house to house in every village, so that no case of individual distress could possibly escape observation. The whole country having been parcelled out into groups of villages, a relief centre and field-hospital were established in each group.

I had been in constant communication with the Lieutenant-Governor, Sir George Campbell, in conjunction with whom I was working in Behar, but I was now obliged to proceed on similar duty to northern Bengal. As the famine in Behar was coming on apace, Campbell himself proceeded thither after my departure, despite his failing health, and supervised the details of the relief operations.

Having studied on the spot the condition of all the distressed districts, I transmitted to Campbell an estimate of the financial cost of the proposed relief operations, on the assumption that the rains would fall propitiously in the coming season, also of the reserve stocks of grain to be provided in event of the rains again failing. He forwarded this to Lord Northbrook, who after a time required us both to revise it by the latest information.

In April Sir George Campbell proceeded to England, and I received charge of the Government of Bengal. The first step was for me to submit to Lord Northbrook my final estimate of the cost of the relief operations, before I quitted my head-quarters and proceeded to the field to personally superintend all the work. This estimate amounted in round numbers to 9 millions sterling in the gross, but then there were to be large recoveries consisting chiefly of the proceeds from the sale of Government grain to the people in the distressed districts, so that the net cost would be only 6⅓ millions. Even this amount was seriously large, and I was thankful for the opportunity thus afforded of obtaining sanction for the estimate from the highest authority. I knew that, even if under Providence these great operations should be blessed with success and should fulfil the humane purpose for which they were designed, critics would cavil at the cost and perhaps demand enquiry. In that case it would be a source of satisfaction to know that the expense had been thoroughly considered beforehand in each and all of its bearings. Afterwards, when this affair had ended with a success exceeding our most sanguine hopes, and exception was taken to the outlay, we congratulated ourselves on having followed the financial maxim of undertaking nothing without an estimate beforehand. In fact we managed to keep the ultimate expenditure just within the estimate.

The month of May had now set in, and the famine had thoroughly declared itself. Employment, agricultural and other, was at a standstill, and there were no wages for the poor to earn. No supplies of grain were brought out and the corn markets were all closed. The Government, before opening its stores, waited to the latest safe day, in order to afford every possible chance to the trade. Its officers were however obliged to sell their grain in vast quantities, the prices being fixed at what were regarded as famine rates. Still starvation stared the people in the face, unless the Government should give them employment and pay their wages in grain. Accordingly many hundred thousand persons were thus employed and paid ; their employment consisting chiefly of road-making. Those who could not work were fed gratuitously, and search was made in every village, house to house, for the infirm and helpless, so that no deserving person should fail to receive succour. The strain in this contest for life or death became more and more intense as week after week rolled wearily on—as in certain battles it has been said that the struggle is even, and it remains to be seen which side has the stiffest back—till the middle of June, when the rain fell with a propitiousness beyond our hopes. A change for the better was felt at once, and tens of thousands of relief labourers went off to their fields. Still the famine must continue for some weeks till the new grain should begin to come in, and the majority of the poor people thus remained on our hands. Soon, too, the authorities found that those who had gone to till the fields had not the means of sustaining themselves when there, until the new harvest should begin to come in. So it was necessary to make large advances of grain to them on their engagement to pay for it after the next harvest. The value of the grain thus advanced was duly recovered after the termination of the famine when plenty had returned.

The rains, having begun well, became suspended for a time, and the worst fears for the future were resuscitated. At the eleventh hour they again descended favourably, before any irreparable harm had been done by their temporary suspension, and thereafter continued propitiously till in the autumn a good harvest was reaped. Thus week after week the poor people who had been for several months on the hands of the Government were discharged, till by the middle of October few of them were left.

The recipients of charitable relief from Government had been chiefly persons who in ordinary times subsist on the private charity of the village folk. The charity, which is thus dispensed in years of average prosperity, redounds to the honour of the Native community. But it is unavoidably suspended during famine, and the many thousands who depend on it must perish unless sustained by Government. These poor people had accordingly been thrown on the hands of the relief officers for several months. But now with returning plenty after the autumn harvest they were sent back in some hundred thousands to their villages, where they began once more to receive charitable support as formerly.

The greater part of the grain procured by Government was used, but a considerable portion remained unused. This was the reserve which had been provided in event of the rains failing for the second time, a failure which, though at one time apparently imminent, had been mercifully averted. The reserve grain then had to be sold, and as by that time the new harvest was coming in abundantly, the sale proceeds proved to be but a small recovery as against the cost which had been incurred.

Some angry criticism soon arose upon the fact of this grain thus having to be sold, as proving that, from some faults in the original calculations, there had been an excess provision. It was immediately shewn that there had been no error whatever, but that as a matter of deliberate policy a reserve had been provided. This reserve, indeed, was not wanted owing to the happy course which events had taken. But if any objections were urged against the policy of adopting this essential precaution, in a case where the lives of millions of people were at stake, they were hardly deserving of refutation.

The people, in the mass, behaved well throughout these critical trials. They proved themselves to be neither demoralized nor pauperized by the receipt of relief. Their zeal and anxiety never slackened for restoring the cultivation and making the most of even momentary opportunities which might offer. Patient courage, unflinching endurance, self-help in extremity, were the honourable characteristics of their general conduct.

In most of these arduous operations for the relief of famine the chief executive officer was Mr. (now Sir Steuart) Bayley, the Commissioner of Behar, who admirably discharged his difficult duties, and next after him in honour and responsibility was Mr. C. T. Metcalfe. The Secretary to the Government of Bengal in the Famine department was Mr. C. E. Bernard (a nephew of John Lawrence); and from him I derived most valuable assistance. The local officers on whom the brunt of the work fell most heavily were Mr. C. H. Macdonnell and Mr. F. C. Macgrath. All the officers mentioned above were members of the Covenanted Civil Service.

Many European officers of the army were employed in this work with the utmost advantage. Native officers also were selected and placed at our disposal by the Commander-in-Chief, Lord Napier of Magdâla, in order that they might render aid in the administration of relief. Their military discipline and training rendered them extraordinarily apt in this work. After the conclusion of the operations, their good conduct was acknowledged publicly.

It became my pleasant duty to prepare a long list of the names of those non-official gentlemen, European and Native, landlords or residents of the distressed districts, who by charitable munificence or unrewarded labours had contributed essentially to the relief of distress.

Conspicuous service was rendered by the servants of the East India Railway Company; indeed without that railway the Government grain could hardly have been conveyed to its destination in time; a more signal instance could scarcely be afforded of the value of railways to India.

Thus the famine of 1874 was over; the deaths from starvation were so few compared to the many millions concerned, that practically there had been no loss of life. The health of the people had been sustained, agriculture was unimpaired, the resources of the country remained uninjured, even the revenues were nearly all realized. But there had been a large expenditure, which however had been exactly foreseen, and to which the Government had made up its mind beforehand.

But when the immunity from loss of life is chronicled it must be thankfully remembered that there was no epidemic of cholera, small-pox, fever, or the like. Indeed throughout this trying time the public health was remarkably good. This is very unlike the experience of other famines, when these fell diseases have come to aggravate the misery arising from want. Such freedom from collateral or concomitant calamity cannot be wholly explained by any known circumstances. One fortunate cause however was this, that in Behar the streams rising in the lower ranges of the Himalayas, while no longer navigable, had yet a good supply of drinking water. The fact, that in time of drought the water supply often becomes impure, is one reason why cholera prevails usually during famine.

Despite success which owing to the mercy of Providence had been unique in the history of Indian famines, and exceeded any hopes we ever dared to entertain, there emanated from some quarters an unaccountably bitter criticism, directed chiefly against the expense. By an irony of fate it was actually argued that the danger of famine could not have been extremely urgent because it had been successfully overcome. This argument was hardly worth considering in the face of the patent, indeed the notorious, facts of the time as known to a host of witnesses. It were bootless perhaps to divine the reasons of that hostility; the criticism possibly arose from the disappointment felt by some traders who thought that if the Government had not interposed so effectually some further opportunities might have presented themselves to trade. In fact, however, the

Government had offered every chance to trade, and had interfered only when, under the peculiar circumstances of the threatened or distressed country, the commercial resources were demonstrably insufficient or wholly impotent. It was observable also that, during this time, trade had been extraordinarily active in all the districts which it could reach, and where, but for it, there would have been scarcity.

It was indeed most unfortunate that the drought visited in its worst form the densely peopled tracts which were far away from the nearest railway. These tracts depended for their communication upon the very water carriage which from the nature of the case was cut off on this dire occasion. Thus it happened that the trade became powerless and Government was obliged to supply the needful. The lesson to be learnt therefrom was this, that such tracts must not be left without communication by rail. Had a railway existed in Behar and northern Bengal in 1874, countless cares and labours would have been avoided, and a large part of the relief expenditure saved. The lesson has indeed been learnt with effect, for those tracts of country now have their railways, which advantages they doubtless owe to the famine of 1874.

Afterwards in 1880, when the Indian Famine Commission was sitting, the evidence shewed that had railways existed there in 1874, offering due facilities to trade, perhaps half of the total expenditure incurred by Government on that occasion might have been obviated.

It may indeed be conceded to the critics that the relief given to the distressed was liberal and unstinted, that the object was to secure effectually the preservation of life, and that for the complete attainment of this object neither labour nor expense was spared. This was the policy which, to the best of our understanding, we were ordered to pursue, and which we unhesitatingly pursued. The object, then, was absolutely attained; a contest with famine was undertaken and was won conclusively. Whether any lesser resistance to so dread an enemy as famine would have sufficed is doubtful; and the doubts which might be felt on this point will have been increased by subsequent experience. Whatever may be the merits or demerits of particular measures, it must be acknowledged that in some other instances large expenditure has been humanely allowed by the State and yet there has been loss of life. In this instance the money was liberally spent indeed, but then all the lives were saved. If there are to be great expenses, it is well to make sure of success for the sake not only of the material results, but also of the moral advantages. Not only were the lives of the people saved, but also their lasting thankfulness was earned. Such national gratitude must add fresh stability to the foundations of British rule.

The manifestation of their gratitude by the people was conspicuous in various ways. The Native press, both English and vernacular, teemed with commendations of the policy prescribed by the Government and of the proceedings taken by its officers during the famine from first to last. At every place I ever visited in the provinces under the Government of Bengal during the year of the famine, or in subsequent years, whether within or beyond the area which was then distressed—there were addresses presented which included, among many other things, strongly worded allusions to the measures adopted for averting the consequences of famine. Too much stress must not indeed be laid on such addresses, but inasmuch as they contained remarks on local topics, which topics varied in each locality and consequently in each address—the fact of the happy prevention of famine being the one and only constant theme proved that it was uppermost in the popular thoughts. On my return to Calcutta after the conclusion of relief operations, the Native chiefs and gentry of Behar presented a congratulatory address specifically alluding to each step which had been taken and every measure adopted. If it were supposed that Behar Native gentlemen were naturally disposed to entertain and express favourable sentiments on the policy which Government had followed, still that supposition cannot apply to the British Indian Association which represents the Zemindars or landlords of Bengal. These Bengali Native gentlemen are notoriously outspoken and independent in their utterances, so much so that they have often been blamed for evincing an undue willingness to criticize the Government and its officers. Yet they also presented an address declaring in the strongest and warmest terms their gratitude on behalf of the Natives, their belief in the necessity of what had been done and their appreciation of the manner in which it had been effected.

CHAPTER XVIII.

(1874–1876.)

THE GOVERNMENT OF BENGAL.

Administration of Sir George Campbell as Lieutenant-Governor of Bengal—Locomotion in the rainy season—Voyage on the great rivers of Bengal—The country boats—Floating cities—Deltaic forests—Chittagong and the eastern frontier—The sights of Orissa—The aspect of Calcutta—Elective franchise in its municipality—The Bengal legislature—Sketch of the principal Native gentlemen—Christian missions—The Brahmo sect—Merits and demerits of the high education—Improved standard of morality—Death of Bishop Milman—Interior of the country—Security of life and property—Agrarian affairs—The Courts of Wards—The peasantry of Behar—Popularity of the Civil Courts—Summer residence at Darjiling in the Himalayas—Scenery of Sikhim—Terrific cyclone in the estuary of the Megna—Departure of Lord Napier of Magdâla—Visit of His Royal Highness the Prince of Wales—Lord Northbrook is succeeded by Lord Lytton as Governor-General—My departure to join the imperial assemblage at Delhi.

British India is eminently a country of large jurisdictions, and Bengal is the largest of them all. The official term "Bengal" comprises several provinces, which at this time were Bengal Behar and Orissa, comprising the territories assigned by the Muhammadan emperor to Clive and other provinces subsequently acquired. It had once comprised Arracan which had been transferred to British Burma, Sambalpur which had been incorporated in the Central Provinces, and Assam which had just been formed into a separate administration under a Chief Commissioner. The Bengal jurisdiction was still, however, very vast, for it contained an area of 204,000 square miles, and a population stated according to the last enumeration to be 63 millions, but ascertained by a subsequent census to be 67 millions. Its revenues and receipts of all sorts pertaining to the Government and to local funds amounted to nearly 20 millions annually.

It had been formed twenty years previously into a Lieutenant-Governorship by Lord Dalhousie in 1854, since which time there had been four Lieutenant-Governors, Sir Frederick Halliday, Sir Cecil Beadon, Sir William Grey, men of the highest eminence in the Civil Service, who had received their early training in Bengal itself, and Sir John Peter Grant who, though originally trained in the North-west, had long served in Bengal. Of these, Halliday is now a member of the Indian Council in London; Grant and Grey both held subsequently the Governorship of Jamaica. The fifth was Sir George Campbell, who, though he had learnt his profession in the North-western Provinces and the Panjab, had been a judge in the High Court at Calcutta, and president of the commission of enquiry regarding the famine in Orissa. He had conducted the Government for three and a half years, when being obliged by ill-health to return to England, as mentioned in the last chapter, he was succeeded by me at the end of April 1874.

Having entered advantageously into the labours of his distinguished predecessors, Sir George Campbell handed over to me the administration in a state of high efficiency. As a basis of knowledge necessary for devising administrative measures, he caused a regular census to be made, for which the people were counted in a single night, the result being that the population proved to be more numerous by one-third than had been previously believed, that is, more than 60 millions instead of more than 40 millions. He then did much for the collection of statistics generally, and of vital statistics especially. He took up the subject of village schools in the organization of which a beginning had been made in Sir John Peter Grant's time. He was the great promoter of primary education; he brought most of the old indigenous schools under State supervision, set up additional village schools in great numbers, and caused village schoolmasters to be trained in normal institutions. He gave much impulse to these normal schools, and considered them to be the homes of vernacular learning. He bestowed special attention on the instruction of Muhammadan youth, arranging that certain endowment funds, belonging to the community of Islam, should be applied to the support of Muhammadan colleges and schools. He passed through his local legislature the law for imposing a light cess on the owners and the non-proprietary holders of land, despite all the opposition which might have been anticipated. The proceeds of the impost were to be devoted to the maintenance of local roads and schools. A good beginning with the actual levy of this useful cess was also made in his time. He desired that in addition to the Native medical men educated in the Medical Colleges, there should be a body of Natives trained in a secondary though still efficient degree for service in the hospitals and dispensaries which had been already founded or were being established throughout the provinces. With this view he founded a Medical School at Calcutta, which bears his name, and is separate from the fine Medical College long existing there. He enlarged the executive machinery in the interior of the country, developed the existing plan of parcelling out each district or country into administrative "sub-divisions," and created new classes of subordinate Native officials. He introduced the competitive system for the admission of Natives to all grades of civil employ, and instituted regular examinations for that purpose, thereby sacrificing much patronage. He spent great labour in passing through his local legislature an elaborate scheme for rural municipalities, which would have had the effect, among many other things, of promoting sanitation and improving the water supply among the villages; but it failed to receive the assent of the Governor-General (Lord Northbrook) because it seemed likely to add unduly to the burdens of the people and provoke discontent. He bestowed much thought upon prison discipline and the construction of Central Jails. He gave, as might be expected, close attention to public works, such as the canals in Orissa and Behar, the railway in northern Bengal, the pontoon bridge over the Hughli at Calcutta, the drainage and reclamation of swampy tracts, and the public buildings at the capital, such as colleges, court-houses, hospitals. He kept a kindly and sympathetic eye fixed on the peasantry of Bengal, discountenanced rack-renting and other oppressive conduct on the part of Zemindars or landlords, and rough-hewed several measures of agrarian reform which were carried into effect by his successor. His moral influence on behalf of tenant-right throughout the country was marked and even decisive. In fine, with personal diligence consistently exerted, he succeeded in imparting a constant movement to every part of an extensive administration. Such a policy was not calculated to win the approval of some classes who not unnaturally dreaded improvement, though as time rolls on it will be regarded with grateful appreciation by the middle classes and the masses of the people for whose benefit it was designed.

My imperative duty on assuming the government was, as seen in the last chapter, to minister to the needs of nearly one-third of the whole population, vast as it was, and to provide bodily sustenance for them, before adopting measures for their moral and material advancement. The necessity of being in camp or on the move, supervising the operations of relief and commanding vast establishments in the field for several months, made it difficult for me to conduct simultaneously an extensive and complex administration, and to despatch punctually a mass of current business. In these affairs the utmost assistance was received from Mr. Rivers Thompson, the principal Secretary at the head-quarters of Bengal, a most able officer. He was afterwards appointed by Lord Northbrook to be Chief Commissioner of British Burma, and is now a member of the Governor-General's Council.

Steuart Bayley and C. T. Metcalfe have been already mentioned in the last preceding chapter with reference to their services in Behar. In the Secretariat at Calcutta excellent service was performed by Ross Mangles, who received the Victoria Cross for gallant conduct near Arrah during the events of the mutinies in 1857; also by Herbert Reynolds, who had won honours at Oxford. Mangles is the son of the East India Director so well known in former days. The statistical bureau was managed by Henry Cotton, an officer of remarkable promise. The burden of preparing the elaborate projects of law, for submission to the Legislative Council, devolved on Henry Lucius Dampier, to whose experienced aid I was much indebted.

When the distressed population had safely passed through the burning heat of May and June and the rains had fallen bounteously everywhere, the crisis of the famine was seen to be over for the moment at least, though utter want still prevailed, for which the relief organization had to be maintained. There would at all events be some slight respite for a time, so I determined to seize the opportunity of making a tour in Bengal.

The rainy season was now at its height, the rivers were in flood, the swamps and marshes flushed with water, and the masses of floating vapour surcharged with moisture. In all other parts of India except Bengal, this would be the very last season which any one would choose for a tour; on the contrary this is the close time when all people both European and Native stay at home. The roads are impassable or passable only with extreme difficulty, the carts are shut up and the draught cattle sent away to graze. The transport being impeded or stopped, trade is slack and all work out of doors, excepting agriculture, is suspended. The husbandman is working in his fields close to his own door; but those, whose avocations ordinarily carry them to long distances, rest for a while till the weather shall become open, the rivers subside and the roads be dry.

But the inhabitants of Bengal have a practice which is diametrically opposite. Bengal is essentially a river-kingdom; it possesses but few roads in comparison with other Indian provinces, but then it has for its highways the rivers threading and permeating the country like a network, and constituting natural channels of communication on a magnificent scale. These rivers, then, are during the winter and summer shallow, full of shoals, and not conveniently navigable. The great navigation begins towards the end of June, comes into full play during July and August, and slackens after the middle of September. During the winter and summer many of the boats are laid up, but all are brought out in July; and then the inland traffic of Bengal bursts into life. The husbandman, village artisan, pedlar or market-gardener does not keep a cart; he has a boat instead, in which he sculls along the watery ways with his produce or his wares. Even the labourer or menial learns to paddle his canoe.

The tours of Anglo-Indians are made mostly when the sky is azure, the landscape in the foreground being coloured brown or ochre, but in the distance having hues of orange, pink or bluish-grey ; and the water—what little there is of it—becoming clear, even transparent. But now for some months consecutively I was to see an almost changeless grey in the sky, an unbroken green in the landscape, and a dull mud-brown colour in the waters. Nevertheless this circuit of Bengal in the rainy season afforded not only a novel but an unique experience of journeying in India, and presented spectacles of which perhaps few countries in the world afford an example.

With this view, full use was made of the state barge, the *Rhotas*, belonging to the Government, for the purpose of seeing Bengal. I went on board of her on the 15th of June on the Ganges within the limits of Behar, lived in her for three months and a half, that is, till the beginning of October, and disembarked from her with regret. She was a barge towed by a steamer the *William Peel*, named after the naval commander who did such good service in the war of the mutinies; and she belonged to a class of vessels called "flats." Before the introduction of railways all the Government stores and much other valuable produce used to be conveyed on the Ganges and its branches by vessels of this character, as far as Allahabad, and are still carried on the Brahmaputra river to Assam. The *Peel* was a powerful steamer with small draught ; the commander was trained to handle her with much skill, turning her in and out of the tortuous channels, despite her great length, and also the length of the barge attached to her.

The *Rhotas* then was a barge with a large clear deck, at the end of which was a dining saloon. Below deck she had a series of cabins for the Lieutenant-Governor, his suite and guests. Steamer and barge together made up a floating and movable Government House. As the principal stations and towns are on the banks of the rivers, the Lieutenant-Governor thus steamed at a quick rate from place to place, seven miles an hour against stream, and at a much quicker rate with it. Indeed when the Brahmaputra was in flood and the *Rhotas* was steaming full speed down stream, she would for several hours cover the same distance as a railway train. But she must always cast her anchor at sunset, and could hardly weigh it before sunrise. Thus, arriving at a station the Lieutenant-Governor would not only entertain, on board, the European community of the place, but also hold a ceremonial reception ("durbar") for the Native chiefs and gentry on the deck. Under several successive Lieutenant-Governors on this very deck proclamations have been read to the Natives, titles conferred, rewards declared, honours awarded. Sometimes we used to take large parties of Native gentlemen for a short trip on the river, and this kind of entertainment was more popular with them than any other which could be given. When the barge and her steamer were illuminated for a social gathering, if there be such a thing as a fairy-like scene it was this, when she lay a mass of party-coloured light on the bosom of the river. One night an entertainment was given at the close of the famine in honour of the officers engaged in the relief operations; it was kept up all night and shortly after the lights were extinguished we steamed away to keep other engagements.

Once Lord Northbrook honoured the *Rhotas* by holding a vice-regal reception on her deck for Europeans and Natives at Dacca, the capital of Eastern Bengal, on the occasion when he laid the foundation-stone of the new waterworks in the city there. For these works a munificent donation had been made by Nawâb Abd-ul-Ghani, a wealthy Muhammadan gentleman of that place.

As a part of the establishment we had a little steam launch, *The Fanny*, with which we could enter creeks and channels in order to study the country and its ways, while the larger vessel lay at anchor mid-stream of some mighty river; many of the most interesting of our detailed inspections were made in this way.

Sometimes we cast anchor during the cool of the afternoon in order to man a rowing boat. On one occasion Bishop Milman, who was among our guests on board, steered for us.

The river scenery was essentially flat, being the very opposite of that which has been described in chapter XI. regarding the Central Provinces. For many miles we appeared to be permeating a waste of waters, as the inundation spread over the rice-fields, and the villages built on mounds, stood out like islands. But we knew that underneath this seeming waste there was a marvellous fertility being nourished. Though far inland, we would be almost tempted to exclaim "nihil est nisi pontus et aer." Often the expanse of river was motionless like a mirror; or again we were

> "Lost in a maze of sluggish and devious waters."

But sometimes the wind lashed up the river into waves, "fluctibus et fremitu assurgens marino," enough to give an undulating motion to our barge and steamer. Or there were opposing currents, as for instance where the mighty Ganges and the mightier Brahmaputra collide in fierce encounter near Goalundo, making quite a maelström. Then indeed there is an example of Greek meeting Greek with the strain of aquatic contest. Once when massive breakwaters and other engineering works had been thrown out to protect the terminal railway-station and engine-house there, the river descended tearing away the costly structures as if they had been made of frail brittle materials, and confounding the devices of the ablest engineers. We approached to within sight of this scene, and watched the whirlpools eddying and surging.

Again, during a wild night the lands of whole parishes would be swept away by an "erosion," as it was called, and shortly afterwards would be thrown up as islands in the watery expanse. The disputes between the people of the villages parishes or hundreds can be imagined, as the new land comes to be distributed among them. But as the disappearance and reappearance of riparian lands are constant phenomena, the villagers become practised in identification and the authorities in adjudication.

All this time the boats of Bengal, the "country craft" as they are termed, with their striking varieties of build and rigging, afforded frequent diversion. Some, with their light structure, swelling canvas and airy movements, seemed like birds as they flitted past us. Anon, as a flotilla of a larger class approached, the long line of horizon would be broken by objects which loomed as moving towers of brilliant white, but which were the lofty sails set one above the other. Again, the boats in a string would draw up near a village to moor for the night, their painted hulls and red-coloured sails being set off against the dense foliage of bamboo and plantain. Or in some sheltered creek many hundreds of boats would be crowded together, their bare masts standing like a leafless thicket in mid-winter, while close by were the branchless trunks and leafy canopies of the cocoa-nut palms. On festal occasions, races were held at Dacca for each of the several classes of country boats before a great concourse of Natives. The river then was gay with all the diversified circumstance of an Oriental regatta.

At two points on the Brahmaputra, the smaller boats, navigating its upper course in Assam, tranship their cargoes into larger boats which can bear the stormy and dangerous navigation of its lower course after the junction of its great affluent the Megna, and so pass through the wide-spreading delta to Calcutta. The principal of these two points of transhipment is called Serâj-ganj, there the boats of all sizes in thousands are moored and lashed together, thus constituting stages, almost roadways along which people can move to and fro. Tens of thousands of boatmen, workmen and traders are congregated; this concourse induces villagers and tradesmen to bring supplies on board the boats; the merchants find it convenient to arrange their transactions on board also. Thus a floating city is actually formed on the river for several months in the year; on board of this vast flotilla, markets are held, goods disposed of, even rates of exchange settled, and transactions proceed as if on land. But, as already explained, the river-banks and the temporary islands mid-stream change every year, therefore the floating city, while it keeps its name, has not a local habitation. It has been not inaptly termed "a town without houses." It assembles at a certain season and remains, so to speak, in session for so many months, then disperses and reassembles the following year at some other point in the river, though it hovers around the same neighbourhood as nearly as possible.

At several places on the river-bank there are building-yards entirely belonging to Natives where these boats are built in the various forms and styles suited to the broad rivers with their storm-waves, the swift rivers with their treacherous currents, the shallows with their shifting shoals, the creeks with their tortuous windings. The bustling activity of these yards, the contrivances designed to meet the exigences to which the vessels are liable, afford a good notion of indigenous enterprise and skill in the shipwright's art.

Of all the river wonders, the most striking is that afforded by the joint delta of the Ganges and Brahmaputra, called "the Sundar-ban" (commonly but incorrectly written "the Sunderbunds") on the northern shore of the Bay of Bengal. There, the absolutely flat surface of alluvial deposits is clothed with a forest dense but low, extending over many hundreds of square miles. Whether this forest is truly primeval is a question for the geologist and antiquarian; for at rare spots deep underneath the surface, remains have been found of solid buildings indicating the sites of perhaps buried cities; nor would it excite surprise if from under the river-bed traces of vegetation were to be disinterred. In the present age, however, the closeness of the thicket, and the abundance, though not the size nor the altitude, of the timber trees, are the all-pervading characteristics. The channels of varying breadth permeate this low forest in all directions; the term network would give but an imperfect idea of this particular river system, which might better be called a labyrinth. If a boatman or a stranger without a compass were to become separated from his companions in cloudy weather, he must be lost. The intricacies of the channels would bewilder him, and the walls of forest on both banks would prevent his perceiving anything beyond; being unable to see the sun, he would lose all idea as to whither he was wending. He would thus perish slowly, though perhaps many boats unseen might be near, unless he were meantime snatched up by some of the tigers which infest these jungles.

Nevertheless certain channels running through these tracts are navigated by boats in vast numbers, and the boatmen from long habit can recognize every turn and twist in the several routes, and discriminate the difference in their aspect, though to a stranger they very much resemble one another. Under the guidance of Native pilots our barge and steamer used to go safely to and fro.

There was at that time a particular reason for observing the Sundar-ban," which means "the sundar forest," the sundar being a tree much used for building the Native boats above described. Inroads had been made in many directions upon this broad growth of sundar, without any arrangement for reproduction. Happily the heart of the forest was still intact, and the wasteful cutting had not gone so far as to render recovery hopeless. Still if this process should continue unchecked the exhaustion of the sundar trees must ensue in time, and thereby an almost fatal blow would be struck at the river navigation of eastern Bengal. The old supply of timber close at hand would fail, and new supplies, if procurable at all, must come from a distance at a higher cost. Our trip was fruitful in results for forest conservancy, as a large deltaic area previously unpreserved was placed under the able Conservator of forests, Dr. W. Schlich. By that measure there was secured the future supply not only of the best and cheapest timber for boat-building, but also of fuel for the markets of Calcutta.

The mass of the population—cultivators, fishermen, boatmen, small traders, artisans—in the regions of eastern Bengal, which have just been described, is Muhammadan. It is by their hands that the jute fibre used in the Dundee factories is produced. These Bengali Muhammadans are not less than 20 millions in number, and are not ethnologically or physically distinguishable from the Hindu people of the rest of Bengal. They must have been converted *en masse* by force or influence under the Mogul empire. If the idea of so large a conversion shall seem surprising, it is to be remembered that in those days the population hereabouts was sparse, consisting of hardy boatmen with a few husbandmen clearing the jungle, perhaps under the auspices of Muhammadan rulers; it was during subsequent generations that the population attained the growth which we now see. The ordinances of Islam are followed by these people in the most perfunctory way; the village mosque is a barn of bamboo matting, and a few texts from the Koran translated into Bengali suffice for the service. Their social condition is low, the marriage tie having but little permanency or effect, and legislation was being undertaken with the view of providing machinery for the regulation of their marriages and divorces.

The landlords however (with the exception of a few great Muhammadan families such as that of Abd-ul-Ghani already mentioned) are Hindus, as also of the officials and the lawyers. Near Dacca, the capital of eastern Bengal, is the town of Bikrampur, scattered among miles and miles of groves, the ancestral home of a larger number of educated Hindus, in the service of Government, than any other place in the country.

In eastern Bengal we observed the people to be robust and sturdy, though somewhat stunted in stature. But towards the centre of the province the extensive swamps and marshes had grievously impaired the health and strength of the inhabitants, prostrating them with fevers periodically, even causing them at times to subside gently from life into death without any violent disease or distress, and

> "sink into darkness
> As when a lamp is blown out by a gust of wind at a casement."

The reclamation of the marshy tracts was an object of constant solicitude to the Government of Bengal; to this end some important measures were adopted, but the progress was small relatively to the numerous and extensive areas of swamp, inasmuch as much capital and combination among neighbouring proprietors had to be secured.

In many places the villages cluster thickly in the neighbourhood of malarious hollows. The Bengali village is very unlike ordinary Indian villages, which with their mud walls and tiled roofs present in the aggregate an arid mass of ochre colouring, with one or two shady trees near at hand. In Bengal the village viewed from a short distance seems like a dense grove of palms and bamboos; entering the grove the traveller finds that nestling in the deep shade are the cottages of wicker-work with thatched roofs covered by climbing plants and creepers.

Shortly afterwards we crossed the Bay of Bengal by an ocean-going steamer to visit Chittagong, thence ascending in a small steamer the river Karnaphûli to near the Lushai frontier, for the purpose of settling questions regarding the defensive post on the British frontier. The tribes that inhabit the adjoining territories, though quite different from those on the North-west frontier, described in previous chapters, are yet in their way troublesome and even martial. The river scenery was here very unlike that just described in eastern Bengal, and though less strange and imposing, was much more beautiful, in the ordinary sense of the term. The channel wound through low hills with gently sloping sides covered with vegetation in tropical luxuriance, from the ferns and grasses to the timber trees which stretched their broad arms over the stream and spread leafy canopies over its waters.

> "The meeting boughs and implicated leaves
> Make network of the dark-blue light of day
> . . . . the translucent wave
> Images all the woven boughs above."

On the opposite shore of the Bay of Bengal we visited Orissa —sailed up the new canal from the coast to Cuttack, the capital of the province, passing by means of a lock the massive dam constructed in order to form a great reservoir opposite the city —noted the value of the irrigation works in progress for the prevention of famine—galloped over the sands of the sea-shore towards the Black Pagoda, a landmark on the coast—saw the famed car of Jaganath which through British humanity is no longer allowed to pass over the bodies of the devotee-victims —held a state reception for the neighbouring hill chiefs to whom were to be handed patents of privileges which had been conferred upon them by Government—had an interview with the Raja at Puri, little thinking that despite his sacred character he would one day stand at the criminal bar on a charge of homicide and aggravated cruelty—saw the surging of a fanatical multitude at the grand temple of Bhuvaneshwar, which the Brahmins illuminated in commemoration of our brief sojourn in the province—wandered through rock-cut temples less carved and ornamented but more antique than those of the Deccan—and observed how the province had not only recovered from the famine of ten years previously, but was actually richer than ever.

As the winter, called locally "the cold weather," approached it was necessary to return to Calcutta, and to stay for several months at that place as being the head-quarters of the provincial Government. In other parts of the empire, the provincial Governors are usually absent from their head-quarters during a great part of the winter months. But in Bengal the general interests centred in Calcutta are so great, the European community is so influential, and the business of local legislation so considerable, that the Lieutenant-Governor must be there during the winter, which is the busy season. It is further very desirable that he should be at hand, as the Government of India are residing at Calcutta during this season. Again he is *ex officio* a member of the Governor-General's Legislative Council, which is in session there also. Thus I lived mainly at Calcutta for two winters consecutively, and found it a charming place of residence during this, the brisk season. The official mansion is named Belvedere, and well it deserves the name, being situated in a richly wooded suburb where the bamboos in fine profusion throw up their tall stems, tapering to the most delicate sprigs, and bending so as to over-arch the roads and lanes. There, too, the plantain puts forth its great leaves, several feet long, in form like a scimitar, and with a sheen on the surface resembling green satin. Outside the grounds of Belvedere, the new Zoological Gardens were then being laid out in a style that might please the landscape gardener as well as the naturalist. Close by is the racecourse, three miles round, with galloping-ground of green turf that never withers even under the hottest sun.

Being now answerable for the local Government of Calcutta I had to examine the place carefully, and found it much changed for the better from the Calcutta of 1847, which has been briefly described in the previous chapter II.

The long line of villas on the bank of the Hughli, so famous in Anglo-Indian history as "Garden reach," was indeed spoiled because the ex-King of Oudh, with his motley host of retainers, had been allowed to take up his residence there. In every other direction, however, the city was marvellously improved. Instead of the unwholesome water from tanks and wells, there was a fine supply conducted by pipes from filtering beds fifteen miles distant. The open pestiferous drains were being gradually replaced by closed sewers underground, and masses of sewage were pumped daily by machinery into channels leading to a distance. The health of the dwellers in the city and the sailors in the port was improved in a proportionate degree; and cholera, though occasionally appearing, was no longer endemic. Jetties, landing-places and warehouses were being constructed along the river-bank for the accommodation of the trade, and chain moorings had been provided for the vessels. A handsome commodious Sailors' Home had been provided. A broad roadway was being arranged across the Hughli by pontoons from Calcutta to Houra on the opposite bank, which was becoming to the capital what Birkenhead is to Liverpool. In the outskirts of the city many factories with their tall chimneys were springing up for the manufacture of jute fibre. Public structures, court-houses, or rather palaces of justice, postal and telegraphic head-quarters, museums, colleges, university halls, market-places, had been or were being built in every direction. Statues of statesmen and generals had been erected in conspicuous places. The Eden gardens were artistically laid out with serpentine water, carved pagodas and tropical plants.

The constitution of the Calcutta municipality was at this

time being keenly, perhaps acrimoniously, discussed. The municipal corporation had charge of the conservancy, the local taxation and the police. Sir Stuart Hogg (brother to Sir James Macgarel Hogg) was its chairman; he was a very able and zealous officer, so the business was efficiently done, and the whole place kept in good order. Still the constitution of the municipalty was not popular; the members of the corporation being all appointed by Government, the tax-paying citizens were becoming generally dissatisfied with this arrangement. In fact an educated middle class had arisen which objected to the exclusive power heretofore pertaining to the upper class, and desired to have a voice and share in the urban administration. A bill was therefore passed through the Legislative Council, whereby only one-third of the members were to be appointed by Government and the remainder elected by the rate-payers. This measure was, as might be expected, displeasing to the upper classes among the Natives, and even to the Europeans, who apprehended that, with so great a numerical preponderance of Native voters, none but Natives would be elected. The Government, however, having the power of appointing one-third of the members, was thereby enabled to secure a due proportion of Europeans in the municipality. At first the rate-payers seemed hardly to comprehend the liberality of the concession which had been made to them, being careless in exercising their new franchise. The candidates elected often failed to give practical attention to progressive measures for the improvement of the place. Subsequently, however, there must have arisen that benefit which cannot fail to arise from the Natives having some power over and interest in their munipal affairs. The moral effect too must be beneficial in forming their national character, and making them feel jointly responsible with the Government for the improvement of their city which comprises so many interests.

The business of legislation was, on the whole, the largest and most important of any that pressed on my attention at this time. It has been explained in the previous chapter VIII. that a Legislative Council was established for Bengal separate from the Legislative Council of the Governor-General. The Bengal Legislature then consisted of some ex-officio members, the other members being appointed by the Lieutenant-Governor, who was also the President. They were partly European and partly Native, official and non-official; their number was small, being limited to thirteen. One or two would be chosen from among the European members of the Chamber of Commerce or of the Trades Association, and some few from among the Native noblemen or gentlemen of Bengal. It was quite possible for an independent member to bring in a bill; but this was rarely done. In the main it was the duty of Government to propose all the laws; and the bills were brought forward by the officials who were members of the Council. The Act of Parliament, when constituting this local legislature, gave it full power to legislate for everything requiring legislation, save certain specified matters. But as its Acts required the assent of the Governor-General before becoming law, the Government of India had full control and would not allow it to legislate in respect to anything for which the Governor-General's Council had legislated. Thus there were many restrictions upon its proceedings; even with this limitation, however, there was an extensive field open for its operations relating to the internal affairs of Bengal. The Native members took great part in the discussions, and their speeches were criticized by the public outside. Thus the Native community was induced to take an interest in framing the laws under which they lived.

Among the Native members the most useful in my time was Kristo Das Pal, and if there was such a thing as the functions of a legitimate opposition they were ordinarily exercised by him. The proceedings being conducted in English he was a good speaker, with a very correct pronunciation, and more fluency than most Englishmen; as a debater, too, he was ready and acute. He was, on the whole, next after Sir Madhava Rao, mentioned in chapter XIII., the best-informed Indian whom I have ever known; his assistance in legislation was really valuable; and in public affairs he had more force of character than any Native of Bengal. He belonged to a caste below that of Brahmin and was the editor of the *Hindu Patriot* newspaper, published in English. This paper was the organ of the Bengal Zemindars, and was in the main sustained by them, but it had a large circulation otherwise both among Europeans and Natives, being conducted with independence loyalty and learning.

Another Native member was Molavi (now Nawâb) Abd-ul-Latîf, the most progressive and enlightened among the Muhammadans of Bengal. He believed that unless the rising generation among his co-religionists exerted themselves intellectually with more effect, they would be utterly outstripped by their Hindu fellow-subjects in the race of life. He was the prime mover in the Muhammadan Literary and Scientific Society, which gave an annual *soirée* in the Town Hall with an extensive display of objects in science and art.

As a member of the Legislature was ordinarily appointed for two years, it followed that in course of time nearly all the eminent Natives of Bengal passed through the Council.

There were two leading clans of high caste at that time in Calcutta, namely, the Tagores and the Sobha Bazaar family. The Tagores have during the last half-century done more for the moral and mental progress of their countrymen than any family which has yet been seen under British rule. From them sprang the Hindu religious reformers, whose lives have been so well summarized recently by Monier Williams, and from whom the Brahmo sect really had its origin. They were at this time represented by Ramanath Tagore, a man possessing some of the fire and forcefulness of disposition characteristic of his race; being well stricken in years he was regarded as the Nestor of Bengal. Next after him was Jotendro Mohan Tagore, on whom the rank of Maharaja has since been conferred; he was a man of milder disposition perhaps, but independent in spirit and liberal in thought; quite an *élève* of the new school, yet without the forwardness and self-assertion which sometimes characterize it. He combined the polished politeness of the old school of Natives with the educational accomplishments of the new, and in him this combination was more complete than in any other man of that time.

The Sobha Bazaar family had historic antecedents dating from the battle of Plassey and the political arrangements made by Clive. The head of this family was Raja Kali Krishna, a pattern of Hindu orthodoxy and an exemplar of the virtues which characterize the Hindu race. A firm believer in the ancient religion, he laboured to assist in preserving its purity and efficacy. Yet his mind was always receptive of light from modern and Western ideas. His scholarship extended to English and European learning and to the classical languages of his own country. His literary taste displayed itself in translations of English poetry into the Indian vernacular and in the composition of Sanscrit verses. His rank and wealth, his public worth, his social merits, endeared him to his countrymen and earned for him the regard of the European community.

After his lamented death in 1874, the leading members of this important family were Narendra Krishna, since dignified with the rank of Maharaja, Kumal Krishna and Harendra Krishna. They too had the refinement of former times together with the modern culture, yet as Hindus of the highest caste they carried great weight socially, and were thoroughly loyal men.

These were all Zemindars, though they were city men as well, being influential both in town and country.

Below these families in rank, but still holding a position of some consequence, was Degumber Mittra, who was more completely a landlord than any. He understood the management of estates and all affairs relating to the peasantry better than most of his contemporaries. By his premature death Bengal lost a loyal liberal independent and useful member of the community.

The Maharaja of Bardwân, a highly educated though retiring and unobtrusive man, employed his vast wealth in works of munificent charity among his tenantry and dependents.

Much regard was attached to the memory of two Native Judges, Anukul Mukerji and Dwarkanath Mittra, who had both sat on the bench of the High Court. Their learning and character reflected honour on their race and on the Western education by which they had been trained.

Of the Muhammadans the most prominent figure was Nawâb Amir Ali; he was one of the old school, and afforded a complete example of its virtues and merits; he never even learned to speak the English language. He made his fortune at the Native Bar, and during the war of the mutinies was deputed on political service to the disturbed province of Behar. He afterwards became manager for the estate of the ex-King of Oudh. Entire trust was placed in his loyalty and fidelity, and next after Salar Jang (mentioned in chapter XIII.) he was the best Muhammadan I have ever known.

In eastern Bengal the most influential Muhammadan was Nawâb Abd-ul-Ghani, of Dacca, already mentioned. The fortune of his family had been made chiefly by trade, and he had great landed possessions. He also was a man of the old school, munificent in disposition and loyal in conduct. His son seemed to have inherited the paternal qualities, but was somewhat more a man of the new school.

Rajendra Lal Mittra, the most effectively learned Hindu of that day, both as regards English and Oriental classics, was preparing his great work on the Antiquities of Orissa. He felt a justifiable pride in the wondrous achievements of the Hindus of old, and doubtless grieved over their political decadence.

The Brahmo preacher Keshub Chander Sen had long been very prominent at the capital; he was still in the zenith of his usefulness, with hardly any symptom of decline, though some of his views were regarded as extravagant and rhapsodical. He was much esteemed by all classes; his English oratory was listened to with rapt attention by Bengalis, and thought excellent even by English auditors. He and his immediate followers maintained a gentle and conciliatory manner, carefully avoiding the display of anything like aggressiveness towards their Hindu fellow-countrymen.

Among the Native Christians the foremost was the Reverend Krishna Mohan Banerji, a clergyman of the Church of England. Though zealous for the faith and ready to attack incisively what he regarded as the pseudo-Christianity of the Brahmos, he yet retained much influence with the middle classes among the non-Christian Hindus. Sprung from the highest caste, he learnt from Christian teaching to feel a catholic charity for all the humbler castes of his countrymen, and seemed to perceive that one mode of propagating Christian principle among the heathen, is to let them feel the warmth of Christian sympathy. Though his influence was perhaps not acknowledged by the upper classes, it really was considerable among the numerical majority of educated Hindus at the capital. In this respect I have never known his equal among the Native Christians. One of his daughters was married to the Reverend Mr. Wheeler; afterwards Mrs. Wheeler undertook, at the instance of Government, the inspection of the Zenana mission classes, and rendered much service in that way.

The Reverend Lal Behari Dey, one of the earliest converts made by the Scottish missionaries, was professor in a Government college. His character was marked by firmness, independence, and ambition for doing good in his generation. Having been in intimate communication with the missionaries he possessed an exact knowledge of the best points in the European character, and his writings displayed much insight into the thoughts and ways of the poorer classes among his countrymen. He possessed much literary skill and wrote English prose with purity and perspicuity.

Of all persons in Bengal, the most munificent was a widow lady Rani (now Maharani) Sharnomoye. She was a strictly orthodox and devout Hindu, much given to works of piety, but ever ready to dedicate some part of her great wealth to works of practical benevolence. Her gifts were generous, not only for the relief of famine, but also for the alleviation of suffering in every form; nor were appeals for help in promoting objects of public utility ever made to her in vain. I have had the pleasure of holding communications with her, not in an interview face to face, but by audience with a curtain drawn between us. She has, by the gracious favour of the Queen, been admitted to the order of the Crown of India. Her career used to remind us of the historic record of the good Mahratta princess Ahalya Bai of Central India.

Liberality in contributing towards works of public usefulness was eminently displayed by a rich firm of Native bankers who, though domiciled in Bengal, were Mârwaris from Rajputana. The honoured heads of that family were Dhanpat and Ganpat: much of the trade in lower Bengal was managed by them.

Solicitous care was given by Government to the training of young chiefs, during their minority, often with good results, but not always with success, and sometimes with discouraging failure. In these days there were three young men who, after receiving an education according to Western principles, had just been or were about to be inducted into the management of large territories; their total rental being not less than half a million sterling annually. These were the chiefs of Kûch Behár, Darbhanga and Hatwa; each of whom gave the fairest promise regarding his future career.

I carefully inspected in those days the Christian missions among the Kols, Santhals, and other aboriginal tribes on the western borders of Bengal, and found the results of the work to be very considerable. There were many thousands of converts, and whole tracts of country were inhabited by Native Christian families. The mission schools became largely attended by heathen as well as by Christian children. The influence of the missionaries in those wild districts was a power for good, and the political effect of their presence proved to be excellent. Hence also many Native Christians went forth to labour in the tea-gardens of Assam, where they would doubtless spread a knowledge of their faith among their comrades.

At that time Colonel Dalton was quitting for ever this home of the aboriginal races, where his long administration had endeared the British name to the people, while his learned researches had illustrated their idiosyncrasy and ethnology.

Among the educated Natives, the first-fruit of the new education was an improved standard of rectitude and integrity. The men themselves saw that this was the case, and attributed it unhesitatingly to educational influences. Much, happily, was due to this cause, much also was assignable to other causes, such as the improvement of official and professional prospects for those who had character as well as ability. The change for the better was perceptible with the utmost distinctness in the upper classes of the Native officials, especially in the judicial department. When I had first known Calcutta, more than twenty years ago, honesty among these men was, according to common repute, the exception; now by the same repute, dishonesty was the exception and honesty the rule. Indeed I scarcely then expected to live to see the change for the better in these respects which I now saw.

There was, on the whole, an upheaval of the Native mind in Bengal consequent on the spread of secular education, although the influence of Christian missions, however great elsewhere, was not much felt in Calcutta. The principal factor was the Brahmo sect, of which the adherents gathered largely at the capital and were scattered throughout the country. In religion they followed the precepts of the Bible without acknowledging the divinity of Christ; but they accepted in addition many doctrines of the Hindu sacred writings. There had been a Hindu Synod named the "Dharma Sabha" instituted to counteract these innovations by recalling the thoughts of the faithful to the ancient ways; many organs of opinion also spoke as if the old belief survived. But it was doubtful whether any resistance, passive or active, would long withstand the advance of new opinions. The existing tendencies were rendering educated Hindus less submissive in tone and language than formerly, more erect in mental and moral stature in the presence of Europeans, even jealous of the superior positions held by Europeans in the country, not altogether disposed to acquiesce in their present status, but rather inclined to criticize the conduct and policy of the Government and to demand increased privileges. Without going so far as to ask for representative institutions, they aspired to have a greater share than previously in governing themselves, though they had not formed exact ideas as to how that share was to be secured. They perhaps desired in effect to have the satisfaction of ruling the country while the Europeans had the labour of defending it. They had an overweening notion of their own intellectual ability, believing themselves to be in this respect equal to any nation and superior to most races. They cherished the notion that wherever brain-work might be absolutely required in India they would rise like oil to the surface of water.

This uneasiness and restlessness—all the more irksome as arising from no definable cause, and not being susceptible of any specific remedy—found vent in the vernacular Press. Of these utterances some were certainly disloyal or even worse, while others were merely captious, peevish, fractious, petulant. On the other hand there was frank outspoken criticism of men measures or policy, which was not to be confounded with disloyalty, and which did good every way, as exercising the faculties of the critics and pointing a moral to those criticized. There was also much, which if rightly interpreted was tantamount to real loyalty such as freemen owe to their liege.

It was probably the contemplation of these faults which induced many observers to deprecate the high or superior education which was being given. Some critics recommended that Government should withdraw from taking part in high education, leaving it to private enterprise, and devote to the promotion of primary education all the resources which could be afforded by the State. So far from coinciding in that view, however, we strove to foster alike both kinds of education, higher and lower. We diffused superior instruction by the establishment of additional colleges in the interior of the country, at the same time developing the village schools and adding tens of thousands every month to the number of children under primary instruction. The policy was to refrain from supporting any branch of education entirely by the State resources, but to induce the people themselves to contribute at least half. This proportion was maintained for the whole educational expenditure, and also for the education of each sort, upper or lower.

The real fault in the high education was the undue and disproportionate attention devoted to literature and philosophy, as compared with physical science and the cognate branches of practical instruction. This caused the legal judicial and administrative professions to be overcrowded, while the scientific and practical professions relating to civil and mechanical engineering, to chemistry botany agriculture and the like were starved and neglected. It was impossible at that time to remedy this fault without the co-operation of the Calcutta University. But this institution relating to other provinces besides Bengal, and being under the Government of India, was not amenable to the Government of Bengal. Meanwhile the difficulty which very many highly educated men, even graduates of the University, found in obtaining suitable employment, was producing discontent.

The memory of the learned and accomplished Archdeacon John Pratt was cherished by all classes European and Native.

Among our educational officers the most popular was Henry Woodrow, an old schoolfellow of mine at Rugby. His sudden death, shortly after he had been appointed Director of Public Instruction, was lamented not only by his European friends but also by all classes of educated Natives throughout the country.

Remarkable services were rendered to education, not only among Europeans and East Indians but also among Natives at the capital, by the Jesuit fathers of St. Xavier's College under the direction of Archbishop Stein. One of the best teachers of physical science in the country was the Reverend Father Lafont, who was much esteemed by the non-Christian Natives as a secular instructor.

The completion of the Bengal Gazetteer, an important work in twenty volumes, was expedited under the supervision of Dr. W. W. Hunter, who brought remarkable accomplishments and ability to the task.

The Bishop of Calcutta, Dr. Robert Milman, while most zealous for the faith, was also much respected by the members of other religious communities. At Calcutta almost every religion in the world is more or less represented, so occasionally at the *soirées* in the Bishop's Palace there used to be gathered the ministers of all these religions, and the liberal sympathy thus evinced produced much moral effect. The public grief was keenly excited by Dr. Milman's untimely death from fatigues and exposure during his episcopal visitations in an enormous diocese under various climates and often at insalubrious seasons of the year. This melancholy event led to the creation of a new bishopric for northern India, namely that of Lahore.

There was some agitation at that time under the benevolent auspices of Archdeacon Baly on behalf of the children of "poor whites" at Calcutta, Europeans and East Indians, many of whom were growing up in ignorance. Most of them, being Portuguese in origin, were much intermingled with the Natives by blood. Assistance was rendered by Government to the several religious communities in order to mitigate this evil.

In the interior of Bengal proper, the change for the better in the condition of the peasantry within the last generation was remarkable. Though the police had still many faults, its efficiency had been improved by the infusion of European blood, so to speak, into its body, and by the ameliorated condition of its Native officers. The crime of gang-robbery had ceased, which within living memory was the midnight scourge, hated by all yet resisted by none, and the dread of which was the skeleton in every villager's closet. Armed ruffianism no longer stalked abroad to harry terrify and plunder those who had an unlimited capacity for fear but no stomach for self-defence. Rack-renting and lawless oppression were comparatively rare; and peasants garnered their crops without the surveillance of land-agents, each man resting with comparative comfort under his own bamboo-clump, or his cocoa-nut tree, or the eaves of his thatched roof with its festoons of creepers. Not indeed that the lot of the peasantry had been altogether raised out of degradation, still it had improved and was yearly improving.

On the other hand a new evil had during recent years arisen, and was at this time assuming formidable proportions. In several districts of northern and eastern Bengal agrarian riots had broken out under the instigation of known agitators, some landlords had been murdered under circumstances reminding us of less favoured lands, and a cry arose not only for diminished rents but for no rent at all. However we passed a law to strengthen the machinery for determining rents, exercised our legal power of quartering police on turbulent villagers at their expense, urged on the Zemindars the expediency of moderation in demand and procedure, and made it clear to the tenantry that unlawful conduct on their part would be repressed with the whole force of the executive arm. Thus the agrarian storm, after much muttering and growling of thunder and some flashing of electricity, passed off.

The Court of Wards, by managing the estates of minors and others who from any cause were unable to manage their affairs, was conducting quite a gigantic business. In some districts the properties of embarrassed chiefs were being brought under an Encumbered Estates Act. Still in the main the Zemindars were administering their estates fairly well, though perhaps disposed to spend too much time at the capital and too little in their villages. The territorial circumstance most noteworthy in recent times is the increase of small properties; during the last two generations the tendency has been for the large estates to split up; and the Bengali barrister, lawyer, official, litterateur, trader, while following diligently his calling in the city, contrives to acquire his bit of land.

In Behar as the clouds of confusion caused by the famine cleared away they disclosed a peasantry much lower in status and in economic condition than their brethren in other provinces. It appeared too that the usual rights of cultivators hardly existed or at least had not been respected, and that in some classes of cases the law was so strained as to become an engine of oppression. Such evils, having grown gradually through several generations, seldom admit of an immediate remedy, still remedial measures were at once set on foot.

The condition of indigo-planting in Behar was at times threatened with dangers similar to those which beset the culture of this valuable dye in Bengal, as explained in chapter VIII. The European planters, however, were disposed to profit by the experience of their brethren in Bengal, and to make timely and judicious concessions to the Native planters.

The difficulties had not, however, been fully overcome up to the date of my departure, though I learn with thankfulness that they have since been much mitigated.

The insalubrity of many among the jails, and the high death-rate shewn by the returns of prisoners, caused constant anxiety. In so far as these sad results were traceable to overcrowding, remedies were applied by the construction of additional buildings. Originally the jails had been built without due regard to ventilation. Great improvements had some years previously been introduced by Dr. Mouatt, formerly Inspector-General, whose humane and philanthropic efforts were directed with administrative skill, and who is to be numbered among the benefactors of Bengal.

The sanitary measures adopted by us in different parts of the country were largely based on the information laboriously gathered and the principles scientifically expounded by Dr. Norman Chevers, who was one among the many ornaments of the Medical Service.

No change was to my eye more noteworthy than the increased popularity of the Civil Courts. In former days they were thought to be arenas where the rich would overbear the poor, but now their existence was respected as the ægis and palladium of the just rights and interests of the weak against the strong. The hopes and fears of the people seemed to be centred in the proceedings of these courts and the results of judicial action. The Native judges were, as might be expected, often criticized in regard to their decisions opinions or arguments, but rarely or never distrusted in respect to the uprightness of their intentions.

I had the pleasure of giving at Belvedere a farewell banquet to Sir Richard Couch, the Chief Justice of Bengal, on his retirement. In provinces where civil justice is more than ordinarily important to the social life of the people, it is essential that the relations between the Lieutenant-Governor and the Chief Justice should be cordial, and so they were at that time. The High Court at Calcutta supervises the examination of Natives for admission to the bar and the bench; it nominates Natives in the first instance for appointment to the judicial service, and upon its report the Government mainly depends for information in respect to the promotion of the Native judges from one grade of the service to another. In these matters great assistance used to be derived from one of the Judges of the High Court, a very able man, Mr. (now Sir Louis) Jackson.

At intervals between these cares and labours I visited Darjîling in the eastern Himalayas during two summer seasons, and derived much advantage from the companionship of John Ware Edgar, the head of the local administration there. That region including both British and Native Sikhim, is one of the most beautiful in the world, and the admirable description of it published by Sir Joseph Hooker more than thirty years ago is still applicable. Its mountains form a division territorially between the Buddhist and Brahminical religions, like the watershed between two vast river systems. On one side of them there tinkles the bell of the temple belonging to that faith which spreads southwards through India to Cape Comorin. On the other side there resounds the gong of the chapel appertaining to the religion which extends northwards through Thibet and China to Pekin. A fresh interest, from an economic point of view, has been excited by the rapid extension of tea-gardens representing what is now a great industry, and by the establishment of cinchona plantations where cheap quinine is produced for the fever-stricken millions. While at Darjîling I took occasion to improve our communications along the border between Sikhim and Nepal, a truly wonderful line adorned with the most splendid rhododendrons. Here are comprised in one matchless panorama the groups both of Everest and of Kinchinjanga, the two loftiest snowy mountains yet discovered on earth. Again, I examined the frontier line between Sikhim and eastern Thibet, where the two empires of Britain and of China meet, and where a series of lovely lakes embosomed amidst the snow-tipped gneiss rocks is to be seen at altitudes ranging from ten to fifteen thousand feet above the sea. Passing to and fro we visited the monasteries of Sikhim, gazed at the countenance of the Buddha, impassible with mystic calm, and watched the processions of abbots and monks in their purple vestments. Or again while enveloped in the rain-cloud and unable to discern any object whatever we listened to the roar of countless cascades and cataracts around us. Then as the wind rolled away the mist-curtain we saw Kinchinjanga and his attendant peaks

> "Lift through perpetual snows their lofty and luminous summits."

There too we admired the quasi-tropical vegetation which is to be seen in no other part of the Himalayas—the graceful cane, the tree-fern, the flowering magnolia, and the climbing plants which swinging from the great arms of lofty trees

> "Hang their ladder of ropes aloft like the ladder of Jacob."

Once too, having much official business with the authorities in Assam, I proceeded thither in the State barge *Rhotas* which has been already described. Thus we passed along the broad Brahmaputra having hills on both sides, and exceeding in grandeur either the Indus or the Ganges, with snowy peaks in the distance. We inspected the tea-gardens on the banks, and then leaving the quasi-tropical vegetation ascended in one ride to the pine forests on the heights of Shillong.

Subsequently while steaming down the Brahmaputra for the last time, I received reports of a terrific cyclone having just occurred in the deltaic district, near the estuary of the Megna, desolating populous tracts of country. Taking a large supply of provisions on board the *Rhotas* and a force of police to render aid, I proceeded as fast as possible to the scene of disaster, and fortunately was the first authority to arrive there. The storm-wave had subsided, leaving the fertile and thickly peopled territory a complete wreck. In some places the ground was strewn with corpses like a battle-field, everywhere dead bodies of human beings and cattle in horrid confusion lay festering in the sun. The cottages were falling to pieces, the gardens were turned into saline swamps, the villages presented a ghastly and sickening spectacle. The evening before the occurrence, the people, about 300,000 in number, retired to rest as usual. Before midnight the wind suddenly freshened, soon there arose a cry "the water is on us," and a wave several feet high burst over the country, followed by another and again by a third. The people were thus caught up by the surging flood and many were lifted on to the trees which surrounded their homesteads. Those who became stopped by the branches were saved, those who were not thus stopped must have been swept away and lost. The cyclone with its gyrations first drove the salt water from the Bay of Bengal into the Megna, banking up the river and flooding its banks, then blowing from the opposite direction propelled this mass of water back again across the country towards the sea; hence the succession of destructive waves over the doomed villages. Everything that medical skill could suggest or administrative resources provide was bestowed to relieve the sufferers.

In those days Lord Napier of Magdâla was about to resign his high office as Commander-in-Chief of the army. A public meeting was held in the Town Hall at Calcutta, when due honour was done to the manifold achievements of the departing General; and arrangements were made for erecting a statue in his memory by public subscription.

The auspicious visit, with which His Royal Highness the Prince of Wales honoured Bengal, took place in December 1875. His Royal Highness, on landing at Calcutta, was saluted by a vast concourse of people, and was received by the Viceroy, Lord Northbrook, at Government House. The city and all the grand buildings, standing in an amphitheatre round the plain of Calcutta, were illuminated. The Natives founded useful institutions for literature, science and art, as permanent memorials of the royal visit. The principal Native rulers and chiefs from Central India, Rajputana, the Panjab, Oudh, Nepal, joyously assembled at the capital in order to render homage to the Prince of Wales, and to many of them separate interviews were graciously granted by His Royal Highness. A chapter of the Order of the Star of India was held in a stately camp pitched on the great plain, when the Prince invested several persons European and Native with the insignia of the Order in the name of Her Majesty the Queen. The Natives of Calcutta were privileged to receive the Prince of Wales at an entertainment wherein all their resources of Oriental ornamentation were displayed. The European inhabitants gave an entertainment in the Western style at the Town Hall in honour of His Royal Highness.

After leaving Calcutta the Prince of Wales stopped for a few hours at Patna, the capital of Behar. There the Native chiefs and gentry marshalled their elephants and paraded them before His Royal Highness with a very imposing array. Then were presented to His Royal Highness the officers, European and Native, who had rendered good service during the recent famine.

Nowhere in India did the royal sojourn make a more profound and happy impression than among the Natives of Bengal.

Soon afterwards it became known that Lord Northbook would be shortly leaving India for England, and would be succeeded by Lord Lytton. As the day drew near for Lord Northbrook's departure from Calcutta, a public meeting was held at the Town Hall in order to consider the most suitable means of doing him honour. It was then decided that a statue of him should be erected at the capital.

Having conducted the Bengal Government for more than two years, I received through the Marquis of Salisbury then Secretary of State an offer of the Governorship of Bombay, which I accepted. During these years the various things relating to the administration had been claiming attention—the progress of canals already under construction and the elaboration of new projects for irrigation—the preparation of plans for branch railways—the repair of embankments—the execution of drainage works—the designs for the reclamation of swamps—the assessment and levy of cesses already authorized by law for roads and schools—the founding of new colleges, the opening of additional medical schools and the development of primary education—the legislation regarding the land, the partition of joint undivided states, the registration of possessory titles, the determination of agrarian disputes—the extension of the forest laws to many hundred square miles of woods and jungle—the organization of the rural post—the improvement of the village police—the development of the statistical department—the constitution of the municipality at the capital on the basis of the elective franchise—the modification of the procedure in the department of civil justice—and the limitation of the licence of appeal by providing new appellate courts in the interior of the country with power of deciding finally.

By this time I had formed a favourable estimate of the people of Bengal. Many classes among them are milder in disposition and less robust physically than the other Indian races with which I had been brought in contact. But these evinced an assiduity in self-discipline, and a power of intense mental application, rarely to be found in any race. Many classes again in the eastern districts are sturdy, wiry, and courageous. A number of the principal men in Bengal accompanied me to the imperial assemblage at Delhi, and received titles or other honours on that auspicious occasion. I was then completing the annual administration report, and my description of the character of the people concluded thus—subject to the exceptions which must be remembered whenever generalization is attempted respecting a vast population consisting of diverse elements :—

"At heart and in the truest sense the Bengalis are thoroughly loyal. In this respect there are not in British India better subjects of the Crown. Under all circumstances, adverse or propitious, they evince a steady industrious and law-abiding spirit which must command regard and esteem from every Englishman who knows them. Their sentiments of reverence for the British Crown and respect for the British nation will have been enhanced by the State ceremonies instituted for proclaiming the imperial title."

CHAPTER XIX.

(1877.)

THE AFFAIRS OF SOUTHERN INDIA.

My deputation to the distressed parts of the Madras Presidency to make enquiries and offer suggestions—Communications with the Governor, the Duke of Buckingham—Condition of the drought-stricken districts in the north—The ruined city of Bijayanagar—Famished fugitives betake themselves to the city of Madras—Condition of the southern districts—Arcot, Trichinopoly, Madura and Tinnevelly—Christianity among the Natives of the southern peninsula—Bishops Sargeant and Caldwell—The Roman Catholic clergy and community—The Native State of Mysore—Substance of my report on the famine in southern India during its earlier stages—Destruction of the forests—Conduct of the people during the distress.

In April 1876 Lord Lytton succeeded Lord Northbrook as Viceroy and Governor-General. During the Christmas week of that year the ceremonies, receptions and festivities of the Imperial Assemblage at Delhi, were being conducted, under Lord Lytton's auspices, with a grandeur not to be surpassed. The title of Empress of India assumed by Her Majesty the Queen was becoming memorable for ever in the minds and hearts of the vast Native population throughout the empire. The Native Princes and chiefs felt that the bonds between themselves and the supreme head of the empire were being strengthened. All men from the highest to the humblest realized better than before their position as members and subjects of an imperial State.

During the autumn there had been reports of famine in the Deccan districts of the Bombay Presidency. But as the season wore on, it became apparent that famine to a much larger extent impended in southern India, embracing much of the Madras Presidency and the greater part of Mysore. Already the Madras Government, of which the Duke of Buckingham was the head, had begun to purchase grain as a reserve supply, and to open relief works which were attended by many thousands. While we were all assembled at Delhi Sir John Strachey, who was then Financial Member of the Government of India, asked me whether I could proceed to the Madras and Bombay Presidencies on deputation from the Government of India in communication with the Madras Government, in order to visit the distressed districts, to examine the relief works already begun or yet to be opened, and to suggest for the consideration of the local authorities whatever measures might seem necessary or desirable. I replied that my time and exertions were at the command of the Governor-General; and the next day I received instructions from Lord Lytton to proceed on this deputation. My functions were purely those of examining, reporting and suggesting; I was not vested with any executive authority, and it rested with the provincial Government to decide as to what action should be taken on any recommendations I might make.

This deputation would last for a short time only as on the 1st of May following, 1877, I was to assume charge of the Government of Bombay. Meanwhile it was necessary that another Lieutenant-Governor of Bengal should be appointed in my stead. Lord Lytton accordingly chose the Honourable Ashley (now Sir Ashley) Eden, who has been already mentioned in chapter XVII. I then proceeded to the Madras Presidency about New Year's Day, 1877, on my new deputation, accompanied by C. E. Bernard, who was chosen to be Secretary, and has been already mentioned in chapter XVII. as having special experience in all that pertained to the relief of famine.

We travelled by rail to the districts of the Bombay Deccan, stopping a short time to examine the effect of the drought there and the operations in progress for the relief of famine. This done we proceeded to Hyderabad, the Nizam's capital, by railway, the very line for the construction of which I had to obtain the Nizam's sanction, as explained in chapter XIII. Thence we journeyed by post to the northern frontier of the Madras Presidency where the most serious phase of the distress was likely to be found.

I had previously some general acquaintance with the Madras Presidency, having visited it several times officially. Thus I already knew its grand works for irrigation and navigation in the deltas of the Godavery, the Kistna, and the Cavery—the great rivers dammed up as they issue from the mountain ranges, their waters being by these means diverted to supply the canals—the water channels first supplying moisture to the crops, and then conveying the produce to market—the school of hydraulic engineers who acquired their training in this wide sphere of experience—the lakes, tanks or reservoirs of various sizes and capacities, maintained in every group of villages throughout the country—the equitable settlement of the land revenue and the consequent expansion of cultivation together with the growth of the agricultural community—the natural wealth and fertility of the Malabar coast, with its coffee plantations, spice gardens, cocoa-nut groves, and its numberless coasting vessels.

On entering the Madras Presidency I duly placed myself in communication with its Governor, the Duke of Buckingham, and during my stay in his jurisdiction I received from His Grace and his officers of all grades the utmost courtesy and assistance. I transmitted to him reports of the enquiries which were made, and of the suggestions which seemed desirable. The various recommendations received prompt consideration from him and from all concerned. The hospitable kindness of the Madras officers was indeed such as to impress itself indelibly upon my memory.

My inspection began, in January 1877, on the bank of the river Tumbadra, dividing the Madras Presidency from the Nizam's dominions, and extended through the Madras territory known as the Ceded districts.

Near this point are the unfinished works of the project undertaken by the Madras Irrigation Company at the instance of Sir Arthur Cotton for conducting a large canal from the Tumbadra.

The aspect of the country at that time was dreary and desolate in the extreme. The plains of black soil stretched widely, but were for the most part without vegetation, whether crops or herbage, and the surface of the earth preserved its dusky colour. The country, too, was for the most part treeless; here and there stood a solitary tree, a clump, or a grove, but literally for miles together the fields were destitute of hedge-rows, or of any plant save their periodical crops, which crops had now perished. The contour of the country was not, indeed, monotonous; on the contrary, it was frequently diversified by hills and masses of granitic rock. The town of Adoni, near the border of the Madras Presidency, on the main line from Madras to Bombay, was the centre of perhaps the greatest distress. Close by there rose up from the dark-coloured plain a noble mass of granite bearing on its face various hues of red and orange. So also at Bellary, the capital of these districts, a very fine cliff overhangs the town and is fortified as a citadel; the rocks of its scarped sides are rounded off and smooth; and from its summit a survey was obtained of the drought-stricken country around. The great hill fortress of this neighbourhood is Gûty, which rises more than a thousand feet above the plain. Once it thoroughly commanded the surrounding country, being elaborately fortified according to the best Asiatic skill by successive dynasties, Hindu, Muhammadan, Mahratta; and the possession of this stronghold was the mark of dominant sovereignty. The British Government held it for a long time, after receiving possession of the district. From its bastions were fired the minute guns at the funeral of the Governor, Sir Thomas Munro. Some years ago, however, its occupation was deemed unnecessary, and in order to save the cost of maintenance it was effectually dismantled. To us the ascent was severe under the hot sun, but the scarps and precipices were very fine, and from the top could be seen the general configuration of the country about to become the scene of so much suffering. The military value of such forts as those of Gûty and Bellary, once potential in wars and politics, is much affected by the opening of the railway which runs near their base. The territory is fraught with associations and memories of Sir Thomas Munro, who was its first British administrator after the cession. Among his assistants was Mr. Robertson, who became afterwards the head of the district administration. Robertson was keenly alive to the utter want of trees in an otherwise fine territory, and caused numerous groves to be planted in suitable places. He died in the district, and on his tombstone there is a record of his labours to restore shade and verdure to the land. Of these beautiful groves many are preserved, while others have been injured and some even destroyed. It was in one of these umbrageous woods, so grateful in a bare and treeless tract, that Sir Thomas Munro was encamped when he was seized with the cholera which rapidly carried him off. We encamped for two days on the very spot, and there many thousands of poor people, candidates for relief, were assembled for our inspection.

Some years previously cotton-mills had been successfully established in the Bellary district, and were once busily at work. But now, owing to failure of the cotton supply, the factories were closed and the machinery was at a standstill.

In these districts the most interesting place is the site of the ruined Hindu city of Bijayanagar, near the present village of Hamphe. These famous ruins, extending over many square miles, are in the very first rank among the sights even of this wonderful empire. The kingdom of Bijayanagar comprised the best part of southern India, and for some time stemmed the tide of Muhammadan conquest. It was subdued at length by an alliance of the several Muhammadan kings of the Deccan, and with its fall the last hopes of Hindu autonomy in the peninsula were extinguished. The style of its architecture is for the most part primitive, but the quaintness is very attractive. We observed with admiration the remains of gateways, cisterns, fountains, terraces, towers, palaces, elephant stables; and were enabled to realize the spots where the Rajputs of old must have held the reviews, pageants, tournaments, festivals, and other spectacles in which Orientals delight. The earliest temples were perhaps not remarkable, but at a somewhat later period some fanes were erected, outside the city, which are deemed by antiquarians to be among the most ornate specimens of Hindu art. Inside the city there is a temple with one of those lofty gateways, called Goparams, towards which hosts of worshippers once marched, and many yet march, by a broad roadway. Standing there we readily imagined the religious processions with the Jaganath cars, the catafalques and other paraphernalia which must have passed along this way in the palmy days of the kingdom. The natural beauties of the place set off the objects of art in an extraordinary degree. The site was originally chosen for the sake of the water supply from the Tumbadra, which here runs through the midst of low hills and granite boulders. The levels being very suitable, channels and watercourses were conducted from the river to all parts of the extensive city. The Tumbadra sometimes courses over its rapids, and then rests in its deep pools which reflect the bright sky and dark rocks. It was once crossed by a viaduct, with monolith granite piers, of which many are yet standing. Several of the old watercourses are still in use, and from them is derived irrigation for the rich soil in the hollows surrounded by granite. After our weary journeyings in aridity, dust and glare, it was passing strange to find ourselves in the midst of gloom, shade and moisture, contemplating the green patches of sugar-cane and listening to the murmurs of the watercourses. The wide-spreading city, once crowded with hundreds of thousands of people, is now tenanted ordinarily by a mere handful of villagers. At this time, however, it was occupied temporarily by a multitude of a different class, for there we found gathered together for our inspection many thousands of poor people who were being employed on the roads in the neighbourhood.

Thus after inspecting the fields villages and market towns, examining the condition of the distressed poor, and the manner in which the able-bodied were engaged, also observing the principles on which relief was being administered to the infirm, we were able to form a precise idea regarding the nature and progress of the famine.

The circumstances fortunately differed from those described in chapter XVII. regarding Behar and northern Bengal. Here a railway was running right through the distressed country from end to end; good roads branched off in every direction; draught cattle and wheeled carriage for trading purposes were abundant; the grain trade was extraordinarily active, and the markets both in towns and villages were well supplied. There was plenty of food in the country, but vast numbers of persons had no means wherewith to buy it, because there was no harvesting, nor any work in the fields, and consequently no wages could be earned. Again, those who were able to sustain themselves were yet pinched, and had no surplus wherewith to support others; therefore the numerous class dependent on alms or some form of subsidy were being left unsupported, and must perish if not assisted extraneously. The necessary employment and assistance were being afforded on a large scale, quite adequate to the circumstances of the moment, and the people were then in good physical condition. Thus while it was absolutely necessary for Government to continue finding employment for the able-bodied and food for the infirm, there was no need whatever for it to import grain as was done in Behar and northern Bengal. Though a small supply had in the first instance been laid in by Government as a reserve, it was decided that there should not be any more importation by the State and that reliance must be placed on the grain trade, which was proving itself to be quite worthy of confidence. On the whole the condition of affairs in the Ceded districts was at that time favourable and satisfactory.

During the famine of Behar and northern Bengal, the remarkable immunity from epidemic sickness has been mentioned in chapter XVII., as partly owing to the excellent and unfailing water supply. In the Madras Presidency, on the contrary, this supply was defective by reason of the drought, and when the wells or tanks became very low the water itself was impure. From this cause, and from the unknown conditions relating to epidemic disease, cholera often broke out as an epidemic among the large gangs of labourers and small-pox frequently appeared. Often the gangs dispersed for a time, flying in abject terror from the deadly pest, although for them to fly was to run the risk of starvation. Mortality thus arose and increased the death-rate in the drought-stricken districts.

A discussion arose as to the wage to be allowed to the people labouring on the relief works. The Madras wage was found to be higher than that which was allowed in the Bombay Presidency. I urged that the Bombay scale should be adopted, the Madras authorities however demurred on the ground that any reduction of their wage would be detrimental to the health and strength of the labouring poor, the Bombay experience notwithstanding. As the Madras sanitary authorities held to their view the chief sanitary officer of Bengal was consulted, who, after examining many of the gangs on the works, decided in favour of the Bombay scale. Accordingly that wage was for a time adopted, but as the season advanced the Madras Government reverted to its original rate.

The Ceded Districts are called Balaghat or "above the mountains," in contradistinction to the rest of the Madras Presidency or the southern peninsula, which is considered to be below them. We travelled then from the Balaghat by rail, through the mountains which are partly clothed with forests. Thereby a grateful contrast was afforded to the bare and desolate country in which we had been sojourning. Below the mountains are Madras, Arcot, Pondicheri and other historic places.

At and near Madras, I found the condition of affairs as regards the famine much less promising. In its vicinity there are extensive territories called "Zemindaris," which are not under British administration, but are ruled by chiefs of their own. These territories, though having some considerable population, are yet poor and their chiefs somewhat resourceless; when the crops failed utterly no system of relief was introduced, and the destitute poor, wandering about, found their way to the Madras city. Again, near the base of the mountains just mentioned, through which the railway passes, there are many sacred places of wide celebrity, to which pilgrims and professional beggars resort habitually in great numbers. These classes are always among the first victims of distress, and they at this time crowded the temple precincts more than ever. The priests, on the other hand, found their resources affected by a sensible diminution in the offerings of the faithful owing to the hard times, and were unable or unwilling to meet extraordinary demands on their bounty. Thus the distressed people, when turned away from these old founts of charity, resorted to Madras. Then the city and suburbs of Madras became crowded with refugees in various stages of misery, among whom many were verging on starvation or were past recovery even by the most humane and skilful treatment. The sentiments of the community at Madras were much moved by the piteous and distressful sights thus presented day after day and constantly increasing in number. The Government and its officers put forth the most strenuous efforts to relieve the sufferers; hospitals and relief camps were established under medical supervision and with all the resources which good management could supply. Still the death-rate in these excellent institutions was very high, inasmuch as when nourishment was given, even with the most judicious moderation, dysenteric affections would but too often supervene whereby the patients were wasted to death.

The landing-places on the Madras sea-shore were loaded with vast consignments of grain imported by sea from Bengal and Burma. At this the centre of the grain trade of southern India, the most enterprising vigour was being displayed.

Near Madras we visited the ruined fane of Mahabalipuram on the very margin of the ocean, sitting on the flight of steps up which the waves surged and dashed. We saw also the rocks near the sea-shore which the ancient Hindu architects hewed into shapely temples, excavating the chambers out of the solid mass. Southey the poet had read of this place as the fabled city of submarine structures. The realities as testified by the remains might justify all the invocations, as he has imagined them, in honour of Bali, the tutelary deity of the place.

I took the opportunity while at Madras to pay a short visit to the Governor of Pondicheri, and received much kindness and hospitality from His Excellency. Relatively to the size of the territory, the French institutions there are numerous and appear to be well conducted according to the best Indian standard. For many miles around, the lands are cultivated in an assiduous and careful manner, indicating that the cultivators must be in the possession of rights well defined and efficiently protected.

From Madras I proceeded northwards along the coast to Nellore. There I inspected the gangs of relief labourers, many thousand in number, who were working on the broad channel then in course of construction along the coast, in order to connect Madras with the canal system of the Kistna delta. This beneficent project was undertaken under the auspices of the Governor and now named after him "the Buckingham Canal." This is the district which is watered by the Pennaar river, and in which Sir Arthur Cotton designed a project whereby the waters of that river should be utilized for irrigation.

It then became necessary to inspect the districts which lay along the base of the Ghât mountains already mentioned.

Of these the first was that of North Arcot in which are situate the historic towns of Arcot and Vellore. In both these towns the walls, fosses, gateways, bastions and towers remain, enabling the student to follow the military events which happened there in the last century. The memory of such events ought to be perpetually kept alive in the minds of Indian officers, civil and military, in order that if required to dare and suffer for the empire, they may be encouraged by the knowledge of what men in the last century were inspired to do. In this neighbourhood there are many fine lakes for irrigation, but their waters were very low after the drought, and it was melancholy to see many rich fields lying temporarily wasted, being deprived of their customary irrigation. In the sandy beds of streams the cultivators dug wells from which they pumped up water for their thirsty fields; indeed they had improvised means of irrigation in various ways, and thus in the midst of the parched tracts there were green oases of crops in every direction. The district is interspersed with hills from the summit of which we could see the effects of dry weather upon a fertile and populous district, and also the efforts which the people were making to sustain their cultivation notwithstanding the general desolation. Many Hindu shrines of celebrity were situated in this district, and consequently there were half-famished pilgrims and devotees wandering about. It was difficult to manage these people, as they refused to become inmates of poor-houses, and preferred to run the risk of starvation rather than accept relief from the authorities.

In this part of the country hand-loom weaving is a very large manufacture, producing a great variety of beautiful fabrics and employing tens of thousands of hands. But the people in the main were now wearing out their old clothes instead of purchasing new, so the demand upon the manufacturers slackened. Wages were not forthcoming at all for many work-people, and those who still earned some wages, though much less than usual, found the earnings insufficient for their support when the price of food was more than doubled. The weavers and their families then came very largely upon State relief.

Here also cholera was rife, causing much mortality and arousing alarm in the public mind. Some idea of its prevalence may be gathered from the fact that in one day no less than five men in my own suite, Natives employed with the horses, were stricken by this malady.

The next district was that of Salem, of which much mention was made in the Life of Sir Thomas Munro, and which is situated near the base of the Mysore plateau. Indeed some of its outlying portions being on that plateau were suffering very severely from the drought. We ascended the fine group of the Shevaroy hills, which are near the town of Salem, and on the heights of which many coffee plantations have been established with success.

Travelling westwards I came to the districts of Coimbatore, which is the favourite among all the districts of the Madras Presidency and is one of the most interesting tracts in the country. It consists of a broad undulating plateau with the Nilgiri mountains on the north, the Palni group of hills on the south, and on the west the mountain pass called the Pâl Ghât, through which the railway runs from Madras on the Coromandel to Beypur on the Malabar coast. At other times I should have been tempted to pay at least a flying visit to the Nilgiri hills, so close at hand—to behold once more the tropical vegetation and finely engineered road of the Konûr pass—the botanic gardens of Utacamand—the coffee plantations of the Ochterlong valley with the blue Nilgiri peak and the glittering sea in the distance—the Cinchona gardens of Nîdawattam—the Wynaad hills rolled about like the waves of the ocean and interspersed with coffee culture. I had seen these things before, however, and now there was no leisure for aught save the inspection of hospitals, relief camps and gangs of labourers in thousands working upon roads.

On my journey thence to the southern peninsula, the first station at which I arrived was Trichinopoly, with the temple-crowned granite cliff rising straight out of the cultivated plain, and with the town nestling around the base of the rock. From the top a striking view is obtained of the rich valley of the rivers Câvery and Colerûn, with their banks fringed by avenues and groves, and the wooded island of Sri-rangam celebrated for its groups of Hindu temples with their tall gateways. Few places have been more enriched by Hindu art than this island of Sri-rangam. Though this district is not largely irrigated, it contains the head works of the canal system which has made Tanjore the best-irrigated district in the empire, perhaps in the world. Here again I should in other circumstances have been tempted to look once more at the antiquities of Sri-rangam, and the engineering works which have made Arthur Cotton and his school household words to millions—to visit Tanjore again with its grand pagodas, its fine city, and its canals spreading like veins and arteries through a province which they have converted into a garden. But these things I had known previously, and after enquiring into some outlying tracts which had suffered from drought, I passed rapidly through Tanjore without stopping to visit Negapatam on the sea-coast, where quantities of imported grain were being landed by the trade ; it being necessary to see whether these stores were rapidly carried into the interior by the railways.

Thence we proceeded to Madura, a district where drought had prevailed, in a degree which might prove serious unless timely showers should be vouchsafed in the spring. Though not so favourite a district as Coimbatore, Madura is second only to it in beauty and interest. Indeed the city of Madura is not equalled in southern India, being justly famed for the palace of Tirumal-Naik, with its colonnades, rotunda and banqueting-hall, the finest existing specimens of Hindu civil architecture—and also the temples with the perspective of carved figures down their grand corridors. These fanes are not desolate, but on the contrary are crowded with throngs of worshippers, sightseers, and men buying or selling jewelry, tinsel, flowers, fancy-work, in the precincts of the holy places. The old palace is being restored tastefully by the Madras Government, and fitted up for courts of justice and public offices. In this district are the Palni hills some 8000 feet above sea-level, affording a summer resort for Europeans; we ascended them by a road leading up the bed of a stream which presented a series of cascades. Thence we had a view of the numerous tanks for irrigation which seemed to dot the Madura district like little mirrors. Just then welcome showers were falling and we noticed the tanks gradually becoming filled.

The last district I visited was Tinnevelly, which forms the southern apex of the peninsula and reaches to Cape Comorin, the drought having extended even so far south as this. We travelled through parched tracts by rail to the port of Tuticorin, saw Cape Comorin itself in the distance, and then stopped for a short time at Tinnevelly, where once again the eye was relieved by the sight of well-watered fields and rich crops.

At Tinnevelly I made the acquaintance of the Reverend Mr. Sargent of the Church Missionary Society, who was about to proceed to Calcutta together with the Reverend Mr. Caldwell of the Society for the Propagation of the Gospel, in order that they both might be consecrated missionary Bishops. It was interesting to hear from Mr. Sargent the real effect which Christianity was producing upon the conduct and character of the Native Christians who were now forming an extensive community. I learnt much on this subject from many authorities, some of whom were, while others were not, connected with missions. The Indian Church was being gradually, perhaps in some places rapidly, organized; Native clergymen were ordained, deacons lay-readers and catechists appointed. For the maintenance of this organization, the Native Christians were raising funds according to their slender means. So numerous were the candidates for confirmation and the applicants for admission to the several grades of ecclesiastical service, and consequently so fast was the demand increasing for the exercise of episcopal functions, that the appointment of two missionary Bishops had become necessary, mainly for Madura and Tinnevelly. Subsequently, too, a third Bishop has been appointed for the neighbouring territory of Travancore. As we travelled through the country I met many Native Christians at different times and places, I also passed often by their villages. My conversation with them impressed me with their simple and absolute fidelity, their loyal feeling towards their European pastors, their resolute desire to transmit the faith unimpaired to their children. They seemed quite to feel that they had a religion and a religious system, which served as a light amidst the surrounding darkness, and the idea of keeping that lamp alight was familiar to their imagination. The ancestral sentiment, which in all secular matters has so much sway over them, immediately asserts itself in respect to the faith of their adoption. Many of them referred with pride to the conversion of their fathers or grandfathers, and regarded the early missionaries as heroes who vanquished error. Such feelings will doubtless grow in strength from generation to generation. These Christian communities are now becoming so extensive and wide-spread that an estimate of their character and conduct can be formed with confidence. On that subject I never heard but one opinion from magistrates, civil officers and independent observers, namely this, that these people are well-behaved, law-abiding, free from crime, temperate, harmless; that they are more regular in sending their children to school than their neighbours of other religions, a very important point; that they are amenable to the advice of their pastors, and attentive to religious ministrations; that they never cause scandals to arise, never apostatize, never compromise themselves with idolatrous practices, and yet never engage in feuds or even in disputes with their heathen neighbours. As for their inner life, let any person—who is acquainted with the practical ethics of Hinduism, not as gathered from sacred writings accessible only to the learned, but as displayed in the conduct of public worship and the effect of private example—contrast all that with the pure belief and the virtuous instruction under which they now live. He will then find it impossible to doubt the enormous effect morally and spiritually produced by Christianity on their minds and hearts. But in order to preserve an exact standard of comparison, it must be remembered that these communities, though growing fast, have not yet outgrown the personal control of the European missionary. Their social life and education have still the priceless advantage of European care. But it is not practicable, even if it were desirable, that such supervision should expand equally with the increase of the Christian population, and the desideratum is to train up a body of Native clergy imbued with the qualities which have rendered their European brethren so successful as they prove to be.

I visited at Dindigal, near Madura, the institution belonging to the Society for Christian Vernacular Education. This well-managed and efficient institution is supplying both books and teachers for the schools that have now become numerous.

I also met several Roman Catholic Bishops together with their clergy and visited their establishments, which are very influential and extensive in southern India. The manners, life and conversation of these Native Christians have characteristics similar to those just ascribed to the Protestants, though doubtless there must be considerable differences in religious system or practice. In their congregations there are included many East Indians who have by intermarriage become almost Natives, though retaining European names in memory of their extraction. Among the purely Native population, the Roman Catholics do not appear from the statistics to be making as much progress as the Protestants.

Having been instructed by the Government of India to visit Mysore, where also the drought had been very severe, I proceeded to Bangalore. We were most kindly received there by Mr. C. B. Saunders, who as Chief Commissioner was managing the State until the young Raja should come of age. Extensive reservoirs for water supply, and other public works, were being constructed near Bangalore for the employment of the able-bodied poor, and large establishments had been organized for feeding the infirm and the helpless. The relief of all sorts was being administered with humane care though with due regard to economy, and up to that time (April 1877) no considerable mortality had occurred. That was the third consecutive year of drought or bad seasons affecting at different times one part or other of the whole province. The people had borne up bravely against this protracted misfortune, and no considerable mortality had occurred. But it was felt that if unhappily a fourth season of failure should supervene, then grave emergencies must arise. This question for weal or woe could not solve itself till July, in other words, for two or three months to come; meanwhile hope was being cherished in the public mind owing to the seasonable spring showers which were then falling. After all their sufferings men trusted that there would be a termination with the fourth year, and felt as if "Deus dabit his quoque finem." But the sad event proved afterwards that the end was not to be yet, and that still another trial was to be piled on the heap of trouble.

While in the Mysore province, I visited Nandidûrg, a grand mass of scarped granite rising abruptly out of the cultivated plain. On its summit Sir Mark Cubbon, the well-known Commissioner of the province, used to dwell in the summer months during the latter years of his long incumbency. He left a name which is still a sound pleasantly familiar to the community, both European and Native, and he is revered as having possessed a sympathetic acquaintance with the notions, feelings, sentiments and prejudices of the Natives.

It thus became interesting to see the now deserted mansion where he lived, the study wherein he would hold long conversations with his Native friends, and the terrace wherefrom, as he paced up and down with halting gait or hesitating step, he would gaze wistfully over the broad territories which, after a lifetime of labour, he was about to quit for ever on account of his failing health.

After a very brief sojourn in Mysore I made a general report on the progress of the famine in southern India, and on the means which had been or were being employed for the administration of relief. The calamity had up to that time (the end of April 1877) been encountered by the Madras Government and its officers with devoted zeal and with a considerable, though not an unvarying, measure of success. The relief works had been established everywhere at suitable places, and the numerous gangs of labourers were kept in fair order and discipline, but an increase of professional supervision by experienced engineers was needed. Gratuitous relief was being administered to the infirm and helpless with liberality and care. In all branches of the relief work, the desideratum was European agency, as experience had abundantly shewn that for affairs of this nature the Government cannot depend on Native agency uncontrolled. The Madras Government had strenuously exerted itself to supply European agency accordingly, and to strengthen it as the distress increased. Still the question of the hour was whether the staff of English officers would or could be augmented sufficiently to cope with the famine, which was becoming more and more intense. There had been some mortality from starvation, as already explained, at Madras itself; not indeed that any inhabitants of the capital had starved, but that wanderers from a distance, taking refuge there, had succumbed. Elsewhere the mortality had up to that date been caused in a lesser degree from hunger, but largely from epidemic diseases, such as cholera and small-pox.

It was now necessary for me to quit the Presidency of Madras and proceed to that of Bombay. After my departure there occurred another calamity of season in southern India, the famine became much more intense and the gravest consequences ensued. But being without personal knowledge of those events I do not allude to them further.

The wasteful destruction of trees, woods or vegetation generally, and the necessity of forest conservancy being enforced more efficiently than before, formed common topics of conversation among the most thoughtful and earnest of the Madras officers. The hill ranges in the interior of the country had been utterly denuded of vegetation, and inroads were being made into the forests which still remained in some of the mountains. To these causes was in part attributed the disastrous irregularity of the seasons, whereby the drought in some months was succeeded by rainstorms and by inundation in others. Observant men declared that in many places a sensible deterioration of the climate had resulted from the partial clearance of the forests. Again, woods would be sometimes cut down which had retained or husbanded the moisture forming the supply of reservoirs for irrigation. Then the rain-water unrestrained would rush in superabundance to the reservoirs, silting them up or bursting their embankments ; the water having thus exhausted itself would cease to flow, and thereafter the supply would fail. All this was duly represented to the Madras Government and doubtless many remedial steps were taken. Still, by reason of the treeless state of many districts and the diminution of forests generally, there is danger lest the climatic conditions of southern India, including the greater part of the Madras Presidency and of Mysore, should undergo modifications productive of economic effects often adverse and occasionally disastrous. In respect to the prevention of drought and its train of evils, there is no subject more urgently demanding the attention of Government than the preservation of the forests.

In the social condition of the people in southern India, the most noteworthy feature was absolute preponderance of the Brahmin caste. Elsewhere Brahminical influence, however great, is moderated by that of other castes, for instance by the trading and literary castes in Bengal, by the Rajputs the Kayasths and Muhammadans in the North-western Provinces, the Sikhs in the

Panjab, the Mahrattas in the Central Provinces, the Parsis and the Jains in Bombay, and so on. In the central or southern parts of the Madras Presidency the Brahmins are supreme, the other castes being mentally and morally prostrate before them. In Madras, as in Behar or Bengal, the people amidst all the dread categories of misery consequent on the drought, evinced a courage which was not the less real from being humble and unostentatious. As the Duke of Buckingham justly said, their conduct was patience exemplified in life and death.

CHAPTER XX.

(1877-1880.)

THE BOMBAY PRESIDENCY.

Sir Philip Wodehouse Governor of Bombay—He administers relief of famine —Ruined city of Bîjapur—Plague of vermin—Partial indebtedness of the peasantry—Railways and canals for irrigation—Serious gang-robberies in the Deccan—Preservation of the forests—Native States of Kâthiawar—The Legislative Council—Character of the principal Natives—The University—National education—The High Court—The city of Bombay—Despatch of troops to Malta—The Bombay army—Rajputana and Central India—The province of Sind—The transport for the Army in southern Afghanistan—The railway from the Indus towards Candahar—My return to Bombay and departure for England.

On 1st May, 1877, I received charge of the Governorship of Bombay from Sir Philip Wodehouse, and Sir Ashley Eden succeeded me permanently as Lieutenant-Governor of Bengal. There is a considerable difference between the position of the Governor of a Presidency, and the Lieutenant-Governor of a province or a group of provinces in India. The Governor is the head of the Government of the Presidency, under which is the civil administration and the army, also several extraneous departments such as the guaranteed railways, and almost all State departments. He has two Councils, one for executive business, consisting of the Commander-in-Chief of the army and two members of the Civil Service, which is like a cabinet on a small scale, the other a Legislative Council constituted as described in previous chapters. The constitution of the Government is fixed by the Act of Parliament known as the Indian Councils Act. The Governor has the power by law to act on his own judgment in certain specified kinds of emergency, but ordinarily for every executive proceeding the decision is that of the Governor in Council. In other words, he must obtain the concurrence of a majority of his colleagues; though, as he has the casting vote, the concurrence of one colleague is sufficient. There is thus a considerable check upon him, which in the long run is of great advantage as preventing hasty or ill-considered changes of policy and practice. The Lieutenant-Governor, on the other hand, has no executive Council, though in the case of Bengal he has a Legislative Council: he therefore, in administration, acts and decides alone without any permanent check. He thus has a less varied sphere than the Governor, but within that sphere he is individually more potential. In Bengal, however, the civil administration is so vast that there may be doubt as to whether it ought to be placed in charge of a single individual without the assistance of a Council.

At this time the famine in the Bombay Presidency had been successfully encountered by Sir Philip Wodehouse. I was well acquainted with all the proceedings, having been, as explained in the last chapter, deputed to visit the distressed districts. I therefore knew that, under my predecessor, the able-bodied had been judiciously employed, that the works to which their labour was applied were really useful, that a reasonably full task was exacted from them, that gratuitous relief was administered with discrimination to the infirm, that due precautions were taken to search out the helpless who might otherwise escape observation, and that generally the European supervision over the work was complete and effective. The strong sense, steady judgment and practical ability of Sir Philip Wodehouse had been well seconded by the Secretary, General (now Sir Michael) Kennedy of the Engineers. To sound professional knowledge Kennedy added a general aptitude for civil administrative affairs, and a disposition to cope resolutely and vigorously with emergencies. He continued to afford me the same aid which he had given to my predecessor, until he was appointed to a high position in the Madras Presidency.

The month of May had now set in with famine spreading over the Bombay Deccan just as it had over Behar and northern

Bengal in May 1874, that is, three years previously. The relief operations went on almost like clockwork, and the distress was relieved without any loss of life or other mishap occurring. The relief labourers were to be seen in many thousands building up mighty dams of earthwork, or excavating reservoirs whence irrigation was to be drawn, or digging out the channels of canals—thereby beginning works that should prevent the occurrence of famine in future.

One of the principal centres of these operations was the famous city of Bîjapur, formerly the capital of the Muhammadan kingdom which embraced the greater part of western India. The dome of the great mausoleum there is the largest in the world, and many of the ruins have imposing dimensions and an almost unique style of architecture. Here within the long shadows flung by the cupolas, the lofty minarets and towers, or underneath the overshadowing archways, were assembled tens of thousands of infirm people to receive each man his dole of food, or of relief labourers to take their wages. Or again, a still greater multitude would be mustered in order that any change in their physical aspect for the better or for the worse might be noted. The masses of distressed humanity gathered together, in the midst of the stately ruins, suggested many strange reflections.

At that time plans and estimates were being made for restoring many of these old buildings at Bîjapur so far as to refit them for use. The ancient hall of audience was to become a judicial court crowded with suitors, not for favour as of yore but for justice, the palace chambers were to be converted into public offices, the war ministry into a central police station. More particularly the old waterworks, for which the place was originally famed, were to be rehabilitated, the channels blocked with débris were to run again with water, the shattered reservoirs to be refilled, the broken fountains to play once more. The idea was the same as that which was being so judiciously carried into effect by the Madras Government at Madura, as explained in the last chapter.

The periodical rains descended propitiously in June, and

till the middle of July the prospect was favourable. Then the rain were suspended for a while during a critical part of the season throughout western India, and fears were renewed. These apprehensions grew fast into alarm, when news came daily that the rains had ceased in southern India, that the danger in the Madras Presidency had become aggravated, that drought had spread throughout the North-western Provinces the Panjab, and most of the larger Native States, that, in short, the whole empire was threatened, with the exception of Bengal, Behar, Orissa and British Burma. For several weeks the prospect continued gloomy, and there was more real apprehension of national disaster from famine than at any time within the last two or three generations. Previously when famine had visited some parts of the empire, there had been abundance in others, no fear had been felt for the total supply of food within the country, and no thought entertained of importing grain from foreign countries. But now, with the contingency of general failure, men began to enquire anxiously whether sufficient quantities of food could ever be imported from abroad for the teeming millions of India. The possibility of any such importation, too, was diminished by the grave fact that there was then a severe famine in the northern half of China. Meanwhile the grain trade was more active than ever, the railways were overworked with the transport of food supplies to southern India, and for a time the general traffic, that is, the transport of all articles save food grains, had to be suspended, in order that the entire resources of the lines might be devoted to the relief of famine, whereby inevitable sacrifices were imposed on the merchants. The servants of the Great Indian Peninsula Railway Company fulfilled all the behests of Government with the most commendable zeal. We seized the opportunity of constructing a chord line of railway by Ahmednagar in the Deccan, in order to relieve the overburdened railways.

It was at this time that the Governor-General, Lord Lytton, left his summer residence at Simla and journeyed to southern India, in order to personally examine the relief operations, and support the Madras Government in such measures as might be deemed necessary for meeting the aggravated emergency. He stopped on his way for a short time at Poona, the head-quarters of the Bombay Government. It was then that General (afterwards Sir Michael) Kennedy was transferred from Bombay to Madras for service in the relief operations of southern India.

At last as autumn was beginning, the rains returned in time indeed to avert destruction, but not until much irreparable damage had been done. But the rainfall was now unseasonably heavy and protracted, the ground became excessively moist at the fall of the year, the chills and damps produced fever in an epidemic form, and many thousands, who had been saved by the Government from starvation for all those weary months, were perishing from malignant fever. Nevertheless the crops were gathered, though the people were often in impaired health.

In the following year (1878) the periodical rains were late throughout western India, and were scanty or precarious in several of the districts which had been recently distressed. But again they came copiously in autumn, and in many places the crops were abundant. Now, however, a new plague appeared in the shape of rats by myriads. The mediæval stories of rats in the subterranean buildings of Europe, or in the "maüse-thurm" of Bishop Hatto in the Rhine, were quite feeble in comparison with the strange reality of this vermin in the Deccan. These creatures laid waste not only acres but square miles of flourishing crops; they ate the grain to satiety and ingeniously stored the rest in the holes which they burrowed. The peasants often extracted the grain from its concealment, and thus recovered it for human use. The efforts of Government were immediately directed to inducing the people to combine *en masse* for the extermination of the rats, which were accordingly destroyed literally by millions. Then the periodical rains came and drowned all the vermin that remained.

This succession of plagues, from drought, damp, malaria, and vermin, seriously affected the health or condition of the people in several districts of the Deccan, and inflicted blows on their prosperity from which they can hardly recover for several years to come. The peasant proprietors bore their misfortunes with admirable fortitude; and the punctuality with which they strove to discharge their fiscal obligations to the State was exemplary.

Such misfortunes as these caused us to reconsider the question whether anything could be done by legislation to mitigate the evils which arose from the indebtedness of some classes among the peasantry of the Deccan. There had in 1873 been some agrarian riots in the Deccan, the peasants attacking the money-lenders. This untoward affair was investigated by a special Commission; from their report, and from the evidence they collected, it was found that the indebtedness was limited in extent, affecting only one-third of the peasantry—though even that proportion was serious. Owing to the circumstances as set forth in the previous chapter XII. the peasantry had become extravagant in reference to their normal condition, and had learnt to live beyond their humble income. They had begun to avail themselves of the facility for borrowing afforded by the newly established property in land, which offered available security. The money-lenders had taken advantage thereof to enrich themselves and enslave their creditors by bonds for sums composed in some part of the original principal, but in most of usurious interest. There was careful consideration whether the land revenue settlement (already mentioned in chapter XII.) was in any way defective. No particular fault, however, was found in a system of which the general merits were acknowledged on all hands. On the whole the Government did not see its way clearly to legislating, and deprecated the making of attempts by authority to remedy economic defects which had their origin in the character of the people and the circumstances of the country.

Viewing the case, however, by the light of the misfortunes just described, I and my advisers thought that there were certain palpable faults in the existing law and procedure, and that in consequence of these defects, the ignorant debtors became morally bondsmen to their educated creditors. We accordingly proposed certain changes which would effectually check the evil, without, on the other hand, destroying the credit of the peasant proprietor in the money market, or preventing him from obtaining temporary loans, which he must need just as reasonably as the English farmer needs accommodation from the bank. These proposals touched the general laws relating to civil justice, and therefore required the approval of the Government of India before being introduced to the legislature. They did not receive approval, however, and subsequently a draft bill was prepared in consultation with us, and in due course was passed into law by the Governor-General's Legislative Council. This law did all, and more than all, we ever proposed respecting procedure—perhaps even too much—but failed in our judgment to remedy the fault in the substantive law. So the matter stood at the time of my departure from India, and subsequently some further modifications of the new Act have been contemplated or are being made In the end, some sort of remedy and some degree of improvement in respect to admitted evils will be doubtless attained.

The peasant proprietors of the Deccan deserve well of the State; in hardihood, endurance and industry they are not surpassed by any section of the Indian people. They are little addicted, in this generation, to the military service which their forefathers liked so well. Their preference is for remaining in their fields and homesteads, as agriculture, despite its drawbacks and uncertainties, is regarded as the better employment. If they were to enlist now as of yore, they would prove to be among the good soldiers of the empire. They are often ready to supplement their little income by carrying in their carts the produce for traders, and even by labouring for a few weeks on the public works. During the famine, they for the most part not only sustained themselves, but also paid their land revenue with commendable punctuality. And they comparatively seldom applied for aid from those who had the dispensing of relief among the distressed.

The weak point in the agriculture of the Deccan is the want of irrigation; and yet the configuration of the country supplies the means of supplying the want, if only enough capital shall be laid out by the State on that object. A great impulse was given to beneficent enterprise in this direction by the results of the drought in 1877. Canals were already drawn from a great reservoir near Poona, called Lake Fife after the eminent engineer who designed it. These canals were now extended, a new canal from the Nîra river was begun, and another near Gokak projected; at least seven large reservoirs, having the dimensions of lakes, were in part excavated, of which some were nearly finished. While the famine lasted we obtained imperial funds for these works, as the distressed people were employed thereon. When it ceased the grants were discontinued, but we laid before the Government of India a fresh scheme with the able assistance of Colonel Merriman R.E. our chief engineer for irrigation. A certain capital outlay was to be incurred by the State in a cycle of years for the completion of all the irrigation works which had been designed. We then proposed to guarantee the interest on this outlay from provincial resources, augmented by a very light cess to be laid on the land for this special purpose. Effect was not, however, given to these proposals, and the works were carried on from time to time, with many interruptions, whenever funds were obtainable. Without some financial foundation such as that which we suggested, the progress of these works is unavoidably precarious.

Similarly the occasion of these misfortunes was utilized for the extension of the railway system in the Deccan. The chord line by Ahmednagar has been already mentioned; though constructed partly as a temporary line, still it was kept open. Another line by Bîjapur, already described, was begun; and a third from the coast south of Bombay was proposed. We desired that the coast line should start from the British port of Karwar, but ultimately it was decided that the railway should be taken inland from the Portuguese port of Goa, by reason of the assistance derivable from the Portuguese Government.

If our proposal to base upon local taxation the finance of works, intended for the prevention of famine, had been accepted by the Government of India, we should have included railways as well as canals in the scheme.

It was the distress, thus "long drawn out" through several

seasons, that was really the proximate, though not the original, cause of what became known as the Deccan dacoities of 1879. The crime of "dacoity," being merely robbery, would be ordinarily regarded as a deed of violence and nothing more. But in the Deccan, which is the heart of the country, it is apt to assume a political significance. It was the weapon whereby the Mahrattas of old encountered their Muhammadan conquerors, and with which they would encounter the British to-morrow, if they had the chance. The mass of the people are not disloyal, but there is more of national feeling among the peasantry there than elsewhere; and among the Brahmins, quite a dominant class, many are restless, ambitious, discontented. The Brahmins indeed are not all disaffected, many of them are doubtless good and loyal. But it were vain to shut our eyes to the fact that there are elements of mischief at work which can hardly be eliminated by any policy which the British Government may reasonably be expected to pursue. If it be true that national character is formed partly by physical surroundings, climate and scenery, partly also by historical associations,—then any one who sees the Deccan, and reads its history, will not have far to go in order to discover the reasons why the political tendencies there demand vigilance on the part of the British Government. The events in different parts of the world, wherein the British empire was concerned during 1878-9, had lent a spark of excitement to ignite the combustible materials existing in the Deccan. So when gang-robbery, under known leaders with a certain sort of organization, suddenly appeared, it became necessary for us to take precautions with military force. The Western Ghât mountains run through the territory from end to end, with fertile valleys on either flank. From their summits the robbers swooped down on the villages, carrying off the plunder into fastnesses among the hills; in some cases fights ensued and innocent blood was shed. Emboldened by casual success, they threatened even the highroads near Poona, the capital, and issued a proclamation in the name of a Brahmin leader, declaring that their proceedings were really directed against the Government. The movement was within a few weeks effectually put down, owing to the exertions of the European police officers backed by military force, and its leaders expiated their folly and wickedness, some by death in action or on the gallows, others by penal servitude. Their ignorant followers, peasants of humble caste but of hardihood and courage, were actuated by the hope of gain in times when employment and labour had proved scanty. Still, the readiness with which they answered the mandate of their shadowy and half-mysterious chief, like bees hiving, the apathetic and unsatisfactory behaviour of the people in many villages, and the sympathy known to be felt if not openly evinced by many of the upper classes, were grave circumstances demanding reflection on our part. The conduct of Major Daniell of the police, both as regards personal prowess and detective skill, entitled him to the acknowledgments not only of the Government, but of the community.

An incendiary fire, malignantly planned, broke out in the old palace of the Mahratta sovereigns in Poona just at the time when the gang-robberies were at their height. In a few hours this beautiful building, built mainly of teak wood, perished by the flames; and thus was lost a structure unsurpassed in its wood carvings and in an original style rarely equalled. There was indeed much melancholy in the thought that now the two great monuments of Mahratta palatial architecture had been burnt, one at Nagpur (already mentioned in chapter XI.) by accident, the other at Poona by the hand of Mahratta criminals. If it should seem almost incredible that any Mahratta could be found "with soul so dead" as to destroy such a building, we must remember that at the time it was used by the British Government for public offices. Thus the deed was perpetrated for the sake of doing mischief to the Government, and must have had instigators undetected, who were far more important than the wretched man who was caught and punished. This event occurring at the same time as the gang-robberies outside was certainly fraught with some political significance.

As there are few parts of India more worthy of the attention of politicians than the Deccan, I was careful to inspect the

Western Ghât mountains which form the backbone of that region. Any one who tries "rerum cognoscere causas" will perceive that it was the existence of these mountains which enabled the Mahrattas to overthrow the Mogul empire. The lairs retreats and strongholds, in this mountain range, sustained Mahratta resistance, and baffled the armaments of the Afghan horse or the artillery of the Great Mogul. With the history book in my hand, I used to scan the old fortress lifting its head among the surrounding peaks, clamber up its steep sides, mount the jagged and broken steps to the postern, admire the trap-rock precipices and the ledges on giddy heights, mark the defences skilfully constructed for the warfare of that age, note the glories of the landscape prospect, and observe how completely the position would command the valleys lying far below or the passes by which we had come. Thus the political events which had occurred in this scene, and the combinations arising from them, became intelligible with a clearness which reading alone could never afford. Such fortresses were not few in number, but were dotted at brief intervals along the range for 400 miles, and made up a military line which the Muhammadans never succeeded in effectually breaking or in permanently wresting from the Mahrattas. The case is different now, for the British Government has pierced the heretofore inaccessible range by many well-engineered lines of road with zigzags and gradients, by which not only the wheeled traffic of commerce but also troops, guns and munitions can pass. Again, the mountains have already been crossed by two lines of railway, and will yet be crossed by a third. Thus the range has been deprived of its old resources for sustaining rebellious resistance on a large scale. But it is still capable of assisting mischief of a lesser sort, and the Government should ever strive to develop communications across it, remembering that every roadway opened in this region adds to our political strength.

The marching along the hills afforded ample opportunity of studying the forests. Additional measures for preserving them were being adopted under the recently enacted Forest Act, with the zealous supervision of Mr. A. Shuttleworth the Conservator.

Beyond the main range of the Western Ghâts, the Deccan was denuded of its vegetation as completely as the most treeless parts of the Madras Presidency, already described in chapter XIX. Within the range, however, many forests happily remained and were being diligently conserved. The cattle-grazing which ordinarily proved injurious to the forests was being restricted to particular "blocks" or areas, so that the vegetation might spring up on the remaining areas. Here were perceived all the ordinary reasons for preserving forests, the husbanding of the vegetation as a part of the national wealth, the permanent supply of the timber and fuel markets, the improvement of climatic conditions as affecting the regularity or irregularity of the periodical rains, the retention of moisture in a land where aridity prevails for several months in the year. In addition to these, however, there was a special reason in that from the mountains spring many rivers or streams which had been or were to be utilized for the storage of water in large quantities for irrigation. If the vegetation be preserved, the waters near the sources are retained to supply the canals; but if it be destroyed the waters become exhausted or evaporated and the canal must be left unsupplied. The destruction in the past of some forests, and the wasteful use of others, must be regretfully accepted as a proof that formerly neither the Government nor its officers adequately appreciated the value of scientific forestry. The Natives have been wholly blind to the subject, and find difficulty in opening their eyes to it now. Whatever privileges of a definite character they possess will be secured to them by law, whatever wood is needed for agriculture or domestic purposes they are welcome to take. But they often want more than that, and seek to enter forests in order that they may lop or fell, not for their own use but for the purpose of exportation or of sale. This they have never been entitled to do without control—nevertheless they often succeed in doing it by pretending that the wood is wanted not for the market but for themselves. If this were to be permitted in the future, as it has too often been allowed in the past, then the exhaustion of the forests would be only a question of time. The private forests are by the terms of the land revenue settlement recognized as the property of the people. The public forests, which comprise most of the tracts that are well stocked with timber, are by law under the control of the State. The object is to treat the vegetation on the same principle as that which is applied to money by a financier, who takes care of the capital and lives on the interest. The State forester is always cutting wood, large or small, and sending it to market, whereby the public really draws interest from the store of forest wealth. But he is careful to leave enough for reproduction, the decrement from felling is replaced by a corresponding increment from fresh growth, and the corpus of the forest, as representing principal, is preserved. The public, however, if left to itself would carve and hack the woods and forests without any care for reproduction or any regret for wastage, in the end destroying uselessly as well as consuming, and would treat the national wealth just as a spendthrift would treat his money, who lived on the capital for momentary convenience without thought for interest thereafter.

The scenery of the Western Ghât mountains leaves a series of pictures imprinted on the tablets of the memory—the basaltic and plutonic cliffs rearing their heads wreathed in mist, the marvellous stratification of the rocks, the long layers of indurated lava; the fortresses crowning scarped precipices and standing as silent yet most eloquent witnesses of daring deeds in times past; the deluging rainfall followed by cascades bursting forth and leaping down the hillsides; the viaducts with lofty piers spanning deep ravines, the roadways blasted out of the solid rock, the interminable strings of laden carts creaking and straining throughout the moonlight hours in this wild scenery; the distant ocean descried from summits and glistening under the light of the declining sun; the forests of the broad-leaved teak, of the arrowy trees used for masts of ships, the terminalia some with black and rough bark, others with smooth bark, arranging their trunks like a row of marble columns on the water's edge.

Between the base of this great range and the sea, lies the

littoral tract named the Concan, which being comparatively free from vicissitudes of season is flourishing better than the Deccan. The redundancy of population makes this tract the best recruiting ground in western India, and the infantry of the Bombay army is chiefly drawn from it. I had to visit the many harbours which are formed by the indentations of the coast, to arrange marine surveys, to provide accommodation for the country boats, and to note where navigable estuaries were being silted up with the débris carried by rivers that flow through hills denuded of their forests.

The most prosperous division of western India is Guzerat, an alluvial tract lying along the coast north of Bombay; which is not only the best part of the Bombay Presidency, but also one of the richest tracts in the Indian empire. With it the name of Mr. Theodore Hope (now Financial Secretary to the Government of India) is honourably associated. The trunk line of railway running through it has been already described in the previous chapter XI. Branches were being carried from this line to the outlying tracts which produce cotton and other exportable articles. One of the largest towns in this tract is Surat, which was famous in the early days of the East India Company, but has within the last century become commercially quite secondary to Bombay. For many years past a discontented spirit has existed in this city, and its annals have been more than once disfigured by the records of disturbance. Now in 1878 we had to levy the license-tax, imposed by a law which the Government of India had enacted for the whole empire. Without any reason beyond this, that the tax was disliked by the townspeople, the mob of persons not touched by the tax, doubtless at the instigation of some among the tax-payers, rose in insurrection very early one spring morning, attacked the railway station, the telegraph office, and other public departments in the city. They would have proceeded to burn the houses of the European civil officers had they not been stopped by a body of Native troops, but they stoned the soldiers and retired only when fired upon, and after blood had been shed. The political excitement of the time, extending as it did to so many parts of the world, was one out of several causes which gave birth to this disturbance.

This occurrence ought to be considered together with the affair, already described, of the Deccan gang-robberies and the Poona fire. These are weak points, in our tenure of the Indian empire, which ought to be remembered when the many strong points in that tenure are summed up. They may also be cited as instances shewing that the British Government must maintain its political prestige undiminished in the eyes of the Indian people.

Adjoining Guzerat is the peninsula of Kâthiawar, which is occupied by a cluster of Native States. When Foreign Secretary, I had seen many reports whereby it was manifest that these States had long remained in an unsettled and lawless condition which retarded their material progress, despite their natural advantages. I now found that the turbulence had been overcome and disorder composed, that the chiefs lived in neighbourly amity and combined in peaceful federation for preserving order from one end of the peninsula to the other. The richer among them were devoting a part of their income to works of public utility, roads and communications. The result was manifest in cultivation expanding, inland traffic increasing, harbours crowded with vessels, exports growing, and the cotton becoming a source of untold wealth. An excellent college had been established for the education of the sons and relations of the chiefs. The territory had recently suffered from drought with its attendant scarcity, and had narrowly escaped through timely showers from a much worse disaster. Use was being made of this dearly bought experience in order to promote the construction of railways. Some progress was made at once with the work, leaving still much to be done, which will doubtless be accomplished in due course. My immediate predecessors, Sir Philip Wodehouse and Sir Seymour Fitzgerald, had bestowed special attention to these Native States. Among the Political Agents, in the peninsula, Colonel Richard Hart Keatinge, distinguished in other fields of duty besides this, and Mr. J. B. Peile, were conspicuous. The position of Kâthiawar is a signal instance of what may be effected in Native States by political management, firm and persevering, yet judicious and conciliatory.

The course of internal affairs in the Presidency was regulated very much by legislation. The establishment of the Legislative Council for Bombay has been already mentioned in chapter XII. The Council was performing its duties with much efficiency in my time; many elaborate Acts were passed, such as the consolidation of all the revenue regulations, the laws relating to canals of irrigation, the rules concerning tenant-right in the Concan, the amendment of the Acts regarding excise, municipalities, and other subjects. The Native members were zealous in representing the interests of their countrymen. A prominent part in the debates (conducted in English) was taken by Vishwanath Narain Mandlik, already mentioned in chapter XII.; and he held much the same position as that ascribed in chapter XVIII. to Kristo Das Pal in the Bengal Council. He was a man exemplary in private life, and possessed great talent for public affairs; he was a Concani Brahmin of that class which once was the mainspring of the Mahratta empire; he enjoyed the confidence and respect of his countrymen, and altogether was one of the ablest Natives I have ever known. Bêchardas Ambaidas, though he usually gave silent votes, watched the proceedings with keen interest; he was a Guzerati banker, of the old school indeed, but a friend of education and disposed to observe closely the effects of the new civilization. There were two Parsi gentlemen in the Council, namely Dosabhoy Framji, one of the most faithful, trustworthy and experienced among the servants of Government; and Sir Jamsetji Jijibhoy, who had recently acceded to his title, and was a young man of excellent promise. The Muhammadan members were, first, Muhammad Ali Roghè, a man of the new school, acute in perception, frank and outspoken in manner, acquainted with foreign countries, and disposed to criticize the British Government; then Syud Idrûs of Surat, a good example of the old school, courtly in language and manner, a man of proved fidelity, esteemed by me as one of the most loyal Muhammadans I ever met.

Besides those who served in the Council, there were several eminent Natives, namely Sir Mangaldas Nathubhai (already mentioned in chapter XII.); Balwant Rao Venaik Shastri, a loyal and enlightened man, a chief of rank in the Deccan and the son of a father who lost his life in what was virtually the British cause; Nanabhai Haridas, a judicial officer of high character and ability, who was more than once appointed to act as a judge of the High Court; Atmaram Pandarang, a medical practitioner, distinguished for the wise liberality of his views, who served for a year as Sheriff of Bombay; Manockji Cursetji (previously noticed in chapter XII.), who laudably persevered in his efforts for promoting female education, and Nouroji Fardûnji, a municipal commissioner who became, as it were, a tribune of the city people.

The University was answering fully the expectations with which it had been established; its senate comprised all the highest talent, literary and scientific, that existed in western India. Its best interests had suffered, in the same manner as the Calcutta University, from the insufficiency of the attention allowed to physical science. After careful discussion the senate decided to grant degrees in science after the model of those granted by the London University, whereby an impulse was given to scientific studies among the Natives. Mr. James Gibbs (member of the Bombay Government) and Mr. Raymond West (a Judge of the High Court) were successively Vice-Chancellors; the Governor himself being the Chancellor, while Mr. Peterson was the learned and able Registrar. The Elphinstone College at Bombay was under the care of a distinguished Principal, Mr. William Wordsworth. This College and the Deccan College at Poona being the only affiliated institutions, it was decided to establish a third College at Ahmedabad for the Guzerat province, with the help of public-spirited Natives. The commercial and agricultural depression of the time affected education generally; the number of those seeking the superior and the middle-class instruction remained stationary; while primary education declined for a time, the first instance of retrogression as yet experienced in western India, breaking the continuity of progress. A real beginning however was made with practical instruction in agriculture, partly through the experienced aid of Mr. Robertson of Madras, whose services were lent to us temporarily by the Governor (the Duke of Buckingham). The Natives of Guzerat evinced a remarkable aptitude for this important branch of study. Much progress was made with the instruction in civil engineering and in science generally, under the able management of Dr. T. Cooke.

The School of Art was for a time supervised by Major Charles Mant, R.E., during the absence of Mr. Griffith an accomplished artist. Major Mant had a genius for architecture; he designed many important structures in various parts of India and completed some of them. His premature death caused a great loss to the public service.

Several Medical Schools were established in the interior of the country—separate from the large Medical College at Bombay—mainly through the exertions of Dr. J. G. Hunter, the Surgeon-General, and Dr. T. Beatty; both these gentlemen were ornaments of their profession, having zeal and benevolence commensurate with their learning and talents.

The sanitary department was subjected to a severe strain owing to the plagues and epidemics already mentioned; it was efficiently conducted by Mr. Lumsdaine, and then by Dr. Hewlett a most meritorious officer who rendered signal services in the relief of famine.

In 1879 the Indian Famine Commission held some of its sittings at Bombay. Colonel Richard Strachey was President; among the members were Mr. James Caird (from England) and Mr. H. S. Cunningham. The Bombay Presidency was represented in the Commission by Mr. J. B. Peile and Mahadeo Wasudeo Barvê, Minister of the Kolhapur State, a Native gentleman of the highest character and attainments, indeed one of the best Mahratta Brahmins I have ever known.

The maintenance of good relations between the Government and the High Court of Judicature is very important for the public well-fare, and happily those relations were excellent. The Chief Justice Sir Michael Westropp, having formerly served as Advocate-General, had great experience regarding the needs and interests of the community, and applied his high attainments not only to the adjudication of complex and difficult causes, but also to the aid of the general administration.

Bishop Mylne, besides supervising the ecclesiastical establishments in his See, laboured with signal success in the cause of Missions to the heathen.

The city of Bombay itself, with its vast and varied interests and its fast-growing importance, claimed constant attention. The police (under the able management of Sir Frank Souter, the Commissioner) was a really efficient body and popular withal. Allusion has been made in the previous chapter XII. to the municipal improvements effected there under Sir Bartle Frere's administration. The public structures, begun or designed then, were advanced towards completion, and although these shewed a goodly array, still not a year passed without several new buildings being undertaken, as the demands of an advancing community in a great seaport are incessant. The stream of Native munificence continued to flow, though somewhat diminished in comparison with former times by reason of the agricultural and commercial depression consequent on the famine. A marble statue of the Queen had been erected by the Native community on the esplanade. Sir Albert Sassoon presented to the city a bronze equestrian statue of the Prince of Wales, in memory of the visit of His Royal Highness. The new "Sailors' Home," built partly through the munificence of Khunde Rao, Gaekwar of Baroda, in honour of the visit of His Royal Highness the Duke of Edinburgh, had become a noble institution. The new wet dock, accommodating the largest ships, was named "The Prince's Dock" because the first stone of it was laid by the Prince of Wales. This fine work was designed by Thomas Ormiston as part of a scheme for improving the whole foreshore of the harbour. The project was first undertaken in Sir Bartle Frere's time, as already mentioned in chapter XII., by the Elphinstone Reclamation Company. Under the administration of his successor, the Right Honourable Sir Seymour Fitzgerald, the property of the company was purchased by the Government, the scheme was enlarged, the wet dock undertaken, and a harbour trust established. Progress with this great work was made under his successor, Sir Philip Wodehouse. In my time the dock and its subsidary works were finished and opened for traffic. It was found, however, that neighbouring docks which were private property interfered with the general management of the foreshore; therefore these also were purchased for the State, and the constitution of the harbour trust was further developed after the model of the trust which succeeds on a much larger scale for the Mersey at Liverpool. The Vehar lake for supplying Bombay with water, already mentioned in chapter XII., being found insufficient for the growing community, the formation of an additional lake was undertaken in the time of my predecessors; the work was completed in my time, and the water was conducted to the city at a higher level than before. Much had already been done at great cost and labour for the drainage of the city; still a mass of sewage entered the harbour to the great detriment of all concerned. So additional drainage works were undertaken for diverting the sewage to a quarter where it would not be hurtful.

The elective principle had been introduced into the municipality of Bombay by Sir Seymour Fitzgerald and established by Sir Philip Wodehouse, and I found it to operate advantageously. The citizens and ratepayers exercised their franchise judiciously, electing good and able men, Europeans and Natives, to serve on the municipal corporation.

The English Press at Bombay was strong in talent; Mr. J. M. Maclean of the "Bombay Gazette" prepared an admirable handbook of the city; Mr. Grattan Geary of the "Times of India" was an author as well as a traveller.

The resources of Bombay were tested when in 1878 an expeditionary force was despatched to Malta. Within fourteen days after the receipt of orders from the Governor-General in Council (Lord Lytton), the Bombay Government (of which Sir Charles Staveley, then Commander-in-Chief, was a member) engaged 48,000 tons of merchant shipping then in the harbour, despatched 6000 men and 2000 horses, with two months' supplies of provisions and six weeks' supply of water. They all arrived at their destination in good condition, and after some months returned equally well; still the risks attending the navigation of the Red Sea, with sailing ships towed by steamers, caused us anxiety. Signal service was rendered by the Quartermaster-General's Department under Colonel Burrows and Major (now Brigadier-General) Hogg, also by the Marine Department under Lieutenant Searle.

During the next year, 1879, the Commission, appointed to enquire into the army expenses in India, addressed many questions to us regarding the numbers and distribution of the Bombay army, especially the Native forces. In these deliberations I received great assistance from the then Commander-in-Chief, General H. Warre. We were obliged to deprecate any reduction of the Native troops, in reference to the vast area requiring to be occupied at its strategic points by military strength, and the many elements of danger existing in western India. All I saw and heard of these troops, in the territories beyond the Indus and elsewhere, gave me a very favourable impression of their discipline, fortitude and endurance.

With the help of Admirals Macdonald, Cockburn and Gore Jones, successively, the defences of the Bombay harbour were maintained in provisional safety.

The Volunteer movement made progress during these years. From among the servants of the Great India Peninsula Railway Company a strong and effective battalion was formed; a lesser though also an effective force was embodied from among the employés of the Bombay, Baroda and Central India Railway. A new battalion, of considerable numbers and efficiency, was obtained from among the European community of Bombay.

I cannot omit to mention with grateful regard the names of my colleagues in Council, James Gibbs (now a member of the Government of India), Lionel Ashburner and Edward Ravenscroft. Among our secretaries C. Gonne, J. B. Peile, J. Nugent and Colonel Macdonald rendered us special assistance. It is truly said that in the interior of Indian provinces the Magistrates and Collectors are really the local governors. Among this important class of officers, the most notable of that day in the Bombay Presidency were G. Pedder, W. Propert, G. Norman, E. H. Percival, J. G. Moore, A. Macdonald, G. F. Sheppard, J. B. Richey. Nor can I forget to mention the good service of C. Pritchard, the Collector of Customs.

I several times visited the Baroda State, and especially on the occasion of the young Gaekwar's marriage, and witnessed all the good work of Raja Sir Madhava Rao the Minister. The State was under the care of the Governor-General's Agent, Mr. Philip S. Melvill.

Next I visited the stations in Central India and Rajputana, which are held by troops of the Bombay army. The first of these was Mhow, near Indore, the capital of the Maharaja Holkar, who has been already mentioned in chapter XIII. I had visited this place in former days, passing by the fortress of Asirgarh, the key of the Satpura range, holding the passage between Bombay and Calcutta, crossed the Nerbadda at points where its rock-bound bed is overlooked by temples, spires and palaces, and then rode up the steep road of the Vindhya range to Mandû, a ruined Muhammadan city. Here, according to an authentic tradition, a tigress with her cubs was found in what once had been the apartment of queens, and I, while sketching the remains of an old reservoir, heard a tiger roaring at sunset on the other side of the water. Now, however, the journey was rapid and easy, as we travelled by railway and admired the engineering works on the flank of the mountain. After visiting the several military cantonments we passed through Oodeypur, famous for its lake surrounded by the tasteful structures which the Rajput princes and priests love to build. The wooded islets in this lake, with their edifices reflected in the water, are objects in which nearly all the natural and artificial beauties characteristic of India will be found. The Rana has the bluest of all the blue blood in Rajputana, that land of Indian kings in the heroic age. He had just been inducted into his responsibilities after being educated under European supervision. He had the good manner of the old school combined with that of the new. His appearance was prepossessing, as might have been expected from his lineage. We visited in this neighbourhood Chitôrgarh, a citadel on an isolated hill famed for its peculiar yet beautiful structures called "towers of victory." There we marked the spots where the Muhammadan besiegers erected batteries, sapped, undermined, stormed, where the Rajputs, staunch to the bitter end, fell almost to a man, king, chiefs, soldiers, retainers, and where their women killed themselves to avoid falling into the hands of the victors. We made the acquaintance of the Ulwar chief, a promising young man, fond of manly pursuits. Several times I met Faiz Muhammad, next after Salar Jang, the best Muhammadan administrator whom this generation has beheld. Returning to Bombay we visited Abu, fondly called "majestic Abu" by the men of western India—observed the grand masses of granite, the walks and rides frequented by Tod, by Henry Lawrence, and other eminent men of the past, and the sanitarium where the children of Europeans are brought up in health and vigour.

The affairs, arising out of the second Afghan war, compelled me several times to visit Sind. Generally the sea voyage was preferred; once, however, I journeyed thither by the desert route, galloping along the seashore bestrewn with myriads of dead locusts, or jolting on a camel's back up and down the sandy billows, with heights and hollows alternating, like the crest of waves and the trough of the ocean. Nothing can be more hopelessly hideous than the ordinary landscape of Sind, the expanse of undulated soil interspersed with scrub, the lands desolated by inundations and clothed with rank vegetation as with a ragged garment. For several months in the year even the canals are waterless, and look like extensive trenches. Karachi, the capital on the sea-coast, has one of the best climates in all British India, and with its harbour, its public buildings, its streets and its municipal arrangements is worthy of its position as a rising seaport. For the harbour works the public owes much to the labours of Mr. Price, the Engineer. But the heat of Upper Sind is truly terrific, exceeding that of the most torrid regions in the East. Nevertheless, the European officers, who serve there, love the province; nowhere in the empire is local attachment more intense than in Sind. Apparently the Indus permeating the country from end to end, rolling down in mighty volume the drainage from Himalayan and trans-Himalayan regions, and bestowing at least a partial fertility upon rainless regions—affects the imagination of educated men. The traditions survive of Alexander and his matchless Macedonians; the name of Nearchus, the navigator, is still a living memory. Every desert, too, has its oasis; as the heat waxes, the waters are swollen from snows melted in far-off climes, the dry canals begin to fill, and are shaded by groves and avenues in the midst of a dreary land. There is one great lake, many square miles in extent, the surface being covered with aquatic plants and skimmed by water-fowl, the air at times almost darkened by the circling flights of birds. The Indus is generally "liber et exultans" amidst alluvial deposits; at one point only is its course cribbed and confined between low hills. There the town of Sakkar on one bank, of Rôri on the other, and the rocky island of Bakkar in mid-stream, make up one of the best pieces of river scenery in the empire—especially when illuminated. Elsewhere the river runs along the foot of the Lakki cliffs, along the side of which the railway is carried.

The Natives of Sind are Muhammadans, tall and broad in stature, but somewhat enfeebled in health, and neither long-lived nor prolific. Notwithstanding security and good government for more than a whole generation their numbers hardly increase, and remain scanty for so broad an area. Existence is probably harder for them than for any Indian race; they never know from one season to another whether the Indus will leave them high and dry or submerge them entirely; their lands are alternately enriched by deposits of silt, or torn up by destructive floods; during the summer they swelter in the ardent heat, in autumn they languish in the exhalations from the subsiding floods, in the winter they might regain vigour were it not that the sharp cold is biting and nipping to enervated frames. The tendency to pneumonia and pulmonary complaints is aggravated by the national habit of wearing cotton clothes; the man who may succeed in teaching them to wear woollen will be a benefactor of their race. Despite persistent and costly efforts, the survey and settlement operations are not so far advanced as in most parts of India. The cultivation in almost every part of the province depends upon the canals, many old and some new, laboriously maintained, supplied with water from the Indus, and spreading like veins and arteries throughout the country. To protect the channels great embankments were thrown up for many miles along the river-bank. With the improvement of these canals the name of Colonel Fife is honourably associated. Owing to the vagaries of the great river the injuries to the works are constant and prove disheartening to the engineers. Often after the completion of head works for irrigation, with much cost and trouble, a sweep of the Indus current will destroy them all, leaving a wearisome task to be repeated the next year.

Despite drawbacks and disadvantages, the administration of Sind begun by Sir Charles Napier, and carried on by his successors, especially Sir Bartle Frere, had comprised all the improvements ever introduced into the other Indian provinces which enjoyed far greater facilities and advantages. Under General John Jacob—a man of marvellous resource, self-denial, and persistency—the frontier, in respect to all its affairs, civil, political, military, had been managed in a manner honourable to the British name. He had been worthily succeeded by Sir Henry Green. In Sind Sir William Merewether was at this time the able and popular Commissioner. He was ultimately succeeded by Mr. Erskine, an excellent administrator. Among those who had spent their lives in the service of the province were Lambert, Dunsterville, Wallace, Haig, Crawford, all "soldier-civilians" as Sir Charles Napier would have called them.

Beyond the frontier of Sind lie the dominions of the Khan of Khelat. My visits to that territory from 1878 to 1880 were caused by the necessity of helping to provide transport for the army operating in southern Afghanistan, and of arranging for the construction of the railway from the Indus towards Candahar.

Owing to the severity of the climate, the inhospitable

character of the country, the difficulty of finding or laying in supplies of fodder, the dislike felt by the camel-drivers for the work, the climate alternating at different times and places between the extremes of heat and cold,—it happened that the losses of camels by death, and desertion on the line of march, were enormous. Not only did thousands of these animals perish from fatigue and hunger, but thousands also were driven away by their owners who deserted. At one time there was anxiety regarding the food supplies of the army, though it was afterwards dispelled by the vigorous arrangements of the Commander, Sir Donald Stewart. The Government of India decided, for the sake of safety, to store reserves of food within the mountains, and I was enjoined by the Governor-General (Lord Lytton) to see personally that all losses of transport were replaced, and that no failure occurred in the arrival of supplies. I accordingly galloped backwards and forwards across the desert, intervening between Sind and the Khelat mountains, to organize the halting-stages and the supply-depôts of the military transport. Very able aid was rendered by my Military Secretary Major Stirling Rivett Carnac. I also inspected the Bolan Pass, greatly admiring its bold bluffs, its pellucid streams, and its grand background, all doubly welcome after the dreary expanse of the desert. The principal chiefs of the Khelat country presented themselves, and the improvement in the relations, between them and their liege the Khan, was manifest. The Khan himself I did not see, but had met His Highness at the Delhi Imperial Assemblage. Formerly the strife between him and his nobles threatened to tear his State to pieces; but now everything wore the aspect of order and stability. The Political Agent to the Governor-General was Sir Robert Sandeman, whose labours were most laudable and successful in preserving peace throughout the Khelat territory, and in vindicating British authority or influence among the predatory tribes in its neighbourhood. The perfect security, with which quantities of British stores streamed along the Bolan Pass and other wild parts of the Khelat territory, redounded to the honour of the Khan and his subjects.

The province of Sind is rich in camels and in cattle; still its resources were severely strained on these occasions. It furnished 30,000 camels, and then its supply was exhausted. It also provided 6000 pairs of draught bullocks, and could have supplied many more if necessary. The carts were made in Bombay, and sent by sea and rail to the frontier; the animals were purchased in the delta of the Indus. This carriage and its draught bullocks joined for the first time on the frontier of Khelat.

The military transport was most ably managed by General, now Sir Robert, Phayre, and remarkable service was rendered by Major (now Brigadier-General) Hogg, already mentioned.

When in the autumn of 1879 the news was flashed of the destruction of Cavagnari's mission at Caubul, the energy, capacity and resolution with which Lord Lytton's Government faced the emergency elicited general admiration and sustained the public confidence.

Shortly afterwards Lord Lytton directed me to cause a railway to be constructed from Sakkar on the bank of the Indus to Sibi near the foot of the Bolan Pass. This railway was begun on the 5th October, 1879, and was opened on 14th January, 1880, the time being 101 days, and the distance being 133½ miles, shewing a daily average of 1⅓ mile. The progress was for some weeks together at the rate of a mile a day, and for some days consecutively at the rate of more than two miles a day. The work was of a temporary description; the ground was generally flat and easy; the difficulty was to collect rapidly the stores and materials from distant parts of the empire, and to supply water in the heart of the desert to many thousands of workpeople. The Chief Engineer, to whose skill and energy much of the success must be attributed, was Colonel James G. Lindsay.

I was further instructed by Lord Lytton to arrange for continuing the line through the mountains to Pishin on the border of southern Afghanistan, in view of a further extension to Candahar. With the assistance of Colonel the Marquis de Bourbel, of Colonel Lindsay and Sir Robert Sandeman, I caused the surveys to be made, through rugged passes leading up to heights of 6000 feet (above sea-level), the line to be marked out by the engineers, and the rails with other materials to be carted to the necessary points within the mountains. I then rode on to Candahar, to confer with General Sir Donald Stewart there, and to satisfy myself that all the requirements for military transport were being met, so far as they depended on the basis of supply in Sind.

On these long rides, the scenery which I saw was generally striking and sometimes beautiful, leaving pictures imprinted on the memory of such views as those of the fertile basin of Quetta, closely environed by bare rocks (10,000 feet above sea-level)—the lofty walls formed by narrow rifts and chasms through which the rivers pass in their course from the elevated plateaux to the plains beneath—the landscape seen from the historic crest of the Khojak Pass—the undulating desert of southern Afghanistan, dotted with abrupt granitic hills—the dust-storms rising against the blue sky in vast columns and then careering along till earth and air are enveloped in obscurity—the city of Candahar, with smiling cultivation around, and boldly shaped hills standing like a row of sentinels behind it—the clear-running Argandab, with long lines of fruit-gardens on one side, and a distant view stretching to the Hazara mountains on the other.

Having completed all the arrangements for organizing the military transport from the Indus to Candahar, for securing the commissariat supplies, for carrying on the railway towards the Afghan border, and for despatching the reinforcements of troops, according to Lord Lytton's instructions,—I returned to Bombay. It was shortly afterwards necessary for me to quit India suddenly, for I had already accepted an invitation to stand for East Worcestershire (my native county) at the general election, and in the first week of March 1880 the news of the dissolution of Parliament was flashed to India by telegraph. I sailed from Bombay on 13th March, 1880, regretting all my good friends there, but feeling that, inasmuch as at that moment all was well in the Bombay Presidency from end to end, with its interests stretching from the border of Mysore in southern India to the frontier of Candahar, I was officially "felix opportunitate mortis."

CHAPTER XXI.

CONCLUSION.

Important questions relating to the effect of British rule upon the people—Their material condition now as compared with former times—The new or Western education—Originality of mind in the Natives—Progress of Christianity in reference to the heathen religions—Ambition and aspirations of educated Natives—Array of political forces on the side of, or militating against, British rule—Loyalty and trustworthiness in many classes, elements of trouble in others—Substantial safety of British rule—Sources of its stability and causes of its permanency.

In the foregoing chapters no attempt has been made to discuss questions relating to the condition or prospects of the country and of the people, lest disquisition should interrupt the course of the narrative. Nevertheless a consideration of the events, which have occurred during this generation, seems to present several questions as deserving a specific answer. Such questions are so comprehensive in their character and so grave in their import, that to substantiate and illustrate fully the answers would require a volume. Much matter, too, bearing closely upon them has been set forth in my former work 'India in 1880.' Still, as doubts on these subjects frequently recur in the public mind, it may be well to give here, by way of recapitulation, a summary of the conclusions at which I have arrived as the results of study, observation and experience. The questions then, which have been suggested to me, may be stated thus:—

First.—What is the economic and financial effect of British rule upon the masses of the people; that is to say, are they growing poorer or richer, irrespective of the question whether India as an empire is increasing or decreasing in wealth and prosperity?

Secondly.—Has the English or Western education elevated the character of the cultivated classes of the Natives? Has this elevation been obtained at the cost of originality in the Natives, and has it lessened the chance of their self-development upon natural and therefore Asiatic lines? Ought the education to be in English or in the Indian vernaculars?

Thirdly.—Is the Western education subverting the several existing religions; and if so, is Christianity advancing sufficiently to take their place? How far is the system of caste shaken?

Fourthly.—Are the highly educated Natives likely to become discontented with their existing status socially and politically, and to ask for privileges which the British Government can hardly consent to grant?

Fifthly.—Is there any dislike to British rule felt by considerable sections of the Native population; is it deeply seated, and has the Government any serious consequences to fear from it?

Sixthly.—On the whole, is British rule in a state of accidental equipoise, balanced between forces some favourable others unfavourable, or is it substantially safe and based upon a foundation of permanent stability?

The first question, then, runs thus: what is the economic and financial effect of British rule upon the masses of the people; that is to say, are they growing richer or poorer, irrespective of the question whether India as an empire is increasing or decreasing in wealth and prosperity?

There is indeed every reason to believe that as an empire India is rising in wealth and prosperity, inasmuch as population increases, cultivation expands, trade internal and external grows apace, quantities of food grain are exported, prices rise invariably, wages generally—but not always—are augmented, large amounts of foreign capital are invested, the diminution in the rate of interest attests the accumulation of Native capital and the strengthening of security, new industries more than replace the old industries decaying or extinct, communications by rail road and river are improved, irrigation is extended, a higher standard of domestic comfort is perceptible even among many of the humbler classes.

This being so, it follows that at least a large portion of the people must be better off than formerly, and that some classes must be considerably enriched. Nevertheless, it is very possible that some classes may be impoverished, and that even the masses may not be improving in condition. It is therefore well to see what classes come under this category, and what are the masses. To assist the view in this respect, the following table is extracted from the report of the Indian Famine Commission, regarding the occupations of the adult males, who amount to 62 millions out of the whole population of British India, about 200 millions.

	Occupation.	Per Cent.	Number of Adult Males.
I.	Commercial	5·2	3,224,000
II.	Professional, including Government service	3·6	2,232,000
III.	Domestic	6·2	3,844,000
IV.	Independent and non-productive	3·4	2,108,000
V.	Industrial	13·1	8,122,000
VI.	Agricultural	56·2	34,844,000
VII.	Labourers	12·3	7,626,000
		100	62,000,000

Now of these, the classes I. and II., commercial and professional, comprising nearly 9 per cent. of the whole, are decidedly flourishing more than formerly. The classes III., IV., and V., domestic, non-productive, and industrial, comprising 23 per cent.

of the whole, are in much the same condition as before. The industrial class has in some respects declined, in others it has risen. The real doubt then refers to classes VI. and VII., agricultural and labourers, comprising 68 per cent. of the whole. The two classes may well be considered together, for the labourers are mostly employed on the land. Of the agricultural adult males, 34 millions in all, about half, or 17 millions, are either proprietors, great and small, or else have proprietory rights. These are all unquestionably richer and more comfortable than formerly, they are the yeomanry and the flower of the peasantry, and are to the population what the phalanx was to an army of old. The remainder of the agricultural males, or 17 millions, are set down as farmers, tenants, cultivators, though of these many possess a sub-proprietory status or tenant-right in some shape. Perhaps half of them are thus situated: and they are, equally with the proprietors, much more prosperous than of old. The other half are tenants at will, some of whom after paying their dues to the proprietor, have a narrow margin only for subsistence. Still their condition improves in each succeeding decade. The labourers, 8 millions, chiefly employed in the fields, have very low wages, notwithstanding the rise in prices, but then they do not need to purchase food, their main item of expense, whenever their wages are paid in kind, as is often perhaps generally the case. They are not appreciably better off than formerly, but then they are at peace and in safety, whereas in the old days of war and revolution they must often have perished from various causes, while in times of famine they were left to their fate. They doubtless are under these circumstances multiplying; still they are not pauperized, as they all work hard for their living. Those who know the historic details of the ravages committed by armed violence during the century preceding British rule, like the darkest hours of night before the dawn, and in some centuries before that—can realize what the misery of the helpless poor must have been. Exemption from that misery is a palpable benefit, which must be taken into account in a comparison between their past and their present.

From this brief analysis it appears that 50 per cent. of the people, namely, commercial 5·2, professional 3·6, three-quarters of the agricultural or 42—are decidedly much more prosperous than in former times. Then 22·7 per cent. of the people—namely, domestic 6·2, independent 3·4, industrial 13·1—are in much the same condition as formerly on the whole, with a slight degree of improvement. Lastly, 26·3 per cent. of the people—namely, one-quarter of the agriculturists, or 14, and labourers 12·3—are in a doubtful case. They are not flourishing, poor people; they have never flourished under any Government; and their lot is in some respects hardened amidst the general prosperity, while in other respects it is softened by the effects of a civilized order. In general terms, then, the condition of half of the whole people, comprising the most intelligent, vigorous and progressive classes, is decidedly ameliorated by British rule; the condition of one-quarter is nearly stationary with a slight improvement, while that of the remaining quarter is in a dubious stage, with only that sort of improvement which arises out of security from the consequences of tumult and bloodshed, and a comparative, though by no means an entire, immunity from the consequences of famine. Upon the whole, there is a clear gain on the side of British rule.

Calculations have been made on independent data to shew that about one-fifth of the population is insufficiently nourished. These estimates are based mainly upon a consideration of the density of the people in certain areas, and the production of food in those areas. Manifestly, such estimates must be subject to manifold qualifications. Still it may be at once admitted that some of the poorest classes are insufficiently nourished. But, alas, similar classes are insufficiently nourished in many other countries besides the Indian empire. In India, however, owing to the mildness of the climate, poverty of sustenance causes much less suffering than in colder climes. My impression is that very poor people in India do not endure nearly as much misery as very poor people in the British isles or in the north of Europe.

The answer, then, to the question comes thus: while the empire generally is increasing in wealth and prosperity, and several large and important classes are proportionably prospering,—the better sections of the masses are also growing richer, while the humbler sections of the masses are in a doubtful stage, certainly not deteriorating below the standard which in all ages has been low for them, but improving very slowly.

The second question stands thus: has the English or Western education elevated the character of the cultivated classes of the Natives? Has this elevation been obtained at the cost of originality in the Natives, and has it lessened the chance of their self-development on natural and therefore Asiatic lines? Ought the education to be in English or in the Indian vernaculars?

Now, the English or Western education has greatly elevated the character of the Natives who have come within its influence. It has taught them truthfulness and honour both morally and intellectually. It has made them regard with aversion that which is false and dishonest. It has imbued them with a love of abstract truth and a desire to exercise the reason with fearless impartiality, to insist upon knowing the why and the wherefore for the faith they may be required to accept. They will no longer tolerate superstitions or any absurdity whatsoever. This improvement is conspicuously manifest in their public conduct, and in all those relations of life which may be called external in contradistinction to domestic. It must doubtless affect beneficially their home life also, but regarding that an European has but little means of judging. In one essential part of domestic conduct they are exemplary, and that comprises the efforts put forth by them to impart the new education to their sons. The sacrifices they make, and the self-denial they undergo, for this object, will hardly be surpassed in the most advanced nations. How far the education of itself has endowed them with amiability, with charitable sentiments and other gentle virtues, may be doubtful; for it will probably be held that they possessed these virtues before. They take hopeful views of the life to come after the death of this body, and respecting the eternal destiny of man. They form positive conceptions regarding the human soul and its expansive capacities under other conditions of existence. They acknowledge their responsibility to God for their thoughts, words and deeds.

Some few of them have been charged with yielding to intemperance, a vice which is not confined to the West, but has always existed in the East also. But this fault has never been enough to detract from the repute of the education and the educated. As a rule the young men are temperate, steady and capable of mental effort long sustained.

The education is imparted directly or indirectly in two ways. The primary way consists of definite instruction in ethics or the science of human duty, of the inferences derivable from Western history and literature, of the mental training from logic and mathematics, and (most important of all) from daily contact and conversation with European professors. The secondary way consists in the contemplation of the example set by the British Government in India in its wise legislation, its dispensation of justice between man and man, its humane administration, its scientific and mechanical achievements, its conscientious efforts for the good of the people. The educational effect of these things upon the population at large may be greater than is, perhaps, imagined by those who are engaged in the thick of affairs.

The effect of this education, direct and indirect, undoubtedly was in the first instance to suppress the natural originality of the educated. Formerly, they ofttimes, indeed, kept their minds at a fairly high level, observing a right standard. But ofttimes they descended to the depths of moral and mental degradation; from such slough they have been extricated by education, and now breathe a purer air. For a time, bewildered by the superiority of the new civilization, they sought nothing beyond it. They crammed their memories with bare facts; they learnt the noblest prose or poetry by rote and repeated it mechanically. But this tendency, militating against their originality, operates less and less forcibly with every decade, and its disappearance after one or two generations may be anticipated. They no longer accept a doctrine secular or religious merely because it is a result of Western civilization. They search for new standards of their own, outside Europe and its ways. For that purpose they go far afield, reverting to the remotest periods of Asiatic philosophy, and in spirit crossing the Atlantic to grope for light in the New World. Their antiquarian research is frequently (though perhaps not always) conducted after a method quite their own. Despite their Western preoccupations, it is towards their own traditions that their loving gaze is turned. Their study of Shakespeare, Milton, Bacon, Locke does not in the least diminish their reverent allegiance to the Asiatic heroes, poets, saints and law-givers of old. Morally, almost spiritually, they approach Christianity, verging actually towards its very borders. But though they venerate its efficacy, they decline to profess it as a religion. Their interpretation of the poetry in nature differs from ours; while learning our notion of "the unseen universe," they do not adopt it unreservedly. They will study the writings of philosophers and economists as Bentham or Malthus, and criticize the conclusions therein set forth. Their ideas regarding the theory of punishment and several branches of civil and criminal law, differ essentially from those which we strive to impress upon them by our legislation. They frequently controvert the economic conclusions which we assert regarding the material condition of their country. In such arguments they often apply the established doctrines of political economy to complex statistics in a manner which, if not just, is really original. The "enthusiasm of humanity" is one of the principles which Christianity introduced into the world; and they have caught some of its sacred fire. But, once touched by this hallowed sentiment, they have followed its dictates with an earnestness all their own. Numberless instances of their far-sighted munificence might be cited in illustration.

In former ages there was little of philosophizing in respect to Indian art, but much of real art existed. In later times there has been much philosophizing but less of actual art. At one moment there was danger lest the very life of Indian art should be stifled by European influence. The European instructors, however, awoke to the danger in time, and now full play is allowed to the fine originality of the Native genius.

The British system, in which the Native administrators are now trained, does at first suppress their natural originality. On the other hand it may be argued that some of the salient features in our system have their prototypes among the Indians—for instance the settlement of the land under Todar Mall, the Minister of Akber the Great, is in several respects a model for British arrangements. The Native States, indeed, copy much that belongs to the British Government, and curiously appropriate English official designations for every department civil or military. Yet they retain in their management very much which, being their own, must be regarded as original, and which is thought by some, rightly or wrongly, to be better suited to the Natives than our own method. Of living statesmen among the Natives, Salar Jang of Hyderabad perhaps has become Europeanized in his method of administration. But Dinkar Rao of Gwalior was quite original, so was Kirpa Ram of Jammu, and more especially Jang Behadur of Nepal, who governed after his own fashion with hardly any tincture of European notions. Madhava Rao of Baroda, too, though Anglicized to some extent is quite Asiatic *au fond*, and, if left to his own resources entirely, would evince striking originality.

The Mahratta Brahmins, again, some of the very ablest among the *élèves* of the modern education, keep their minds riveted upon national models, and would strenuously repudiate the notion of their inner thoughts being transformed by what they have been learning. They must perforce admire much of all the moral and intellectual novelties to which they have been introduced. On the other hand, it is to be feared that nothing can shake many of the prepossessions, favourable to their own ideas and adverse to ours, which have gained strength from father to son through many centuries. They will learn much from us, and may even acquire new faculties, for all that, as a race, they will retain their individuality. Their association named the Sarva Jânik Sabha may be hypercritical, but is certainly original.

In authorship the educated Natives are prolific even in English, and in the vernacular the mass of current literature is known to few Europeans save those who, like Garcin de Tassy, make it their special study. Native authors have produced some works of original merit, but not so many as might have been expected.

Respecting physical science, they are already apt in verifying its teachings by experiment. Whether they will become discoverers cannot be predicted, for as yet our State education, though now improving fast, has been quite deficient in all branches of this science, except the medical where it has always been excellent. Nor can any forecast be hazarded as to whether they will be inventors, for as yet their natural ingenuity has been but little developed by mechanical instruction. But the constant spectacle of wonder-working mechanism, under British management, must stimulate their thoughts.

The new religious sects which have arisen or are arising—the Brahmos of the east and north of India, the similar communities in the west—are essentially original, notwithstanding that they owe their origin to the new education. There is a philosophic mysticism, a transcendentalism, about them which so far from being derived from the Western teaching given them, is positively opposed to it. They gather all they can from European instructors in Christianity, and then apply the instruction after a manner of their own.

Taking all these considerations together, we may trust that the English or Western education will not impair the originality of the educated, nor lessen the chance of their self-development. It would be sad if these men were confined to springs of thought belonging not to themselves but to their masters; in that case their mental growth would be sickly and stunted. We can never desire that they should be intellectually prostrate before us in servile imitation. But there is no probability of this happening; on the contrary, while abandoning some things of their own, and adopting others from us, they are likely to cherish the essence of nearly all that is indigenous. Already this development of theirs is moving in what must be called Asiatic lines—as the lines are not exactly European—and will probably diverge still more in an Oriental direction. So far from lessening this chance for them, our instruction has been the main factor in producing it. The education has furnished them mentally with wings; and though fledgelings as yet, they are essaying flight, and none can now foresee how high they will soar. Without it, no such possibility would have been opened out for them. For they had lost all power of self-improvement when British rule dawned upon their horizon. By reason of the invasions from without, the disturbances from within, the disruption of ancient systems, the submergence of learning by floods of violence, they had long lost all means of recovering themselves.

Female education offers the greatest field now open to benevolent effort; in no other respect socially is there so much which needs doing, and which might practically be done. Doubtless some great result will ere long be attained and that will affect mightily the coming generation. It is not likely that the Western education will at all extinguish the originality of mind which Indian women often have, notwithstanding the repressive influences of centuries. The flashes of ability and the sparks of character which have emanated from them—despite disadvantages which to European women would seem incredible—afford indications of what they may become hereafter, when their minds shall be freed.

As to whether the superior education generally ought to be in English or in the Indian vernaculars—it may be said that while English is, and must be, the medium of imparting much of the best and highest education,—the various vernaculars, eighteen in number, will probably continue as at present to be the media for instructing the masses. The cultivation of the vernaculars does certainly strengthen originality among the Natives. Despite their thirst for Western literature, the educated classes, in common with the rest of their countrymen, venerate their own languages, whether classical or spoken. As the old vernacular literature is both scanty and obsolete, the necessity of providing food for the mind of the rising generation is evoking, and will yet further evoke, the original talent of Native authors. The Government has responded to the popular sentiment by promoting the culture of the vernaculars to a degree unknown even among the best of the preceding Native governments. Indeed, the successful vigour, with which this is done by the British in India, is a fact probably unique in the history of conquering races.

The third question is stated thus: is the Western education subverting the several existing religions, and if so, is Christianity advancing sufficiently to take their place? How far is the system of caste shaken?

The Western education has not affected the Muhammadan faith. It has subverted the Hindu faith, or the Brahminical religion, among the educated classes of Hindus, but not among the masses. The educated people on abandoning what may be termed the religion of mediæval Hinduism, do not become irreligious, but revert to the primitive Hindu faith, or else adopt some form of theism. Christianity is not advancing sufficiently to take the place of the heathen religions whenever they are renounced. It is growing, however, absolutely fast, though it still covers but a small part of the ground relatively to the vastness of the population. But the number of Native Christians has increased at the rate of fifty per cent. in every decade for the last thirty years, or one generation, and with the existing missionary agencies, some considerable ratio of increase will probably be maintained. Whether any decided expansion shall occur, must depend upon the efforts of the Christian Churches. It may occur largely if the missionary zeal and the resources of the Churches shall increase. Meanwhile the results, as compared with the agency employed, are quite satisfactory to all concerned. Christianity wins no rapid way among the educated classes by reason of their education. Some of them become Christians, some also among the humbler classes; the proportion of high-caste and humble-caste men among the Native Christians probably does not differ from the proportion of the same castes in the population generally. On the other hand the Missions may, if their means be adequate, effect decisive progress among the aboriginal races and others who are outside caste, numbering in all 27 millions. The conduct of the Native Christian communities, now reckoning nearly half a million of souls (Protestants), is good, and worthy of the faith they profess. With judicious guidance and encouragement from Europeans, there is every chance of a Native Christian Church being organized with Native clergy and deacons sustained by the congregations. Such a Church may have liberty to grow in an Indian or Asiatic manner suitable to the circumstances of the East.

Respecting caste, it is shaken somewhat among the educated classes, and inroads in various directions have been made into its well-guarded pale. Many tendencies of the age, too, militate against its prevalence. Nevertheless it is as yet quite unshaken among the masses, and it possesses social as well as religious force.

The fourth question is in this wise: are the educated Natives likely to become discontented with their existing status socially and politically, and to ask for privileges which the British Government can hardly consent to grant?

In the Native States, which comprise statistically one-fifth of our empire, and should be estimated morally at a higher proportion—the educated Natives are not at all likely to become discontented with their status socially and politically. On the contrary they are there finding already, and will find still more as time rolls on, a scope and a sphere for their ambition and their energies. But in the British territories they are now feeling this discontent, and may perhaps feel it in an increasing degree. It has sprung up within twenty years and has grown somewhat during the last decade. British rule being what it is, the presence of Europeans in all, or almost all, the important posts is absolutely essential, and must necessarily bar a career of the best sort for the educated Natives, who, seeing this, must sooner or later become dissatisfied. This disadvantage under our Government is being, and may yet further be, mitigated, but cannot be wholly avoided. Nor does this fact, *per se*, prove any superiority on behalf of the Native States over British rule. For it is the British paramount power that enables the Native States to be what they are; without the ægis of England, they would relapse into the barbarism whereby education is stamped out under the iron heel of violence and careers are closed to all save the stalwart.

Socially, the educated Natives probably feel discontent at not being admitted more than they are to European society in India. But they will doubtless secure this admission more and more, as they become qualified for it. On the other hand, Europeans have been in a still stricter degree debarred from Native society. But as the dominion of caste recedes and as Native ladies become educated, there may possibly be a social union between Europeans and Indians such as no previous era has witnessed.

The educated Natives will ask for much that the Government can concede, such as improved status and emoluments in the public service, besides opportunities of influential usefulness by serving in honorary capacities for the welfare of the community as gentlemen serve in England. The progress, which the Government has secured for them in these directions within the last generation, is an earnest of similar benefits to come. It is to be hoped that they will entreat the Government to give a more practical turn to several branches of the higher education, and to impart scientific instruction more largely and efficiently than heretofore, so that they may acquire the knowledge necessary for carving out new careers.

Our object should be to educate the character as well as the intellect, teaching the non-official Natives to feel public spirit and the official Natives to bear responsibility. Hitherto we have succeeded most in training Natives to rise to high posts in the judicial service. Our ambition should be, however, to train them for the executive posts demanding the sterner qualities on which Englishmen justly pride themselves. Most of those posts must needs continue to be held by Europeans; it would be dangerous to place such duties in the hands of Natives. Still there are many posts of a responsible character which Natives might occupy, if only they were endowed with the more robust qualities. It should be the aim of the Government to endow them with such qualities, by means of education direct and indirect.

They will also ask for some privileges which the British Government cannot concede in full, inasmuch as they will express a desire for representative institutions in the English sense of the term. They seldom formulate such requests very specifically, for, although they themselves understand the meaning of "representation," they remember that the vast majority of their countrymen do not. They perhaps would like an oligarchical council to be formed from among themselves by some State procedure, or else that the power of electing should rest with the educated only, who form but a very small minority of the people; but they have never, probably, thought out such schemes. They certainly wish to have the power of the purse, which power would dominate the internal administration, while they are quite content to leave to the Government the duty of external defence.

Now the Government, believing that the elective franchise had a good moral effect upon those who are reasonably qualified to exercise it, has already entrusted, subject to an ultimate control by the State, the municipal administration of the capital cities of Calcutta and Bombay to corporations elected by the ratepayers, and has extended or is likely to extend the principle to the largest municipalities in the interior of the country. Further, the Government seems disposed to entrust some share of power respecting local and provincial finances to elected representatives; but here it cannot relinquish its controlling authority. The Native members of the Legislative Councils are at present appointed by the Governor-General. Possibly they might be elected, if only any constituency for such a purpose could be devised, which would indeed be difficult to devise. At all events, however, the Government could not allow them to have anything approaching a majority or equality in the Council. That source of power it must retain in its own hands.

Some observers may hold that if high education tends to political discontent, the Government should prudently refrain from imparting it. But such a view could not be maintained in the nineteenth century. Surely it is our bounden duty to give to the Natives the benefit of all that we know ourselves. If we admit that there are cases in which plain dictates of duty must be followed and reliance placed on Providence for the result, then here is an example of the strongest kind. Politically we are so secure that we can afford to be generous in imparting knowledge, even though in some respects disaffection were to spring up in consequence; but in fact true loyalty and contentment in other and more important respects will thereby be produced or confirmed. At all events this is an occasion for putting into practice the maxim, "be just and fear not."

The fifth question is in these words: is there any dislike of, or hostility to, British rule felt by considerable sections of the Native population; is it deeply seated, and has the Government any serious consequences to fear from it?

In order to answer this question, the population may be classified thus, respecting degrees of loyalty or otherwise:—

Actively loyal	I. The Princes and Chiefs of the Native States.
	II. The banking, trading and industrial classes.
	III. The Zemindars or landlords of permanently settled estates.
Loyal but passive	IV. The peasant proprietors, and the cultivators.
	V. The labourers.
Many loyal, but some the reverse	VI. The educated classes.
	VII. The Native aristocracy in the British territories.
	VIII. The Hindu and Muhammadan priesthood.

Excitable or ready for mischief	IX. The fanatics. X. The hangers-on of courts and camps. XI. The mob.

The most potential numerically are classes IV. and V., which comprise two-thirds of the whole population, and constitute the backbone of the body politic. In the main, they are attached to British rule, so far as their nature is capable of political attachment. They cheerfully acquiesce in it, and have everything to gain by its continuance. They are sure not to do anything against it; if it be threatened, they will show it such favour as they secretly or quietly can without compromising themselves. But they cannot be depended upon to fight for it, or to make any vigorous efforts on its behalf. It is melancholy that such should be the case; but this is the consequence of invasions having swept like waves over the country at frequent intervals during many centuries. The succession of conquerors, and the change of masters from time to time, may be expected to produce an apathetic and submissive character in the people, which is transmitted from generation to generation. They will give the British Government their hearty goodwill, so long as it can hold its own; but if it begins to stagger under hostile blows, they will try to make terms, or at least to be on a friendly footing, with the party that may possibly be victorious. On the other hand, the securing of their contentment is primarily important, because in the last resort they would rise against oppression, and if, without being actually oppressed, they were discontented, their dead-weight would be thrown into the scale of our opponents, which for us would be a serious contingency.

Outside this solid and stolid mass, which, though not immovable, is hard to move, there are political forces, some operating for British rule, others militating against it, some, too, having a doubtful and vacillating movement.

The princes and chiefs in the Native States (I.) are at heart among the best friends we possess; their relations with the British Sovereign have within this generation become more close and cordial than before, and they are proud of being the feudatories of a world-wide empire. The Native States, the commercial community, and the landlords of permanently settled estates (I., II. and III.) being actively loyal, it follows that the time-honoured traditions which powerfully affect the popular imagination, the capital and enterprise of the country, and a large portion of its territorial influence,—are all arrayed on the side of British rule, and afford truly immense advantages. But then the landed aristocracy, in the British territories, cannot possibly have the same status now which it had under the preceding Native rule; the educated classes have unsatisfied aspirations; the priesthood dread the new education; therefore these three sections VI., VII., VIII., are in a fitful mood in respect to the existing state of things. They all acquire advantages under British rule, and many of their impulses are loyal; among them are many good and faithful men, while some (we must hope they are but few) are to be counted as undoubtedly inimical. Lastly, the fanatics (IX.)—not numerous, but capable of making their shrill and angry voices heard—the men who prefer service as armed retainers rather than more industrious employment (X.), and who on the morn of revolution issue forth like insects on a summer's day—the mob (XI.) among whom ruffianism is not subdued by peace and revolution—all are fermenting under British rule, and entertain towards it a hostile feeling, not because they have any assignable reason therefor, but because we are foreigners able to stop mischief and to answer for order. If any nucleus of rebellion were formed, the disaffected sections would rally round it; nevertheless, as a rule, they are inapt at combining, or else their combination would be unstable and ineffective.

The Native army, being composed of various elements, reflects nearly every phase of the thoughts which pervade these several sections of the community. If it were to become overgrown, as was once the case, it would on occasions assert itself with dire effect amidst the conflict of the diverse elements described above. But if it be kept low, as at present, in proportion to the European forces, it will be faithful in obedience, and will remain an important factor in the might wielded by the British Government.

Thus upon a reckoning up of forces for and against us, there seems to be a clear balance in our favour—when this vast population is considered in the aggregate.

Then, added to this preponderance on our side within the country itself, there is the priceless advantage of the clear head, the stout heart, the strong arm, all directed with that unity of will which peculiarly characterizes the English in comparison with Asiatic races. Moreover, there are the appliances and contrivances of western science, which are many times more potent than physical power.

The answer to the question, then, comes thus: there is no dislike of or hostility to British rule felt by any considerable section of the Native population. But while some sections are actively loyal, others have a mixed character, partly loyal, partly unsatisfactory, while some again are excitable and ready for mischief. The hostility, in so far as it exists, is deeply seated, still the Government has not any serious consequences to fear from it, so long as the just rule and the European armament, now existing, shall be maintained.

The sixth question is: on the whole, is British rule in a state of accidental equipoise, balanced between forces some favourable others unfavourable? Or is it substantially safe, and based upon a foundation of permanent stability?

The answer to the last preceding question has shewn that British rule is not in a condition of bare equilibrium politically, and that it does not fall within the category of those institutions whose

> "lives are kept in equipoise
> By opposite attractions and desires."

On the contrary, it has within the country and among the people a clear balance in its favour. By its just administration, and by its right arm, it renders this balance quite overwhelming. It is, therefore, substantially safe; indeed it is grandly secure at the present time.

But whether it is based upon a foundation of absolutely permanent stability, no well-informed man can say; perhaps this cannot be said of any foreign rule in a conquered country. Certainly it has not founded, nor is in the way of founding, political institutions for the sake of which the people will, if need be, turn out to fight; for it, such a task is probably impossible. Neither has it acquired that hold upon the affections of the Natives, which an indigenous Government, identical with its subjects in colour, creed, tongue, race, and custom, may possess. It has given them many noble institutions, and many boons which are calculated to secure their fealty, and for which they ought to do battle, "sua si bona nôrint." It must not be over-confident, however, of receiving all the gratitude which it really deserves. At the very least, it is rooted in the respect and regard of the great majority, and that is a cardinal point; nevertheless implicit reliance must not be placed upon such a basis. Again, all the thriving classes, which are by far the most numerous, remain bound to the Government by ties of material advantage. Still entire confidence must not be placed even on this, for such ties may be snapped suddenly if a whirlwind of fanaticism or of passionate nationality were to come.

The empire is safe, provided that vigilance is unceasingly exercised. It is fraught with elements of trouble and surrounded with dangers, of a secondary degree perhaps, but yet enough to be serious, if our affairs were to take any untoward turn. But with the necessary vigilance, the Government is quite master of the situation. British rule has two supporting pillars—just administration and physical power. But this physical power must in the main be European; in other words, an European army must be maintained decisively superior to all the other armed bodies in combination. This plain truth became obscured, or was overlooked for many years, and the gravest consequences at length occurred in 1857. There are abundant signs to shew that like consequences might recur, if ever the European army were allowed to fall below that strength, which is wisely established at present. Without a just administration, and with a discontented people, not even an European army would keep India down. But with good government, and with a people contented in the main, as at present, the European army, together with the favouring influences within the country, will keep the Government settled as on a rock.

The atmosphere of settled peace must conduce to the material prosperity of the Natives, and the sense of being in a direct relation to the British Crown, as subjects towards their Sovereign, must arouse and elevate the sentiments of which their imaginative temperament is susceptible. Thence arises an imperial responsibility to move the conscience of all British born people,

> "Who love
> Our ocean-empire with her boundless homes,
> For ever-broadening England, and her throne
> In our vast Orient, and one isle, one isle,
> That knows not her own greatness."

FINIS.

INDEX.

LONDON: PRINTED BY WILLIAM CLOWES AND SONS, LIMITED, STAMFORD STREET AND CHARING CROSS.